THE NEW CRIMINAL JUSTICE THINKING

The New Criminal Justice Thinking

Edited by
Sharon Dolovich and Alexandra Natapoff

NEW YORK UNIVERSITY PRESS
New York

NEW YORK UNIVERSITY PRESS
New York
www.nyupress.org

© 2017 by New York University
All rights reserved

References to Internet websites (URLs) were accurate at the time of writing. Neither the author nor New York University Press is responsible for URLs that may have expired or changed since the manuscript was prepared.

ISBN: 978-1-4798-3154-8

For Library of Congress Cataloging-in-Publication data, please contact the Library of Congress.

New York University Press books are printed on acid-free paper, and their binding materials are chosen for strength and durability. We strive to use environmentally responsible suppliers and materials to the greatest extent possible in publishing our books.

Manufactured in the United States of America

10 9 8 7 6 5 4 3 2 1

Also available as an ebook

To Jody, for everything

Always for Raphael

CONTENTS

ACKNOWLEDGMENTS

This book has been many years in the making, from conversations to conference to the final product. We are deeply grateful to our home institutions of UCLA School of Law and Loyola Law School, Los Angeles, as well as to NYU School of Law, for making the endeavor possible. It has been a pleasure and an honor working with the authors in this collection. They have taught us an enormous amount. Special thanks to our editor Ilene Kalish and to NYU Press for having faith in the project. And our gratitude to our cite-checkers Scott Dewey and Ben Woolley, and to our proofreaders Samantha Abelove, Jessica Blatchley, Jessi Bulaon, Rusty Klibaner, Rowan Meredith, Flinn Milligan, Susanna Pfeffer, and Sydney Truong.

Introduction

Mapping the New Criminal Justice Thinking

SHARON DOLOVICH AND ALEXANDRA NATAPOFF

This is a pivotal moment for the American criminal system. Police violence is squarely on the public agenda. Mass incarceration, until recently viewed with indifference if it was noticed at all, is now broadly recognized as a national crisis and an expensive mistake. The system's racial skew is openly acknowledged at the highest levels of government. States are experimenting with decarceration, decriminalization, and alternative forms of punishment. Liberals and conservatives alike condemn the enormous economic costs and questionable public safety benefits of the current system. After 30-plus years of our "war on crime"—with its exponential growth in arrests and convictions, increasingly harsh sentences, unprecedented prison building, and profligate use of probation and other noncarceral penalties—there is an emerging willingness on all sides to question, challenge, and rethink our existing approach to preventing and punishing crime.

Such change requires new ways of thinking. If we are to fix the current criminal system—a vast enterprise affecting millions of lives and costing billions of dollars—we need a complete and nuanced understanding of what exactly this system *is*: What social and political institutions, what laws and policies, does it encompass? How do the stories we tell ourselves about the criminal system diverge from the way it actually operates? What does the system really do every day in the name of criminal justice, and how does it do it?

There are high moral stakes in getting the answers right. The criminal system is integral to our democracy, performing vital social functions while inflicting considerable pain and suffering on the individuals it targets. Its operations and failures impact not only its direct subjects but also their families and communities. And its harmful effects are lasting and corrosive, promoting and exacerbating conditions of socio-economic and political marginalization. Any adequate account must therefore attend honestly to these effects and to the mechanisms by which they are achieved and justified, as well as to the daily realities of those people most burdened by the state's exercise of its penal power.

To do so, we must recognize law's profoundly situated nature. Law does not function in the abstract. It is always implemented within institutional contexts inseparable from their own social, political, and economic realities. The law of policing, for example, cannot be understood apart from how, and against whom, American police officers enforce their power. In the same way, the law regulating punishment can be fully appreciated only by surveying how, as a practical matter, the state's agents mark, burden, and exclude those it labels as criminal. To understand the law governing the criminal context, we need to understand the rich and conflicted relationship between law's implementation (the law in action) and the terms set down by various legal sources (the law on the books).

This collection reveals the American criminal system in all its multilayered complexity; at every moment, there are numerous actors, institutions, and dynamics operating on multiple fronts. A system this complicated requires a roadmap and techniques for navigating its typography, and the essays in this volume provide these tools—legal and institutional as well as sociological and moral. In essence, they reflect new, richer ways of thinking about criminal justice. Challenging the standard view, with its formalistic and linear vision of individual wrongdoers breaking legal rules, the authors in this collection offer a variety of thick and nuanced models for making sense of the legal processes, social institutions, and political dynamics that together shape the reality on the ground. If these essays share a common insight, it is the inescapable need for contextualization. As they show by example, it is only through a richly textured, empirically situated analysis that the daily truths of the American criminal system can be fully understood.

The American Socio-Criminal System in Four Dimensions

The American criminal system is not only complex. It is also massive. At the moment, there are over 2.2 million people behind bars in the United

States and approximately 4.5 million more under some form of community supervision. In 2013, there were 11.3 million arrests, and at least 10 million minor criminal cases were processed through local criminal courts. Fully one third of the adult population has a criminal record of some kind.[1]

Above and beyond this sheer scale, the criminal system can be highly intrusive, and even, for some individuals, omnipresent. The policing of some citizens and communities often commences well before any crime has occurred. For people with criminal convictions, the burdens of punishment continue to be felt long after any formal sanction has been lifted. The system is also a colonizer, relentlessly expanding its reach and blurring familiar boundary lines. If, as a formal matter, there remains a distinction between criminal and civil law, between law enforcement and social work, between penal policy and social regulation, in each case it can be difficult in practice to say where one ends and the other begins.[2] A full understanding of American criminal justice must therefore account for the enormous scope and expansiveness of a system that has grown to define and constitute a wide swath of American social and political life.

In what follows, we sketch what we regard as the four essential dimensions of the American criminal system—four integral but often unacknowledged aspects that must be appreciated as we struggle to comprehend and morally evaluate the system itself. Collectively, these dimensions provide a roadmap that is not only analytically thorough, but also captures the interrelated and profoundly social dimensions of criminal justice that make it such a powerful, and powerfully oppressive, governance mechanism.

First and foremost, space must be made for the entire, protracted, and frequently recursive criminal process as it is experienced by those caught up in it. This first dimension centrally concerns the *actual human experience* of the millions of people who are selected, labeled, managed, and punished as "criminals."

Second is the *full range of relevant law*, defined not only by the standard rules of criminal procedure and formal definitions of crimes and criminal sentences, but also by the laws establishing the terms of the criminal penalties as actually served, along with the civil remedies, collateral consequences and disabilities, and all the laws of all the institutions—civil as well as criminal—that make up the socio-criminal complex.

The third necessary dimension encompasses the *public policies that generate the crime/poverty nexus*, including the institutions, from public schools to private workplaces, responsible for the ongoing collective processes of resource redistribution, social engineering, and power allocation. These civic institutions, long abutting the criminal system, have been enlisted in promoting the mass criminalization of America's most disadvantaged citizens. As a result, public institutions like schools, hospitals, and welfare offices now help to determine not only an individual's economic and social well-being, but also his or her relationship to the penal system.

Fourth and finally, our criminal system is a profoundly American way of *managing social status and power*, acting as both a source and a reflection of historical stratifications and governing cultural norms. As recent events in Ferguson and Baltimore remind us, this final dimension highlights the role that the criminal system has long played in the collective generation and perpetuation of national legacies of racism, sexism, classism, and other forms of systemic discrimination.

Conceptualizing the criminal system in this multifaceted way is a deliberately expansive move. It is an argument that, in order to understand, judge, and ultimately refashion our system of criminal justice, we need to acknowledge multiple dimensions: the system's impact on fellow human beings, its legal rules, its cross-institutional workings, and its caste-perpetuating effects. Omit one of these elements, and you will have missed a vital piece of the puzzle. Our vision is also deliberately unconventional. It locates the criminal process at the center of a far broader set of institutions, procedures, and laws than is typically associated with the state's response to crime. It does so in order to capture the dynamic, interrelated quality of criminal justice on the ground, and to reveal the extent to which much civil law, and many of our basic social institutions, are implicated in the management of the criminal system well beyond what is conventionally thought of as "criminal law." Ultimately, it insists on understanding criminal justice broadly, as a socio-political system that lies at the heart of modern American society and constitutes a full-fledged governance system in its own right.

Each of the essays in this collection contributes in its own unique way to this broader vision of criminal justice. Below, we briefly survey the contours of this expansive understanding, and then describe how each essay pushes us to think in new ways about criminal justice.

The Making and Treatment of Individual Criminals

First and foremost, the criminal system transforms people into "offenders" so as to punish and control them. Part of this terrain is familiar from what might be called the "standard model," which construes the criminal system narrowly as the process that identifies individual wrongdoers, proves their guilt, and then (and only then) imposes penalties. But to fully understand how we decide who will be designated as "criminal" and what actually happens to them as a result, it is not enough to look to formal rules and processes. We must also attend to the reality on the ground—what actually happens every day—as certain classes of criminal suspects are targeted by the police while others are ignored; as some are charged by prosecutors while others are let go; as some defendants deploy significant resources to contest their guilt before judges and juries while others succumb to the pressures to plead guilty; and as convicted offenders are sentenced to and experience wildly disparate punishments.

The official implementation of the criminal law is morally fraught, informed at any given moment by a range of social, political, economic, cultural, institutional, and psychological factors (see Lynch, Kohler-Hausmann). There are many players here—legislators, public defenders, law enforcement officials, judges, correctional officers, parole officers, and so on—and each actor is subject to their own experiences, influences, pressures, and interests, and empowered to make discretionary decisions critical to the ultimate outcomes. To fully and accurately comprehend this central component of the American criminal system— what it actually does to the people it targets, from the moment of police contact through the entire administration of punishment—we must develop a rich account that recognizes and grapples with the experiences and influence of all the parties involved.

The question of who is seen and treated as "criminal" turns heavily on selection by law enforcement (see Barkow). Most Americans violate the law in some way at some time, and law enforcement resources are limited. As a result, the targeted population necessarily reflects a wide variety of selective public policies, resource constraints, and biases (see Richman, Chesney-Lind). Not even all murders are created equal: in some impoverished communities, unsolved homicides languish for years, while in other more privileged venues, resources are lavished on similar cases.[3] And such disparities are not unique to homicides. Assaults against women, for example, are increasingly vigorously prosecuted when labeled "domestic violence," but underenforced when they occur against sex workers. And it is only in recent history that Wall Street's market manipulations have become treated as potential crimes and not just clever money-making schemes.

The power of law enforcement selection is particularly strong in low-level cases (see Natapoff). As New York City's stop-and-frisk debacle demonstrates, police targeting decisions importantly shape the legal significance of crimes. In New York, until the practice was challenged by public outrage and court order, police stopped over half a million people a year, disproportionately young men of color. In some poor Black neighborhoods, every young male resident could expect to be stopped at least once a year. These "order-maintenance" and "zero tolerance" policies amounted to an official decision to treat young men of color in certain neighborhoods as presumptive criminals (see Fagan). And this decision was a self-fulfilling prophecy: racially inflected policing ensured that these men were marked and brought into the system, giving them arrest and conviction records that putatively justified the initial decision to treat them—and the demographic group to which they belonged—as criminals, even in the absence of evidence to this effect.[4]

Similarly, as is by now familiar, the war on drugs has been waged with methods that select and define "criminal" in racialized ways (see Ocen). Although African Americans and whites use drugs—including marijuana—at approximately the same rate, we criminalize those groups at vastly different levels. The national arrest rate for marijuana possession for African Americans is four times that of whites. In some jurisdictions, it has been 10, 20, even 30 times higher.[5]

These policies and practices are fully a part of the criminal law we actually have. Only by evaluating how and why we select our criminals on the front end—and who escapes selection—can we properly understand the scope and significance of the criminalization process.

Yet front-end selection is only part of the challenge. In addition, we need to fully acknowledge all that happens afterward to those labeled as criminals. For those convicted of more serious crimes, the punishment will include incarceration, whether for months, years, or decades. In many states, the death penalty remains an option, and across the country, the imposition of sentences of life without the possibility of parole (LWOP), whether formal or virtual, has reached unprecedented levels. As a consequence, the number of people doing LWOP in one form or another far outstrips the number of people on the nation's death rows. Even people convicted of non-homicide crimes can find themselves serving decades or even life sentences. And although sentence length is a crucial determinant of the weight of the penalty, the degree of harm incarceration represents for prisoners themselves turns as much upon the conditions of confinement as on the length of stay—and perhaps even more so (see Dolovich, Kerr). This is especially true for long-term prisoners, who often endure extreme hardship, the combined effect of many compromising factors, including overcrowding, understaffing, minimal programming, gang control, threats of predation from staff and other prisoners, the proliferating use of solitary confinement, grossly inadequate medical and mental health care, and the radical indifference of society at large to the suffering of those who live under such conditions.[6]

For those millions of Americans convicted of minor crimes, punishment may also involve a custodial term, along with months or years under some form of burdensome and intrusive "community supervision."[7] Low-level offenders are often saddled with fines and fees they cannot pay, a punishment that can lead to long-term debt, deeper impoverishment, family displacement, and even additional incarceration.

And for everyone with a criminal conviction, whether incarcerated or not, the system imposes an endless gauntlet of exclusions, restrictions, obstacles, and prohibitions to be navigated and endured for years, if not forever. These so-called "collateral" consequences include formal restrictions on such crucial matters as housing, employment, access to student loans, voting, jury service, and government contracts.[8] They also include the substantial informal economic costs, psychological burdens, and social stigma that go with being labeled a criminal.[9]

This account intentionally expands the class of conditions and burdens that count as punishment. The Supreme Court has been parsimonious in this regard, but from the perspective of the actual individuals on the receiving end, the punishment inflicted is more than just a fine, probation, or a custodial term. It also includes such practical burdens and personal indignities as denial of the right to vote or serve on a jury, the unwillingness of private individuals to rent them an apartment, and the often insurmountable difficulty in getting a job. These experiences are not "collateral" to punishment. For those subjected to them, they *are* punishment (see Simon).

This expansive understanding has special implications for those who are convicted of minor crimes, an experience that can mark and burden a person for a lifetime in ways that far exceed their culpability. Even brief periods of probation can trap a minor offender in an extended and punitive dance with the state. For the poor, the underemployed, and those with substance abuse or mental health problems, a minor conviction can further derail their lives, undermining the stability of their families and communities and spreading the burden of heavy penalty even to the next generations.[10]

It is crucial here to recognize the cyclical nature of the penal experience. What might be thought of as the "back end" of the system—all the punishments and burdens that follow conviction—is also in important ways a direct conduit back to the beginning of the criminal process. Hardships imposed on people convicted of crimes can steer them back into the criminal system. Prison conditions are famously criminogenic, compromising rather than enhancing the development of pro-social tendencies and skills.[11] And even once people have served their time, the countless formal and informal collateral consequences can make daily life a constant struggle, further marginalizing those subject to them, both socially and economically.[12] This marginalization increases the likelihood of recidivism and helps keep people visible to law enforcement, thus facilitating their readmission into the system.

At the same time, the composition and complexion of the population of convicted offenders shapes front-end enforcement policies. Police point to offense rates to justify stop-and-frisk practices, even though offense rates are a direct function of those very enforcement choices. American culture has long associated criminality with blackness and continues to do so,[13] even though the racial makeup of the criminalized population is itself a result of law enforcement selection and prosecution policies.[14] Focusing on what happens at the back end thus helps explain the many ways the system operates to ensure a steady supply of certain kinds of people coming in through the front.

Even more troubling from a rule-of-law perspective, the question of individual guilt turns out to be only a part—and sometimes a negligible part—of how we decide whom to treat like criminals. Most young men stopped-and-frisked in New York were released without arrest or charge, indicating that the police themselves realized they had gotten the guilt question wrong. Many people who find themselves in jail plead guilty, not because they actually committed the crime, but because they cannot afford bail and do not want to risk the loss of job or home that often attends even short-term incarceration. Or they may plead guilty because the risk of a long sentence after trial is not worth taking when weighed against the certainty of a short plea-bargained sentence. We know that innocent people are marked and punished in these ways, and yet we permit the process to persist. These are hallmarks of a system that is at best careless about guilt.

Our body politic is currently grappling with perhaps the most disturbing and tragic manifestation of this carelessness: the threat it poses to the lives of young Black men. Ferguson was once just the name of a St. Louis suburb, as Selma was once just an Alabama city with a bridge. Today, "Ferguson" represents not only the death of Michael Brown, an 18-year-old unarmed African American killed by a local police officer, but numerous other cases, recent and not so recent, of unjustified police violence against unarmed Black men, among them Eric Garner, Tamir Rice, Freddie Gray, Amadou Diallo, and Abner Louima. Now a cultural symbol of political protest, "Ferguson" stands for a growing anger and frustration over the routine way the criminal system overstates the threat posed by Black men and undervalues their safety and lives.

In sum, any adequate conception of American criminal justice needs to push the boundaries of the standard view, to expose and encompass more of what actually happens on both the front and back ends. This reality is lived by flesh-and-blood human beings, a fact that the standard focus on formal rules and processes tends to ignore, but which must be front and center in any morally adequate understanding of the criminal system (see Bibas, Simon).

All the (Criminal) Law

As the foregoing indicates, the criminal system often operates in ways that contravene the basic values of a constitutional democracy: fairness, equality, impartiality, political accountability. Because existing rules are so often insufficient, ignored, or twisted in practice, it is tempting to shed one's faith in the centrality of rules and the value of changing them. We believe this would be a mistake, both philosophically and pragmatically. In a society that aspires to the rule of law, legal rules form a vital infrastructure for state action and the conduit for legislative and judicial directives to other legal actors (see Dolovich). In the criminal context, rules define crimes; fix penalties; empower and constrain police, prosecutors, and judges; and undergird the effective operation of the adversarial process. In a foundational sense, we rely on the rule of law and the concept of legality to ensure the legitimacy of the state's exercise of its penal power. As the late William Stuntz put it, "this central commitment of American government" requires that "when the state deprives one of its citizens of life, liberty or property, the deprivation is primarily the consequence of a legal rule, not a discretionary choice."[15] Justice Scalia once referred to the principle of *nulla poena sine lege* (no punishment without law) as "one of the most widely held value judgments in the history of human thought,"[16] and later in this volume, Jonathan Simon refers to the legality principle as "the central premise of modernity in criminal law."

To understand the criminal system is thus always in some deep sense to understand its laws. But exactly what law is relevant? American law schools generally operate on a narrow working definition of "criminal law," as that collection of statutes defining which behaviors count as crimes and the legal rules for determining what factual showing is required for conviction. This so-called substantive law is accompanied by the study of the myriad procedural rules, both statutory and constitutional, that govern investigations, trials, and due process more generally, a body of law collectively referred to as "criminal procedure."

Yet once we view the criminal system expansively, the legal distinction between "civil" and "criminal" loses much of its force (see Barkow). The diverse body of law that shapes both the mechanisms by which people are marked for entry into the system as criminals and the full reality of what happens to them once they are so marked is far broader than what law students know as criminal law and criminal procedure. Indeed, many legal regimes more commonly labeled as civil are as fully a part of the criminal system as the basic principles of mens rea.

The front end of the system, where people are labeled as criminal, is driven by many seemingly civil phenomena: the administrative principles that shape prosecutorial and public defender offices, the aggregate settlement dynamics that generate guilty pleas, the contractual market for bail bonds. On the back end, the criminal system includes not only the laws governing sentencing, but also the bureaucratic mechanisms for imposing and administering the various criminal penalties, including prison regulations, the rules governing probation and parole, and the broad discretion accorded probation, correctional, and parole officers.[17] It includes the vast set of legal rules that define and constrain the civic functioning and economic options of the 65 million Americans living with criminal convictions, as well as the rules that enable informal collateral consequences such as the commercial collection of personal data.[18] It even includes regimes explicitly styled as civil, including civil contempt for failing to pay criminal fines and fees, the rules governing (civil) immigration detention, the regime of habeas corpus through which defendants challenge the constitutionality of their convictions and sentences, and the doctrinal standards and framework for challenging prison conditions and other issues relating to the administration of punishment.

The socio-criminal legal regime also indirectly relies on the rules of many civil institutions (see Valverde). Immigration is perhaps the most obvious example, but the criminal law should also be understood to include social regulations like the school disciplinary rules that drive the school-to-prison pipeline, and zoning restrictions that "banish" offenders from public parks and other public arenas and expose repeat violators to jail time.[19] And it increasingly encompasses welfare policies that restrict the civil rights of welfare recipients and refer those recipients to prosecutors when the terms of that (civil) contract are broken.[20]

An expansive view of criminal law also requires that we rethink the constitutional scope of this area, not least because, in our constitutional democracy, the Bill of Rights is an important way that we legitimate the harms imposed in the name of criminal justice. The police procedurals and courtroom dramas of television and film have made generations of Americans experts on various constitutional protections, from

Miranda warnings to the right to a jury trial and the right to counsel. And to be sure, at the front end of the criminal process, even before the determination of guilt, these and other protections deriving from the Fourth, Fifth, and Sixth Amendments are of central relevance. But for those individuals subjected to criminal punishment—who, once misdemeanors are factored in, number in the millions annually—the list of relevant constitutional provisions and principles gets longer. The Eighth Amendment prohibition on cruel and unusual punishment is vital for anyone facing criminal punishment in any form. The Eighth Amendment Excessive Fines Clause looks to increase in importance along with the growing public awareness of the myriad fees imposed by the criminal process.[21] And for the incarcerated, several other constitutional protections also become directly relevant, including First Amendment freedom of speech and association and the free exercise of religion, and the Fourteenth Amendment Equal Protection Clause.

Finally, it bears remembering that criminal procedure and civil rights are flip sides of the same constitutional coin. Although law schools typically distinguish between criminal law and procedure on the one hand, and constitutional law and civil rights on the other, this is a misleading distinction. The urgent civil rights issues embodied in the slogan "Black Lives Matter" are centrally about criminal procedure. Conversely, the criminal system is heavily shaped by habeas corpus, prison litigation, the rules governing constitutional challenges arising from the administration of punishment, and a wide range of civil rights laws and procedures that permit institutional enforcement of conventional criminal rules. All of this law is criminal law, and must be understood as such if one is to fully comprehend the legal foundations of the criminal system.

The Criminalization of Poverty: An Institutional View

In the United States, the criminal process by which we decide who is to be labeled a criminal and what happens to them as a consequence is inextricably entwined with the institutions of welfare provision and the experience of poverty more generally. This is a two-way street: poor people tend to get routed into the criminal process, and brushes with the criminal system tend to make or keep people poor. Understanding the American criminal system thus requires looking specifically at how the criminal process works as an official socio-economic regulator in close cooperation with other features of the welfare state.

Poor people are routed into the criminal system in a number of ways. One way is by formally criminalizing things that poor people do. When we make it a crime to sleep or urinate in public, we turn the homeless into criminals. When we make it a crime to provide unlicensed child care, we criminalize poor parents and their neighbors. As Kaaryn Gustafson has described, when welfare case workers are directed to refer their clients to prosecutors for violation of welfare rules, we criminalize welfare recipients. When we incarcerate people for failure to pay traffic fines or for driving on a suspended license they cannot afford to fix, we criminalize the working poor.

Poor people are also routed into the criminal system geographically, based on where they live. Urban African American neighborhoods are overpoliced, especially for drug offenses. Public housing estates are likewise heavily policed, creating a direct pathway between residency and entrance into the criminal system. Some cities have "million-dollar blocks": concentrated areas in poor urban communities where the incarceration rate "is so dense that states are spending in excess of a million dollars a year to incarcerate the residents of single city blocks."[22]

The welfare institutions that serve children have also become engines of criminalization. In some public schools, internal disciplinary mechanisms have been seeded with law enforcement officers. Children who might otherwise receive detention or a trip to the principal's office find themselves arrested, brought before a judge, and incarcerated for conduct that in another school would be written off as normal behavior for school-aged children. This "school-to-prison pipeline" disproportionately affects children of color: 70% of arrested students are African American or Latino, and minority boys and girls alike are more likely to be arrested, referred to law enforcement, suspended, or expelled than their white counterparts for comparable behavior.[23] In a particularly tragic doubling down, children of incarcerated parents often end up in foster care, where they "are significantly more likely to be abused and neglected . . . than their peers in the general population."[24] Such children are less likely to complete their education and more likely to end up on the streets. The experience of being in foster care "is [thus] one of the best predictors there is that a child will wind up behind bars."[25]

Even as our welfare institutions route the disadvantaged into the criminal system, the criminal process itself functions as a powerful engine of social inequality, crisply labeled by Loïc Wacquant as "a self-perpetuating cycle of social and legal marginality with devastating personal consequences."[26] The mechanisms by which the criminal system contributes to this feedback loop are well understood. People who lack well-resourced lawyers are more likely to be treated unfairly. As many as 80% of those held on bail cannot afford to pay it, and are thus exposed to the financial and personal costs of incarceration: losing their jobs, cars, apartments, or even custody of their children. Increasing attention is being paid to the resurgence of "debtor's prison," as low-income and middle-class people struggle to pay off the numerous fines and fees levied against even minor criminal conduct—including conduct that has been officially decriminalized. Indeed, misdemeanor fines strongly exacerbate the class bias of the criminal system: offenders with financial resources can pay their fines and walk away, while the indigent and underresourced remain at risk of probation, incarceration, and further punishment.[27]

Finally, there are the myriad ways that a criminal conviction may directly impoverish its bearer. A conviction severely undermines a person's ability to obtain employment, African American men being especially disadvantaged in this regard.[28] The collateral consequences of a conviction can include the loss of public housing, student loans, and licenses. Fines and fees can destroy a person's credit, while convictions and failure-to-pay warrants can prevent people from connecting with important support institutions such as banks, police, and hospitals.[29]

These examples are just the tip of the iceberg: a vast literature chronicles the many intersections between criminalization and poverty. The point here is to note the mutually reinforcing relationship between the criminal system and the public institutions tasked with supporting the socially disadvantaged. Any complete understanding of the criminal system must make space for this dynamic relationship.

Perpetuating Social Caste

The criminal process does more than simply manage crime and mete out punishment. It is also a central mechanism by which society marks and controls the socially vulnerable and politically disadvantaged. As the foregoing discussion indicates, it is impossible to describe the reality of the criminal system without including the corrupting effects of racism, class bias, and other mechanisms for institutionalizing disadvantage and conferring privilege. This phenomenon is not an independent dimension of the criminal system; it is woven deep into its every aspect. But it is precisely the constitutive effect of social caste on the criminal system (and vice versa) that makes it necessary to give separate notice to this interaction and the recursiveness it produces. From racially driven police selection decisions to longer prison sentences, from the school-to-prison pipeline to the lasting social burdens and exclusions imposed on offenders, the criminal apparatus imposes and preserves social and economic inequalities—in ways frequently untethered from individual blameworthy conduct.

Race is the most obvious and peculiarly American fault line that we manage and reproduce through the criminal process.[30] As Priscilla Ocen observes in this volume, it is impossible to comprehend the system without reference to the African American experience. But race is not the only basis on which the criminal system marks, controls, excludes, or dehumanizes its subjects. Poverty, drug addiction, mental illness, even residence in public housing or being on welfare: all serve as markers of social disadvantage at once heavily shaped by the criminal system and contributing to its immense scope. If we ever manage to transform our practices so that members of these disadvantaged groups were not disproportionally policed, criminalized, and penalized, we would radically alter the landscape of socio-economic and racial inequality in the United States.

To be sure, this insight is hardly new. As Mariana Valverde writes in her chapter, the criminal system has long been understood as a mechanism for controlling and managing "*misère*." But as many of the authors in this volume explain, the precise rules and techniques by which it currently does so vary widely. As Issa Kohler-Hausmann describes, those rules and techniques change over time and in different contexts. Sometimes rules work to reduce caste and inequality; sometimes they obscure and preserve it. Dan Richman argues that local conditions and politics make an enormous difference, and Mona Lynch similarly emphasizes the impact of individual actors and the cultures of the institutions in which they work. In many ways, this collection reflects a persistent desire to understand not merely how the criminal system operates, but also how it contributes to the most inegalitarian aspects of our culture and society, and ultimately how it might be otherwise.

This Collection

The authors in this book have collectively spent over a century dissecting the criminal process, asking what this process does and how it does it. We invited each of them to think expansively and critically about crucial aspects of the process, and each author has sliced the conceptual question in his or her own way. The resulting essays bring a wide range of perspectives to the enterprise, including administrative law, constitutional law, social psychology, moral philosophy, political theory, criminology, and critical race theory.

In 2013, we organized a conference co-sponsored by UCLA School of Law, Loyola Law School, Los Angeles, and NYU School of Law, at which this interdisciplinary conversation began. Some of the essays in this collection were initially written for that conference; these are accompanied here by shorter essays written in response by one or more conference participants. We subsequently invited additional authors to contribute to the collection; those essays do not have responses.

Each essay and response is a product of years of unique experience and scholarly perspective. They have their own special flavors and reflect a wide range of worldviews. Rather than trying to reduce them to neat categories, we offer the following roadmap to help the reader navigate this collection.

The first set of essays offer *Systemic Perspectives*—conceptual frameworks that we might use to understand the criminal system as a whole. The second set explores *Legal Doctrine in Principle and Practice*, the promises and limitations of legal rules and constitutional principles. The third set is about *Getting Situated*, shining a light on the situational and contextual nature of legal practices and outcomes, and the *Actors, Institutions, and Ideology* that inform their particular shape. The fourth section, *Humanizing the Question*, focuses on the dignitary and democratic values that the criminal system should manifest in practice. And finally, in *The New (Old) Criminal Justice Thinking*, we are reminded that all these questions have been around for a long time in various forms.

As will be apparent even from the brief summaries below, many essays overlap and pick up themes in other sections, which means this collection could have been organized in numerous ways. For example, there is no single section on race because most of the authors engage race and social disadvantage in ways that are integral to their analyses. Similarly, we do not segregate chapters based on the common "substantive" versus "procedural" divide because each essay grapples with the intimate relationship between process and outcomes in its own distinctive manner. Most of the chapters are interdisciplinary in various ways. We think this thematic messiness is appropriate: it reflects the rich, interrelated nature of the criminal justice system on multiple dimensions, and is itself a necessary component of the new criminal justice thinking.

Systemic Perspectives

The first set of essays offers different ways of conceptualizing the criminal system other than the traditional story about legal rules and guilty individuals. Each of these essays and responses is particularly attuned to the institutional realities of the criminal process: who makes the decisions, in what institutional context, and how those variations affect the normative trajectory of the system as a whole.

Rachel Barkow takes aim at the criminal-civil divide by reconceptualizing the criminal process as an administrative bureaucracy. She points out that prosecutors' offices make decisions in ways that are better explained by bureaucratic pressures and institutional history than by crime rates or individualized concerns about culpability or proportionality. Of particular importance is her argument that the explosion of the penal state and our current policies of mass incarceration can be explained at least in part by common principles of bureaucratic expansion and institutional self-interest, which in turn help us understand why the penal system grew so radically even as crime rates fell. As she puts it, in response to "the violence and unrest of the 1960s and 1970s . . . [t]he government created agencies and actors who have a vested stake in resisting any efforts to contract the system and who seek to maintain the rules that make those bureaucracies run most efficiently. The criminal regulatory state is thus a critical and necessary link to understanding mass incarceration in America."

In response, Dan Richman takes Barkow's challenge a step further. He agrees that the penal state can be explained in part by administrative principles, but argues that local variations in law enforcement resources and normative community commitments are powerful drivers that help account for the wide divergences in actual practice. "Why are some counties quicker to fill up prison beds than others? What trade-offs are being made between social welfare expenditures and policing expenditures, between policing expenditures and prosecution decisions? And why?" By reminding us of "the messy decentralized politics that are a hallmark of American criminal justice," Richman links Barkow's administrative model to the variegated realities of criminal practice on the ground.

Also in response, Stephanos Bibas reminds us that the criminal law is supposed to be normatively distinctive. He zeroes in on Barkow's primary conceptual move, in which the penal apparatus loses its special status as an adjudicator of moral culpability and becomes just another agency like the Department of Health and Human Services. While acknowledging that the modern penal state has in practice lost much of its moral compass and connection to public values, Bibas argues that we should fight rather than embrace this trend, and attempt instead to "return [the system] to its roots as a popular morality play." Bibas argues that we once had—and could have again—a more morally grounded, communitarian, and transparent model of criminal justice in which convictions are more tightly linked to individual culpability and community values. Or as he puts it, "What we need more of is not expertise or revolution, but transparent, accountable democracy rooted in the community's moral consensus."

This trio of essays invites a significant departure from the traditional criminal justice model. The conventional story is that legislatures pass statutes defining culpable criminal activity and the executive investigates and enforces those rules against offenders, who are punished only upon a finding or concession of guilt. The legitimacy of the process and ultimate punishment depends on the idea that this sequence defines culpable conduct in advance in a democratically legitimate way, and then accurately identifies people who have engaged in it. This scaffolding underlies most criminal legal theory as well as the standard commitment to due process. Barkow, Richman, and Bibas turn this familiar picture on its head. Their approach suggests that the administrative bureaucracy of criminal justice has itself become the source of penal legitimacy and power, and that it—and not our definitions of guilt or the personal culpability of criminals—best explains the outcomes that the system produces. While Barkow and Richman more or less accept this intellectual turn and Bibas resists it, they all agree that the modern criminal process has lost much of its special connection to the individual culpability of the offender.

Far from uniform, the criminal process works in different ways for different people and for different crimes. Sometimes formal rules clearly determine processes and outcomes, while sometimes social factors seem more salient. Alexandra Natapoff conceptualizes these systemic variations through the model of the "pyramid." The top represents serious felonies, the federal system, wealthy defendants, and the rest of the relatively small class of cases in which rule of law works more or less the way it is supposed to. Defendants who want to contest their guilt can have a trial, counsel have resources, and courts are receptive to arguments based on evidence and law. By contrast, as we move down the pyramid, cases get pettier, defendants get poorer, and counsel gets more burdened. By the time we reach the bottom—the realm of petty offenses and assembly-line courts—race, class, police arrest policies, and prosecutorial plea-bargaining habits best explain what the criminal system does and how it does it. Natapoff traces this dynamic to concrete doctrinal and policy choices. As she writes, "the pyramid . . . illustrates a profound feature of the penal system: sometimes criminal convictions can fairly be justified as a product of law and evidence, while sometimes they are better understood as a product of institutional practices and inegalitarian social relations."

In response, Meda Chesney-Lind notes that the pyramid model resonates with longstanding concerns in criminology, particularly the attempt to measure the effects of race, class, and gender. She offers concrete examples of the pyramid's operation from her own work, which showed that "bias against females was more pronounced at the [Honolulu] district court level (where minor offenses were prosecuted) than at circuit court levels"; in cases involving low-level offenses, women were actually more likely to be jailed than men. Similarly, she notes that "typically many more girls than boys enter the juvenile justice system" for status offenses like running away from home, "because parents are concerned about their daughters' and not their sons' behavior outside the home." Chesney-Lind ends with a challenge to criminology to "increas[e] efforts to describe and document the actual functioning of the criminal system, particularly the system that most U.S. citizens actually experience." In particular, she argues that "the field's traditional bias toward quantitative methods (and large national samples) must be augmented by richer, more detailed descriptions of key parts of the system that most people experience."

In these ways, the pyramid is a heuristic that helps organize a broad range of scholarship as well as widely held intuitions about the criminal process. It mediates the tension between the influence of social variables like race, class, and gender—weaker at the top, nearly dispositive at the bottom—while still acknowledging the vital role of rules. It also upends the usual conceptual hierarchy in which serious cases are treated as paradigmatic, while misdemeanors are dismissed as minor deviations from the due process ideal. Most Americans are criminalized through the misdemeanor process, which means that in reality the sloppy secretive bottom of the pyramid overwhelms the rule-bound transparent top, offering a new way of thinking about the system as a whole.

Legal Doctrine in Principle and Practice

The second set of essays takes aim at the relationship between principle, doctrine, and practice. The criminal system holds a distinctive place in our constitutional democracy, wielding awesome powers over life and liberty. Even as we rely on legal and especially constitutional doctrines to make sense of and legitimate those powers, chasms remain between what the law purports to justify and the everyday reality on the ground. These essays help us understand how that divergence comes about, and what we might do to better realign the way the system actually functions with the values it is supposed to embody.

Sharon Dolovich examines a pervasive contradiction that haunts key doctrines of constitutional criminal law. Throughout this area, the Supreme Court has affirmed basic constitutional principles—such as the right to counsel or the right against cruel and unusual punishment—that courts are to enforce against the state for the protection of individual penal subjects. Yet in practice, the governing doctrinal standards encourage judges in individual cases to affirm the constitutionality of state action seemingly regardless of the facts. As a result, at the precise moment of judicial review, when our constitutional scheme promises penal subjects direct critical scrutiny of their treatment by the state, the system instead delivers almost automatic and uncritical validation of whatever state action produced the challenged conviction, sentence, or punishment. Dolovich shows how this effect is achieved doctrinally, through the Court's repeated deployment of what she calls the three "canons of evasion," and she further identifies troubling questions raised by pervasive use of these canons for the legitimacy of the state's penal power. As she asks, "If the courts are not disciplining the criminal system—a site that presents strong temptations for state officials to cut constitutional corners—who is? And if the answer is no one, what does this mean for the degree to which citizens should regard the outputs of the criminal system as consistent with [our] core constitutional commitments?"

In response, Hadar Aviram considers three intellectual frameworks through which we might understand Dolovich's doctrinal insights. She argues that the classic "legal model," which views constitutional interpretation as a vehicle for furthering core legal values, naively assumes the neutrality of legal institutions. Conversely, the "socio-empirical approach," which treats courts as just one of many socio-political institutions that legitimate and reinforce existing structures of power and inequality, fails to grapple adequately with the nature of law and legal discourse. Aviram concludes that Niklas Luhmann's systems theory offers the most satisfying way to make sense of both the constitution's functions and its limitations. This approach helps us to see law's character as a closed system of communication. Although it is open to evidence from other systems and seemingly able to assimilate that evidence, law is structurally incapable of getting beyond the limitations of its own reductive legal/illegal dichotomy. For this reason, judicial review is ultimately an ineffective vehicle for resolving the complex challenges that typically give rise to constitutional claims. Systems theory, concludes Aviram, "offers us a modicum of modesty when expecting great things from the courts. If what we need are better defense attorneys, juries, and correctional officers, hanging our hopes on the flawed instrument of constitutional communication will prove hollow indeed."

Lisa Kerr provides a case study of the dynamic Dolovich identifies, focusing on U.S. courts' failure to extend maternal rights into the prison context. Highlighting the interest incarcerated mothers have in retaining custody of their newborn infants, Kerr illustrates how courts, although acknowledging that prisoners retain constitutional rights, drain the content of those rights in response to the most minimal justifications advanced by prisons and state officials. One particularly severe implicit consequence of state punishment thus becomes the permanent breaking apart of families. As Kerr shows, Canadian courts have largely adopted the same deferential approach to prison officials as have American courts, including—at least historically—with respect to claims brought by new mothers to remain with their children. But according to Kerr, one recent Canadian case—*Inglis v. British Columbia*—sharply diverged from this tradition. Not only did the judge in *Inglis* rule on the side of the prisoners, but her reasoning departed significantly, even radically, from what one typically sees in judicial rulings on prisoners' constitutional claims, even while resting on wholly recognizable and noncontroversial legal principles. As Kerr writes, "the *Inglis* court pushes for benefits to outweigh costs and demands sensible connections between the long-range goals of the system and its present-day actual operation." Moreover, "[r]ather than treating the prison as an exceptional space, where the difficulties of managing problematic residents can justify any managerial approach, the court constructs penal facilities as ordinary state institutions responsible to the full spectrum of public law commitments and values." In this way, *Inglis* offers a new model for judicial review of prisoners' constitutional claims—new criminal justice thinking for courts—on which "the fundamental rights of prisoners can be . . . bounded by higher law," rather than "the contingent product of local policy trends."

Getting Situated: Actors, Institutions, and Ideology

One of the most fertile aspects of this collection is the robust conversation it introduces between sociology, criminology, and legal theory. Many of the essays draw on multiple fields, but the three pieces in this section take the interdisciplinary challenge head on. They reveal how sophisticated insights from sociology, social psychology, institutional theory, and critical race theory can deeply enrich our understanding—both theoretical and applied—of how the criminal system actually functions.

Mona Lynch offers what she calls a "social psychology of criminal procedure." The term challenges us to understand local criminal justice processes and their outputs in a multivariate way: by considering individual "situated" actors, their institutional contexts, and the ways that rules engage, constrain, and are interpreted by both individuals and institutions. Drawing from sociology, social psychology, and structural legal analysis, Lynch proposes a dynamic model for understanding "local criminal justice systems (and the criminal justice actors and workgroups that people them) [as] hubs that translate and put into motion formal legal change to produce punishment outcomes." By way of example, she dissects a case study on racially disproportionate felony charging practices in Cleveland, Ohio, from the late 1980s until 2009. Lynch argues that in order to fully understand how the criminal process operates, we would need to unpack the specific individual, organizational, and cultural dynamics that produced those felony convictions: "How did the drug paraphernalia felony arrest policy get conceived of, enacted, and routinized . . . ? Why did prosecutors . . . take action to ratify those arrests as felony charges? Why was the practice so resistant to change even after its racially disparate impacts were made clear to system actors?" Such thick descriptions are critical as we rethink the system's institutional commitment to mass incarceration. "[A] full understanding of criminal justice practices," Lynch concludes, "requires fleshing out those fundamental human processes as they are shaped by the specific conditions that comprise the constituent organizations as complex social spaces."

Priscilla Ocen responds by applying Lynch's model to recent events in Ferguson, Missouri, and to the problem of discretionary racism more generally. She asks how a social psychology of criminal procedure might help us understand the situated and influential role of race for all the actors that make up the criminal justice drama, including not only police and prosecutors, but also local residents. Ocen argues that the "situated actor" model should take a page from critical race theory (CRT) and include the historical and "macro-institutional dynamics" of race, because "individuals and institutions [in the criminal system] operate in particular political and historical contexts that are deeply racialized." Specifically, Ocen reminds us that "many of the institutions that comprise the criminal justice system have historically been deployed to contain the 'threat' presented by non-whites, the poor, and other marginalized groups." This history still inflects the many assumptions, inferences and decisions that go into police and prosecutorial decision-making. Ocen also points out that the subjects of the criminal system are themselves situated actors, whose interpretations and operationalization of criminal rules and norms should also be accounted for in empirically rich ways. Ultimately, Ocen argues that Lynch's model and CRT would each gain much from thoughtful engagement with the insights of the other. As she puts it, "Lynch's model can provide an empirical basis for theoretical claims advanced by CRT . . . [including the] claim that race and racism are foundational aspects of the modern criminal justice system. On the other hand, . . . Lynch's model can incorporate some of the normative and methodological insights of CRT. Specifically, . . . the model can engage CRT's normative claim that race and law are mutually constitutive; that law constructs and reinforces racial inequality."

Like Lynch, Issa Kohler-Hausmann calls for a thicker understanding of the criminal system. She cautions us against the framework of surprise, in which we waste precious time dissecting the "surprising" fact that "law in action" diverges from "law on the books." Instead, she reminds us that law is a situated phenomenon, one that can never be fully explained or encompassed by its rules. Rather, "[t]he actors populating living criminal justice systems are working with (or under) all types of legal rules—those detailing proscribed behavior and authorized sanctions, those conferring powers and capacities, those defining roles and statuses, and many others difficult to categorize." To understand what law does, "we want to ask what exactly the frontline legal actors are doing with legal rules and how they interpolate them into an ongoing course of meaningful (although not necessarily beneficial) social action." Kohler-Hausmann then brings this question to two exemplary contexts discussed in the first section: the determinate sentencing/mandatory minimum regime (Barkow), and the lack of attention to individual guilt in low-level misdemeanor courts (Natapoff). In each example, she shows how practices diverge from legal mandates in significant and revealing ways that can be fully grasped only by examining the actual operations, histories, and outcomes of the process. Kohler-Hausmann concludes that "we must understand the particular commitments, constraints, and conceptualizations of current legal actors working with the rules we hope to change if we wish to change the outcomes produced by those rules."

Humanizing the Question

As Stephanos Bibas reminds us in the first section, the criminal system has moral, not just instrumental aspirations. Here, Jonathan Simon argues that whatever our moral commitments have been in the past, going forward, the modern criminal system should adopt the value of dignity as its governing ideal. Simon argues that the legality principle—once a primary engine for strengthening the criminal system's democratic legitimacy—has exhausted its sociological and jurisprudential power. Surveying 150 years of criminal legal commitments, Simon shows how the legality principle rose to prominence as a vehicle for reform and accountability, and then fell under pressure from mass incarceration and institutional racism. He concludes that, "with the proliferation of harsh criminal laws, even the demand for formal legality has become a weapon of the strong to streamline conviction and harden punishment." Accordingly, we need to supplement the legality principle with a dignity principle, "an increasingly prominent value in legal systems internationally since the middle of the 20th century." Simon traces the quiet development of various forms of dignity in Supreme Court jurisprudence, from police procedure to prison conditions, determinate sentencing, and mental health. He ends with a call to action: "the great banner reading 'nulla poena sine lege' must now be, not lowered, but joined by another banner of 'no crime and no punishment without respect for human dignity.'"

In response, Jeff Fagan takes Simon's project a step further by exploring the emotional dimensions of individual interactions with state actors. It is a step fueled by Fagan's own work in procedural justice in which he, along with Tom Tyler and others, examines the procedural legitimacy of legal institutions and how certain forms of official treatment are more or less likely to incline citizens to respect the state's authority. In this essay, Fagan considers the dignitary implications of official maltreatment, focusing in particular on the dignity-injuring potential of unjustified, racially motivated, or otherwise abusive police stops. Such interactions not only personally humiliate, but they also deny the targeted individuals "basic and essential recognition" as social and political equals, instilling instead "a profound sense of loss." In line with Simon's vision, Fagan calls for a jurisprudence that "recognizes the emotional highway between dignity and legitimacy." This approach would "internalize[] the central role of dignity and respect to regulate the relations between citizens and criminal legal actors," and condemn the "everyday indignities" inflicted even by officers whose conduct is "perfectly compliant with constitutional requirements."

The New (Old) Criminal Justice Thinking

Mariana Valverde wraps up the collection with a historical overview of the discourses that got us here in the first place. She explains that modern criminology has its roots in a long tradition of what she calls "miserology," the study of that "hybrid of moral degradation, physical ill health, spatial marginality, and collective despair . . . found among the new urban proletariat." It is an illustrious history, spanning Engels's focus on the "nameless misery" of British factory workers, great 19th-century novelists like Charles Dickens and Victor Hugo, Christian anti-poverty activism, modern welfare dependency discourse, and even *The Wire*. But criminology, like much of criminal theory, has lost touch with those deeply situated inquiries. Valverde points to the mid-20th century as a moment of schism between the professional study of crime and crime rates—what we now call criminology—and the study of housing, alcoholism, public health, mental health, and other poverty-related phenomena. But the early miserologists were engaged in a project that looks cutting-edge today; among other things, they recognized the role of criminogenic social conditions, understood crime as just one facet of a larger social reform project, and developed ideas about "spatialization." Valverde concludes that "further research in the intellectual history of criminology may well restore the social reformers, philanthropists, socialists, journalists, and assorted organic intellectuals of the 1830s and 1840s to their proper place as the pioneers of 'criminology.'"

* * *

We thought Valverde's essay—particularly her interest in de-centering crime—was an apt conclusion to a collection that in many ways seeks to do just that. Each author, in his or her own fashion, invites us to transcend the narrow framework of "crime" and "criminal" and to think in an institutionally, socially, and empirically situated way about what the criminal system does, how it does it, and to whom. Indeed, Valverde made us wonder whether Black Lives Matter might not itself be a new and timely iteration of "miserology," a call to recognize the pain and lived experiences of those most burdened by the criminal system. In many ways, this demand for a more just and equitable criminal process captures something profound about the current historical moment, in which the criminal system of the 21st-century United States has become a primary battleground for civil rights and social justice. The essays in this collection not only make sense of this terrain, but the conceptual tools they offer will, we believe, help point the way toward meaningful change.

NOTES

1 Bureau of Justice Statistics, Dep't of Justice, Correctional Populations in the United States, 2012 1 (2013), *available at* www.bjs.gov; Minor Crimes, Massive Waste: The Terrible Toll of America's Broken Misdemeanor Courts, at 11, Nat'l Assoc. of Criminal Defense Lawyers (NACDL), April 2009, *available at* www.nacdl.org; Michelle Natividad Rodriguez & Maurice Emsellem, Nat'l Emp't Law Project, 65 Million Need Not Apply: The Case for Reforming Criminal Background Checks for Employment (Mar. 2011).

2 Alexandra Natapoff, Gideon's *Servants and the Criminalization of Poverty*, 12 Ohio St. J. Crim. L. 445 (2015).

3 *See, e.g.,* Jill Leovy, Ghettoside: A True Story of Murder in America (2015).

4 *See, e.g.,* Jeffrey Fagan, Garth Davies & Adam Carlis, *Race and Selective Enforcement in Public Housing*, 9 J. Emp. Leg. Stud. 697 (2012); Amanda Geller & Jeffrey Fagan, *Pot as Pretext: Marijuana, Race, and the New Disorder in New York City Street Policing*, 7 J. Emp. Leg. Stud. 591 (2010); Tracey Meares, *The Law and Social Science of Stop and Frisk*, 10 Ann. Rev. L. & Soc. Sci. 335 (2014).

5 Am. Civil Liberties Union, The War on Marijuana in Black and White 40 (June 2013).

6 *See* Sharon Dolovich, *Two Models of the Prison: Accidental Humanity and Hypermasculinity in the LA County Jail*, 102 J. Crim. L. & Criminology 965, 992–

1012 (2012); Sharon Dolovich, *Foreword: Incarceration American-Style*, 3 HARV. L. & POL'Y REV. 237 (2009).

7   *See* Fiona Doherty, *Obey All Laws and Be Good: Probation and the Meaning of Recidivism*, 104 GEO. L. J. 291 (2016); Michelle Phelps, *The Paradox of Probation: Community Supervision in the Age of Mass Incarceration*, 35 L. & POL'Y 51 (2013).

8   Gabriel J. Chin, *The New Civil Death: Rethinking Punishment in the Era of Mass Conviction*, 160 U. PA. L. REV. 1789 (2012).

9   *See* Wayne Logan, *Informal Collateral Consequences*, 88 WASH. L. REV. 1103 (2013); *see also* National Inventory of the Collateral Consequences of Conviction *at* www.abacollateralconsequences.org (national database documenting over 38,000 formal collateral consequences).

10   Alexandra Natapoff, *Misdemeanors*, 85 S. CAL. L. REV. 1313 (2012).

11   *See* Dolovich, *Incarceration American-Style*, *supra* note 6.

12   *See* Bruce Western & Becky Pettit, *Incarceration & Social Inequality*, DAEDALUS (Summer 2010) 8 (explaining that prisoners have collectively become "a group of social outcasts," whose "[s]ocial and economic disadvantage, crystallizing in penal confinement, is sustained over the life course").

13   *See* KHALIL GIBRAN MUHAMMAD, THE CONDEMNATION OF BLACKNESS: RACE, CRIME, AND THE MAKING OF MODERN URBAN AMERICA (2010).

14   *E.g.*, ACLU, WAR ON MARIJUANA IN BLACK AND WHITE, *supra* note 5.

15   Daniel A. Skeel & William J. Stuntz, *Christianity and the (Modest) Rule of Law*, 8 U. PA. J. CONST. L. 809, 809 (2006).

16   Rogers v. Tennessee, 532 U.S. 451, 467–68 (2001) (Scalia, J., dissenting).

17   *See, e.g.*, Lisa Kerr, this volume (describing how imprisoned mothers lose custody of their newborn infants at the discretion of prison officials).

18   *See* JAMES B. JACOBS, THE ETERNAL CRIMINAL RECORD (2015).

19   KATHERINE BECKETT & STEVE HERBERT, BANISHED: THE NEW SOCIAL CONTROL IN URBAN AMERICA (2011).

20   *See* KAARYN S. GUSTAFSON, CHEATING WELFARE: PUBLIC ASSISTANCE AND THE CRIMINALIZATION OF POVERTY (2012).

21   *See* Beth A. Colgan, *Reviving the Excessive Fines Clause*, 102 CAL. L. REV. 277 (2014).

22   *See* Spatial Information Design Lab, *Million Dollar Blocks (2006)*, *at* http://spatialinformationdesignlab.org.

23   KIMBERLÉ CRENSHAW, PRISCILLA OCEN & JYOTI NANDA, BLACK GIRLS MATTER: PUSHED OUT, OVERPOLICED, AND UNDERPROTECTED (2015); CATHERINE Y. KIM ET AL., THE SCHOOL-TO-PRISON PIPELINE: STRUCTURING LEGAL REFORM (2010); *see also* Samantha Buckingham, *A Tale of Two Systems: How Schools and Juvenile Courts Are Failing Students*, 13 U. MD. L.J. RACE, RELIGION, GENDER & CLASS 179, 189–90 (2013).

24   NELL BERNSTEIN, ALL ALONE IN THE WORLD: CHILDREN OF THE INCARCERATED 145–46 (2007).

25   *Id.* at 147.

26 *See* Loïc Wacquant, *The New "Peculiar Institution": On the Prison as Surrogate Ghetto,* 4 THEORETICAL CRIMINOLOGY 377, 384 (2000).

27 Alexandra Natapoff, *Decriminalization,* 68 VAND. L. REV. 1055 (2015).

28 DEVAH PAGER, MARKED: RACE, CRIME, AND FINDING WORK IN AN ERA OF MASS INCARCERATION (2007).

29 BECKETT & HERBERT, *supra* note 19; ALICE GOFFMAN, ON THE RUN: FUGITIVE LIFE IN AN AMERICAN CITY (2014); Sarah Brayne, *Surveillance and System Avoidance: Criminal Justice Contact and Institutional Attachment,* 79 AM. SOC. REV. 367 (2014).

30 MICHELLE ALEXANDER, THE NEW JIM CROW: MASS INCARCERATION IN THE AGE OF COLORBLINDNESS (2012); LOÏC WACQUANT, PUNISHING THE POOR: THE NEOLIBERAL GOVERNMENT OF SOCIAL INSECURITY (2009).

PART I

Systemic Perspectives

How should we conceptualize the criminal system as a whole? The traditional response—that it is first and foremost a system of rules—is a famously impoverished answer, not least because it fails to account for some of the system's most powerful dynamics and doesn't begin to explain its wildly variable outcomes. In these essays, the authors offer richer, broader frameworks, with insights borrowed from administrative law, political theory, legal realism, critical race theory, criminology, and various other disciplines.

Rachel Barkow, The Criminal Regulatory State

Daniel Richman, Disaggregating the Criminal Regulatory State: A Comment on Rachel Barkow's "The Criminal Regulatory State"

Stephanos Bibas, Improve, Dynamite, or Dissolve the Criminal Regulatory State?

Alexandra Natapoff, The Penal Pyramid

Meda Chesney-Lind, Linking Criminal Theory and Social Practice: A Response to Natapoff

1

The Criminal Regulatory State

RACHEL BARKOW

When people describe the criminal justice system in the United States today, the topic often turns to mass incarceration. We now have more than 2.2 million people in prisons or jails, and nearly 7 million people under criminal justice supervision.[1] With 716 out of every 100,000 people incarcerated, our incarceration rate leads the world.[2]

Given its glaring dimensions, it is no wonder so many scholars have sought to make sense of how we arrived at this point. Commentators have pointed to broad cultural and political dynamics to explain the punitive turn in America.[3] In this essay, I have a more modest goal. I want to explain a mechanism that has helped translate these larger political and cultural dynamics into the expansive system we have today: the regulatory nature of American criminal law. Only by seeing the criminal justice system as a regulatory system can one fully appreciate how the system has expanded in the manner it has. Authors have persuasively pointed to political and cultural responses to the violence and unrest of the 1960s and 1970s to explain the turn to punitiveness. But to understand why the system did not contract—and in fact expanded—even as crime rates fell and its impact disproportionately fell on poor communities of color, one cannot ignore the bureaucracies created in that initial response to violence. The government created agencies and actors who have a vested stake in resisting any efforts to contract the system and who seek to maintain the rules that make those bureaucracies run most efficiently. The criminal regulatory state is thus a critical and necessary link to understanding mass incarceration in America.

To begin, in addition to thinking of mass incarceration as an undifferentiated mass, it is important to keep in mind the ways in which its subpopulations may matter. One stark feature of this system is its disproportionate impact on people of color.[4] African Americans make

up almost half of the people incarcerated, nearing one million people.[5] African-Americans and Hispanics combined make up 58% of the
prison population, even though they are only 25% of the U.S. population.[6] Between 6.6% and 7.5% of all black males ages 25 to 39 were
imprisoned in 2011.[7] More than 20% of black men born since the late
1960s have been incarcerated for at least a year, and typically two, for
a felony conviction.[8] In some cities, more than 40% of black men are
under the supervision of the criminal justice system.[9] If current trends
continue, almost one-third of black men can expect to be incarcerated during their lifetimes, while only 6% of white men face the same
expectation.[10] Race, then, is a critical part of the story of American
criminal justice, as even a modest understanding of American history
makes plain.[11]

In addition to understanding its racial dimensions, it is also important to pay attention to the different types of crimes that the system
covers. A large proportion of individuals serving time are doing so for
serious crimes. It is, of course, difficult to define with precision what
constitutes a serious crime, and reasonable people can disagree about
what would qualify. But there is no denying that a large portion of offenders are there for the kinds of crimes that take the greatest toll on
victims and society. Of those serving time in state prison, 53% are there
for violent offenses.[12] And, indeed, it was the rise in violence in the
1960s, continuing into the 1970s and 1980s, that provides the most natural explanation for the uptick in incarceration from the 1970s until the
early 1990s, precipitating what I will refer to as the first wave of mass
incarceration.[13] In understanding the mass incarceration of this period,
a logical starting point would be to question the reasons for the rising
crime rates to which it responded. That is not to say whether or not the
response was commensurate or proportionate, or whether lesser sentences for these offenders could be just as effective from a deterrence
perspective.[14] But the general contours of the story during this period
and with this population are not particularly puzzling. In the face of
widespread violence and serious thefts, it is easy to see why a society
would respond by seeking incapacitation of the individuals who commit
such crimes. Studies have shown that incarceration during this period
decreased crime, even if there is disagreement on the extent.[15] And even
if lesser sentences could achieve the same deterrence at a lesser cost, one

can understand why the public might still demand longer sentences as a matter of retributive justice for these serious crimes.

A more comprehensive story has to account for the other large group of offenders in the system. Most of the remaining offenders serving time are doing so for low-level crimes, including drug crimes. Many of these individuals came into the system during what I will call the second wave of mass incarceration that started in the mid-1990s and continues to the present day. The rate of incarceration ballooned in this period, even with declining crime rates,[16] and it had continued largely unabated until the recent budget crisis signaled what could be the modest start of a shift. Studies of this second wave show no statistically significant relationship between the growth of the prison population and the reduction in violent crime.[17] In fact, they show diminishing returns as incarceration increases.[18] As one study puts it, "beyond a certain point, [prison expansion] will no longer serve any reasonable purpose. It seems that that point has been reached."[19]

Joanna Shepherd, analyzing prison population growth studies from before and after the mid-1990s concludes that the reason this second wave may not yield crime-fighting benefits is because the increase was largely driven by offenders committing drug offenses and other low-level crimes.[20] She notes that for this group in particular, the crime-increasing effects of incarceration might outweigh the crime-decreasing ones. The longer people are incarcerated, the greater the difficulty they will have in maintaining family ties and obtaining employment upon release, and thus the greater the risk they will reoffend.[21] In addition, longer prison stays have detrimental effects on communities by disrupting family structures and removing a large proportion of adult males, a dynamic that has been shown to lead children in those communities to commit disproportionately more crimes.[22] The net effect is that, for low-risk offenders, shorter terms of incarceration reduce crime more than longer terms, and sentences with no prison time are more effective at reducing crime than sentences of incarceration.[23]

This second wave thus presents one of the biggest puzzles of American mass incarceration: why the carceral state has continued to grow to include more offenders committing drug and nonviolent crimes, even when studies show that it is counterproductive at fighting crime, imposes enormous fiscal and social costs, is particularly concentrated on poor communities of color, and does not serve the same retributive ends.

It is this aspect of American criminal justice that motivates this essay. I do not claim here to have an overarching theory that trumps or displaces any other. Nor do I want to suggest that the dynamic I will describe applies in all contexts or all places. Instead, I have a more modest goal. I want to add to our existing understanding by highlighting one feature of criminal justice that both eased its expansion from the first wave to the second wave and made that expansion appear routine: its function and operation as a regulatory system.[24]

The criminal justice system in the United States is a mass bureaucracy, and like other mass bureaucracies, it has certain hallmarks. The system has vested and powerful regulators who may fail to appreciate the tradeoffs and downsides when they pursue their goals because of a type of tunnel vision that develops. In addition, the system, because of the mass number of cases it must process, places a premium on efficiency.[25] This demand for efficiency, coupled with a commitment to treating like cases alike, leads to skepticism about—if not hostility to—individualized assessments. So there is a push for mandatory, one-size-fits-all sanctions that focus on the offense, not the offender.

To be sure, there is no single criminal justice system in the United States, so nothing here should be taken to mean there is a single bureaucracy that governs all of them. Undoubtedly, there are important differences among jurisdictions. But the general shift in thinking to eliminate sentencing discretion by judges and parole officers and to routinize and streamline case processing is something that characterizes attitudes in prosecutors' offices, legislative chambers, and sentencing and corrections agencies throughout the country. It is the dominance of that mindset and the resulting regulatory scheme it creates that I mean to highlight here. There may be exceptions to this way of thinking here and there, but there is no denying that it accurately describes a general shift in thinking in the United States.

Critically, unlike other regulatory systems, this system lacks traditional administrative checks to keep it from going beyond its initial mission or pursuing its goals when the costs outweigh the benefits. This regulatory dynamic helps explain the ease with which the system expanded from the first wave to the second wave, despite the very different prison populations encapsulated and the increasing evidence that the expansion had an enormous and concentrated effect on poor communities of color, ceased yielding crime-fighting returns, and cost an enormous sum of money to maintain.

This essay will explore the regulatory aspect of the criminal justice system in four parts. First, I describe how the politics produced during the first wave of mass incarceration paved the way for the massive bureaucratic system of criminal justice that is detailed in the second part. The third part then explains why that regulatory system may be prone to expand even when doing so fails to achieve crime fighting goals or incurs higher costs than benefits. Fourth and finally, I conclude by observing how some recent developments may be early signals that parts of this regulatory system are changing.

The Politics of the Criminal Regulatory State

Sweeping, persuasive accounts by scholars such as David Garland and William Stuntz explain how the modern politics of American criminal law grew out of massive disorder and violence in American society in the 1960s.[26] In the face of urban riots and spiking homicide rates, the public was dissatisfied with a criminal justice system it perceived as ineffectual and too lenient. This public concern set in motion a new political economy of criminal justice that has remained largely unchanged to the present day. Elected officials came to realize they could win voters by demonstrating that they understood their fears and would respond by being tough on those who were violent and socially disruptive. They also realized the converse was true, and they could lose voters if they were perceived as soft on crime and unresponsive to basic demands for public safety. While Republicans were the first to embrace this strategy, Democrats followed suit. If the lesson was not immediately clear to Democrats, it certainly became so after the Willie Horton ad campaign helped sink Michael Dukakis's bid for the presidency.

The major parties' tough-on-crime posture is not solely in response to public concerns with crime. It is also responsive to the demands of other key groups like prosecutors, rural communities that may depend on prisons for jobs, private prison companies, corrections unions, and victims' rights organizations.[27] And of course it plays to the media's focus on the most heinous crimes.[28]

The voices most likely to oppose this expansion have been relatively weak. Would-be criminals are hardly going to self-identify, and, in any event, most likely underestimate the likelihood that they will be caught and punished.[29] Those who have already been charged and convicted of crimes are not well positioned to lobby for change because they tend to be poor and disorganized, and, in some places, are disenfranchised from voting.[30] Their families and friends also tend to suffer from resource constraints.[31] And although the effects of mass incarceration have devastating economic and social effects on particular communities and blocks,[32] many individuals in these same communities have also supported a strong punitive response to stem the pervasive violence.[33] Similarly, although mass incarceration has hit communities of color particularly hard, racial justice groups have faced a conflict about how to address the issue, both because individuals in these communities are divided on how to deal with it,[34] and because these justice groups have competing missions that make it hard to put criminal justice at the forefront.[35] As a result, thus far they have largely focused on greater rights for law-abiding citizens and have shied away from focusing on criminal justice concerns. Because the politics of crime are so one-sided, they have likely seen focusing on criminal justice as a losing battle.[36]

Given this political imbalance, it is not hard to see why there is still a worry among many elected officials about being perceived as soft on crime, even as crime has faded in prominence as a public concern. Powerful, well-organized and well-financed groups have lined up on one side of the issue, so it appears costly to go against them. And there may seem little to gain politically in looking for innovative solutions to criminal justice issues because there are few identifiable constituent groups that would appreciate such efforts and reliably bring votes or donations in response.

In this political climate, it is also easy to see how criminal law expands—and how it does so across jurisdictions in America. Politicians seeking to demonstrate that they are responsive to social problems and unrest need tangible proof of that responsiveness. Passing new criminal laws is often the easiest path. The politics in this arena are so lopsided that passing criminal legislation is often the best avenue for getting something tangible accomplished before the next election cycle. Criminalizing a problem thus becomes commonplace, as Jonathan Simon astutely observes in *Governing through Crime*.[37] Instead of thinking about building new regulatory structures or improving existing ones, our society has grown accustomed to thinking of a criminal response as the solution to just about anything, from the financial breakdown,[38] to massive environmental damage,[39] to juvenile misbehavior,[40] because that is the political model they have seen time and time again.

The end products of this political landscape are sweeping criminal codes with duplicative and overlapping offenses that in most cases give prosecutors license to choose from a menu of options and to treat a wide swath of behavior as criminal. These codes also include severe and mandatory sentencing provisions that put the bargaining leverage in the hands of the government.

The Sweep of the Criminal Regulatory State

The political economy of crime described above has led to more than the extension of criminal law into new areas. It has also created an enormous and powerful criminal justice bureaucratic state.

Perhaps the most obvious example is the proliferation and expanded power of agencies responsible for regulating punishment. The most important of these are, without question, prosecutors' offices. The prosecutor's office increasingly operates like a traditional regulatory agency, as Judge Jerry Lynch has vividly described.[41] In many offices, an emphasis is placed on processing as many cases as possible because of crushing caseloads.[42] As a result, instead of the trial process dominating the system, more than 95% of cases are handled by an informal plea process that moves cases through the system quickly. The breadth and severity of the criminal code and the lack of a judicial check on plea bargaining mean that prosecutors have tremendous bargaining leverage to extract pleas.[43] A defendant who wants to exercise his or her trial rights will likely face a sentence after trial that is far greater than the sentence being offered at the plea bargaining stage.[44] With mandatory minimum sentences, prosecutors have direct control over the sentencing outcome after conviction; even in the absence of mandatory punishments, prosecutors typically have a range of statutory offenses to choose from in making their charging decisions, thus giving them a menu of sentencing ranges to choose from as well. Faced with an enormous trial penalty and overburdened defense lawyers who may lack the appropriate incentives to take cases to trial, the end result is that just about everyone takes whatever prosecutors are willing to give them.[45] In 95% of the cases, then, prosecutors are adjudicators as well as law enforcers. They are the key decision-makers in just about every criminal case.

Prosecutors have used this power to take on a legislative role as well. In addition to exercising enormous influence over the content of legislation and penalty provisions,[46] the terms of plea bargains have themselves become more regulatory in nature. Pleas are no longer just about agreeing to certain conditions of confinement or fines or restitution. They often involve much broader conditions, including insisting that defendants give up their right to appeal[47] or their rights to DNA testing, or mandating the preservation of DNA evidence.[48] In the corporate sphere, prosecutors use the threat of criminal punishment to change—or, more pointedly, regulate—corporate behavior. Prosecutors have adopted terms in non-prosecution or deferred prosecution agreements that require companies to fire officers, change business practices, disclose financial information otherwise not required by law, or even to stop marketing certain products.[49]

But the regulatory nature of criminal justice today does not stop with prosecutors. The rise in problem-solving courts is another example of how the bureaucracy of criminal justice has spread. Judges, often with input from prosecutors, take on key policymaking roles, determining how to deal with problems of drug addiction, mental illness, returning veterans, and domestic relationships, not to mention all the issues associated with reentry, from employment to education.[50]

Taken together, these problem-solving courts are a backdoor way of regulating the problems associated with poverty that, before the first wave of incarceration, were largely dealt with outside the criminal justice system. Indeed, many of these problems were core concerns of the War on Poverty. As that war was surrendered and gave way to the War on Drugs, the problems remained, but the strategies shifted. Instead of targeting as a general matter the problems of addiction, mental illness, unemployment, lack of job skills, and educational deficits that were particularly pronounced in poor communities, now the system focuses on these problems on a piecemeal basis as it deals with individuals who get entangled in the criminal justice system. As that group broadens—and with ten million misdemeanor cases being filed yearly,[51] it is, indeed, a relatively large population—more and more people receive services under the aegis of the criminal regulatory system. But the key ticket to entry remains the commission of a crime.

Prosecutors and judges are not the only key administrators in the criminal justice regulatory state. Other agencies, such as forensic agencies and corrections departments, play important roles as well.[52] And in terms of expanding the criminal regulatory state, another key development has been the demise of parole boards and the rise of sentencing guidelines. Although unheard of before the 1980s, sentencing commissions now exist in more than one-third of the states[53] plus the federal system, and guidelines operate in 21 jurisdictions in the United States.[54]

Guidelines are a critical part of the criminal regulatory state because they are, along with criminal statutes, the key substantive regulations. Before their advent, it was often hard to know exactly how much time an individual would serve. Sentences were indeterminate, with the ultimate release date governed by parole determinations and based on the individual defendant's progress. This model placed faith in the ability of punishment to rehabilitate offenders. That model came under attack in the 1970s as individuals on the right and left side of the political spectrum lost faith in rehabilitation. The end result was that many jurisdictions did away with parole and indeterminate sentencing and turned to a determinate model that was not tailored to individual offenders, but was instead keyed to the nature of an offense.

This new model thus required the identification of the key factors underlying an offense that would determine a sentence, with particular emphasis on those factors that are easiest to quantify and put into rules, such as loss amounts and drug quantities. The move to guidelines and determinate sentencing thus had a substantive effect, because it tended to place greater weight on the kinds of factors that were easiest to reduce to rules and tables.

Guidelines also changed the politics of sentencing. Just as agency regulations are easier than agency adjudications to police,[55] so too are guidelines easier to oversee than the individualized determinations that came before. As Frank Zimring predicted, the shift to determinate sentencing made it easier for legislative bodies to raise sentences because it became clear what the sentences actually were.[56] These guidelines are thus another critical component of the criminal regulatory state because they make it easy for legislative overseers to examine and, if they desire, change the policies. And legislators have been quick to do so because they have not traditionally viewed these decisions as requiring specialized expertise that requires any kind of deference to sentencing commissions or judges.[57] Thus, guidelines and statutory sentences tend to move in one direction—greater severity and sweep—because the politics in this area are so one-sided.

It is for that same reason that the criminal regulatory state itself has by and large moved in one direction—expansion. When all of the political forces line up on one side, it is a recipe for constant growth, unless some countervailing force holds the system in check. As the next part explains, those checks have, for the most part, been quite weak in the criminal regulatory state.

The Lack of Limiting Forces

The regulatory scope of the criminal justice system is comparable to any number of vast administrative regimes. But there is a critical difference with other civil regulatory agencies: the traditional administrative state has key features that keep regulatory agencies in check that are absent in the criminal regulatory state.

First, as noted, there is the political process. The political interests tend to be more evenly matched in most regulatory arenas than they are in the criminal context. Indeed, in most other regulatory contexts, it is the regulated entity that often has the upper hand and is well positioned to block laws that are too sweeping. It is commonplace these days to hear complaints in the civil sphere that regulatory targets "capture" their regulatory overseers. Whether or not that is true, it is clear that regulated entities tend to be well-organized and well-financed to fight against overreaching regulations.

It is equally clear that the dynamic in the criminal context is the opposite. The regulated targets—criminals—are among the weakest political groups (if not the weakest) in society. They not only tend to be poor, but poorly organized and with few allies that hold any political sway.

The regulators hold all the power, at least insofar as they want to regulate, because their legislative overseers stand ready to check underregulation but seem not to care about overregulation. So if prosecutors want a law to be broader or a sentence to be mandatory in order to increase their bargaining power, they tend to get their way.[58]

The second major difference is the role of the courts in policing the two regulatory states. Judicial review in the civil regulatory context is fairly robust, with courts standing at the ready to make sure agencies draw lines in rational ways, consistent with their statutory limits and purposes. Arbitrary and capricious decisions are not tolerated. While the standard is deferential, it is hardly a rubber stamp, and many regulations are remanded to agencies for more careful line-drawing and explanation for why the policy is consistent with the statute.

As with the politics, the contrast with the criminal regulatory state is stark. Judicial review of criminal justice agencies is almost nonexistent. There are effectively no limits on prosecutors, except for bars on unconstitutional discrimination, which is so hard to prove that successful actions are almost impossible to find. There is no general review for rationality in prosecutorial decision-making, and courts leave plea bargaining to the parties without providing substantive oversight. Prison regulators get a kind of super deference.[59] And even sentencing commissions—the agencies most like traditional civil regulators—do not face traditional arbitrary and capricious review.

The third key difference is review within the executive itself. Most state and federal administrative agencies must separate adjudicative and enforcement functions within the agency.[60] Civil regulatory agencies face considerable review of their regulations elsewhere in the executive branch.[61] For example, at the federal level, agencies face intense review at the Office of Information and Regulatory Affairs to see if the benefits of their regulations outweigh the costs.[62] In arguing for the need for this kind of cost-benefit analysis review, Christopher DeMuth and Douglas Ginsburg wrote in 1986 that a regulatory agency "will invariably wish to spend 'too much' on its goals. An agency succeeds by accomplishing the goals Congress set for it at thoroughly as possible—not by balancing its goals against other, equally worthy goals."[63] Thus, they argued in favor of "some countervailing constraint" in the form of review "by an office that has no program responsibilities" to generate more balanced regulatory decisions.[64] Indeed, just as the massive criminal justice regulatory state was emerging, a simultaneous movement was taking place to shrink the civil regulatory state, and this cost-benefit analysis was a critical part of that movement.

But the focus on fiscal constraint and a concern with government overreaching largely bypassed the criminal regulation state. There is generally no comparable review of any of the policies of the criminal regulatory state. Most escape review because they fall into the adjudicative category that escapes cost-benefit review in all cases. But even regulations such as sentencing guidelines fail to go through the process.

The end product of this regulatory structure has been the expansion of the criminal regulatory state without much thought as to whether its expansion is rational or yields benefits that outweigh its costs. There are no structural mechanisms in place to check for rationality or sound policymaking. The main limits on this criminal regulatory state are the individual judgments of prosecutors and budgets that are not boundless.

Understanding the operation of this bureaucratic state thus helps put in focus how the first wave of mass incarceration led to the second wave. In many ways, this shift took place with little thought to the very different populations it was addressing or the racial disparities it was producing. Instead, the expansion took on a life of its own because of the absence of any effective checking mechanisms to take a look at what the overall system was doing. Instead, the system forged ahead, one case at a time, without the kind of overall look at the big picture that characterizes the oversight of the civil administrative state.

Conclusion: The Future of the Criminal Regulatory State

The story so far, then, is one of a large regulatory state with all the strong political forces pushing in favor of maintaining that state. A key question that emerges is what, if anything, could break this dynamic and shift the direction of this system.

One possibility would be a change in the politics that produced the initial wave of mass incarceration. If public attitudes were to shift so that a tough-on-crime position became a losing political proposition, or so that the public valued politicians taking a smart-on-crime approach just as much, one would expect the operation of the criminal regulatory state to shift course. A massive system of incarceration is financially costly as well, so as the political system focuses more on costs, politicians might pay more attention to whether the money spent on incarceration could be better spent on alternatives and still yield the same deterrent benefits (or even greater ones). And because these costs are particularly concentrated in certain communities—and disproportionately communities of color—there are racial justice concerns as well.

There are some signs that the politics may be shifting. Racial justice concerns appear to be having a greater influence on criminal justice policy. The Fair Sentencing Act of 2010, for example, reduced the disparity in how crack and powder cocaine are treated at the federal level. Concern for the racial disparities the differential treatment created was a prime motivator for the change. And states have increasingly paid attention to the costs of incarceration and sought less expensive but equally effective alternatives for certain categories of offenses and offenders.[65] Prominent voices on both sides of the political spectrum have raised concerns about the fiscal and social costs of criminal justice policies and the need for rationality.[66] Individuals motivated by religious convictions and libertarian concerns have also become increasingly active in criminal justice reform.[67]

This movement is likely to have its greatest success addressing the population swept up in the second wave. It is less clear whether there can be a debate in the legislative space about sentence length, diminishing marginal returns, and the costs and benefits of penal responses for crimes other than nonviolent ones. Similarly, with respect to the expansion of criminal laws to cover nonviolent behaviors, drug offenses, and less serious crimes, the issue is whether they naturally get lumped in with more serious crimes as part of a discussion of "criminals" or "felons," or whether the politics can become more granular, so that the public separates out more serious threats from less serious threats and can understand the value in taking a less punitive approach with some offenses, given the costs and benefits of using incarceration and the criminal system. That all remains to be seen.

It is unclear how many of the changes can take place strictly in legislatures. Politics at the legislative level in the U.S. tends not to be particularly nuanced; generalities and powerful anecdotes are the order of the day. But that is part of why the administrative state was born: to work out the details and to administer general commands in the face of more specific situations and with a close eye toward data. The administrative state is all about making distinctions and drawing lines between categories so that rules are crafted only insofar as they achieve their statutory goals and/or their benefits outweigh their costs. But the administrative state works at this level of detail only because the checking mechanisms described above force it to engage in careful line-drawing. Those checks have been absent in the criminal context, which accounts for the sweeping expansion we have seen.

So even if the politics start to shift, fundamental changes would require a shift in the regulatory edifice as well. But here, too, there are some early signs that indicate such a shift may be starting to happen. In particular, a concern with evidence-based decisionmaking and cost-justified decisions in criminal law is starting to emerge and spread throughout the country.[68] If this takes hold and changes the way criminal justice agencies operate, it will incorporate a kind of rationality review that dominates in the civil regulatory space. And it will likely have a disciplining effect on the scope of criminal policies because many of them are not cost-benefit justified.[69]

Another nascent trend may be more court oversight. The Supreme Court in recent terms has shown a greater willingness to take a look at criminal policies. Although limited to juveniles, its Eighth Amendment jurisprudence is just starting to give non-capital sentences the kind of inquiry it has given death sentences.[70] It has also recently recognized the importance of plea bargaining in the system and the fact that the ability to take a case to trial is not a sufficient safeguard if a client receives ineffective assistance of counsel at the plea stage.[71] It has also held that the Sixth Amendment places limits on the ability of legislators to create mandatory sentencing guidelines that bypass the jury's role as a check in the system.[72] Taken together, one can see these policies as the beginning of a kind of judicial review of the criminal regulatory state. To be sure, it is far less than the oversight that exists in the civil sphere, but it could signal the start of a trend, either in constitutional law, or, more likely, in statutory developments that place a greater role with the courts.

Of course it remains to be seen how far these trends will go, or whether they are really trends at all. But whatever the future holds, it is clear that attention to the criminal regulatory state is critical for anyone seeking to understand the system as it actually operates.

NOTES

Thanks to Ariel Werner and Robbie Pollack for excellent research assistance.

1 LAUREN E. GLAZE & ERIKA PARKS, BUREAU OF JUSTICE STATISTICS, CORRECTIONAL POPULATIONS IN THE UNITED STATES, 2011, at 3, tbl.2, *available at* http://bjs.ojp.usdoj.gov.

2 Vikrant P. Reddy & Marc A. Levin, *The Conservative Case against More Prisons*, AMERICAN CONSERVATIVE (Mar. 6, 2013), *available at* www.theamericanconservative.com.

3 For a sampler, MICHELLE ALEXANDER, THE NEW JIM CROW (2010); DAVID GARLAND, THE CULTURE OF CONTROL (2001); JONATHAN SIMON, GOVERNING THROUGH CRIME (2007); WILLIAM STUNTZ, THE COLLAPSE OF AMERICAN CRIMINAL JUSTICE (2011); DO THE MEDIA GOVERN? (Shanto Iyengar & Richard Reeves, eds., 1997).

4 David Garland, *Introduction: The Meaning of Mass Imprisonment*, 3 PUNISHMENT AND SOCIETY 5, 6 (2001) ("Imprisonment becomes *mass imprisonment* when it ceases to be the incarceration of individual offenders and becomes the systematic imprisonment of whole groups of the population.").

5 NAACP, Criminal Justice Fact Sheet, *available at* www.naacp.org.

6 *Id.*

7 E. ANN CARSON & WILLIAM J. SABOL, BUREAU OF JUSTICE STATISTICS, PRISONERS IN 2011, at 1 (2012), *available at* bjs.ojp.usdoj.gov.

8 *See* BRUCE WESTERN, PUNISHMENT AND INEQUALITY IN AMERICA 19, 26 (2006).

9 *See* Alfred Blumstein, *Racial Disproportionality of U.S. Prison Populations Revisited*, 64 U. COLO. L. REV. 743, 744 (1993).

10 BUREAU OF JUSTICE STATISTICS, CRIMINAL OFFENDER STATISTICS, LIFETIME LIKELIHOOD OF GOING TO STATE OR FEDERAL PRISON, *available at* www.ojp.usdoj.gov.

11 For a compelling account of the historical relationship between race and the politics of crime, *see* WILLIAM STUNTZ, THE COLLAPSE OF AMERICAN CRIMINAL JUSTICE (2012).

12 E. ANN CARSON & WILLIAM J. SABOL, BUREAU OF JUSTICE STATISTICS, PRISONERS IN 2011, at 1 (2012), *available at* http://bjs.ojp.usdoj.gov. The estimated number of prisoners sentenced for violent crimes under federal jurisdiction as of December 31, 2010 was 15,000 out of 190,641, or just under 8%. Combining these figures with those in the text, the estimated number of prisoners sentenced for violent crimes under state and federal jurisdiction as of December 31, 2010 is just under 48%. CARSON & SABOL, BUREAU OF JUSTICE STATISTICS, PRISONERS IN 2011, at 10 tbl. 11 (2012), *available at* http://bjs.ojp.usdoj. gov. Another 17% of offenders are there for property offenses. *Id.* at tbls. 10, 11.

13 Joanna Shepherd, *The Imprisonment Puzzle: Understanding How Prison Growth Affects Crime*, 5 CRIMINOLOGY AND PUBLIC POLICY 285, 292 (2006) (de-

scribing studies of prison population growth using data from 1971 until 1989 or 1993 that showed a negative relationship between prison growth and crime and explaining that this increase in prison population largely consisted of individuals committing violent crimes and property crimes).

14 For example, because offenders generally have short criminal careers—10 to 12 years in length—and age out of criminal behavior, longer periods of incarceration may not bring any additional reductions in crime if the individual's criminal career would have been over in any case. Shepherd, *supra* note 13, at 290. So for some of these offenders, their sentences may not be serving deterrent or incapacitative purposes beyond a certain point, leaving the question of whether their sentences are justified as a matter of retributive justice.

15 *See, e.g.*, Thomas B. Marvell & Carlisle E. Moody, *Prison Population Growth and Crime Reduction*, 10 JOURNAL OF QUANTITATIVE CRIMINOLOGY 109 (1994) (finding a reduction in index crimes with increased imprisonment); Steven D. Levitt, *The Effect of Prison Population Size on Crime Rates: Evidence from Prison Overcrowding Litigation* 111 QUARTERLY JOURNAL OF ECONOMICS 319 (1996).

16 Crime reached its high point in 1991 and declined thereafter, with violent crime dropping a full 33% between 1991 and 2000. *Compare* Uniform Crime Reports: 1991, at 10, with Crime in the United States: 2000, at 11.

17 *See, e.g.*, Tomislav V. Kovandizic & Lynne M. Vieraitis, *The Effect of County-Level Prison Population Growth on Crime Rates*, 5 CRIMINOLOGY AND PUBLIC POLICY 213 (2006) (finding "no evidence that increases in prison population growth [correlate] with decreases in crime"); Shepherd, *supra* note 13, at 286.

18 Raymond V. Liedka et al., *The Crime-Control Effect of Incarceration: Does Scale Matter?*, 5 CRIMINOLOGY AND PUBLIC POLICY 245 (2006).

19 Liedka, *supra* note 18, at 272.

20 Shepherd, *supra* note 13, at 292.

21 *Id.* at 291.

22 *Id.*

23 *Id.* This explains John DiIulio's shift from declaring prisons a "bargain by any measure" in 1996 to stating in 1999 that policymakers should strive for zero prison growth. John J. DiIulio, Jr., *Prisons Are a Bargain, by Any Measure*, N.Y. TIMES (Jan. 16, 1996), at A17; John DiIulio, Jr., *Two Million Prisoners Are Enough*, WALL ST. J. (Mar. 12, 1999), at A14.

24 I am not the first person to highlight the administrative nature of the criminal justice system or to offer insights from administrative law that apply to criminal law. For rich accounts, *see* Daniel Richman, *Prosecutors and Their Agents, Agents and Their Prosecutors*, 103 COLUM. L. REV. 749 (2003); Gerard E. Lynch, *Our Administrative System of Criminal Justice*, 66 FORDHAM L. REV. 2117 (1998); Dan M. Kahan, *Is Chevron Relevant to Federal Criminal Law?*, 110 HARV. L. REV. 469 (1996); Ronald F. Wright, *Sentencers, Bureaucrats, and the Administrative Law Perspective on the Federal Sentencing Commission*, 79 CAL. L. REV. 1 (1991). In other work, I have explored the relationship between administrative law and

criminal law in greater depth than the space of this short essay allows. See, e.g.,
Rachel E. Barkow, *Prosecutorial Administration*, 99 U. VA. L. REV. 271 (2013);
Rachel E. Barkow, *Institutional Design and the Policing of Prosecutors: Lessons from
Administrative Law*, 61 STAN. L. REV. 869 (2009); Rachel E. Barkow, *The Ascent
of the Administrative State and the Demise of Mercy*, 121 HARV. L. REV. 1332
(2008); Rachel E. Barkow, *Separation of Powers and the Criminal Law*, 58 STAN.
L. REV. 989 (2006); Rachel E. Barkow, *Administering Crime*, 52 UCLA L. REV.
715 (2005).

25 For an expanded analysis of this concern with speed and efficiency, see STEPHA-
NOS BIBAS, THE MACHINERY OF CRIMINAL JUSTICE (2012).

26 GARLAND, *supra* note 3; STUNTZ, *supra* note 3.

27 Barkow, *Administering Crime*, *supra* note 24, at 728.

28 *Id.* at 749–50.

29 *Id.* at 726.

30 *Id.*

31 *Id.*

32 Jennifer Gonnerman, *Million-Dollar Blocks*, VILLAGE VOICE (Nov. 9, 2004),
available at www.villagevoice.com.

33 James Forman, Jr., *Racial Critiques of Mass Incarceration: Beyond the New Jim
Crow*, 87 N.Y.U. L. REV. 21, 36–45 (2012).

34 *Id.* at 42–44.

35 ALEXANDER, *supra* note 3, at 54, 211–17.

36 *Id.* at 211–17 (describing how the professionalization of civil rights organizations
"enhanced their ability to wage legal battles but impeded their ability" to address
caste in the criminal justice system, and explaining that civil rights advocates seek
"stories of racial justice" that evoke sympathy and defy stereotypes, which criminals do not).

37 SIMON, *supra* note 3, at 89–106.

38 *See, e.g.*, Mary Kreiner Ramirez, *Criminal Affirmance: Going Beyond the Deterrence Paradigm to Examine the Social Meaning of Declining Prosecution of Elite
Crime*, 45 CONN. L. REV. 865, 872 (2013) ("[G]iven what is known, one would
expect some criminal actions by the DOJ."); Colin Barr, *Where Are the Subprime
Perp Walks?*, CNNMONEY.COM (Sept. 15, 2009), *available at* http://money.cnn.
com (observing that "three years after the housing bubble popped, federal prosecutors have yet to bring a case against the executives whose firms took part in
some of the worst excesses of the subprime mortgage market," despite no "shortage of abuses to investigate").

39 *See, e.g.*, Amy DeLine, *A Century of Criminal Law and Criminology*, 100 J. CRIM.
L. & CRIMINOLOGY 309, 315 (2010) ("Lawmakers and citizens alike are calling
for criminal charges for BP and its top executives."); Joshua Fershee, *Choosing a
Better Path: The Misguided Appeal of Increased Criminal Liability after Deepwater
Horizon*, 36 WM. & MARY ENVTL. L. & POL'Y REV. 1, 3 (2011) (noting calls
for laws making it easier to prosecute companies for environmental disasters and

arguments for the imposition of strict criminal liability); Faisal A. Shuja, *Federal Criminal Issues Presented by the British Petroleum Oil Spill*, 9 LOY. MAR. L.J. 115, 115 (2011) ("BP should be held criminally liable rather than simply viewing the oil spill as a business loss."); David M. Uhlmann, *After the Spill Is Gone: The Gulf of Mexico, Environmental Crime, and the Criminal Law*, 109 MICH. L. REV. 1413 (2011) (presenting a comprehensive argument for the criminal prosecution of BP, Transocean, and Halliburton).

40 Deborah N. Archer, *Introduction: Challenging the School-to-Prison Pipeline*, 54 N.Y.L. SCH. L. REV. 867, 868 (2009/2010) (noting that "the often misguided approaches of our criminal justice system . . . are bleeding into our schools"); India Geronimo, *Systemic Failure: The School-to-Prison Pipeline and Discrimination against Poor Minority Students*, 13 J. L. SOCIETY 281, 281–82 (2011) (observing "increases in school-based arrests, student suspensions and expulsions, the adoption of zero tolerance policies, the use of disciplinary alternative education programs, and the criminalization of students for minor schoolyard misconduct"); Elizabeth E. Hall, Note, *Criminalizing Our Youth: The School-to-Prison Pipeline v. The Constitution*, 4 S. REGIONAL BLACK L. STUDENTS ASS'N L.J. 75, 76 (2010) (noting students arrested in school for a temper tantrum, failure to clean up, using a knife from home to cut food at lunch, making a cell phone call during class, texting during class, and throwing an orange at a classmate); Ann M. Simmons, *12-Year-Old Arrested in Vandalism of Middle School*, L.A. TIMES (Mar. 13, 2013), *available at* http://latimesblogs.latimes.com.

41 Lynch, *supra* note 24.

42 Adam D. Gershowitz and Laura R. Killinger, *The State (Never) Rests: How Excessive Prosecutor Caseloads Harm Criminal Defendants*, 105 NW. U. L. REV. 261 (2011).

43 Barkow, *Institutional Design and the Policing of Prosecutors, supra* note 24.

44 *Id.* at 880–81 (noting federal sentences are three times longer after trial).

45 *Id.* at 881–84.

46 Barkow, *Administering Crime, supra* note 24, at 728–29.

47 Alexandra W. Reimelt, Note, *Unjust Bargain: Plea Bargains and Waiver of the Right to Appeal*, 51 B.C. L. REV. 871 (2010).

48 Samuel R. Wiseman, *Waiving Innocence*, 96 MINN. L. REV. 952, 957–58 (2012).

49 Rachel E. Barkow, *The Prosecutor as Regulatory Agency* 180–81, in PROSECUTORS IN THE BOARDROOM: USING CRIMINAL LAW TO REGULATE CORPORATE CONDUCT (Anthony S. Barkow & Rachel E. Barkow, eds., 2011).

50 Pamela M. Casey & David B. Rottman, *Problem-Solving Courts: Models and Trends*, 26 JUST. SYS. J. 35 (2005); Judith S. Kaye & Susan K. Knipps, *Judicial Responses to Domestic Violence: The Case for a Problem Solving Approach*, 27 W. ST. U. L. REV. 1 (1999–2000) (calling for domestic violence courts in the problem-solving court model and describing New York's alternative courts); Michael L. Perlin, *"The Judge, He Cast His Robe Aside": Mental Health Courts, Dignity and Due Process* (NYLS Legal Studies Research Paper No. 12/13 #53; NYLS Clinical

Research Institute, Paper No. 31/2012, 2013), *available at* http://ssrn.com; Erik Eckholm, *Courts Give Addicts a Chance to Straighten Out*, N.Y. TIMES (Oct. 14, 2008), at A1 (describing Seattle's drug court program); Mosi Secret, *Outside Box, Federal Judges Offer Addicts a Free Path*, N.Y. TIMES (Mar. 2, 2013), at A1; Note, *Designing a Prisoner Reentry System Hardwired to Manage Disputes*, 123 HARV. L. REV. 1339, 1351 (2010) (describing the emergence of reentry courts designed to improve reintegration of offenders into the community, often overseen by probation officers and judges with the participation of public defenders and prosecutors). For Judge John Gleeson's discussion of federal drug court programs in the Central District of California, the District of Connecticut, the Central District of Illinois, the District of South Carolina, the Western District of Washington, and the Eastern District of New York, see Statement of Reasons for Accepting Deferred Prosecution Agreement Dismissing Charges Entirely, United States v. Emily Leitch (2013), *available at* www.talkleft.com.

51 Alexandra Natapoff, *Misdemeanors*, 85 S. CAL. L. REV. 101, 103 (2012).

52 At the federal level, prosecutors play a lead role in these areas because of the placement of these agencies within the prosecutorial-dominated Department of Justice. Barkow, *Prosecutorial Administration*, *supra* note 24. The federal criminal regulatory state is perhaps the broadest of all criminal regulatory systems.

53 Rachel E. Barkow and Kathleen M. O'Neill, *Delegating Punitive Power: The Political Economy of Sentencing Commission and Guideline Formation*, 84 TEX. L. REV. 1973, 1994 tbl.1 (2006) (listing states with sentencing commissions).

54 Rachel E. Barkow, *Sentencing Guidelines at the Crossroads of Politics and Expertise*, 160 U. PA. L. REV. 1599, 1560 (2012) (listing 20 state guideline regimes in addition to the federal system).

55 Rachel E. Barkow & Peter W. Huber, *A Tale of Two Agencies: A Comparative Analysis of FCC and DOJ Review of Telecommunications Mergers*, 2000 U. CHI. LEGAL FORUM 29, 67–71 (describing the ways in which it is more difficult to review adjudications than regulations).

56 Franklin E. Zimring, *Making the Punishment Fit the Crime*, 6 HASTINGS CENTER REPORT 13 (Dec. 1976).

57 Barkow, *Administering Crime*, *supra* note 24, at 734–35.

58 To the extent the laws regulate judges by curbing discretion over sentencing, judges are also not well primed as regulatory targets to fight back. *Id.* at 724.

59 Sharon Dolovich, *Forms of Deference in Prison Law*, 24 FED. SENT. REP. 245 (2012).

60 Barkow, *Institutional Design and the Policing of Prosecutors*, *supra* note 24, at 888 (discussing federal agencies). States with Administrative Procedure Acts modeled on the federal version, which is most of them, have the same or similar requirements. Michael Asimow, *Contested Issues in Contested Cases: Adjudication under the 2010 Model State Administrative Procedure Act*, 20 WIDENER L. J. 707, 723 (2011) ("American agencies typically are subject to internal separation of functions.").

61 JASON A. SCHWARTZ, INSTITUTE FOR POLICY INTEGRITY, 52 EXPERI-
   MENTS WITH REGULATORY REVIEW (2010), *available at* http://policyintegrity.
   org. Although this review varies greatly among states, it is far more robust than
   anything in the criminal sphere.
62 Exec. Order No. 12,866, Exec. Order No. 13,563.
63 Christopher C. DeMuth & Douglas H. Ginsburg, *White House Review of Agency
   Rulemaking*, 99 HARV. L. REV. 1075, 1081–82 (1986).
64 *Id.*
65 Rachel E. Barkow, *Federalism and the Politics of Sentencing*, 105 COLUM. L. REV.
   1276 (2005).
66 George Will, Opinion, *Leahy and Paul Plan on Mandatory Sentencing Makes
   Sense*, WASH. POST (June 5, 2013), *available at* www.washingtonpost.com;
   Richard A. Viguerie, Op-Ed, *A Conservative Case for Prison Reform*, N.Y. TIMES
   (June 10, 2013), at A23; Justice Safety Valve Act of 2013, S. 619, 113th Cong. (2013).
67 *See* Neil King, Jr., *As Prisons Squeeze Budgets, GOP Rethinks Crime Focus*, WALL
   ST. J. (June 20, 2013), *available at* http://online.wsj.com.
68 Organizations like Vera and PEW are working with states to make greater use of
   cost-benefit analysis, along the lines of what Washington does with the Washington State Institute for Public Policy. *See* PEW, Results First, *available at* www.
   pewstates.org; Vera Cost-Benefit Analysis Knowledge Bank, *available at* http://
   cbkb.org.
69 *See*, for example, the kind of analysis the Washington State Institute for Public
   Policy has performed to evaluate various programs and criminal justice policies
   in the state, *available at* www.wsipp.wa.gov.
70 Graham v. Florida, 130 S. Ct. 2011 (2010); Miller v. Alabama, 132 S. Ct. 2455 (2012).
71 Lafler v. Cooper, 132 S. Ct. 1376 (2012); Missouri v. Frye, 132 S. Ct. 1399 (2012).
72 United States v. Booker, 543 U.S. 220 (2005); Apprendi v. New Jersey, 530 U.S. 466
   (2000).

2

Disaggregating the Criminal Regulatory State

A Comment on Rachel Barkow's "The Criminal Regulatory State"

DANIEL RICHMAN

Rachel Barkow commendably goes straight to the hardest criminal justice puzzle: While the story of the massive increase in the U.S prison
population between the 1970s and the early 1990s—what Barkow calls
the "first wave of mass incarceration"—is inextricably intertwined with
the massive increase in violent crime and serious thefts during that
period,[1] what about the "second wave of mass incarceration," which
started in the mid-1990s and, notwithstanding declining crime rates
and current fiscal pressures, continues until this day? While modestly
disclaiming any overarching explanatory theory, Barkow suggests that
the "function and operation" of criminal justice as a regulatory system
"both eased its expansion from the first wave to the second wave and
made that expansion appear routine." With a recognition of the criminal
justice system as the wild and tangled criminal counterpart to the rational regulatory state will come, she suggests, the promise of balance and
reform, because we will think more productively about how to oversee
this bureaucracy.

I quite agree that there are considerable positive and normative pay-
offs to seeing police officers and prosecutors as subspecies of street
bureaucrats and to looking through an administrative law lens at the
strange world that gets constituted, but not ordered, by substantive
criminal statutes. Recognizing how penal laws often end up being just
subsidies for prosecutors to cash out for plea bargains, how the absence
of political support for moderation skews the legislative process, and
how enforcement dynamics can lead legislators to prefer harsh criminal
statutes to civil regulation—these are preconditions for clear-eyed assessment of that world.[2] But in our sprawling county-based criminal

justice system, there are limits to how far thinking in broad "regulatory state" terms will take us in understanding how we got into our national predicament, and how we will get out.

Consider some basic findings from John Pfaff's astute recent work on national imprisonment data: prison populations have indeed climbed during the 1990s, but "time served per admission" has not. Harsh sentencing numbers regularly get thrown around by legislators and doubtless have had an effect on plea bargaining. But Pfaff reports that sentence lengths do "not appear to have changed much at all between 1977 and the early 2000s, and that "to the extent that there has been any change since then, it has been in the direction of *leniency*."[3] Nor, according to Pfaff's analysis, have arrests driven the "second wave" of incarceration. Rather, the driver has been decisions by prosecutors to seek felony charges, which has in turn increased prison admissions and populations.

How do we explain the increased readiness of prosecutors, as an aggregate nationwide, to translate arrests into felony prosecutions resulting in prison (not jail) time? Macro regulatory failures will do some work on this score: "[p]rosecutors are county officials, but the state pays to incarcerate the [felony] defendants they convict; we should thus expect prosecutors to 'overuse' prison beds, since neither they nor their constituents bear the full cost."[4] And while states were left to pick up the bill, Pfaff suggests "that state-level officials may have been willing to tolerate these moral hazard costs [as] they do not appear to have crowded out spending on other programs."[5] To the extent that Barkow's "second wave of mass incarceration" has been driven by unreflective "buying" decisions by county officials, interventions like California's 2011 Public Safety Realignment Act, which shifted "virtually all of the responsibility for monitoring, tracking, and imprisoning lower-level felons previously bound for state prison to county jails and probation,"[6] can lead only to better decisionmaking.

Yet if one sticks with aggregate figures, one will miss the interesting action at the county level. On the eve of Realignment, David Ball recently reported that California

as a whole is divided between counties which persistently use prison resources at high rates and those which use prison at low rates. The counties with the highest rate of prison usage have, as a whole, below-average violent crime rates. They also have lower property and "Part I" crime rates. The argument that prison usage is driven by violent crime rates has no statistical support.[7]

One also finds radical discontinuities in New York State between New York City and Upstate.[8] While the routinizing and streamlining that Barkow describes is surely occurring, the connection between mass processing and unreflective deployment of punitive sanctions may be a lot more complicated than she suggests.

Why are some counties quicker to fill up prison beds than others? What trade-offs are being made between social welfare expenditures and policing expenditures, between policing expenditures and prosecution decisions? And why? There are limits to how far Barkow's sweeping "regulatory state" framework will get one here, in such a patchwork system insulated by strong norms of local autonomy. And I wonder what the "policy review" she envisions would look like. Must the disciplining interventions she calls for occur at the statewide level? And if at the county level, by (usually elected) county judges, why should we imagine "policy" judgments that differ from those of the elected prosecutors? Moreover, even putting aside the complexities of county-level regulation, I'm less sanguine than Barkow about judicial competence, at any level (including federal), to review discretionary enforcement decisions with an eye to the rationality of the policies that undergird them.

We do need to think harder about enforcement policies, however. And Barkow is quite right to push us to do so. The United States may lack the "police science" that Markus Dubber cogently describes,[9] but we do have a variety of police or prosecutorial "projects"—case-spanning decisions about what behavior and which neighborhoods should be policed in what way, with the formal criminal law playing only a regulatory, and not a proscriptive or defining, role. Actual violent crime need not be the only target of criminal enforcement projects, but it does provide a standard against which other projects and the intensity of their targeting ought to be measured.[10]

I suspect, however, that the reassertion of balance and proportionality that Barkow rightly seeks is more likely to come from the way in which the world of criminal enforcement differs from other slices of the "administrative state" than ways in which Barkow would (against all odds) make it more like them. Before turning to exogenous cost-benefit calculators, we might thus give more thought to the peculiar missions and outputs of the criminal justice system. Although police and prosecutorial projects—giving citizens a sense of security, protecting property, solving murders, disrupting terrorist plots—may vary, all are hostage to community participation, for tips and cooperation, for prospective jurors, as well as for funding and political support. Even as the extent to which citizen participation has been woven into the warp and woof of our decentralized regimes makes Germans blanch and leads Frenchman to decry our barbarism, we ought not forget the ways in which this participation can be a source not only of risk—of racism and political opportunism—but of balance. One need not valorize localism as much as Bill Stuntz did[11] or (on the other hand) deny the messiness of local equilibria—just consider the Bronx[12]—to recognize that in many of the same features that distinguish American visions of criminal justice from the Regulatory State lie the promise of regulation and improvement.[13]

The links between communities and "community policing" will vary from place to place and over time, as will the links between "community policing" strategies and actual prosecutions. But they are unavoidable—at least in the absence of a massive reconfiguration of the American criminal justice system—and, I suggest, worthy of celebration, particularly now that data collection and analysis has become not just a tool of policing and prosecutorial management but a means of monitoring and assessing the exercise of penal authority.

What makes Barkow's valorization of a hypothetical, hypercompetent Regulatory State particularly odd is that the pathologies of our actual Regulatory State drive considerable chunks of our current federal criminal docket. Of the 79,386 defendants sent to federal prison in 2013, 24,952 were immigration cases, 24,967 were drug cases, 8,057 were firearms, and 7,788 were fraud.[14] Regardless of any reader's specific normative views on immigration, drugs, firearms, and white-collar malfeasance, I'd be surprised if he could articulate a strong defense of the current allocation of enforcement resources between the criminal and regulatory regimes in any of these areas.[15] Indeed, far from simply offering a patient for treatment, the federal criminal docket itself offers lessons in the recalcitrance of certain policy spaces to cost-benefit analysis. So while I don't deny that rigorous cost-benefit analyses of the type

Barkow prescribes might well lead to more rational sorting at the civil/ criminal divide, I do wonder what lessons the actual Regulatory State offers in fraught policy spaces.

Let me end on a hopeful note, however. On criminal justice matters, as in so many others, the United States is a place of both underreaction and overreaction. When violent crime spiked in the 1960s and 1970s, we underreacted. As John Pfaff reports: "by 1977, violent crime had already risen by 257 percent since 1960, while prison populations had increased by only 31 percent, and had even decreased in absolute number every year between 1962 and 1968 (and again in 1972), just as crime rates were starting to rise."[16] Then we overcompensated, and prosecutors developed charging patterns that appear to have continued even as the tide of crime began to recede. (It's worth noting that "despite two decades of steadily declining crime, the rate of violent crime in 2010 was still 151 percent higher than in 1960, and property crime 94 percent higher."[17]) And—even though much of the decline can be attributed to California's forced reduction in prison admissions—there is increasing evidence that incarceration rates are starting to recede as well.[18]

That fiscal constraints appear to be driving recalibration processes in states and counties around the country is not surprising, because the political economy of criminal justice expenditures, particularly at the state level, is not as one-sided as Barkow suggests. The voices of criminal defendants may not be loud in the political process, but those of voters wanting to spend scarce dollars on schools, hospitals, and roads can be.[19] Moreover, voters' desire to pay for prison beds may be changing as well. Even in 2000, Francis Cullen, Bonnie Fisher, and Brandon Applegate reported that, although there was "no evidence" that citizens were "clamoring for a reversal of current correctional policy," the data did suggest that they wanted "their correctional system to be more than a machinery for inflicting harm."[20] And according to at least some 2012 polling, voters are quite ready to support less punitive polities, at least for non-violent offenders.[21]

To the extent politics do shift, Barkow suggests that the way out of our current state lies in some combination of legislated sentencing reform and a "regulatory edifice" that would promote evidence-based and cost-justified decisionmaking. Perhaps, but not necessarily. Consider California's Realignment Act. To be sure, the measure was sparked by judicial mandate because of prison overcrowding, and not by an ideological conversion experience. And the experiment has not run long enough to assess its impact on both incarceration rates and recidivism. But the county-level dynamics forced by Realignment are both a far cry from the optimal administrative process that Barkow envisions and a lot truer to the messy decentralized politics that are a hallmark of American criminal justice.

Without changing any statutory sentencing lengths, California simply transferred responsibility for housing or supervising thousands of non-serious, non-violent, and non-sexual cases to its fifty-eight counties, putting "few limits" on how they could spend the accompanying funding, and leaving them free to pick some mix of policing, jail, supervision, and treatment expenditures. Not surprisingly, a "study of the counties' first year Realignment spending plans found that they vary tremendously in terms of how their funding is allocated and the issues that they have prioritized."[22] Yet even in the absence of the reporting and outcome measurement that a rigorous "experimentalist" regime would call for,[23] I don't think it Pollyannaish to expect that over time (and notwithstanding deficiencies in the way Realignment was rolled out[24]), county decisionmaking will internalize inescapable information about fiscal and public safety outcomes. The process probably won't be pretty, and one can easily imagine the political backlash if (or more likely, when) someone who arguably "but for" Realignment would be in prison commits some heinous crime. But in California and, indeed, across the nation, local politics and messy conversations among local stakeholders ought to be embraced, not targeted—particularly when administrative rationality can't be counted on to make things right.

NOTES

1 John F. Pfaff, *Waylaid by a Metaphor: Deeply Problematic Account of Prison Growth*, 111 MICH. L. REV. 1087, 1089 (2013) ("Between 1960 and 1991—the heart of the boom in prison populations—violent crime rose by 371 percent and property crime by 198 percent.").

2 *See, e.g.*, Daniel Richman, *Federal Criminal Law, Criminal Law, Congressional Delegation, and Enforcement Discretion*, 46 UCLA L. REV. 757 (1999); Daniel Richman, *Prosecutors and Their Agents, Agents and Their Prosecutors*, 103 COLUM. L. REV. 749 (2003); Daniel Richman, *Overcriminalization for Lack of Better Options: A Celebration of Bill Stuntz, in* THE POLITICAL HEART OF CRIMINAL PRO-

CEDURE: ESSAYS ON THEMES OF WILLIAM J. STUNTZ (Michael Klarman, David Skeel, & Carol Steiker, eds. 2012).

3   John F. Pfaff, *The Causes of Growth in Prison Admissions and Populations* (Working Paper No. 1884674, 2011), *available at* http://papers.ssrn.com; *see also* John F. Pfaff, *The Myths and Realities of Correctional Severity: Evidence from the National Corrections Reporting Program on Sentencing Practices*, 13 AM. L. & ECON. REV. 491, 494 (2011).

4   Pfaff, *Causes, supra* note 3 at 21; *see also* Robert L. Misner, *Recasting Prosecutorial Discretion*, 86 J. CRIM. L. & CRIM. 717 (1996).

5   Pfaff, *Causes, supra* note 3 at 21.

6   Joan Petersilia & Jessica Greenlick Snyder, *Looking Past the Hype: 10 Questions Everyone Should Ask about California's Prison Realignment*, 5 CALIF. J. POLITICS POLICY 266 (2013); *see also* Joan Petersilia, *California Prison Downsizing and Its Impact on Local Criminal Justice Systems*, 8 HARV. L. & POLICY REV. 801 (2014).

7   David Ball, *Tough on Crime (on the State's Dime): How Violent Crime Does Not Drive California Counties' Incarceration Rates—and Why It Should*, 28 GA. ST. U. L. REV. 987, 998 (2012).

8   JAMES AUSTIN & MICHAEL JACOBSON, HOW NEW YORK CITY REDUCED MASS INCARCERATION: A MODEL FOR CHANGE? (2013), www.brennancenter.org.

9   *See* Markus D. Dubber, *The New Police Science and the Police Power Model of the Criminal Process*, 73, *in* THE NEW POLICE SCIENCE: THE POLICE POWER IN DOMESTIC AND INTERNATIONAL GOVERNANCE (Markus D. Dubber & Mariana Valverde, eds., 2006).

10 *See* Daniel Richman, *Federal White Collar Sentencing in the United States—A Work in Progress*, 76 LAW & CONTEMP. PROBS. 53 (2013) (exploring challenges of setting sentences for white-collar crime in world of unduly constrained civil regulatory enforcement).

11 *See* WILLIAM J. STUNTZ, COLLAPSE OF AMERICAN CRIMINAL JUSTICE (2012).

12 *See* Ailsa Chang, *Cycle of Mistrust Leaves Crimes Unprosecuted in the Bronx*, WNYC NEWS (Aug. 22, 2012), www.wnyc.org; *see also* William Glaberson, *Faltering Courts, Mired in Delays*, N.Y. TIMES, Apr. 13, 2013, *available at* www.nytimes.com (noting that "Bronx jurors are famously skeptical of the police" and that, in 2011, "Bronx prosecutors won only 46 percent of their jury trials").

13 *See* Tom R. Tyler & Jeffrey Fagan, *Legitimacy and Cooperation: Why Do People Help the Police Fight Crime in Their Communities*, 6 OHIO ST. J. CRIM. L. 231 (2008).

14 U.S. SENTENCING COMM'N, FINAL QUARTERLY DATA REPORT, FISCAL 2013. Tbl. 18, at 30.

15 On immigration, *see* David Alan Sklansky, *Crime, Immigration, and Ad Hoc Instrumentalism*, 15 NEW CRIM. L. REV. 157 (2012); Mariano-Florentino Cuéllar,

The Political Economies of Immigration Law, 2 UC IRVINE L. REV. 1 (2012); on firearms, *see* Daniel Richman, *"Project Exile" and the Allocation of Federal Law Enforcement Authority*, 43 ARIZ. L. REV. 369 (2003); on white-collar offenses, *see* Daniel Richman, *Political Control of Federal Prosecutions: Looking Back and Looking Forward*, 58 DUKE L. J. 2087, 2108–20 (2009) (discussing political economics of corporate crime enforcement); Daniel Richman, *Corporate Headhunting*, 8 HARV. L & POLICY REV. 901 (2014).

16 Pfaff, *Waylaid by a Metaphor, supra* note 1 at 1099.

17 *Id.*

18 PEW PUBLIC SAFETY PERFORMANCE PROJECT, U.S. PRISON COUNT CONTINUES TO DROP, Mar. 8, 2013; Petersilia, *Downsizing, supra* note 6, at 807.

19 John F. Pfaff, *The Empirics of Prison Growth: A Critical Review and Path Forward*, 98 J. CRIM. L. & CRIM. 547, 562 (2008) (noting relative strength of lobbies "whose access to funding is threatened by prison growth").

20 Francis T. Cullen, Bonnie S. Fisher, & Brandon K. Applegate, *Public Opinion about Punishment and Corrections*, 27 CRIME & JUSTICE 1, 67 (2000).

21 PUBLIC OPINION ON SENTENCING AND CORRECTIONS POLICY IN AMERICA (March 2012), www.pewstates.org.

22 Petersilia, *Downsizing, supra* note 6, at 809.

23 *Id.* (noting that the California legislature did not require counties "to report any results to the state or to measure the outcomes of their programs"); *see also* Charles F. Sabel & William H. Simon, *Minimalism and Experimentalism in the Administrative State*, 100 GEO. L. J. 53 (2011).

24 Petersilia, *Downsizing, supra* note 6, at 813 ("Our interviews elicited a portrait of counties struggling, often heroically, to carry out an initiative that was poorly planned and imposed upon them almost overnight, giving them little time to prepare.").

3

Improve, Dynamite, or Dissolve the Criminal Regulatory State?

STEPHANOS BIBAS

Rachel Barkow has been one of the most perceptive critics of American criminal justice in recent years, comparing its features to those of administrative agencies to highlight its structural flaws. Her chapter in this volume, "The Criminal Regulatory State," continues to mine that seam of ore. In many respects, she notes, criminal justice professionals behave like bureaucrats on a mission, maximizing enforcement without pausing to weigh the costs of overpunishment. Her account highlights how poorly fiscal and political constraints and executive and judicial review check overbroad criminal codes. The emphasis on prosecution and conviction as metrics of success leads police and prosecutors to overarrest, overprosecute, and overpunish low-level drug and other crimes in many cases. The impact lands hardest on minority communities and threatens the legitimacy of the criminal justice system in their eyes.

Critics agree far more on the broad outlines of the problem than on what to do about it. In this short essay, I want to sketch out three broad ways that one could respond. The first approach is to refine the system's bureaucratic tools to make criminal justice more like an administrative agency. That meliorist approach is the one Barkow favors, as she gestures toward cost-benefit analysis and similar reforms borrowed from administrative law, but it may simply grease the gears of a broken machine. It seeks to improve the means of criminal justice, rather than trying to reorient its ends. In reaction to meliorism, a radical critique seeks to smash the criminal justice machine in order to destroy its power imbalances; it condemns lesser reforms as papering over injustice. That radical approach is impractical. Instead, I want to advocate a third approach: loosening or dissolving the machine. Instead of relying more on expertise and wonkish incremental reforms or repudiating the whole exercise, I advocate a return to criminal justice's populist moral roots as the system's guiding star. What we need more of is not expertise or revolution, but transparent, accountable democracy rooted in the community's moral consensus.

Refining the Bureaucratic Machine

The criminal justice system is a mess, particularly when one views it through the lens of administrative law. It grew up haphazardly, contains little centralized decisionmaking, does a poor job of balancing costs and benefits, and has too few checks and balances or levels of review. An administrative-law scholar would naturally seek to refine the criminal justice system to approximate the institutional design of administrative agencies. Structural reforms could bring more bureaucratic rationality to the system, emphasizing evidence-based decisionmaking and a technocratic focus on the costs of enforcement.

As Barkow notes, one of the central reforms to the administrative state has been the introduction of systematic cost-benefit analysis to discipline agencies' overregulation. Agencies, she notes elsewhere, tend to pursue their primary mission at the expense of secondary missions and other values and tradeoffs;[1] outside review can check that tendency. The Office of Information and Regulatory Affairs (OIRA) within the Office of Management and Budget (OMB) forces federal agencies to justify their rules in cost-benefit terms.

One could try to introduce similar rationality in criminal justice, but substantial differences stand in the way. OIRA reviews agency rulemaking that reaches a substantial threshold of cost, but criminal justice is a matter of enforcement actions that rarely flow from any rulemaking at all. To make cost-benefit analysis meaningful in criminal law, one would first have to guide and constrain decisions to arrest, prosecute, and plea bargain with rules in the ways that sentencing guidelines have constrained decisions to sentence. Rick Bierschbach and I have proposed such a notice-and-comment approach to the decisions that culminate in sentencing.[2] Once that significant reform was in place, a centralized agency might then be able to analyze rules, if not enforcement actions, in terms of benefits and costs. Some state sentencing commissions, notably Minnesota's, apply similar criteria in evaluating sentencing rules, but one would need to rely on more supervision and internal policies within police departments and prosecutors' offices to serve as OIRA for arrest, charging, and plea-bargaining decisions. The costs and benefits of individual enforcement decisions would also be worth considering, but it would be impractical to systematize cost-benefit analysis for each enforcement decision.

Other reforms would flow from an emphasis on bureaucratic rationality. One is better data-driven decisionmaking. Criminal justice agencies are often decades behind in their information technology, making it hard for them to measure and improve their actual performance. Computer systems like CompStat have revolutionized policing in many cities, but most prosecutors' offices still lag behind. One area that cries out for better use of data is that of disparate impacts on minority communities. In some circumstances, data may indicate that racially disparate impacts are justified by greater rates of offending or violence. In others, better analysis may show that racial impacts flow from particular enforcement priorities, tactics, or biases that could be reformed. Either way, the debate is muddied by the lack of fine-grained data about what police officers and prosecutors are doing in particular situations and why.

Another set of refinements that could work well within the administrative framework is better personnel policies and incentives. Many criminal justice agencies do not think carefully enough about the kinds of people they want to hire and promote, the kinds of training they need to impart, and the monetary and non-monetary incentives needed to encourage effective performance. As I have argued, prosecutors' offices should take a page from the management literature, learning how successful companies hire, fire, train, promote, and compensate their employees to cultivate the right traits and performance.[3] Prosecutors' offices could also use performance evaluations and feedback to assess employees, reward their strengths, and address their weaknesses.[4]

Probably the deepest structural deficiency in criminal justice is that it lacks the checks and balances that are built into the administrative state. Plea bargaining bypasses juries and sidelines judges, so there are few external constraints on line prosecutors' unilateral sense of justice and efficiency. Nor are there many internal constraints. Unlike most bureaucracies, most police and prosecutors' offices require little or no approval by supervisors, leaving almost unfettered discretion in the hands of the lowest-level line officials. Shared office culture may still influence police and prosecutors' norms and sense of going rates, but that may not be enough to rein in outliers' idiosyncratic priorities and senses of justice.

Various reforms could introduce more checks and balances both within and outside police and prosecutors' offices. Internal office policies could require supervisory prosecutors to review and approve charges, plea bargains, cooperation agreements, and sentence recommendations according to specified criteria.[5] External checks would substitute for the disappearance of jury trials as effective constraints on enforcement discretion. For example, judges could take more active roles in plea bargaining, to provide unbiased perspective and rein in excessive charges and bargaining threats.[6]

These refinements all have much to recommend them. But the improvements they bring would be incremental. They would not likely assuage critics' deeper concerns that American criminal justice is misguided, broken, or out of control. To critics, this bureaucratic tinkering would resemble oiling a broken engine or straightening deck chairs on the *Titanic*, distracting attention from what is actually sinking the ship.

Smashing the Bureaucratic Machine

A more profound critique of the criminal justice machine is founded in wealth and power. On this view, the criminal justice system oppresses the poor and minorities. It uses punishment not primarily to effect justice or to protect public safety, but to rein in deviance and disorder, especially among the underclass. Though it pays lip service to justice and fairness, in practice it is a coercive tool of social control designed to maintain the status quo. Underneath the rhetoric of jury trials and constitutional rights lies a speedy plea-bargaining machine that uses conviction and punishment to control mostly poor, predominantly minority defendants.

Exhibit A in this critique is the underfunding and overwork that hobble indigent defense. *Gideon v. Wainwright* is a ringing endorsement of indigent felony defendants' Sixth Amendment right to appointed counsel. In practice, *Gideon* means much less than it does in theory. Voters are far less willing to fund criminal defense than criminal prosecution, because defense lawyers threaten to get guilty defendants off. Thus, public defenders are paid substantially less than prosecutors. Private appointed counsel receive low flat fees or hourly rates subject to inadequate caps, forcing them to plea bargain cases in rapid succession, often at the initial appearance. Contract attorney work is awarded to the lowest bidder, not the most vigorous or effective advocate. As a result, the best and most experienced criminal defense lawyers typically gravitate toward representing privately retained clients. And there is little funding for the paralegals, private investigators, psychiatrists, and forensic scientists needed in many cases to mount a vigorous defense.[7]

Compounding inadequate defense lawyering is inadequate criminal discovery. The adversarial system promotes trial by surprise and largely relies on each side to build its own case. Prosecutors have police, subpoena powers, and search warrants to build their cases, while defense lawyers often lack the time, powers, and private investigators needed to even the scales. Yet criminal discovery rules are much stingier than civil ones, counting on trials to air each side's case. *Brady* and *Giglio* entitle the defense to exculpatory and impeachment material, but not to the incriminating witness testimony that is central to evaluating the prosecution's case. In a world where most cases plead out before trial, the defense must bargain largely in the dark.[8] A third complaint is that enforcement focuses not only on violent and property crime, but on other offenses such as drug and low-level crimes, as Barkow objects. Drug enforcement is not limited to traffickers and violent gangs. It reaches down to low-level addicts dealing drugs to support their habits, inflicting long mandatory penalties regardless of violence or harm caused. Indeed, critics charge that prosecutors' use of confidential informants and cooperating witnesses offers leniency to wrongdoers with information to trade while perversely punishing those too inoffensive to have information to trade. It subverts loyalty and coopts minor miscreants as tools of a police state.[9]

What is to be done? Michelle Alexander favors having public defenders start a plea-bargaining strike to crash the system.[10] The Stop Snitching movement, popular in minority communities, discourages cooperation with police and prosecutors in making cases.[11] Paul Butler argues that minority jurors should nullify the law and refuse to convict minority defendants in nonviolent cases.[12] The American Bar Association recommends that public defenders refuse to accept appointments beyond the caseloads recommended by ABA standards.[13] And the Holy Grail of systemic critics is wholesale decriminalization or legalization of illegal drugs, effectively ending the War on Drugs. Failing that, large-scale diversion of criminal cases to drug courts, mental health courts, re-entry courts, and the like could effectively recast crimes as public-health and public-safety concerns.[14]

The system is indeed broken, and profound frustration is entirely understandable. But it is wishful thinking to believe that a revolution can bring the system to its knees. Collective action is notoriously difficult to enforce, and it is unethical to sacrifice a current client's chance of a favorable plea bargain or cooperation deal in the hope of benefitting future clients. Structural-reform litigation or public-policy advocacy cannot hope to achieve the massive funding increases that would be needed to lower caseloads, increase support services, and level the playing field.[15] Americans are unlikely to support drug decriminalization or legalization any time soon, except perhaps for marijuana users.

The other problem with this critique is its cynicism, its rejection of the system's professed ideals. Moral justice remains an American aspiration, even if we repeatedly fall short of it. Most crimes continue to threaten public safety and require some punishment and condemnation. And though race and poverty may partly explain certain crimes, they hardly excuse them. The solution is not to discard the ideal of equal justice under law, but to live up to it.

Loosening or Dissolving the Criminal Justice Machine

My critique of incremental bureaucratic refinements differs from that of the radicals. Cost-benefit analysis might be helpful but is not a panacea, in part because it flattens out the relevant values and policy considerations. As I have argued elsewhere, in many ways criminal justice places too much emphasis on a narrow vision of efficiency, stressing, in particular, speed, cost, and volume.[16] What we need is not a more efficient system but a more effective one that incorporates a range of softer values often overlooked by criminal justice professionals.

Thus, I want to advocate a third approach: loosening or dissolving the expert-run criminal justice machine by injecting more local democracy and more popular moral judgment. Superficially, this approach resembles the first approach because it too promotes reforms rather than revolution. But whereas Barkow emphasizes bureaucratic refinements to enhance the power of professional experts, my proposal is to reorient criminal justice's ends as well as means. The goal is not to destroy the system or to promote technocratic evolution, but to return it to its roots as a popular morality play. Many reformers want criminal justice professionals to act more like expert bureaucrats, guided by cost-benefit analysis, whereas I focus on loosening their grip.

At the root of modern criminal justice, I have argued, is a large principal-agent gap. Prosecutors and police supposedly represent the people and victims of crime. Yet the system is opaque and insular, running on auto-pilot and largely insulated from oversight and input from the community.[17] My goal is to scrape away the bureaucratic rust, myopia, and entrenched mindsets of criminal justice professionals to allow lay voices to reenter the conversation. The community-policing and community-prosecution movements gesture in this direction, but in many cases they are largely symbolic or honored in the breach.[18]

Professionals, fixated on speed and efficient plea bargaining, overlook various other values beyond crime control that also matter to victims and the public. For example, Tom Tyler has argued powerfully that the fairness of the process greatly influences its legitimacy in the eyes of the public, and Paul Robinson likewise shows that the substantive fairness of its outcomes bears heavily on the law's moral credibility.[19] Better informing and including the public in individual cases could promote both legitimacy and moral credibility.

There are many ways to limit experts' dominance and their relentless focus on efficiency and quantity to the exclusion of the quality of the process. For starters, the system could reopen roles for laymen, especially at the retail level of charging, plea bargaining, and sentencing individual cases and formulating local policies. This could involve eliminating the most dishonest forms of plea bargaining, such as charge bargaining and fact bargaining; better publicizing enforcement data; consulting with community groups on enforcement priorities; soliciting and incorporating feedback from victims, defendants, and the public; and restorative-justice measures.[20] Victims, defendants, and the public could not only see justice done but have a role in doing it themselves, giving them the satisfaction of their (brief) day in court.

Fiscal constraints can also play a role. When locals must weigh crime enforcement and prison building against funding local schools and hospitals, they may make more nuanced tradeoffs, experimenting with less costly alternatives for less dangerous wrongdoers. A greater emphasis on federalism and devolution can assist this weighing. California's realignment law, for example, forces counties to internalize the costs as well as the benefits of incarcerating or otherwise punishing defendants who have not been convicted of violent, serious, or sex crimes.[21] At the local or neighborhood level, criminal justice costs loom larger, and national media frenzies give way to local appreciation of enforcement priorities and costs.

Finally, this lay focus might support a loosening of lawyers' excessive focus on due process and procedural rules that lead to sclerosis. Inviting laymen to speak their piece, even briefly, could reorient the system back to more of a morality play and less of a technical game. Legal rules are a means to fair process and substantive judgments but are not ends in themselves. They should not obscure the broader goals of moral judgment, substantive justice, and serving the substantive goals of punishment.

This reform agenda is more ambitious and thus harder to implement than technical, incremental bureaucratic reforms. But it resonates with many people's dissatisfaction with the system, without having to smash the entire edifice. Our goal, in the end, should be neither to refine nor to destroy the system, but to loosen or dissolve it enough to return it to its common-sense roots as a transparent, participatory morality play.

NOTES

Thanks to Sharon Dolovich, Sasha Natapoff, and the participants in the conference entitled *Theorizing the Modern Criminal System: Law and Sociology in Conversation* for a stimulating discussion, and especially to Rachel Barkow for the opportunity to comment on her fine paper.

1 *See* Rachel E. Barkow, Prosecutorial Administration 33–37 (Jan. 2013) (unpublished manuscript) (on file with author).
2 Richard A. Bierschbach & Stephanos Bibas, *Notice-and-Comment Sentencing*, 97 MINN. L. REV. 1, 37–47 (2012).
3 Stephanos Bibas, *Prosecutorial Regulation versus Prosecutorial Accountability*, 157 U. PA. L. REV. 959, 996–1011 (2009).
4 *Id.* at 1011–15.
5 *Id.* at 1000–7.

6 See Albert W. Alschuler, *The Trial Judge's Role in Plea Bargaining* (pt. 1), 76 COLUM. L. REV. 1059, 1123–34 (1976). *Cf., e.g.*, FED. R. CRIM. P. 11(c)(1) (forbidding federal judges to take part in plea discussions).

7 See, e.g., Stephanos Bibas, *Plea Bargaining Outside the Shadow of Trial*, 117 HARV. L. REV. 2463, 2476–86 (2004).

8 See, e.g., Stephanos Bibas, Brady v. Maryland: *From Adversarial Gamesmanship toward the Search for Innocence? in* CRIMINAL PROCEDURE STORIES 129, 140–42, 146–51 (Carol S. Steiker ed., 2006).

9 Daniel C. Richman, *Cooperating Defendants: The Costs and Benefits of Purchasing Information from Scoundrels*, 8 FED. SENT'G REP. 292, 292–93 (1996); *contra* Frank O. Bowman III, *Defending Substantial Assistance: An Old Prosecutor's Meditation on* Singleton, Sealed Case, *and the Maxfield-Kramer Report*, 12 FED. SENT'G REP. 45, 47 (1999) (reporting lack of empirical data supporting the hypothesis that kingpins are more likely to receive substantial-assistance discounts than small fry).

10 See Michelle Alexander, *Go to Trial: Crash the Justice System*, N.Y. TIMES, Mar. 11, 2012, at SR5.

11 U.S. DEP'T OF JUSTICE, OFFICE OF COMMUNITY ORIENTED POLICING SERVICES, THE STOP SNITCHING PHENOMENON: BREAKING THE CODE OF SILENCE (2009), *at* www.cops.usdoj.gov; Jeremy Kahn, *The Story of a Snitch: Across Our Inner Cities, The Code of Omerta Has Spread from Organized Crime to Ordinary Citizens*, ATLANTIC MONTHLY, Apr. 2007, at 80.

12 Paul D. Butler, *Racially Based Nullification: Black Power in the Criminal Justice System*, 105 YALE L.J. 677, 715–22 (1995).

13 NORMAN LEFSTEIN, ABA, SECURING REASONABLE CASELOADS: ETHICS AND LAW IN PUBLIC DEFENSE (2011), *at* www.americanbar.org; ABA STANDING COMM. ON ETHICS & PROF'L RESPONSIBILITY, FORMAL OP. 06-441 (2006); ABA, TEN PRINCIPLES OF A PUBLIC DEFENSE DELIVERY SYSTEM 2 (2002).

14 Though supporters of problem-solving courts do not frame the purposes of these courts as back-door decriminalization, critics charge that is exactly what drug courts and similar problem-solving courts do. *E.g.*, Morris B. Hoffman, *Problem-Solving Courts and the Psycholegal Error*, 160 U. PA. L. REV. PENNumbra 129, 138–39 (2011–2012); Morris B. Hoffman, *Therapeutic Jurisprudence, Neo-Rehabilitationism, and Judicial Collectivism: The Least Dangerous Branch Becomes the Most Dangerous*, 29 FORDHAM URB. L. J. 2063, 2096–97 (2002).

15 A few courts, however, have allowed class actions challenging public defenders' underfunding and excessive caseloads to proceed. *E.g.*, Luckey v. Harris, 860 F.2d 1012, 1016–18 (11th Cir. 1988); Hurrell-Harring v. State, 930 N.E.2d 217, 222–24 (N.Y. 2010). And a few have allowed public defenders who are already overburdened to refuse to accept further court appointments. *E.g.*, Public Defender, Eleventh Judicial Circuit of Florida v. State, Nos. SC09–1181, SC10–1349, 2013 WL 2248965, at *6-*15 (Fla. May 23, 2013). *But see* State v. Clark, 624 So.2d 422

(La. 1993) (upholding contempt finding against private appointed attorney who refused to accept his fifth felony appointment over the course of four months because the volume of work was harming his private practice).

16 STEPHANOS BIBAS, THE MACHINERY OF CRIMINAL JUSTICE 30–34, 39–40, 110–14 (2012).

17 *Id.* at 29–48.

18 *Id.* at 146–47.

19 TOM R. TYLER, WHY PEOPLE OBEY THE LAW 94–108, 125–34, 146–47, 161–70, 178 (1990); Paul H. Robinson & John M. Darley, *The Utility of Desert*, 91 NW. U. L. REV. 453, 457, 474, 483–85, 488 (1997).

20 BIBAS, *supra* note 16, at 144–64.

21 *See, e.g.,* Magnus Lofstrom et al., Pub. Pol'y Inst. of Cal., *Evaluating the Effects of California's Corrections Realignment on Public Safety*, Aug. 2012, at 5.

4

The Penal Pyramid

ALEXANDRA NATAPOFF

Introduction

The American criminal system has a profoundly conflicted relationship to legality. At its best, the process is peerless in its lawfulness. Defendants have robust rights and can demand exacting scrutiny of the evidence against them. Federal courts peer over prison walls to enforce constitutional rules. U.S. police departments have become increasingly professionalized; data collection and scientific advances play a growing role in investigations.

Such careful rule-bound practices infuse legal theory with relevance. In this world, philosophical debates over culpability, due process, and rule of law are not mere thought experiments but robustly connected to ways that the criminal system actually functions.

At the very same time, the system approaches lawless chaos. Hundreds of thousands of suspects are railroaded into guilty pleas with little or no legal assistance. Nearly every month reveals yet another defendant wrongfully convicted of the most serious sort of offense. The public defense bar is sinking under the weight of massive caseloads and underfunding. Police in major cities openly round up young black men based on little more than neighborhood and time of day, while American prisons have become internationally infamous for their harshness, violence, and inhumanity.

In this world, legal rules neither explain nor justify results. Instead, socio-legal theories of power, social control, race, and institutional structure better explain the criminal process and predict its outcomes.

How can both stories be true? How can the U.S. criminal system operate in ways that are rigorously true to its theoretical commitments, and yet at the same time embrace seemingly lawless practices driven by social inequality, political expediency, and institutional habit? Or, to put it another way, how should we understand the competition between legal rules and socio-political fact in shaping the criminal process and determining its outcomes?

This essay proposes a way of conceptualizing the ebb and flow of legality throughout the criminal process. The penal system can be thought of as a pyramid in which law itself functions very differently at the elite top than it does at the sprawling bottom. The top is the world of federal offenses, serious cases, and well-resourced defendants, and here, rules dominate. The process is sensitive to evidence, transparent, accountable, and hypervisible. Lawyers and judges maintain a careful culture in which changes in the rules matter and outcomes are authentically contested. Think of high-profile acquittals like those of the Bear Stearns hedge fund managers, the Duke lacrosse team, and O.J. Simpson.[1] This is the "law" of rule of law, of legal theory, and of law school textbooks, and at the top, it can authentically be said to govern practices and outcomes.

By contrast, at the bottom of the pyramid where offenses are petty and caseloads number in the thousands, such rules hardly matter at all. Instead, outcomes are driven by institutional practices and inegalitarian social relations.[2] Suspects and defendants are handled in the aggregate based on discretionary police and prosecutorial decision-making that may or may not track legal principles. Defense counsel lack resources and incentives to test cases and evidence, rendering the process only nominally adversarial. The bottom of the pyramid is discretionary, weak on accountability and record-keeping, often rife with error, and largely invisible. Think of overwhelmed public defenders who "meet and plead" their clients in mere minutes, or the municipal court in Ferguson, Missouri, which the U.S. Department of Justice described as a place rife with "racial bias" in which poor African American residents are viewed collectively as "sources of revenue."[3] This is the world in which "law in action" bears little relation to the law on the books, in which explanations are social rather than legal, "guilt" is a cover for official action rather than an authentic moral pronouncement, and rule of law does little justifying work.[4]

The culture of the bottom invites mass injustice. Racial profiling, assembly-line convictions, and debtor's prisons thrive in this world where individuated justice is rare, rules are weak, and discretion permits discrimination. These phenomena also pose deep challenges for criminal legal theory.[5] This is because most theories of culpability, punishment, and procedural justice assume, if not always explicitly, the existence of a functional rule of law. Scholars argue over what the substantive law should say, or how procedures should work, because they believe that those rules and procedures will drive eventual outcomes. In effect, the morality and political legitimacy of individual punishments goes hand in hand with the belief in the existence of rule-bound decision-making.[6] When outcomes don't actually flow from rules, legal theory is left scrambling for explanations.

Not everybody thinks about criminal justice in terms of rules and rule of law. Sociology and other socio-legal studies offer powerful, extra-legal explanations for why the criminal system behaves the way it does, including race, class, the impulse towards social control, or what is sometimes described as the move toward an actuarial or risk-based system.[7] The pyramid is a useful heuristic in this regard because it illustrates why such social explanations often seem accurate but sometimes don't. Depending on where you are in the pyramid—closer to the top or lurking near the bottom—the influence of race and class, and the explanatory power of the social control model ebbs and flows vis-à-vis the classic explanatory power of legal rules and individual culpability. In other words, at the top, criminal law and its condemnation of crime actually explain and predict outcomes, giving doctrine and legal theory more purchase. At the bottom, social facts unrelated to defendants' guilt exert more influence over practices and outcomes so that socio-legal theories do a better explanatory job. And in the murky middle, some combination of legal rules and social facts generate outcomes that cannot be fully explained by either alone.

The pyramid thus illustrates a profound feature of the penal system: sometimes criminal convictions can fairly be justified as a product of law and evidence, while sometimes they are better understood as the result of institutional practices and inegalitarian social relations. In other words, sometimes people are convicted *because* they committed a crime and the rules require that they be punished, while sometimes people are convicted *because* they are poor, black, live in a heavily policed neighborhood, lacked counsel, or for other reasons that have nothing to do with rules or guilt.

To be clear, even at the top where rules work, convictions are not necessarily moral or fair. The U.S. Sentencing Guidelines and mandatory drug minimums, for example, famously produce unfair outcomes in serious cases even when people are actually guilty and all the rules have been scrupulously observed.[8] The most carefully litigated capital case might still be inherently unjust. But our system routinely produces convictions that are divorced even from those rules—fair or unfair—through processes untethered from standard criminal procedure. This is a different sort of systemic wrong—about how law manifests in practice—and it is the wrong that the pyramid helps elucidate.

The pyramid also helps explain why so many types of criminal scholarship seem to talk past each other. Some work focuses on the rules and the careful culture of the top: here, social facts are analytically secondary, treated as distortions of what would otherwise be sound outcomes. But for inquiries that start with the power dynamics at the messy bottom, formal rules are at best one piece of a largely sociological puzzle, and at worst post hoc justifications for socially determined outcomes.

This longstanding dispute over the causal role of rules goes to the heart of the criminal system's moral claims to legitimacy. It is, in effect, a way of asking whether personal culpability and actual guilt determine criminal justice outcomes. This is no mere formality. The old-fashioned idea that the criminal system is driven by moral concerns about individual culpability plays a powerful legitimating role with the public, the Supreme Court, and in the political and scholarly sphere. This remains true even as vast swaths of the criminal process openly jettison fidelity to that idea and to the procedures it demands.[9] The pyramid shows why. Because those ideals function relatively well at the top in full public view—for the wealthy, the well-represented, in white collar and other high-profile cases, for example—they validate many of the system's moral and theoretical claims about what it does. At the same time, the erosion of those legitimating ideals further down the pyramid takes place in ways that are harder to see, generates less political heat, and slips beneath the radar of the criminal system's own record-keeping and accountability mechanisms.

Any effort to model the criminal process in broad brush strokes must contend with its inherent diversity. There is no one "system," but myriad institutions, players, and local variations. The pyramid is shaped by innumerable pressures, from local budgets to election cycles.[10] But there are at least five factors—classics, if you will—that capture much of the dynamic and explain how the law often works differently for different people under different circumstances. Those five phenomena are *offense severity, race, gender, class,* and *defense counsel,* and they have each generated large literatures in their own right. Two have received the lion's share of attention. Race famously skews practices and results, and lack of defense counsel is often blamed when innocent people are convicted or the process fails to adhere to the law. But neither fully explains the ebb and flow of lawfulness throughout the system. Class and wealth affect the availability of legal process, while also regulating the roles of race and gender, and the legal culture of serious cases differs radically from the world of misdemeanors. Only by considering all these factors collectively can the concrete relationships between law, practice, and outcome be fully evaluated.

Of course these factors intersect in one particularly infamous way: African Americans tend to be poor, poor people tend to get less representation, and the criminal system treats poor African American men particularly harshly. In a pinch, the whole theoretical edifice might be summed up by the general proposition that people who are socially disadvantaged get treated badly by the criminal system. But this generalization shortchanges a complicated story. First, it is sometimes untrue in interesting ways. For example, in some jurisdictions an elite public defense bar provides stellar representation to the very poorest black defendants. Second, the generalization papers over important variations within the story, like the unique ways that we criminalize girls and women of color, or the special threats to undocumented offenders.

Third, the generalization obscures a key theoretical question: How exactly does law intersect with social context to produce all the different criminal practices that make up the system we actually have?[11] The question is key—and the central focus of this book—because a robust theory of criminal justice demands specificity about the circumstances under which law does or does not work, and why. And the influence of race, class, counsel, and other factors are not ghosts in the machine: they affect specific institutions, practices, and decisions that alter what rules mean, how rules are applied, and the outcomes they generate.

This chapter explores how offense severity, social status, and defense counsel together shape the penal pyramid. As a matter of intellectual discipline, the pyramid unites three basic fields: substantive criminal law (serious versus petty offenses), defendant socio-political vulnerability (race, gender and class), and criminal procedure (the right to counsel). Whether a crime is serious or petty greatly affects the degree to which formal rules determine its adjudication. Defendant race, gender, and class help explain why some defendants get the benefit of legal rules while others don't. And the availability of counsel—the right that enables all others—regulates the extent to which any defendant will be treated according to rule. While each arena has developed its own approach to questions of fairness and legitimacy, collectively they offer a dynamic picture of rule of law as a resource that is unequally distributed throughout the criminal system for explicable reasons and in quite specific ways.

The pyramid is more heuristic than formula. It does not let us calculate the precise impact of any particular variable, although criminology has an illustrious history of trying to do just that.[12] Rather, it is a way of organizing our thinking about major features of the criminal process that influence lawfulness and fairness, and our intuitions about whether criminal convictions are robust or suspect. It conceptualizes the system as a hierarchy in which we expect more lawfulness at the top than at the bottom, based on predictable interrelated reasons. It also accommodates the fact that the process is dynamic and highly situated: some minor cases involving poor minority defendants are rigorously litigated, while some serious cases with white defendants receive cavalier treatment. But in the main, the pyramid captures the average reality that wealthy white defendants with good lawyers and resources are likely to be treated in ways that comport with the law, whereas poor defendants of color, especially those facing minor charges, will likely have trouble getting the rules to work for them. More abstractly, it offers a bridge between the competing world views of legal theory and sociology, drawing out specific relationships between rule of law and socio-political fact, and a working story about the complex dynamics that generate millions of criminal convictions every year.

Part I of this essay describes the characteristic features of the top and bottom of the penal pyramid, and the combinations that make up the middle. Parts II through IV explore each of the classic factors—offense severity, defendant social status, and the provision of defense counsel—and locate them within larger conversations about how the law is supposed to work, in contrast to socio-empirical descriptions of the actual criminal process. Part V takes a step back and engages sociology's contention that law itself is an ideological—and often suspect—construct. The piece concludes with some thoughts about the mediating roles of transparency and the socio-political challenges of the bottom.

I. The Best and Worst of Times: Legality at the Top and Bottom of the Pyramid

For some people and under certain circumstances, the U.S. criminal system functions in exquisite compliance with formal law and procedure. The paradigmatic example is the trial of a serious offense conducted by skilled, well-resourced counsel in federal court. As a matter of practice, we expect to see such trials—or plea bargains worked out in their robust shadow—in white-collar cases where companies or individual defendants can afford and have the incentives to fully litigate their liability. We also see them in connection with serious drug or violent crimes where experienced defense counsel and prosecutors go head to head. Such cases might involve numerous motions, experts, appeals, publicity, and all the other procedural explications that accompany complex litigation. If one side violates a rule or misses a trick, the other side is likely to exploit it. Federal judges, drawn as they are from the elite ranks of the bar, expect and understand the invocation of a panoply of legal and ethical rules, and the expectations of the professional bar are likewise finely tuned to legal detail and compliance.

Of course this is not to say that such attorneys and judges are perfect, that they never slack off, break the rules, or make mistakes. It is rather to identify a culture that adheres to rules and understands that there are public and professional checks that enforce such adherence in a wide variety of ways. Often referred to as "highly regulated" and "exacting,"[13] the culture represents an ideal, to be sure, but it is also alive and well in some parts of the system.

It is here that the bedrock legitimating values of criminal justice are at their strongest. At the top, the criminal system can assert with a straight face that it proceeds according to rule and is centrally motivated by the culpability of defendants. The presumption of innocence, the right to counsel, due process, and the expressive moral value of criminal cases are at their height. This is the fodder for most Supreme Court cases and for much traditional legal scholarship devoted to analyzing what the law is and how it works. This is also where fears of a certain kind of miscarriage of justice are strongest: that the rich get more process than they are due, that criminals will escape on a technicality, or, until relatively recently, that serious white-collar offenders will be treated too leniently by legal decisionmakers who share their class outlook.

As we proceed down the pyramid, things start to look different. Offenses are lower profile and less serious; defendants and their counsel have fewer resources and greater incentives to plead rather than fight. Defendants have prior criminal records, making trials risky and reducing the stigmatic impact of yet another conviction. The public cares less, as do some of the judges and lawyers involved. As the threat of appeal and public scrutiny recedes, so does diligence in record-keeping and information gathering. While some posit two justice systems, one for the rich and one for the poor,[14] in practice there is no bright line. A host of pressures erode adherence to rules, resulting in fundamental if gradual changes to the way the criminal system does its work.

By the time we reach the bottom of the pyramid, the criminal system has become an entirely different animal. This is the universe of petty offenses, crowded dockets, and so-called "assembly line justice." Trials are nearly extinct and their shadows weak, as is the adversarial culture that is supposed to battle over rules and evidence. Instead, public defenders and prosecutors bargain wholesale over disposition of hundreds of cases, often in minutes. In many cases, there is no defense counsel at all and defendants encounter prosecutors alone.[15] Defendants who cannot make bail often languish in jail for months and may eventually plead guilty just to get out. Case outcomes (almost always guilty pleas) are governed not by the evidence in cases, details of substantive law, or the Bill of Rights, but by police and prosecutorial discretion and local bargaining habits. Down here, it is hard to maintain that the system is authentically motivated by defendant culpability because the players rarely stop to check whether defendants are innocent or not; instead it is presumed that everyone who enters the system is guilty in some way.[16]

If the top of the pyramid is adversarial, law-bound, and transparent, the bottom is bureaucratic, discretionary, and opaque.

As the pyramid metaphor implies, the top of the system is smaller than the bottom. While there are important counter-stories discussed below, the pyramid model rests on some basic empirical facts about U.S. criminal justice. The federal system, the best resourced and most transparent version of American justice, comprises only about 10 percent of U.S. cases. Felony convictions receive the lion's share of litigation and attention—nationally, two to three million felony cases are filed every year in contrast to approximately ten million misdemeanor cases. Most criminal defendants are poor—80 percent cannot afford counsel—so the vast majority rely on a public defense system that spends an average of $12 per capita.[17] The pyramid is thus an artifact of the unequal distribution of resources, attention, and transparency that attach in practice to only a small fraction of cases.

In a very general sense, the pyramid is old news. Sociologists and legal theorists alike have long noted that a privileged few receive far more legal process and attention than do the majority of disadvantaged defendants. But there is no consensus on the mechanics of how social disadvantage actually erodes the workings of legal rules, or precisely what ingredients go into shaping the pyramid. There is also no agreement on how to conceptualize rules and sociological insights as a whole.[18] The factors discussed below have each received their share of blame; taken together, they reveal more precisely the inner workings of criminal justice and the variable role of law itself.

II. Severity

Offense severity is arguably the least appreciated and most important factor determining the extent to which criminal cases are decided according to law. It is underappreciated in part because petty offenses are the second-class citizens of criminal theory, lacking the kind of attention lavished on serious felonies and seemingly paradigmatic cases like homicide and rape. But the misdemeanor system occupies far more of the criminal landscape than its felony counterpart. With ten million petty cases filed every year, most Americans experience the criminal system through the misdemeanor process. More specifically, the misdemeanor system is the engine of the urban policing phenomenon that sweeps hundreds of thousands of young black men into the criminal process every year, fueling not only the massive size of the criminal system but the initial stages of the racialization of crime itself.[19]

Offense severity constitutes the pyramid in a number of ways. First, it makes the top of the pyramid small because severe offenses are less common. Of approximately 1.1 million felony convictions issued every year, violent felonies represent approximately one fifth, homicide and rape cases comprise around 2 percent,[20] while death sentences now issue in only around one hundred cases per year, i.e., in less than 2 percent of all murders.[21] By contrast, the ten million misdemeanors cases filed annually constitute around 80 percent of most state dockets.[22]

Constitutionally speaking, severity triggers certain legal entitlements: grand jury presentments, jury trials, and the right to counsel being the most common, the enhanced procedural mechanisms accorded the death penalty being the most prominent. As a result, the more severe the offense and punishment, the more "law" a defendant becomes entitled to.

Serious offenses also command more law for political and institutional reasons. The public expects serious cases to be taken seriously, and prosecutors and defense offices devote more resources to them.[23] As a result, litigation is more common, bargaining is constrained by rules and evidence, and the law matters more. As William Stuntz once put it, "For crimes at the top of the severity scale, law defines both criminal liability and punishment," whereas for lesser crimes like drug offenses, crime and punishment are "defined by district attorneys and the police with whom they work, not by state legislators. In that kind of environment, law's marginal effect on plea bargains is, well, marginal. It may not exist."[24]

At the very bottom of the severity scale, the misdemeanor process is infamously light on both substantive law and legal process. The substantive content and statutory language of criminal statutes such as trespassing and loitering are routinely ignored. This is in part because such offenses are not motivated by the actual harms of trespassing or loitering but are better understood as general grants of power to police to manage certain social environments.[25] It is also in part because the legal processes surrounding such offenses tend to be quick and dirty, rarely resulting in serious litigation or appeal, permitting unlawful arrests and convictions to occur easily without challenge.[26] Likewise, procedural rights such as Fourth Amendment constraints, discovery, or evidentiary accuracy receive short shift in an environment where "[g]uilt is typically presumed in a process too rough-and-ready for the parties to develop and consider it properly."[27] In these various ways, law and traditional norms of adversariality and accuracy do less work at the bottom of the pyramid.

By itself, of course, severity does not explain why the criminal system so often loses touch with its own legal moorings. Even in serious felony cases, law sometimes fails. Stephen Bright famously described capital case outcomes as determined not by severity but wealth and access to counsel: "the death sentence not for the worst crime but the worst lawyer."[28] White defendants who kill black victims, and black defendants with light skin fare better than dark-skinned defendants.[29] Conversely, even the most minor offenses may be thoroughly litigated when defendants have the resources, counsel, and incentives to do so.[30] Severity thus interacts with other factors like race, class, and counsel to shape the process and helps predict when law will govern and when it won't.

Conceptually, severity is connected to core sociological insights about the expressive role of the criminal system. For example, the notion that the criminal process articulates shared moral concepts and reinforces social solidarity depends on the idea that criminal prosecutions and convictions represent moral judgments about defendant behavior.[31] But that idea is strongest in connection with serious offenses, and it depends on some basic doctrinal assumptions: for example, that criminal laws themselves define culpable conduct, and that convictions reliably indicate that defendants have in fact engaged in that conduct. In other words, theories like Durkheim's implicitly rest on a pretty traditional set of assumptions about what the criminal system actually does as a doctrinal and mechanical matter.[32]

At the top of the pyramid, such assumptions are relatively safe: serious offenses tend to define morally culpable conduct, and, notwithstanding the now constant stream of exonerations, serious convictions tend to demand evidence of guilt. But the bottom of the pyramid is a different story. Offenses like trespassing, loitering, and disorderly conduct are morally amorphous at best; the moral import of common offenses like marijuana possession is heavily contested.[33] Moreover, even if such offenses define shared moral prohibitions, the evidentiary processes of the misdemeanor system are so sloppy that no one can say with certainty whether misdemeanor defendants actually engaged in the prohibited behavior.[34] Instead, it is fairer to say that many petty offenders sustain convictions because police consider them good candidates for arrest, and that once arrested, the hydraulic forces of the petty offense process ensure that arrests convert to convictions.[35]

The collective condemnation of people who are likely to be arrested is also a form of social solidarity, but not the sort rooted in classic blameworthy individuated criminal conduct. Instead, it is closer to the kind of collective social marking and group control identified by a different strain of sociological thinking, one in which criminal processes constitute an exercise of social power over the disadvantaged who are presumed to be dangerous.[36] As Malcolm Feeley and Jonathan Simon once described it, "[a]ctuarial justice invites [the underclass] to be treated as a high-risk group that must be managed for the protection of the larger society."[37] In sum, depending on the severity of the offenses and their corresponding spot on the pyramid, different socio-legal descriptions gain or lose purchase.

III. Defendant Social Status: Race, Gender, and Class

Unlike severity, race has long occupied center stage in the debate over why criminal principles fall away in practice, giving rise to unequal justice and legally unjustified outcomes. The U.S. criminal system is routinely conceptualized and criticized as a not-so-covert system of racial control, with canonical tomes devoted to explaining how racism misshapes the criminal law and has produced the most racially disproportionate criminal system on the planet.[38] To a large extent, the discussion of racism in the criminal system addresses the experiences of black men. Because African American men are incarcerated at far greater rates than either white men or African American women, and because the black male experience represents for many the paradigmatic example of what ails the system, this focus is appropriate.[39] But gender shapes the pyramid in many ways. For one, the criminal system is heavily invested in defining, controlling, and often distorting the meaning of masculinity in general, and African American masculinity in particular.[40] African American women are punished and burdened in ways unique to the intersections of their race and gender.[41] The criminal law, moreover, has historically been slow to recognize the gendered harms of crimes like domestic violence and sexual coercion. In other words, while poor black men dominate the penal landscape, gender defines that landscape in complex ways.

Ironically, the focus on race has obscured the pyramidic nature of the criminal process because the system discriminates based on race at every stage, for offenses of all severities, against rich as well as poor African Americans. Because even prominent black men with access to good lawyers are discriminated against,[42] race appears indiscriminate in its distortion of all sorts of rules.

To fully understand the influence of race and its contribution to the pyramid, race must therefore be considered in conjunction with class.[43] Wealthy and well-educated African American men may be discriminated against based on their skin color. But their class status, residence in wealthy neighborhoods, speech, dress, knowledge of their rights, and access to counsel buffers them against the harshest impact of systemic discrimination. Their class gives them more access to protective rules and the means to invoke a robust legal response. Conversely, poor, undereducated black men, especially those without a high school diploma, are most likely to be swept up into the criminal system and treated lawlessly when they get there.

As James Forman points out, the class aspects of mass incarceration distinguish it from previous forms of institutional race discrimination like Jim Crow.

[O]ne of mass incarceration's defining features is that, unlike Jim Crow, its reach is largely confined to the poorest, least-educated segments of the African American community. High school dropouts account for most of the rise in African American incarceration rates. [A] black man born in the 1960s is more likely to go to prison in his lifetime than was a black man born in the 1940s. But this is not true for all African American men. . . . [F]or an African American man with some college education, the lifetime chance of going to prison actually decreased slightly between 1979 and 1999 (from 6% to 5%). A black man born in the late 1960s who dropped out of high school has a 59% chance of going to prison in his lifetime whereas a black man who attended college has only a 5% chance.[44]

Similarly, David Cole describes the elite aspects of the criminal system as "predicated on the exploitation of inequality":

> Absent race and class disparities, the privileged among us could not enjoy as much constitutional protection of our liberties as we do; and without those disparities, we could not afford the policies of mass incarceration that we have pursued over the past two decades.[45]

In these ways, race and class inequalities together generate the pyramid, the top of which functions in accord with rigorous legal norms, by creating a bottom in which inequality permits the suspension of those very same norms. Class does a certain amount of work on its own: numerous criminal practices effectively punish poor people of all races, in ways that range from the inability to make bail or pay fines to the heightened risks of job loss and other economic consequences.[46] And while race distorts the workings of legal rules even in the most serious cases and for the wealthiest defendants, its effects are radically enhanced as defendants proceed farther down the penal pyramid, growing poorer, less politically powerful, and less visible.

The most dramatic manifestation of this dynamic appears in the urban misdemeanor arena, where poor young black men are arrested, processed, and convicted of minor offenses with hardly a nod to due process or the substantive demands of legal rules. Specifically, the law fails at the bottom of the pyramid for this class of people and offenses because their race and poverty erode the application of identifiable rules. For example, as several lawsuits in New York revealed, quality-of-life policies encourage police to make arrests for all sorts of reasons—profiling, quotas, or to send messages in high-crime neighborhoods—thereby eroding the rule that arrests require probable cause.[47] Similarly, the rule that jailable misdemeanors trigger the right to counsel is widely ignored in misdemeanor court such that indigent defendants often must negotiate directly with prosecutors over their charges.[48] Such legal practices predictably weaken the force of law in certain classes of cases, permitting decisional factors such as race, poverty, and urban segregation to shape outcomes more powerfully than they otherwise would.

This legal dynamic resonates with a dominant strain in the sociological conversation about criminal justice, which understands the criminal process as a form of social control over African Americans and the poor. For example, Mona Lynch has described criminal law as a kind of subterfuge, where "the state invented the 'war on crime,' then the 'war on drugs' and most recently, the 'war on gangs' all of which are currently waged with harsh criminal statutes that only thinly disguise the target [poor African American] populations."[49]

Even more pointedly, Loïc Wacquant argues that the modern criminal system reflects "the gradual replacement of a (semi-)welfare state by a police and penal state for which the criminalization of marginality and the punitive containment of dispossessed categories serve as social policy at the lower end of the class spectrum."[50] In particular, Wacquant deems the mass incarceration of African Americans to be the fourth iteration of the "peculiar institutions" that have governed and controlled American blacks, after slavery, Jim Crow, and the ghetto.[51] For Wacquant, the confluence of race and class explains the penal process in ways that relegate criminal law to at best a footnote and at worst a manipulative political spectacle.[52]

The pyramid helps put law back into the sociological text, revealing the precise dynamics of law's failure to explain or justify how the criminal system treats poor black populations. In urban neighborhoods, city courts, as well as probation offices and prisons, we can see how institutional dynamics erode specific legal rules in ways that permit social hierarchies to assert themselves in legal outcomes.[53] The pyramid thus highlights how law affirmatively pulls back in certain social locales through identifiable practices of official discretion and noncompliance. This is an important meta-feature of the criminal system: social variables undermine rules and procedures in identifiable ways that make the law look irrelevant in predictable places, even as law remains vibrant and explanatory elsewhere.[54]

IV. Defense Counsel

The right to counsel is criminal law's primary mechanism for eliminating inequality. As the right that ensures that "all other rights of the accused are protected,"[55] counsel is treated by the Supreme Court and many scholars as both necessary and sufficient to level the pyramid: competent counsel guarantees that defendants of all races and class backgrounds receive legally comparable treatment. Indeed, scholars often identify the pervasive lack of counsel—underfunding and over-burdening of public defenders—as a central cause of systemic inequality and error.[56] If everyone had a good lawyer, so the story goes, differences in race, class, education, and other social inequalities would fade and criminal law would apply equally to everyone.

This story is partially true. High-quality lawyering clearly matters, altering outcomes and the availability of legal arguments, among other benefits. The federal public defense system and other elite public de-fense offices are widely lauded as providing quality representation to the poorest and most disadvantaged of defendants.[57] Indeed, good lawyers are often perceived to be so effective at manipulating the law that they can thwart justice on behalf of their clients, exploiting technicalities and impeding accurate convictions of the guilty.[58]

Nevertheless, the mere failure to provide counsel does not fully ac-count for the social inequities of the criminal process. Conversely, as I've described elsewhere, providing counsel alone is not enough to ensure lawfulness for all defendants.[59] This is so for a number of reasons. First is that the criminal system and its impact on individual lives is not lim-ited to the four corners of criminal cases. For example, a vast literature describes the corrosive impact that racially skewed stop-and-frisk prac-tices have on African American men and neighborhoods, long before anyone is charged with a crime or entitled to counsel.[60] More generally, even the Supreme Court has acknowledged that criminal procedure—defense counsel's greatest weapon—is poorly designed to regulate the social control function of policing because police may not care whether arrests result in convictions.[61]

Once people are charged with crimes, defense counsel become more influential actors, but even here their abilities are limited. They can-not control prosecutorial selection bias, overcharging, or judicial bail decisions—powerful factors that pressure defendants into taking pleas. This is due to the negotiated nature of the criminal process in which prosecutors hold nearly all the cards. As Stuntz explained:

> [W]here law does not reign, the district attorney's office generally does.
> This is one point on which I differ with . . . [the view that] defense at-
> torneys "are the linchpins of the plea-bargaining system": improve the

quality of the advice defendants get from their lawyers, and bargains will improve too. There is some merit to that position. But given the array of weapons the law provides, prosecutors are often in a position to dictate outcomes, and almost always have much more to say about those outcomes than do defense attorneys.[62]

In effect, the weaker the shadow of trial, the weaker the role of defense counsel.

Finally, many punitive aspects of the criminal process flow simply from passing through the process itself, captured by Feeley's famous phrase "the process is the punishment."[63] Defendants incur arrests records, undergo pre-trial incarceration, lose time from work, and may even lose their jobs in connection with the mere fact of having been brought into the criminal system. As Issa Kohler-Hausmann has described, even when cases are dismissed—the gold standard of defense lawyering—defendants are often still marked, controlled, surveilled, and burdened in lasting ways.[64] In sum, many of the punitive features of the criminal process are simply beyond counsel's reach.

The right to counsel functions best as an equalizer where laws and rules are important and can be contested. In other words, defense lawyers are most powerful in the robust adversarial process at the top of the pyramid. But much of the criminal system is no longer adversarial in any true sense. Instead, police selection decisions and prosecutorial charging discretion dominate outcomes in ways that marginalize defense skills and tools.[65] Accordingly, while the provision of counsel is a key determinant in how and whether individuals are treated according to law, it remains only one variable.

The right to counsel is the system's primary doctrinal answer to the sociological accusation that criminal law is a mechanism of class control in disguise, treating rich and poor differently.[66] And at the top of the pyramid, it's a pretty good answer. When rules matter, well-resourced counsel can often level the playing field on behalf of even the most disadvantaged client. But at the bottom, where overburdened counsel cannot meaningfully represent clients in the face of massive dockets and prosecutorial dominance, counsel failure is part of the mechanism through which a putatively law-bound system permits legal differentiation between rich and poor. In effect, the maldistribution of counsel resources and the inherent limitations on the role of counsel result in the unequal distribution of lawfulness based on defendant wealth.

V. The Changing Ideological Function of Law

It turns out that the ideological work performed by the criminal law is variable. Legal norms at the top are wildly different from the ones at the bottom and generate a criminal system with an inherently stronger relationship to law. This, in turn, makes legal theory more relevant at the top with respect to serious, well-litigated cases because its primary subject—a law that determines outcomes and meanings—is a more robust part of the criminal process itself. Here, sociological stories about race, class, and power are incomplete: they miss something important if they do not consider the robust role of rules, their power over the way such cases are handled, and their contribution to the social significance of such cases.

At the bottom, by contrast, legal theory has less explanatory power (and sociology more) precisely because legal norms are weaker engines. Here, formal law has run out of steam, so to speak, and other dynamics have taken its place. Notions of social control and institutional power thus offer more persuasive explanations for case outcomes.

Perhaps the deepest conflict between the legal and sociological perspectives is the dispute over systemic motivation. Criminal law contends that we arrest, convict, and punish people *because* they commit crime. In other words, the motivations of the criminal process and its players are driven by the rules of criminal conduct embodied in law and the desire to combat crime and punish the guilty. Sociology, by contrast, implicitly rejects that story by offering myriad alternative explanations and motivations for what the criminal system does, ranging from racial dominance to social control to institutional and group behaviors. It is a fundamental theoretical disagreement about what the criminal system is for.[67]

The pyramid suggests that both perspectives may be right, just in different places. At the top, the system is indeed motivated by classic notions of law, crime, and culpability. But because adherence to those ideals is a scarce resource, akin to what Lawrence Friedman once called the "luxury of slow individuated justice,"[68] it eventually wanes, giving way to other motives and values.

Variables like offense severity, race, class, and counsel reveal the granular ways in which this works. The assembly-line culture of misdemeanor court erodes the relevance of legality. The maldistribution of the right to counsel generates class-based outcomes. Fourth Amendment doctrine affirmatively permits race to infuse police discretion. These are the concrete mechanisms through which social facts influence the meaning of legal rules. Instead of leaving sociology at the door when we enter the castle of doctrine, sociology describes the very pressures and tendencies that lead to well-recognized failures of legal principle.

Conversely, sociology cannot ignore the ideological sway of rules and rule of law. As David Garland argues, law should be understood as a powerful source of social meaning in its own right: "punishment is a form of social action which operates within a legal framework and is deeply affected by legal forms and procedures."[69] In other words, legal forms and procedures—the subject of legal theory—are integral to the influence that criminal justice has on social organization and understandings.

At the top, fidelity to legal principle holds out the promise of a certain kind of fairness. In this vein, Randall Kennedy once famously asserted that "the principal injury suffered by African-Americans in relation to criminal matters is not overenforcement but underenforcement," namely, the failure to protect or provide *enough* law.[70] Kennedy's claim reflects criminal law's universal appeal: the idea that if law worked the way it should, it would go after crime and not classes of people. Kennedy's complaint is that racism deprives African Americans of this ideal. But his complaint presupposes the potential for law to function neutrally and in accord with its universal precepts, in other words, the way it mostly does at the top of the pyramid.[71]

By contrast, at the bottom of the pyramid, law's universality gives way because so many of its defining legal forms and principles such as probable cause and the right to counsel are ignored. Like Herbert Packer's famous "crime control" model, or Feeley and Simon's actuarial paradigm, the lower reaches of the criminal system sidestep classic rules of due process and individual liability and treat the dispossessed through the social logic of "danger management, not individualized criminal justice."[72] In this way, criminal law assumes a different ideological character, motivated by norms of race and class control and relatively indifferent to the seemingly universal values of law and culpability that shape the process at the top.

VI. The Distributive Role of Transparency

The ideas behind the pyramid have been around for a long time. We've always known that the rich get more due process than the poor, that formal law is stronger in some places than others. But the bottom of the pyramid has gotten less than its fair share of attention. This is in part due to the nature of what sits at the bottom: minor cases in which law doesn't do much work, processed in bulk in low-visibility circumstances. Legal theory tends to focus on serious cases in which culpability issues are interesting or where procedural issues are challenging. This sort of sustained attention requires information, something in short supply at the bottom.

A final lesson of the pyramid is therefore that transparency generates more lawfulness: we can view and theorize serious, federal, and/or well-litigated cases because the system produces records about them. By contrast, some jurisdictions do not even count petty convictions, some misdemeanor courts produce no transcripts, and the overall lack of adversarial litigation ensures that records remain thin. In a chicken-and-egg dynamic, traditional law is lacking at the bottom because no one cares enough to keep careful track of what happens down there, and, because there's no law, there's no record of the miscarriages of justice.[73]

By way of example, Chief Justice Jean Hoefer Toal of the Supreme Court of South Carolina recently admitted that her state doesn't bother appointing counsel in many misdemeanor cases even though the U.S. Supreme Court requires it. In her words, she disagrees with the decision in *Alabama v. Shelton*[74] to require counsel.

> *Alabama v. Shelton* is one of the more misguided decisions of the Supreme Court, I must say . . . so I will tell you straight up we are not adhering to *Alabama v. Shelton* in every situation.[75]

In the eyes of this judicial official, the petty cases at the bottom of the pyramid literally do not deserve legality. This judicial view exerts a legal force of its own: at the bottom, in effect, courts are authorized to ignore the rules. Moreover, but for external intervention, this judicial policy would have remained invisible: we learned of it not because of a published opinion or other record produced internally by the legal system but because the National Association of Criminal Defense Lawyers (NACDL) conducted the first nationwide study of the petty offense process. Left to its own devices, the criminal process permits the continued violation of rules at the bottom not only by withholding counsel and the scrutiny that goes with representation, but by sponsoring a culture that openly disregards the law of the top.[76]

The pyramid's waning commitment to transparency embodies the vital relationship between information and social power. Transparency does not merely ensure fidelity to legal rules, although that is one of its core functions, but is itself a sign of social importance. When the system cares about people and cases, it keeps track of them; those who remain undocumented do so precisely because they lack social stature.[77] The opacity at the bottom in turn permits the continued erosion of law. While sunlight may be the best disinfectant, it turns out to be an expensive social resource. Not everyone has an equal claim to attention, for the same reasons that not everyone has an equal claim to the rule of law. If nothing else, this dynamic suggests that paying more attention to sociological insights about the bottom of the pyramid may be an important equalizing force, extending the possibilities of lawfulness into new regions.

Conclusion

As lawyers, ironically, we do not always appreciate how and why the law matters to its most vulnerable subjects. Especially for people accustomed to lawless treatment, getting a full dose of due process can represent more than just a chance to win. Sometimes it means that they are important.[78] As a federal public defender who often lost on the merits, I learned this lesson from many clients. But I learned it first from Perry.[79]

It wouldn't be Perry's first gun conviction but it was about to be mine. Stuck on a long, dark, winding road, Perry had accidentally driven up to the entrance of the heavily guarded military base. With no way to turn around, Perry was stopped and searched by military police who found the illegal weapon. Now Perry was in federal court with me as his newly minted public defender. A quiet, lanky man, Perry was clearly resigned to adding yet another conviction to his lengthy record. But I was pushing a Hail Mary argument that his constitutional rights had been violated by the unavoidable encounter. The judge—a careful jurist—listened thoughtfully, called my arguments "interesting" and "novel," and denied my motion to suppress the gun.

I had failed Perry. Crushed, I turned to him, apologizing for the loss. But Perry's eyes were shining. "No," he said. "Thank you. That was great. I never had anyone make me a constitutional argument before."

At its best, the top of the penal pyramid is not just a well-functioning legal machine. It offers a form of respect and dignity to the poor and the disfavored by treating them with the same careful attention accorded the wealthy and powerful. Conversely, at its worst, the bottom represents a kind of dystopia: a quick-and-dirty assembly line that marks and burdens vulnerable people in bulk without individuated justice, due process, or rule of law. It is an expression of official distrust as well as disrespect, denying broad classes of people their individual worth by withholding those markers of citizenship and entitlement reflected in legal rules and individuated procedures.

Because rules do not work well at the bottom, the cure for the bottom's normative dysfunctions cannot lie simply in promulgating new rules. If the pyramid teaches us anything, it demonstrates that rules do not function in a normative vacuum. Rather, they work best for people about whom the system cares and who are recognized by legal actors as deserving of proper treatment. The bottom needs a dose of that careful, caring culture of the top, a culture that drives judges to schedule hearings for novel arguments, in which lawyers have the time and resources to construct arguments and talk to their clients, and where the fates of all defendants are determined in the same law-abiding spirit. In other words, the bottom needs to matter to everyone who participates in it, from lawyers and judges to legislatures and the public. Only then can we have confidence that legal reform will help those for whom it is intended and those who need it most.

NOTES

This chapter benefitted greatly from comments I received at the University of Illinois, NYU, U.C. Irvine, and Vanderbilt Law School workshops and conferences.

1 Zachery Kouwe & Dan Slater, *2 Bear Stearns Fund Leaders Are Acquitted*, N.Y. TIMES (Nov. 10, 2009); Duff Wilson & David Barstow, *All Charges Dropped in Duke Case*, N.Y. TIMES (Apr. 12, 2007). One Duke lacrosse player who was exonerated from rape allegations commented: "This entire experience has opened my eyes up to a tragic world of injustice I never knew existed. . . . If police officers and a district attorney can systematically railroad us with absolutely no evidence whatsoever, I can't imagine what they'd do to people who do not have the resources to defend themselves."

2 Some scholars might label this array of social practices a form of "law" in itself. *See, e.g.*, Naomi Mezey, *Out of the Ordinary: Law, Power, Culture, and the Commonplace*, 26 LAW & SOC. INQ. 145 (2001).

3 INVESTIGATION OF THE FERGUSON POLICE DEPARTMENT, U.S. Dep't of Justice, Civil Rights Division, March 4, 2015, available at www.justice.gov.

4 *Cf.* William J. Stuntz, *Reply: Criminal Law's Pathology*, 101 MICH. L. REV. 828, 829 (2002) (arguing that "we have a deeply lawless criminal justice system in part because that system is deeply committed to legality").

5 Robert Weisberg, *Reality-Challenged Philosophies of Punishment*, 95 MARQUETTE L. REV. 1203 (2012) (identifying a pervasive "disconnection between theory and social fact regarding American incarceration").

6 *See, e g.*, William J. Stuntz, *Christianity and the (Modest) Rule of Law*, 8 U. PA. J. CON. L. 809, 810 (2006) ("If there is one key condition that must be satisfied for a country to call itself free, it is that no one can be thrown in prison for no better reason than because it pleased some government official to put him there. Legality requires that the law put him there."); *see also* Tom R. Tyler & Jeffrey Fagan, *Legitimacy and Cooperation: Why Do People Help the Police Fight Crime in Their Communities?*, 6 OHIO ST. J. CRIM. L. 231, 239, 253 (2008) (concluding that neutral, rule-bound police procedures influence public perceptions of police legitimacy).

7 *See* Nicola Lacey, *Analytical Jurisprudence versus Descriptive Sociology Revisited*, 84 TEX. L. REV. 945, 980 (2006) (arguing "for a general commitment to theorizing law as a social phenomenon"); *see also* BERNARD E. HARCOURT, AGAINST PREDICTION: PROFILING, POLICING, AND PUNISHING IN AN ACTUARIAL AGE (Univ. of Chicago Press, 2006).

8 *See* Rachel Barkow and Issa Kohler-Hausmann, this volume.

9 Compare Stephanos Bibas and Rachel Barkow in this volume.

10 Carlos Berdejo and Noam M. Yuchtman, *Crime, Punishment and Politics: An Analysis of Political Cycles in Criminal Sentencing*, 95 REV. ECON. STATS. 741 (2013). *See also* Daniel Richman, this volume.

11 *See* Mona Lynch and Kohler-Hausmann, this volume.

12 *See* Meda Chesney-Lind, this volume.

13 Darryl Brown, *The Decline of Defense Counsel and the Rise of Accuracy in Criminal Adjudication*, 93 CAL. L. REV. 1585, 1588–89 (2005); Stephanos Bibas, *Regulating the Plea-Bargaining Market: From Caveat Emptor to Consumer Protection*, 99 CAL. L. REV. 1117, 1119 (2011); *see also* Alexandra Natapoff, *Deregulating Guilt: The Information Culture of the Criminal System*, 30 CARDOZO L. REV. 965 (2008) (describing tensions between the rules and commitments of the trial-centric sphere, plea bargaining, and investigation).

14 DAVID COLE, NO EQUAL JUSTICE: RACE AND CLASS IN THE AMERICAN CRIMINAL JUSTICE SYSTEM (New Press, 2000).

15 AM BAR ASS'N, GIDEON'S BROKEN PROMISE: AMERICA'S CONTINUING QUEST FOR EQUAL JUSTICE 21 (2004); ROBERT C. BORUCHOWITZ ET AL., NAT'L ASSOC. OF CRIMINAL DEFENSE LAWYERS, MINOR CRIMES, MASSIVE WASTE: THE TERRIBLE TOLL OF AMERICA'S BROKEN MISDEMEANOR COURTS 9–17 (2009).

16 MALCOLM M. FEELEY, THE PROCESS IS THE PUNISHMENT: HANDLING CASES IN A LOWER CRIMINAL COURT 296 (Russell Sage, 1979) (describing dominant "presumption of guilt"); HERBERT L. PACKER, THE LIMITS OF THE CRIMINAL SANCTION 158–63 (Stanford Univ. Press, 1968) (describing "crime control" model and noting that it requires a "presumption of guilt" to function efficiently).

17 REPORT: JUSTICE DENIED: AMERICA'S CONTINUING NEGLECT OF OUR CONSTITUTIONAL RIGHT TO COUNSEL, at 30 n.61 (Constitution Project & Nat'l Legal Aid and Defender Assoc., April 2009).

18 Weisberg, *supra* note 5.

19 I've written elsewhere about the misdemeanor process and its contribution to the racialization of crime. Alexandra Natapoff, *Misdemeanors*, 85 S. CAL. L. REV. 1313 (2012). *See also* Alexandra Natapoff, *Aggregation and Urban Misdemeanors*, 40 FORDHAM URB. L.J. 1043 (2013) (on the systemic aggregate production of petty convictions); Alexandra Natapoff, *Gideon Skepticism*, 70 WASH. & LEE L. REV. 1049 (2013) (on the structural limitations on the right to counsel to ensure integrity of the misdemeanor process).

20 SOURCEBOOK OF CRIMINAL JUSTICE STATISTICS ONLINE, Table 5.44.2006, available at www.albany.edu.

21 *DeathPenaltyInfo.org Fact Sheet* at 3, available at www.deathpenaltyinfo.org.

22 Natapoff, *Misdemeanors*, *supra* note 19.

23 Daniel Richman & William Stuntz, *Al Capone's Revenge: An Essay on the Political Economy of Pretextual Prosecution*, 105 COLUM. L. REV. 583, 600–4 (2005) (describing various pressures on state and local police and prosecutors to go after serious cases).

24 William Stuntz, *Plea Bargaining and Criminal Law's Disappearing Shadow*, 117 HARV. L. REV. 2548, 2564 (2004).

25 *See, e.g.*, Katherine Beckett and Steve Herbert, *The Punitive City Revisited, in* AFTER THE WAR ON CRIME: RACE, DEMOCRACY AND A NEW RECONSTRUCTION 109–10 (Mary Louise Frampton, Ian Haney López & Jonathan Simon, eds. 2008) (describing the variety of urban criminal legal tools deployed to "clean up particular urban spaces"); MARKUS DIRK DUBBER, THE POLICE POWER: PATRIARCHY AND THE FOUNDATIONS OF AMERICAN GOVERNMENT (Columbia Univ. Press, 2005) (describing the social control functions of numerous minor policing offenses).

26 Eve Brensike Primus, *Structural Reform in Criminal Defense: Relocating Ineffective Assistance of Counsel Claims*, 92 CORNELL L. REV. 679, 693 (2007) (describing structural impediments to appellate and collateral review of misdemeanor convictions).

27 Josh Bowers, *Legal Guilt, Normative Innocence, and the Equitable Decision Not to Prosecute*, 110 COLUM. L. REV. 1655, 1707 (2010).

28 Stephen B. Bright, *Counsel for the Poor: The Death Sentence Not for the Worst Crime but for the Worst Lawyer*, 103 YALE L.J. 1835 (1994).

29 *See, e.g.*, McCleskey v. Kemp, 481 U.S. 279 (1987); Jennifer Eberhardt, et al., *Looking Deathworthy: Perceived Stereotypicality of Black Defendants Predicts Capital-Sentencing Outcomes*, PSYCH. SCI. (May 2006), vol. 17, no. 6, 383–86.

30 *See, e.g.*, United States v. Horn, 185 F. Supp.2d 530 (D. Md. 2001) (federal drunk driving case relying on the testimony of multiple experts and extensive briefings to exclude field sobriety test evidence under *Daubert v. Merrell Dow*, 509 U.S. 579 (1993)) (litigated by the author).

31 *See* Janice Nadler, *Moral Character, Motive, and the Psychology of Blame*, 97 CORNELL L. REV. 255 (2012); DAVID GARLAND, PUNISHMENT AND MODERN SOCIETY: A STUDY IN SOCIAL THEORY 23–24, 58–59 (Univ. of Chicago Press, 1990) (on Durkheim).

32 GARLAND, *supra* note 31, at 58.

33 *E.g.*, DOUGLAS HUSAK, OVERCRIMINALIZATION: THE LIMITS OF THE CRIMINAL LAW (Oxford Univ. Press, 2008).

34 Samuel Gross, *Frequency and Predictors of False Conviction: Why We Know So Little, and New Data on Capital Cases*, 5 J. EMP. LEGAL STUD. 927, 930 (2008) (on the likelihood of misdemeanor wrongful convictions).

35 DUI offenses are probably an exception to this rule of thumb, in part because the presence of wealthier defendants in the offender pool has elevated the adversarial practice surrounding that offense. *See, e.g.*, Charles Short, *Note, Guilt by Machine: The Problem of Source Code Discovery in Florida DUI Prosecutions*, 61 FLA. L. REV. 177 (2009) (surveying litigation over breathalyzer reliability in numerous states).

36 JONATHAN SIMON, GOVERNING THROUGH CRIME: HOW THE WAR ON CRIME TRANSFORMED AMERICAN DEMOCRACY AND CREATED A CULTURE OF FEAR (Oxford Univ. Press, 2007); LOÏC WACQUANT, PUNISHING

THE POOR: THE NEOLIBERAL GOVERNMENT OF SOCIAL INSECURITY (Duke Univ. Press, 2009).

37 Malcolm Feeley & Jonathan Simon, *Actuarial Justice: The Emerging New Criminal Law*, at 192, *in* DAVID NELKEN, THE FUTURES OF CRIMINOLOGY (Sage, 1994). *See also* DAVID GARLAND, THE CULTURE OF CONTROL: CRIME AND SOCIAL ORDER IN CONTEMPORARY SOCIETY 170–75 (Univ. of Chicago Press, 2002); Feeley & Simon, at 173 ("Actuarial justice . . . is concerned with techniques for identifying, classifying and managing groups assorted by levels of dangerousness. It takes crime for granted. It accepts deviance as normal.").

38 MICHELLE ALEXANDER, THE NEW JIM CROW: MASS INCARCERATION IN THE AGE OF COLORBLINDNESS (New Press, 2012); COLE, *supra* note 14; JEROME MILLER, SEARCH AND DESTROY: AFRICAN-AMERICAN MALES IN THE CRIMINAL JUSTICE SYSTEM (Cambridge Univ. Press, 1997); MICHAEL TONRY, MALIGN NEGLECT: RACE, CRIME AND PUNISHMENT IN AMERICA (Oxford Univ. Press, 1996).

39 Paul Butler, *Black Male Exceptionalism? The Problems and Potential of Black Male-Focused Intervention*, 10 DU BOIS REV. 485, 496 (2013) ("The strongest claim that African American men have to exceptionalism is with regard to incarceration."); Devon Carbado, *Men in Black*, 3 J. GENDER, RACE & JUST. 427 (2000) ("A central project of antiracist discourse is to reveal the extent to which Black men are victims of a racist criminal justice system.").

40 Sharon Dolovich, *Two Models of the Prison: Accidental Humanity and Hypermasculinity in the L.A. County Jail*, 102 J. CRIM. L. & CRIMINOL. 965 (2012); Devon Carbado, *(E)racing the Fourth Amendment*, 100 MICH. L. REV. 946 (2002) (describing how being stopped by police shapes the identity of black men).

41 Priscilla Ocen, *Punishing Pregnancy: Race, Incarceration, and the Shackling of Pregnant Prisoners*, 100 CAL. L. REV. 1239 (2012).

42 *See* Carbado, *supra* note 40; *see also* PAUL BUTLER, LET'S GET FREE: A HIP HOP THEORY OF JUSTICE (New Press, 2010) (describing how his race affected his experience of being prosecuted for assault).

43 In what might be referred to as an intersectionality. Kimberlé Crenshaw, *Mapping the Margins: Intersectionality, Identity Politics, and Violence against Women of Color*, 43 STAN. L. REV. 1241 (1991).

44 James Forman, Jr., *Racial Critiques of Mass Incarceration: Beyond the New Jim Crow*, 87 N.Y.U. L. REV. 21, 54 (2012).

45 COLE, *supra* note 14, at 5.

46 Bridget McCormack, *Economic Incarceration*, 25 WINDSOR Y.B. ACCESS TO JUST. 223 (2007).

47 Natapoff, *Misdemeanors, supra* note 19; Ligon v. City of New York, 925 F.Supp.2d 478 (S.D.N.Y. 2013) (holding New York police practices unconstitutional).

48 BORUCHOWITZ, *supra* note 15.

49 Mona Lynch, *From the Punitive City to the Gated Community: Security and Segregation across the Penal Landscape*, 56 U. MIAMI L. REV. 89, 105 (2001).

50 WACQUANT, *supra* note 36, at 6, 41.

51 *Id.* at 196.

52 "The law-and-order merry-go-round is to criminality what pornography is to amorous relations: a mirror deforming reality to the point of the grotesque that artificially extracts delinquent behaviors from the fabric of social relations in which they take root and make sense, deliberately ignores their causes and meanings, and reduces their treatment to series of conspicuous position-takings." WACQUANT, *supra* note 36, at xii.

53 *E.g.*, Fiona Doherty, *Obey All Laws and Be Good: Probation and the Meaning of Recidivism*, 104 GEO. L.J. 291 (2016); Michelle Phelps, *Mass Probation: Towards a More Robust Theory of State Variation in Punishment*, PUNISHMENT & SOCIETY *OnLineFirst* (May 10, 2016); Sharon Dolovich, this volume (on prisons).

54 *See, e.g.*, WACQUANT, *supra* note 36, at xix (admitting that his analysis focuses on the "lower regions of social and urban space" and therefore "overlooks other forms of offending (such as white-collar, corporate, and regulatory crimes, for instance)"). In other words, Wacquant focuses on the bottom of the pyramid, where law's influence is at its weakest.

55 Penson v. Ohio, 488 U.S. 75, 84 (1988).

56 *See, e.g.*, Ingrid V. Eagly, *Gideon's Migration*, 122 YALE L.J. 2282, 2306 (2013) (discussing the historic understanding of Gideon as a class and racial equalizer); Jonathan A. Rapping, *The Revolution Will Be Televised: Popular Culture and the American Criminal Justice Narrative*, 41 NEW ENGL. J. ON CRIM. & CIV. CONFINEMENT 5 (2015) (on cultural views of the public defender embedded in Gideon); Bright, *supra* note 28.

57 *See, e.g.*, Eagly, *supra* note 56, at 2311–12.

58 See COLE, *supra* note 14, at 2–3 (describing how O. J. Simpson's "dream team" of lawyers were perceived by whites to have distorted the law).

59 *See* Natapoff, *Gideon Skepticism*, *supra* note 19.

60 *E.g.*, Jeffrey Fagan & Amanda Geller, *Following the Script: Narratives of Suspicion in Terry Stops in Street Policing*, 82 U. CHI. L. REV. 51, 62–63, 86 (2015).

61 Terry v. Ohio, 392 U.S. 1, 13 (1968) ("Encounters are initiated by the police for a wide variety of purposes, some of which are wholly unrelated to a desire to prosecute for crime.").

62 Stuntz, supra note 24, at 2558.

63 FEELEY, *supra* note 16.

64 Issa Kohler-Hausmann, *Managerial Justice and Mass Misdemeanors*, 66 STAN. L. REV. 611 (2014) (describing the punitive aspects of New York misdemeanor court in connection with dismissal dispositions).

65 Once a defendant is convicted, the right to counsel continues to fade in efficacy as well as availability. *See, e.g.*, Primus, *supra* note 26.

66 There is also a different, Marxist argument that seemingly neutral rule of law itself is a mechanism of class control—the provision of counsel obviously is no response to that view. *See, e.g.*, GARLAND, *supra* note 31, at 112 (describing a Marx-

ist theory of criminal law as a "bourgeois form of law [that] has been shaped by legal responses to economic development, so that one might say it is economically determined. But [in this theory] the reverse is also true: the legal form provides an important regulative structure which sanctions capitalistic relationships and enforces the appropriate economic rules. At the same time, law provides a powerful ideology which helps legitimize these relationships by phrasing particular economic interests in a vocabulary of universal right.").

67 *See* Lacey, *supra* note 7, at 948, 980 (on the tension between social and analytical descriptions of law); *see also* Hadar Aviram, this volume.

68 Lawrence M. Friedman, *Legal Rules and the Process of Social Change*, 19 STAN. L. REV. 786, 792 (1967).

69 GARLAND, *supra* note 31, at 116. *See also id.* at 130 ("Penality is intimately linked with the legal sphere and is patterned by legal forms and principles. To the extent that the law is a system of ideological display, punishment contributes to its legitimatory functions and effects. Through the medium of penality, state power and state violence can be articulated in legal forms which enlist popular consent.").

70 RANDALL KENNEDY, RACE, CRIME, AND THE LAW 19 (Random House, 1997).

71 *See also* GARLAND, *supra* note 31, at 117 ("If penality serves a class purpose, it does so in a way which enlists support among the subordinate classes and which protects interests which are experienced as being universal rather than specific.").

72 Feeley & Simon, *supra* note 37, at 193; *see also* PACKER, *supra* note 16.

73 I've written more specifically about this dynamic elsewhere. Natapoff, *supra* note 13.

74 535 U.S. 654 (2002) (requiring counsel for the imposition of jailable probation).

75 BORUCHOWITZ, *supra* note 15, at 17.

76 *See* AMY BACH, ORDINARY INJUSTICE: HOW AMERICA HOLDS COURT (Picador, 2010).

77 *See, e.g.,* Devon W. Carbado and Cheryl I. Harris, *Undocumented Criminal Procedure*, 58 UCLA L. REV. 1543 (2011) (on the marginalization of doctrine governing undocumented noncitizens).

78 Tracey L. Meares & Tom R. Tyler, *Justice Sotomayor and the Jurisprudence of Procedural Justice*, 123 YALE L.J. FORUM 525, 527 (2014) ("[P]eople understand the way in which they are treated by legal authorities to provide them with information about how that authority views them and the group or groups to which they belong.").

79 Not my former client's actual name.

5

Linking Criminal Theory and Social Practice

A Response to Natapoff

MEDA CHESNEY-LIND

Natapoff has chosen the metaphor of a pyramid to characterize the social organization of the "criminal system," since she contends that these sets of institutions dispense very different forms of justice depending upon location in a multi-faceted hierarchical structure. Building on a lengthy tradition of research on the actual functioning of the criminal justice system (see Black, 1993, 2010; Smith, 2005), Natapoff's chapter also relies heavily on the author's own work exploring the routine processing of those charged with misdemeanors. In this essay, she explores the differences between what might be described as the "ideal" and the "real" in the U.S. legal system. Her analysis occasionally encompasses the workings of various bureaucratic systems of social control (e.g., the police, courts, and corrections), but she is clearly most interested in the judicial systems of social control.

Natapoff's essay focuses on key ways that the "mechanics" of social disadvantage work in the criminal system, and in her analysis, she directs attention to what she calls three "variables": offense severity, offender "social status" (race, gender, and class), and defense counsel. Natapoff's "variables" are actually quite similar to those routinely used for decades by criminologists seeking evidence of racism or sexism in the criminal justice system, though admittedly, she uses them in a very different way in her essay. This positivist criminological approach to use of these variables was quite simple. Researchers would "control" statistically for the effects for every possible "legally relevant" variable, including things like age, offense type (severity), length of criminal record, and even the presence or absence of a lawyer. After that, the data were reviewed for any effects of race or sex (most commonly) that were still statistically significant. If these were found, this approach concluded that there was evidence of discrimination; if they were not, then this approach concluded that these processes were not affected by either the race or gender of the person facing charges.

Early research on gender bias in sentencing tended to be quite mixed in its results, as did early research on racial bias (see Spohn, Gruhl & Welch, 1981; Raeder, 1993). Some of this was likely a product of the fact that many of these studies focused on felony sentencing, which, as Natapoff has argued, involves a small fraction of all those arrested and processed by the courts. Other research, though, did find evidence of bias. As an example, looking at the outcome of all adult arrests for Part One offenses in the City and County of Honolulu during a four-month period in 1980, researchers found sex "significant" at certain points in the process (Ghali & Chesney-Lind, 1986). Four different data sets, including arrest data, were used in the analysis. Consistent with Natapoff's contention that discrimination is easier to detect earlier in and at the lower levels of criminal processing, we found that the bias against females was more pronounced at the district court level (where minor offenses where prosecuted) than at circuit court levels.

Specifically, Ghali and Chesney-Lind found that women were disadvantaged at the "police" level, with men more likely to be released, while women were more likely to be jailed. Women were also more likely to plead guilty then men, and they were more likely to be prosecuted. It is notable that in 1980, the prosecutor decided to prosecute 99% of all cases forwarded to him by the police, so the police-level decision-making process (which is clearly often opaque and discretionary) is highly consequential. The patterns of gender bias were not nearly so clear in the circuit court cases (where felonies where tried), and in some instances, it appeared that women were getting less severe sentences (e.g., women were more likely to receive probation). Such patterns are consistent with Natapoff's contention that the greatest injustices are hidden in the "minor offenses" tried at lower levels in the system, while researchers seeking evidence of racism or sexism rarely considered these settings.

Looking more globally at these patterns, it is possible to suggest that the very statistical methods that criminologists have long used to explore evidence of bias are themselves problematic. Essentially, researchers are taking variables like "prior arrests" and even "offense type" that, as Natapoff's essay documents, are often proxies for things like poverty, race, and gender; are "controlling" for their effects in judicial process- ing; and then are finding little or no evidence of "bias" in the criminal system. Ultimately, the shortcomings of this approach were in ample evidence when scholars at RAND using this sort of methodology con- cluded there was no racism in the criminal justice system in the late 1980s (Klein, Turner, & Petersilia, 1988). Recall that as this study ap- peared, the United States was well into the war on drugs and was em- barking on a pattern of mass incarceration that would ultimately result in the U.S. having the highest incarceration rate in the world (Liptak, 2008).

The great insight into the role played by race and racism in the crimi- nal system was to sidestep this methodological debate and instead focus on the characteristics of those in prison and the differential impact of imprisonment on particular ethnic and racial communities. This ap- proach was pioneered by the Sentencing Project, where researchers simply began to calculate the odds that young African American males would be incarcerated compared to young males of other races. This important work ultimately documented that three in every ten African American males would serve some time in prison. These crucial com- parisons, as well as others, were later articulated and extended in *Race to Incarcerate*, first published in 1999 and since updated (Mauer, 2006). This approach laid bare the racialized aspects of the carceral state as well as the critical role that the drug war played in these patterns. Along with other works (see Alexander, 2012; Mauer & Chesney-Lind 2002), this research ultimately sidelined efforts to mask these huge raced (and gen- dered) consequences of the "normal" processes of the criminal system. Of course, as the papers in this volume establish, many legal scholars are way past this discussion, unlike mainstream criminology where positiv- ism and presumptively powerful quantitative methods still tend to be privileged.

Certainly Natapoff's work turns a sharp focus on the disadvantages race and class confer, adding a vital new emphasis on the importance of considering both race *and* class. She also briefly notes that gender, particularly the punishing of certain forms of African American mas- culinity and femininity, is an important theme in the policing of race. One could argue, though, that the criminal system is more broadly implicated in the enforcement of male privilege (or patriarchy), as well as other systems of privilege such as ageism (particularly a bias against youthful offenders) and heterosexual privilege. To illustrate this, let me provide some of the evidence that gender, in its own right, operates in ways that are unique—not ones that can be subsumed by race and/or class. Let's start with offense type, one of the issues that Natapoff's paper engages. Her own work on those charged with misdemeanors clearly informs her argument about the types of "justice" meted out at different levels in the criminal system (since these cases are tried at the base of the pyramid), with often pretty terrible consequences for those tried at the lower levels of her pyramid. This discussion will also provide additional support for the contention that the statistical process used in the differential sentencing literature actually functions to mask the bias present in the system.

Consider research on girls' experiences in the juvenile justice system. This work documented the powerful ways in which minor offenses known as "status offenses," particularly running away from home, operated in girls' lives. Feminist historical work documented that the "child-saving movement" was largely about incarcerating immigrant white girls in reform and training schools for offenses like "sexual immorality" and waywardness—the status offenses of their day (Chesney-Lind, 1977; Odem, 1995; Schlossman & Wallach, 1978). Many of these girls were simply sexually active, often with boys or young men that their parents did not approve of. Some of these young women were actually running away from homes filled with abuse, and they were arrested for defying their parents (and ultimately judges who told them they had to stay home and obey their parents no matter how abusive).

Contemporary work notes that while the behavior of running away from home is engaged in by both males and females (if you review self-report data), typically many more girls than boys enter the juvenile justice system for this offense, because parents are concerned about their daughters' and not their sons' behavior outside the home (Chesney-Lind & Irwin, 2007). Of course, both the harsh historical trends as well as contemporary forms of sexism were missed by mainstream criminologists studying "delinquency," since they often eliminated girls and women from their analysis and tended to focus only on boys' offenses (Irwin & Chesney-Lind, 2008).

A second arena in which to consider the interface between the criminal system and gender would be women's imprisonment. When the United States embarked on a policy that might well be described as mass incarceration (Mauer & Chesney-Lind, 2002), few considered the impact that this penological change of course would have on women. Yet during the last decades of the 20th century, the number of women in jail and prison soared (dramatically outstripping male increases), completely untethered from women's arrest rates, which have not increased by nearly the same amount (Bloom, Chesney-Lind, & Owen, 1994). The dimensions of this shift are staggering: for most of the 20th century, we imprisoned about 5,000 to 10,000 women in any given year. At the turn of the new century, we had more than 100,000 women doing time in U.S. prisons (Harrison & Beck, 2004, p. 1). Women's incarceration in the United States not only grew but actually increased eightfold during the past century, and virtually all of that increase occurred in the century's final two decades (Chesney-Lind & Pasko, 2012). Again, offense type was very important as well. At the start of mass incarceration, only one woman in ten was serving time in prison for a drug crime; at its peak, the proportion was one in three (Chesney-Lind, 2006). The war on drugs had translated into a hidden war on women, particularly women of color (see Bloom, Chesney-Lind, & Owen, 1994).

The gendered aspects of this interface between carceral control and gender are also significant to consider. Particularly of note is the fact that in a male-dominated prison system, gender "equality" often translated into the pattern of treating women as if they are men (some have called this vengeful equity). This resulted in distorted and inhumane conditions for women in prison like videotaped strip searches, giving birth in shackles (because men often escape during medical treatment), and female chain gangs (Chesney-Lind, 2006; Ocen, 2012). Clearly, in the two cases above, the carceral systems operated to enforce and undergird patriarchal privilege in ways that complement but do not overlap with the systems of privilege discussed by Natapoff.

Natapoff, at the end of her essay, notes the importance of the "ideological function of law"—that the law is "a powerful source of social meaning in its own right." This invites a consideration of how, exactly, the law became explicitly involved in the policing and criminalization of the poor and marginalized, particularly low-income African Americans.

Actually, the conservative takeover of American political life in the late 20th century owes much to the conscious use of race in the framing of the "crime problem" and "criminals." This likely began with Barry Goldwater's unsuccessful 1964 presidential campaign, which repeatedly used phrases like "civil disorder" and "violence in the streets" in a "covertly racist campaign" to attack the Civil Rights Movement (Chambliss, 1999, p. 14). Both Richard Nixon and Ronald Reagan refined this approach as the crime problem became a centerpiece of the Republican Party's efforts to wrest electoral control of Southern states away from the Democratic Party. Nixon's emphasis on "law and order" and Reagan's "war on drugs" were both built on "white fear of black street crime" (Chambliss, 1999, p. 19). And, as Natapoff notes, the war on drugs in particular was waged, in Mona Lynch's words, using "harsh criminal statutes that only thinly disguise[d] the target populations." As noted earlier, these statutes also laid the crucial foundation for the aberrant U.S. practice of mass incarceration.

Over time, crime emerged as a code word for "race," and crime policy became a staple in Republican attacks on Democratic rivals. When Reagan's vice-president, George H. W. Bush, ran for the White House, he successfully used the Willie Horton incident (in which an African American man on a prison furlough raped and robbed a woman) in his decisive defeat of Michael Dukakis in 1988 (Chambliss, 1999). Bill Clinton, a Democrat, learned the lesson well. No Republican was going to "out-tough" him on crime. While running for president in 1992, then-Governor Clinton interrupted his New Hampshire campaign to return to Arkansas and preside over the execution of Ricky Ray Rector, a mentally impaired black man sentenced to death by an all-white jury for killing a police officer (Sherrill, 2001, p. 1).

The benefits to Republicans from their traditional ownership of the crime issue were evident in both George W. Bush elections. In fact, Bush gained the presidency in part because of felony disenfranchisement, predominantly of African American voters in Florida (Lantigua, 2001). The second Bush campaign continued to talk tough on crime but added an appeal to "moral values" particularly around rolling back women's rights and attacking gay rights. While out of the White House, the Republicans moved a key part of their "moral agenda"—recriminalizing abortion—to various state houses as well as Congress. As a direct result, the last decade saw the number of women living in states clearly hostile to abortion rights increase from 31% (living in 13 states) in 2000 to 56% (living in 27 states) in 2013 (Nash, Gold, Rowan, Rathbun, & Vierboom, 2014).

Initially, the Obama presidency did not appear to signal a major change of course regarding crime and imprisonment issues. During Obama's second term, though, Attorney General Eric Holder began actively taking on key aspects of the legal structure that undergirds the war on drugs. For example, Holder endorsed a proposal to reduce prison sentences for people convicted of dealing drugs, and he separately pushed for the elimination of mandatory minimum sentences for nonviolent drug crimes (Apuzzo, 2014). Finally, there have been some definite shifts in incarceration patterns, possibly due to both state and federal changes in drug policy (see Goode, 2013) and the increasingly burdensome costs of imprisonment during recent economic downturns. Notably, between 2000 and 2009 the rate of incarceration in state and federal prisons declined 9.8% for black men and 30.7% for black women.

Returning to Natapoff's paper, she argues that an antidote to the patterns of privilege she documents is greater transparency to remind us of the "vital relationship between information and social power." For criminologists to assist effectively in this effort, increasing efforts to describe and document the actual functioning of the criminal system, particularly the system that most U.S. citizens actually experience (i.e., the "real" system so powerfully documented by Natapoff), must be added to the agenda. Crucially, the field's traditional bias toward quantitative methods (and large national samples) must be augmented by richer, more detailed descriptions of key parts of the system that most people experience. Issues like bail, jail conditions, parole and probation revocation; the sometimes toxic interface between mental health, emergency rooms, and jails; police encounters on the streets; and, perhaps most importantly, the role of the prosecutors in minor cases should all be added to the already fairly rich literature on jail and prison conditions. Such rich descriptions are increasingly appearing (see, e.g., Phillips, 2012; Sered & Norton-Hawk, 2014) and are vital to the transparency Natapoff advocates.

The damage caused by the conservative framing of the crime problem is irrefutable. For many who enter the system, their experiences of arrest and of court routines are such that these in themselves literally have become a form of punishment (Feeley, 1992), and, most importantly, the U.S. is haunted by a very racialized system of mass incarceration. As many scholars have noted, the increased reliance on what is often called "law and order" strategies to control crime and delinquency run deep within America's culture, economy (see Garland, 2001), and race relations, and, in fact, rest within the larger shift in the U.S. from a "welfare state" to a "penal state" (Wacquant, 2001). Along with this shift, of course, come public attitudes about the crime problem and criminals that reinforce prison as a viable "solution" to the many social problems associated with this nation's long history of racial injustice and increasing income inequality.

REFERENCES

Alexander, M. (2012). *The New Jim Crow: Mass Incarceration in the Age of Colorblindness* (reprint). New York: New Press.

Apuzzo, M. (2014, March 13). Holder Endorses Proposal to Reduce Drug Sentences in Latest Sign of Shift. *New York Times*. Retrieved from www.nytimes.com.

Black, D. (1993). *Sociological Justice*. New York: Oxford University Press.

Black, D. (2010). *The Behavior of Law, Special Edition*. Bingley, UK: Emerald Group Publishing.

Bloom, B., Chesney-Lind, M., & Owen, B. (1994). *Women in California Prisons: Hidden Victims of the War on Drugs*. San Francisco: Center on Juvenile and Criminal Justice.

Chambliss, W. (1999). *Power, Politics, and Crime*. Boulder, CO: Westview Press.

Chesney-Lind, M. (1977). Judicial Paternalism and the Female Status Offender: Training Women to Know Their Place. *Crime & Delinquency*, 23(2), 121–130. doi:10.1177/001112877702300203.

Chesney-Lind, M. (2006). Patriarchy, Crime, and Justice: Feminist Criminology in an Era of Backlash. *Feminist Criminology*, 1(1), 6–26. doi:10.1177/1557085105282893.

Chesney-Lind, M., & Irwin, K. (2007). *Beyond Bad Girls: Gender, Violence and Hype* (1st ed.). London: Routledge.

Chesney-Lind, M., & Pasko, L. (2012). *The Female Offender: Girls, Women, and Crime* (3rd ed.). Thousand Oaks, CA: Sage Publications, Inc.

Feeley, M. M. (1992). *The Process Is the Punishment: Handling Cases in a Lower Criminal Court*. New York: Russell Sage Foundation.

Garland, D. (2001). *The Culture of Control: Crime and Social Order in Contemporary Society*. Chicago: University of Chicago Press.

Ghali, M., & Chesney-Lind, M. (1986). Gender Bias and the Criminal Justice System: An Empirical Investigation. *Sociology and Social Research*, 70(2), 164–171.

Goode, E. (2013, February 27). Incarceration Rates for Blacks Dropped, Report Shows. *New York Times*. Retrieved from www.nytimes.com.

Harrison, P. M., & Beck, A. (2004). Prisoners in 2003. *Bureau of Justice Statistics Bulletin*. NCJ 205335, Washington, DC: United States Department of Justice, Office of Justice Programs, Bureau of Justice Statistics.

Irwin, K., & Chesney-Lind, M. (2008). Girls' Violence: Beyond Dangerous Masculinity. *Sociology Compass*, 2(3), 837–855. doi:10.1111/j.1751-9020.2008.00120.x.

Klein, S. P., Turner, S., & Petersilia, J. R. (1988). Racial Equity in Sentencing. Retrieved from www.rand.org.

Lantigua, J. (2001, April 30). How the GOP Gamed the System in Florida. *Nation*. Retrieved from www.thenation.com.

Liptak, A. (2008, April 23). U.S. Prison Population Dwarfs That of Other Nations. *New York Times*. Retrieved from www.nytimes.com.

Mauer, M. (2006). *Race to Incarcerate* (revised ed.). New York: New Press.

Mauer, M. & Chesney-Lind, M. (Eds.). (2002). *Invisible Punishment: The Collateral Consequences of Mass Imprisonment* (1st ed.). New York: New Press.

Nash, E., Gold, R., Rowan, A., Rathbun, G., & Vierboom, Y. (2014). *Laws Affecting Reproductive Health and Rights: 2013 State Policy Review*. New York: Guttmacher Institute, State Center. Retrieved from www.guttmacher.org.

Ocen, P. A. (2012). Punishing Pregnancy: Race, Incarceration and the Shackling of Pregnant Prisoners, *California Law Review*, 100, 1239–1311.

Odem, M. E. (1995). *Delinquent Daughters: Protecting and Policing Adolescent Female Sexuality in the United States, 1885–1920*. Chapel Hill: University of North Carolina Press.

Phillips, M. (2012). New York City's Bail System—A World Apart. *CJA Research Brief*, 30, 1–6.

Raeder, M. S. (1993). Gender and Sentencing: Single Moms, Battered Women, and Other Sex-Based Anomalies in the Gender-Free World of the Federal Sentencing Guidelines. *Pepperdine Law Review*, 20, 905–990.

Schlossman, S., & Wallach, S. (1978). The Crime of Precocious Sexuality: Female Juvenile Delinquency in the Progressive Era. *Harvard Educational Review*, 48, 65–94. Retrieved from www.eric.ed.gov.

Sered, S., & Norton-Hawk, N. (2014). *Can't Catch a Break*. Berkeley & Los Angeles: University of California Press. Retrieved from www.ucpress.edu.

Sherrill, R. (2001, January 8). Death Trip: The American Way of Execution. *Nation*. Retrieved from www.thenation.com.

Smith, B. P. (2005). Plea Bargaining and the Eclipse of the Jury. *Annual Review of Law and Social Science*, 1(1), 131–149. doi:10.1146/annurev.lawsocsci.1.041604.115948

Spohn, C., Gruhl, J., & Welch, S. (1981). The Effect of Race on Sentencing: A Re-Examination of an Unsettled Question. *Law & Society Review*, 16(1), 71–88. doi:10.2307/3053550.

Wacquant, L. (2001). Deadly Symbiosis: When Ghetto and Prison Meet and Mesh. *Punishment and Society*, 3, 95–134.

PART II

Legal Doctrine in Principle and Practice

We live in a constitutional democracy, yet our many lofty constitutional principles often seem disconnected from the ways that the criminal process is actually permitted to function. Indeed, the Supreme Court itself often validates penal practices that seem to directly contradict basic notions of fairness, equality, and dignity. These essays explore how this dynamic occurs, and the frequently tense relationship between principle, doctrine, and legal practice.

Sharon Dolovich, Canons of Evasion in Constitutional Criminal Law

Hadar Aviram, Taking the Constitution Seriously? Three Approaches to Law's Competence in Addressing Authority and Professionalism

Lisa Kerr, Making Prisoner Rights Real: The Case of Mothers

6

Canons of Evasion in Constitutional Criminal Law

SHARON DOLOVICH

I. Disciplining the State's Penal Process?

Even a passing familiarity with the American criminal system is enough
to make clear that the state routinely falls far short of constitutional
compliance.[1] It is, for example, well known that most people caught
up in this system do not have adequate representation to counter well-
resourced prosecutors; that most people plead guilty without meaningful
due process protections; and that, as a consequence, even people with
strong claims of actual innocence or other grounds for acquittal can find
themselves convicted and branded as criminals. Unchecked discretion
in the hands of police and prosecutors, enabled by expansive legislative definitions of criminal conduct, has helped feed a ballooning penal
system in which indigent African Americans and other poor people of
color are disproportionately arrested, tried, convicted, and punished. A
record number of people of all races are serving unduly long sentences
in carceral facilities that are overcrowded, unsafe, and often insuffi-
ciently equipped to provide even for prisoners' essential human needs.
And millions more are trapped in a tight web of legal restrictions and
burdens, the collective effect of which is often out of all proportion to
the severity of the triggering offense.

This situation raises an obvious question: Where are the courts? In
theory, judicial oversight and review are supposed to discipline the
criminal system and ensure that the state's exercise of its penal power
does not exceed constitutional bounds. But instead of using the threat
of dismissal, reversal, or public condemnation to trigger a virtuous circle
of institutional reform and official compliance with core constitutional
commitments, courts largely affirm the outputs of our plainly compromised criminal system.[2]

The *sine qua non* of legal reasoning is the application of law to facts. For courts genuinely committed to meaningful constitutional review in the criminal context, the essential question—which I will henceforth call *the basic question*—should thus simply be: Given the facts of the case and the basic constitutional values at stake, was the conduct of the relevant governmental actor or institution consistent with the state's constitutional obligations? If, however, this is the question courts are supposed to answer, how is it possible that judges are repeatedly confronting the reality on the ground—lawyers sleeping through trials,[3] African Americans convicted by all-white juries,[4] people sentenced to life without parole for nonviolent crimes, people incarcerated under conditions of severe deprivation, and so on—and yet, in the vast majority of noncapital cases,[5] finding no constitutional problem?

How this happens—how constitutional review courts addressing the merits in criminal cases come face to face with the reality on the ground and still find little if anything to be constitutionally amiss—is the central puzzle this chapter addresses. And the answer, I suggest, is that, without saying so explicitly, Supreme Court doctrine governing substantive constitutional challenges in the criminal context systematically encourages judges at all levels to sidestep the basic question and instead to affirm the constitutionality of state action on grounds having little to do with the facts of the case.[6] This effect is achieved, over and over again, through three basic doctrinal moves, which I call *deference*, *presumption*, and *substitute question*. These evasive maneuvers are transsubstantive and pervasive in constitutional criminal law. They may take different forms depending on the particular issue, and may be explicit or merely implicit. The order of appearance in the doctrine also varies. But very often in the opinions establishing the governing constitutional standards, one will find the Court

- underscoring the need for judicial deference to some state actor or institution—typically the state actor or institution whose conduct or choices are most likely to be challenged as unconstitutional in this context;[7]
- establishing a presumption of constitutionality to apply to whatever governmental conduct or choice is at issue; and

- announcing a substitute question that will be dispositive in most instances—a question with the effect of shifting the inquiry away from the governing constitutional principle and having little if anything to do with the actual lived experience or even the complaint of the individual or class members bringing the claim.

When these pieces are in place, lower courts—both trial and appellate—are effectively guided to reject constitutional claims as baseless without ever needing to analyze the facts in light of the legal standards supposedly designed to manifest the applicable constitutional norms. There are, of course, exceptions; even in the noncapital context, claimants do sometimes prevail. In some cases, moreover, the Supreme Court is willing to address the basic question directly,[8] to establish rules broadening the scope of judicial inquiry and thus of constitutional enforcement,[9] or otherwise to resist the temptation to rely on its familiar canons of evasion.[10] Over the past several decades, however, the overall pattern in the Court's opinions in the constitutional criminal context has been one of retreat from the meaningful application of basic constitutional values, a retreat effectuated by the use of the three evasive moves identified here. As a result, even at the merits stage, the state nearly always wins—almost regardless of the facts.

Yet if courts routinely affirm the outputs of the criminal system—its convictions, sentences, and punishments—as constitutionally sound without ever seriously analyzing the facts of the case (how the conviction was achieved, what the sentence will actually involve, what treatment a prisoner actually received), the fact that a case survives merits review tells us little or nothing about the legitimacy of the state's exercise of its penal power, i.e., the degree to which the exercise of that power is consistent with our core constitutional principles. The routine judicial sidestep of the basic question also casts serious doubt on the idea that judicial review serves any sort of disciplinary function over the criminal justice system, whether motivating institutional reform or incentivizing state actors to remain within constitutional bounds.

At this point, some might object that there *are* no constitutional imperatives beyond what the Supreme Court says there are—that, if the substantive doctrine has evolved toward deference, presumption, and substitute question, the values these moves embody represent the sum total of what the Constitution normatively affords. At issue here is a fundamental disagreement over constitutional meaning. Some commentators have forcefully argued for what has come to be called the "pragmatic" view, on which the Constitution encompasses only those protections provided by the governing judicial doctrine and no more.[11] Others take a more aspirational view, on which the limited constitutional protections typically afforded by courts do not represent the whole of constitutional meaning, but instead indicate an inevitable gap between constitutional meaning and constitutional implementation, some moral remainder between the protections the courts currently afford and those to which citizens are normatively entitled.[12]

As should be clear, I subscribe to the latter, aspirational view.[13] I will not try to justify this view here, but will simply concede that those who do not share it will likely reject out of hand the broadest version of my claim—that, thanks to the Court's deployment of the canons of evasion (among other avoidance strategies), the gap between constitutional meaning and constitutional implementation in the criminal context is a yawning chasm,[14] and that, as a consequence, back-end judicial review is achieving little if any meaningful disciplinary effect on the criminal system. Still, even those inclined to the pragmatic view should remain open to the core claim developed here, i.e., that despite a periodic readiness to declare narrow constitutional principles and announce general standards for their implementation in the criminal context, the Court has over the past several decades persistently deployed the same raft of evasive maneuvers to yield doctrinal standards allowing lower courts to dismiss substantive constitutional claims without ever having to answer the basic question. In this way, I argue, courts avoid confronting facts that would otherwise be strongly suggestive of unconstitutionality even on the Court's own stated principles.[15]

The main focus here is on the evasive mechanisms applied at the merits stage, and then only at the moment of deciding whether the relevant constitutional standard has been violated. It bears emphasizing, however, that in the criminal context, most constitutional claims fail long before this point is reached. The judicial process does not commence automatically; it must be triggered. And in a case involving constitutional criminal law, to get a hearing on the merits, a claimant must navigate

a veritable procedural thicket. For people filing habeas petitions or §
1983 claims (i.e., people constitutionally challenging the various outputs
of the criminal system), these procedural obstacles can include, among
other things, onerous time limits, strict exhaustion requirements, and
complex rules concerning when, how, and in what form claims must
be filed. Because there is no right to counsel on habeas review or for §
1983 prison conditions challenges, and because most people caught up in
the criminal system are indigent, people seeking to bring constitutional
claims through these vehicles largely do so without the help of a lawyer. To make matters worse, most people challenging their convictions,
sentences, or punishments are litigating their cases from inside a prison
or jail, where they are likely to confront innumerable structural obstacles, including those of inadequate law libraries and insufficient legal
assistance if they need help with their claims. And most prisoners do
need such help, whether because they are illiterate, non-native English
speakers, mentally ill, or simply among the more than 95% of American
prisoners who are "unable to read and understand complex documents
or perform tasks that require 'integrating, synthesizing, and analyzing
multiple pieces of information.'"[16] Collectively, these obstacles mean that
even in cases where the outputs of the criminal system warrant contestation, the substantive claims will often be lost (and no constitutional
violation found) well before a hearing on the merits.

Still further obstacles await those prisoners able to get before a judge
with a strong claim on the merits. For example, under 28 USC § 2254 (d)
(1), habeas claimants must show that the state court decision denying
their claim "was contrary to, or involved an unreasonable application
of, clearly established federal law as determined by the United States
Supreme Court,"[17] a standard the Court has narrowly interpreted to
mean that "there is no possibility fair-minded jurists could disagree that
the state court's decision conflicts with the Court's precedents."[18] And
then there are those mechanisms by which claimants are denied relief
even when the court *has* found a constitutional violation. Focusing on
Fourth, Fifth, and Sixth Amendment claims, Carol Steiker identifies
several doctrines that "permit the use at trial of admittedly unconstitutionally obtained evidence."[19] These "inclusionary rules" include, among
others, "standing, the good faith exception to the warrant requirement,
the 'fruit of the poisonous tree,' impeachment [and] harmless error."[20]

Likewise, in the § 1983 context, the doctrine of qualified immunity[21] allows defendants to escape liability even for conduct judged unconstitutional, as long as their actions do not violate "'clearly established statutory or constitutional rights of which a reasonable person would have known'"[22]—a standard that, the Court has held, requires a showing that "every reasonable official would have understood that what he is doing violates that right."[23]

One can thus identify at least three categories of doctrinal moves that keep courts from entering judgment for claimants in the constitutional criminal context, each of which corresponds to a different stage in the judicial process:

(1) procedural and quasi-substantive doctrines that allow courts to avoid reaching the claim on the merits (e.g., procedural default, PLRA exhaustion,[24] *Iqbal's* heightened pleading standard,[25] the Court's narrow reading of § 2254 (d)(1));

(2) procedural and quasi-substantive doctrines that encourage courts to enter judgment for the government despite an affirmative finding of a constitutional violation (e.g., Steiker's "inclusionary rules," harmless error,[26] qualified immunity);[27] and

(3) evasive techniques that steer courts away from answering the basic question at the merits stage, precisely when such analysis is presumably called for (deference, presumption of constitutionality, substitute question).

Taken together, these three categories indicate a prodigious and troubling degree of judicial evasion in the constitutional criminal context. Although each category warrants critical scrutiny, in this chapter, I focus solely on the third, applied when courts self-consciously undertake to determine whether, given the facts of the case, the relevant constitutional norm has been violated. If even here, at the very heart of things, governing doctrine allows and even encourages courts to avoid addressing the essential constitutional inquiry, it is hard to see on what basis courts may be said to be "[i]mplementing the Constitution" at all as regards the criminal context[28]—or through what mechanism, if any, the state's exercise of its penal power is being kept within constitutional bounds.

In what follows, I trace the development of the canons of evasion through four constitutional claims that regularly arise in the criminal context: Sixth Amendment claims of inadequate assistance of counsel (IAC); Eighth Amendment claims of grossly disproportionate sentences; Eighth Amendment prison conditions challenges; and Fourteenth Amendment claims of racial discrimination in jury selection.[29] As will be seen, the three canons are operative as to each case, although the form and order of appearance vary depending on the context. With each example, I offer a close reading of how these canons shape the governing doctrine. Such detail is necessary because the precise workings of each mechanism become vivid only when viewed from inside the doctrinal context in which is employed. Table 6.1 summarizes the form these moves take in each example.

Table 6.1

Claim	Norm Affirmed	Deference to?	Presumption	Substitute question
6th Amendment inadequate assistance of counsel (IAC)	Right to reasonably effective assistance of counsel	Defense counsel	Assistance of counsel is constitutionally adequate (explicit)	How strong was the prosecution's case? (*Strickland*)
8th Amendment disproportionality in noncapital sentencing	No grossly disproportionate sentences	Legislators	Sentences less severe than Harmelin's are constitutional (extreme example)	Did the legislature have a rational basis for authorizing the sentence? (*Ewing*)
8th Amendment prison conditions	Prisoners are entitled to the minimal civilized measure of life's necessities	Correctional officers	Prison conditions are constitutional unless some prison official actually realized the risk of harm (implicit)	Was some prison official criminally reckless vis-à-vis the challenged condition? (*Farmer*)
14th Amendment racial discrimination in jury selection	No purposeful discrimination	Prosecutors	Peremptory strikes accompanied by facially neutral reasons are unmotivated by purposeful discrimination	Was the prosecutor's proffered reason for the strike facially neutral? (*Purkett v. Elem*)

As the table indicates, as to each claim, the Court explicitly announces a basic, albeit narrow constitutional norm. Yet, each time, rather than developing standards for establishing when this value has been violated—the obvious move for a Court wishing to provide guidance to the judges who will make this determination in individual cases—the Court instead crafts doctrine that guides lower courts to find against the claimant without ever really analyzing the facts in light of the governing norm. We turn now to the examples themselves, to see precisely how the Court has achieved this doctrinal sleight of hand.[30]

II. Avoiding the Basic Question: A Practical Guide

A. *Sixth Amendment IAC Claims after* Strickland

The dominant narrative justifying state-imposed criminal punishment assumes that all defendants receive adequate legal representation. This normative principle has a direct constitutional analog in the Sixth Amendment and has been affirmed by the Supreme Court on multiple occasions. In the landmark case of *Gideon v. Wainwright*, the Court held that when a criminal defendant charged with a felony cannot afford a lawyer, the state is obliged to provide one free of charge.[31] Acknowledging that the institutional safeguards of the criminal justice system are not satisfied merely when "a person who happens to be a lawyer is present at trial alongside the accused,"[32] the Court has also made clear that this right is a right to the *effective assistance* of counsel.[33]

With this declaration, the Court neatly framed the basic question for Sixth Amendment right-to-counsel claims: Given what the defense lawyer actually did or did not do during the representation, did the defendant receive effective assistance of counsel? Arguably, to answer this question, one would want to assess the lawyer's performance against appropriate standards of practice—i.e., against what a reasonably adequate defense lawyer would have done under the circumstances. In some situations, determinations of reasonableness would require no elaborate comparisons; reasonably adequate lawyers, it seems safe to say, would not fall asleep during trial, come to court drunk, or refer to their client using racial epithets.[34] In other cases, assertions of adequacy might benefit from a sense of defense counsel's general duties at various stages of the criminal process. Thus, lawyers who fail to investigate a client's defense;[35] fail to ask about the client's criminal history before advising on a plea offer;[36] fail to make "timely objections to significant, arguably erroneous rulings of the trial judge";[37] or fail to put on any mitigating evidence at the penalty phase of a capital trial[38] would raise strong questions as to the constitutional adequacy of the representation provided. As with any legal standard, there would be room for disagreement as to how a given case should come out. But whatever the outcome in each case, answering the basic question would require courts to look squarely at the facts before them, then to consider whether or not the lawyer in question met her minimum obligations to her client.

In practice, however, this is not how courts decide IAC claims. Instead, they follow the two-part test established by the Supreme Court in *Strickland v. Washington*.[39] *Strickland* held that "the proper standard for attorney performance is that of reasonably effective assistance."[40] The two prongs of *Strickland*'s test for reasonably effective assistance are typically framed as "performance" and "prejudice." First, "the defendant must show that counsel's performance was deficient," i.e., that it "fell below an objective standard of reasonableness" judged in terms of prevailing professional norms. Second, the defendant must demonstrate prejudice, by showing "a reasonable probability that, but for counsel's unprofessional errors, the result of the proceedings would have been different."[41] As framed by Justice O'Connor's majority opinion, *Strickland* offers a textbook example of the evasive canons in action.

Deference and Presumption: In the IAC context, both deference and presumption are closely intertwined with the Court's elaboration of *Strickland*'s performance prong. In *Strickland*, the majority acknowledged the Sixth Amendment right to effective assistance and affirmed that defense counsel has basic obligations to the client, including the "duty to avoid conflicts of interest, . . . to advocate the defendant's cause, . . . to consult with the defendant, . . . to keep the defendant informed, . . . [and] to bring to bear such skill and knowledge as will render the trial a reliable adversarial testing process." The Court, however, insisted that "[t]hese basic duties" do not "form a checklist for judicial evaluation of attorney performance," and that "[n]o particular set of detailed rules for counsel's conduct can satisfactorily take account of the variety of circumstances faced by defense counsel or the range of legitimate decisions regarding how best to represent a criminal defendant."

Implicit in this refusal to set standards is the view that counsel must be free to make judgments without fear of being second-guessed by courts after the fact. In dissent, Justice Marshall challenged this position, arguing that "many aspects of the job of a criminal defense attorney are more amenable to judicial oversight." As Justice Marshall put it, "much of the work involved in preparing for a trial, applying for bail, conferring with one's client, making timely objections to significant, arguably erroneous rulings of the trial judge, and filing a notice of appeal if there are colorable grounds therefor could profitably be made the subject of uniform standards." But the *Strickland* majority maintained that there are "countless ways to provide effective assistance in any given case," and that "[e]ven the best criminal defense attorneys would not defend a particular client in the same way." The Court thus held that "[j]udicial scrutiny of counsel's performance must be highly deferential"; that "counsel is strongly presumed to have rendered adequate assistance and made all significant decisions in the exercise of reasonable professional judgment";[42] and—in case the point was lost—that "the defendant must overcome the presumption that, under the circumstances, the challenged action 'might be considered sound trial strategy.'"

In support of this last proposition, the Court cited *Michel v. Louisiana*,[43] a case that plainly illustrates how easily this presumption, applied in a "highly deferential" way, enables a lawyer's avoidable error to be recast as deliberate "trial strategy" and thereby transformed into effective assistance of counsel for Sixth Amendment purposes. In *Michel*, three African American co-defendants were convicted of aggravated rape and sentenced to death. On appeal, defendants challenged "the composition of the grand juries which indicted them," on grounds of "systematic exclusion of [African Americans] from the panel."[44] This being Louisiana in the early 1950s, this allegation could well have been founded, but no hearings were ever held on the issue because none of the defendants had raised a timely objection. At the time, Louisiana law gave defendants until three days after the grand jury term expired to object to its composition.[45] Though this period may sound short, and indeed would have been for those individuals indicted on the last days of a term, this deadline in practice left plenty of time for defendants indicted earlier in the life of a grand jury to challenge their indictments.

This was the case for Michel's co-defendant, Edgar Labat. Labat was indicted in December 1950, and "Mr. E.I. Mahoney" was appointed as his lawyer on January 5, 1951.[46] The grand jury term expired in March 1951, which at a minimum left Mahoney eight weeks to file a motion to quash Labat's indictment—a reasonably adequate period for any competent attorney, as the *Michel* Court found. But Mahoney filed no such motion during that time, thereby forfeiting Labat's claim. Labat alleged ineffective assistance, introducing evidence that Mahoney, who "was 76 or 77 when he took the case," was "ill in bed during several months of [1951]."

Without knowing more, it is impossible to say whether Mahoney's illness prevented him from filing the motion, although Labat's IAC claim implies as much. But the *Michel* Court saw no reason for further inquiry, finding that the facts did not support an inference of lack of effective counsel. For one thing, the Court emphasized, "Mr. Mahoney was a well-known criminal lawyer with nearly fifty years' experience" who had been honored by the New Orleans bar for his accomplishments and character.[47] And, the Court contended, "the mere fact that a timely motion to quash was not filed" does not in itself signify ineffective assistance, since "*the delay might be considered sound trial strategy*, particularly since the codefendant could not be found."[48]

For anyone wanting to determine whether as a matter of fact Labat had had adequate assistance of counsel, these reasons would be wholly insufficient. Mahoney may well have had an illustrious career, but if he was too sick to file a motion on Labat's behalf before the deadline passed, it seems fair to conclude that Labat did not in fact receive reasonably effective assistance. It is, moreover, hard to see how forfeiting a constitutional challenge to the initial indictment could benefit a client at trial—whether or not the co-defendant was present and accounted for. And in any case, the point is not that Mahoney's failure to timely file necessarily demanded a finding of ineffective assistance. It is rather that the facts Labat introduced—of an elderly, infirm lawyer close to the end of his life,[49] bedridden for months during his year as Labat's counsel—at a minimum raised a real possibility that Mahoney's failure to file the motion was due not to strategy but to incapacity. And if incapacity was indeed the reason, the claim of ineffective assistance would have been incontrovertibly valid.[50] Yet in *Michel*, the Court allowed a presumption of effectiveness and a wholly unsupported hypothesis of deliberate strategy to supplant inquiry into the actual reasons for Mahoney's failure, rendering the facts of the matter entirely irrelevant to the legal conclusion.

Michel's treatment of Labat's claim implicitly presumed the adequacy of counsel. Almost 30 years later, *Strickland* transformed this implicit presumption into an explicit doctrinal directive. Courts may and do continue to see past *Strickland's* idealized construction to the facts of the cases before them. But the idea that one person's incompetence might be another's strategic maneuvers has proved a potent formula for dismissing IAC claims.[51] And more generally, the strong presumption of adequacy, applied alongside the imperative of judicial deference, creates pressure against finding inadequate performance and allows courts—as in *Michel*—to reject IAC claims without ever subjecting the facts to close critical scrutiny.[52]

Substitute Question: If *Strickland's* "performance" prong pushes courts to presume adequacy, its "prejudice" prong replaces what would seem to be the relevant inquiry (i.e., what kind of representation the lawyer actually provided) with a different inquiry, one focusing not on the quality of counsel but on the strength of the prosecutor's case. To demonstrate prejudice under *Strickland*, claimants must show "a reasonable probability that, but for counsel's unprofessional errors, the result of the proceeding would have been different."[53] And to do so, a court "must consider the totality of the evidence before the judge or jury."[54] The stronger the evidence of guilt, the harder it will be for the defendant to meet "the burden of showing that the decision reached would reasonably likely have been different absent the errors."[55]

In other words, even when the lawyer's performance was so poor as to lead courts to resist the combined pressures of the deference imperative and the explicit presumption of adequacy and actually to find counsel's performance to have fallen below the (low) constitutional bar, the prejudice prong instructs courts still to reject IAC claims when the strength of the evidence was sufficiently strong to make it reasonably probable that the defendant would have been convicted even with competent counsel. With this second prong, the Court thus pivots away from the quality of counsel altogether, effectively substituting the question of the strength of the prosecutor's case for that of whether counsel's performance was constitutionally deficient. Moreover, *Strickland* makes clear that courts able to dispose of cases on the prejudice prong should do so,[56] thereby making the strength of the prosecutor's case—and not the quality of the representation—the primary issue.

Some might argue that this additional inquiry is in fact the more appropriate focus, since if the evidence of guilt is overwhelming, no error by counsel would have made a difference. As a quasi-harmless error standard—albeit one putting the burden on the defendant[57]—this prong seems to guard against judicial vacation of convictions due to rights violations not likely to bear on the reliability of the verdict. Yet if the client did not in fact receive reasonably effective assistance of counsel, there is no way to fairly assess the strength of the case against the defendant, since the content and quality of the record will have been shaped from the outset by defense counsel's inadequate performance.[58]

Interestingly, embedded in this substitute inquiry is a second implicit presumption—that the record before the review court is trustworthy. *Strickland* leaves no room to challenge this second presumption on IAC grounds, making it effectively irrebuttable. That this second, irrebuttable presumption is necessarily dependent on the first (i.e., that counsel has "rendered adequate assistance and made all significant decisions in the exercise of reasonable professional judgment"[59]) means that *Strickland* relies on what might be termed *stacked presumptions*. The combined effect of these presumptions is to enable—indeed to direct—courts to dismiss IAC claims as unfounded, without ever meaningfully scrutinizing claims that, whether out of incompetence, laziness, or more likely lack of sufficient time or resources, defense counsel provided nothing close to the level of assistance necessary to ensure "the proper functioning of the adversarial process" and thereby to "produce[] a just result."[60]

B. Eighth Amendment Disproportionality Claims after Harmelin and Ewing

Common sense tells us there are moral limits to the severity of the criminal sentences the state may impose. We do not, for example, give a person life in prison for stealing a paperclip, or even for stealing a car. To be sure, not every case will be so straightforward. (Is a ten-year sentence for armed robbery too long?) But the presence in the Bill of Rights of a prohibition on "cruel and unusual punishment" and the subsequent recognition by the Court that this prohibition precludes at a minimum grossly disproportionate sentences[61] have together made this inquiry a matter of judicial review. This assignment seems fitting; after all, courts are often called upon to apply general standards to particular situations, obliging them to determine on what side of the line a case falls.[62]

Just as the Court expressly affirmed the right to effective assistance of counsel, it has explicitly acknowledged a right against grossly disproportionate punishment. Unlike the IAC context, however, governing precedent here does offer a set of standards that reviewing courts might bring to bear on the basic question for noncapital Eighth Amendment disproportionality claims. In *Solem v. Helm*, Justice Powell identified three factors that might guide judicial deliberations in this area: (1) "the gravity of the offense" (to be weighed against "the harshness of the penalty"),[63] (2) "the sentences imposed on other criminals in the same jurisdiction" (a.k.a. the intra-jurisdictional comparison), and (3) "the sentences imposed for commission of the same crime in other jurisdictions" (a.k.a. the inter-jurisdictional comparison).[64] As to the first factor, *Solem* went still further and noted a range of considerations that might help to determine where on the spectrum a given offense might fall in terms of "gravity"; as Justice Powell noted, with reference to what he plainly took to be widely shared intuitions, "non-violent crimes are less serious than crimes marked by violence or threat of violence," "[s]tealing a million dollars is viewed as more serious than stealing $100," a "lesser included offense should not be punished more seriously than the greater offense," "attempts are less serious than completed crimes," "an accessory after the fact should not be subject to a higher penalty than the principal," and "negligent conduct is less serious than intentional conduct."[65]

A decade after *Solem*, in *Harmelin v. Michigan*, the Court narrowed the factors to be used by courts addressing the basic question in this context, deeming the second and third (the intra-and inter-jurisdictional comparisons) appropriate to take into account only when "a threshold comparison of the crime committed and the sentence imposed leads to an inference of gross disproportionality."[66] Still, this formulation preserved *Solem*'s first factor—essentially the basic question for this context—as the central inquiry, and did not overtly repudiate Justice Powell's considerations for gauging the severity of the crime. Thus, even after *Harmelin*, the doctrine directed courts to answer the basic question for the Eighth Amendment disproportionality context: Is the punishment imposed grossly disproportionate to the crime committed?

Yet, after *Harmelin*, it is a rare case in which courts have upheld claims of unconstitutionally disproportionate sentences.[67] The reason why cannot be that the sentences meted out by the American criminal justice system are by and large measured and appropriate. Judging from the facts of cases raising Eighth Amendment disproportionality claims over the past 30 years, numerous people have received grossly disproportionate sentences[68]—especially considering the state of the country's prisons and the consequent harshness of the conditions under which carceral penalties are to be served.[69] Still, in case after case, judges have confronted people sentenced to extremely long prison terms, not infrequently for relatively minor crimes, and repeatedly found no constitutional issue. They have typically done so, moreover, with little if any attention to the culpability measures Justice Powell identified in *Solem*—or any other relevant features of either the offender's personal blameworthiness or the experiential implications of the penalty—despite the fact that *Harmelin*'s modified test plainly directs courts to carefully weigh the crime committed against the sentence imposed.

There are several aspects of the governing precedent that in theory could explain this phenomenon.[70] In practice, however, the most potent explanation lies in the way the Court has channeled reviewing courts toward upholding challenged sentences without pausing to consider the basic question—here, whether the penalty imposed could be said to be grossly disproportionate to the offense committed.

Deference: First, there is the Court's repeated insistence on judicial deference to legislative prerogatives as to sentencing. Across all the relevant precedent, the Court emphasizes that the judgment involved in the "fixing of prison terms for specific crimes . . . is 'properly within the province of legislatures, not courts,'" and thus that reviewing courts must take an extremely deferential posture toward these claims.[71] In the 1980 case of *Rummel v. Estelle*,[72] the majority seemed strongly inclined to foreclose entirely all excessiveness challenges to noncapital sentences. But it found an obstacle in *Weems v. United States*, the 1910 case that struck down a noncapital sentence in part because it found the penalty in question to violate "a precept of justice that punishment for crime should be graduated and proportionate to the offense."[73] The *Rummel* majority thus had to settle for emphasizing that "[o]utside the context of capital punishment, successful challenges to the proportionality of particular sentences have been exceedingly rare" and insisting, *Weems* notwithstanding, that "one could argue without fear of contradiction by any decision of this Court" that "the length of the sentence actually imposed is purely a matter of legislative prerogative."[74]

Subsequent Supreme Court cases reiterated this imperative of judicial deference to legislative determinations. In his dissent in *Solem v. Helm*—in which five justices voted to strike down Helm's sentence of life in prison without parole (LWOP) for a seventh nonviolent offense—Chief Justice Burger condemned the overriding of "the considered action of legislators under the guise of constitutional interpretation[.]"[75] In his controlling opinion in *Harmelin*, Justice Kennedy identified as the first principle to "give content to the uses and limits of proportionality review" the need for "'substantial deference to the broad authority that legislatures necessarily possess in determining the types and limits of punishment for crimes.'"[76] And in her opinion in *Ewing v. California* upholding a 25-year sentence for a nonviolent third strike under California's three-strikes law, Justice O'Connor cautioned repeatedly that "the legislature . . . has primary responsibility for making the difficult policy choices that underlie any criminal sentencing scheme," and that the Court "do[es] not sit as a 'superlegislature' to second-guess these policy choices."[77]

Perhaps the strongest signal the Court has provided as to the need to defer to legislatively authorized criminal penalties came just one year after *Rummel*, in *Hutto v. Davis*. Davis was convicted of two counts of possession with intent to distribute approximately nine ounces of marijuana and sentenced to 40 years in prison.[78] On habeas, the District Court struck down the sentence, finding it to be "so grossly out of proportion to the severity of the crimes as to constitute cruel and unusual punishment in violation of the Eighth Amendment[.]"[79] A panel of the Fourth Circuit reversed, but the case was reheard *en banc* and this time, the District Court order was affirmed.[80] The Supreme Court granted *certiorari*, vacated the judgment, and remanded for reconsideration in light of *Rummel*.[81] On rehearing, the *en banc* court again affirmed the District Court,[82] and the Supreme Court again granted *cert*.

As noted, the *Rummel* Court had emphasized that, outside the death penalty context, "successful challenges to the proportionality of particular sentences have been exceedingly rare."[83] To the dissenting justices in *Hutto v. Davis*, it was obvious that the appellate judges who voted to affirm the District Court a second time viewed this as "one of those 'exceedingly rare' cases[.]"[84] But the *Davis* majority, comprised of the same justices as the *Rummel* majority, roared as if it had been stung. Not only did it decisively reverse, criticizing the Fourth Circuit for "sanction[ing] an intrusion into the basic line-drawing process that is 'properly within the province of legislatures, not courts'"—i.e., on grounds of deference— but it all but accused the Fourth Circuit of willfully defying the plain holding of *Rummel*.[85] According to the Court, in affirming the District Court after *Rummel*, the *en banc* court "could be viewed as having ignored, consciously or unconsciously, the hierarchy of the federal court system created by the Constitution and Congress." [86] It is hard to imagine a clearer directive to lower courts to forbear from exercising the judgment called for by the basic question.

Presumption: In the IAC context, the presumption of constitutionality, like the imperative of judicial deference, is explicitly stipulated. By contrast, in the Eighth Amendment disproportionality context, the Court instantiates this presumption—and thereby pushes lower courts away from engaging the basic question—by sheer force of example. Since 1980, the Court has heard six cases raising disproportionality claims. Reasoning aside, the facts of these cases read like a laundry list of penalties constituting grossly excessive punishment:

- life in prison for obtaining $120.75 by false pretenses (*Rummel v. Estelle*)
- 40 years in prison for possession with intent to distribute nine ounces of marijuana (*Hutto v. Davis*)
- LWOP for passing a bad check for $100 (*Solem v. Helm*)
- LWOP for possession of 672 grams of cocaine (*Harmelin v. Michigan*)
- a 25-year mandatory minimum for the theft of three golf clubs worth $399 each (*Ewing v. California*)
- a 50-year mandatory minimum for the theft of video cassettes worth $154 from two Kmart stores (*Lockyer v. Andrade*)

Yet in all but one of these cases (*Solem v. Helm*), the Court upheld the sentence as constitutional—and even in *Solem*, four justices joined a vociferous dissent.

Call this *presumption by extreme example*. These examples serve as strict guideposts for all courts hearing Eighth Amendment claims of excessive sentences. If even *these* penalties were not found by the Supreme Court to be unconstitutionally disproportionate, then most other sentences must also be upheld. True, in *Solem*, the Court struck down Helm's LWOP sentence as unconstitutionally excessive. But *Solem* was decided close on the heels of *Rummel* and *Davis*, two cases upholding very long sentences for equally minor offenses, and the only meaningful difference lower courts seemed able to discern post-*Solem* was that Helm, unlike Rummel and Davis, had received LWOP. As a consequence, courts after *Solem* seriously considered granting relief only in cases involving LWOP sentences—and, even then, did so very rarely. And in any case, any ambiguity *Solem* created was handily resolved in *Harmelin*, when the Court upheld an LWOP sentence for a *first offense* of possession of 672 grams of cocaine. All by itself, Harmelin's sentence has provided a sufficiently extreme example to push courts to uphold as constitutional virtually any sentence that might be authorized by the legislature. There is no death penalty in Michigan, which means that, as Justice White pointed out in his dissent, Harmelin received "the harshest penalty available" in that state.[87] Moreover, unlike Rummel, Helm, and Ewing, Harmelin had no prior convictions to muddy the analysis. Yet even here, Justice Kennedy in his controlling opinion had no difficulty finding that Harmelin's sentence "[did] not give rise to an inference of gross disproportionality[.]"[88] If Harmelin's sentence is within constitutional bounds, virtually any sentence short of death[89] for any crime but the most petty must likewise be presumed constitutional,[90] even for first-time offenders. Thus, notwithstanding *Harmelin*'s formal standard, in most cases, judges need scarcely contemplate the actual facts before them before disposing of Eighth Amendment disproportionality claims as without merit.

Substitute Question: Notwithstanding the Court's repeated insistence on deference and despite the strong presumption of constitutionality *Harmelin* creates, the doctrine after *Harmelin* retained the basic question as the putative center of judicial analysis. But as the District Court and the Fourth Circuit demonstrated in *Davis*, so long as the door to the basic question remains open, however slightly, the possibility remains that some judges will exercise their own judgment and strike down sentences on gross disproportionality grounds. Thus, in *Ewing v. California*, the first post-*Harmelin* Supreme Court case to raise this issue, the Court loosed its final evasive arrow, substituting for the basic question an alternative inquiry that narrowed still further the possibility of success on these claims (if not foreclosing it altogether). In *Ewing*, the defendant argued that his 25-year mandatory minimum sentence was unconstitutionally disproportionate to the offense of conviction: the theft from a pro shop of three golf clubs worth $399 each. Writing for the majority, Justice O'Connor made as if she were applying *Harmelin*'s threshold factor, announcing her intent to "address the gravity of the offense compared to the harshness of the penalty."[91] As to the gravity of the offense, Justice O'Connor discussed the theft on its own,[92] and at greater length argued that "[i]n weighing the gravity of Ewing's offense, we must place on the scales not only his current felony, but also his long history of felony recidivism."[93] As to the severity of the punishment, Justice O'Connor said little, although she did concede that, "[t]o be sure, Ewing's sentence is a long one."[94] But then, as Youngjae Lee nicely puts it, Justice O'Connor "simply changed the subject."[95] Rather than explicitly attempting to weigh the offense against the penalty, as *Harmelin*'s threshold factor requires, Justice O'Connor instead concluded that Ewing's sentence was "justified by the state's public-safety interest in incapacitating and deterring recidivist felons, . . . reflect[ing] a rational legislative judgment, entitled to deference, that offenders who have committed serious or violent felonies and who continue to commit felonies must be incapacitated."[96]

Framing the issue this way cleanly shifts attention away from the basic question animating the prohibition on grossly disproportionate punishment and toward judicial inquiry into the legislature's reason for authorizing the sentence. After *Ewing*, a court's finding that the legislature had a rational basis for authorizing the challenged penalty will end the matter—as, indeed, it did in *Ewing* itself.[97] Moreover, Justice O'Connor's opinion made clear that this inquiry into legislative purpose is to be extremely deferential, since "the Constitution 'does not mandate adoption of any one penological theory.'"[98] This shift away from the basic question and toward a deferential inquiry into whether the legislature had a rational basis for its sentencing policy allows courts to find a sentence not to be constitutionally excessive with only the most glancing reference to either the offense the defendant committed or the punishment she consequently faces.[99]

C. Eighth Amendment Prison Conditions Claims after Farmer

In our constitutional system, it is widely agreed that the state may not, in the name of criminal punishment, inflict torture or "other barbarous penalties."[100] Nor may accepted forms of punishment be applied in ways that cause gratuitous pain and suffering. As the Supreme Court has recognized, such treatment would both itself amount to torture and serve no legitimate penal purpose.[101] It would therefore represent an abuse of the state's penal power.

As with the right against grossly disproportionate punishment, the right against torture and the infliction of gratuitous harm has a constitutional analog in the Eighth Amendment prohibition on cruel and unusual punishment. The Supreme Court has explicitly acknowledged as much, holding that, under the Eighth Amendment, the state is obliged to provide prisoners with "the minimal civilized measure of life's necessities,"[102] and to protect them from the "substantial risk of serious harm"[103]—by, among other things, treating their serious medical needs[104] and keeping them safe from violence at the hands of other prisoners.[105] Plaintiffs bringing Eighth Amendment prison conditions claims must therefore show that the state failed to provide for and protect them to this extent. But to succeed on these claims, prisoners must also demonstrate some "sufficient culpability" on the part of state actors for the harm they suffered. It is not prisoners' suffering alone that is unconstitutional under the Eighth Amendment; it is suffering arising from a deprivation for which the state is responsible.

In *Farmer v. Brennan*, the Court emphasized the duty prison officials have under the Eighth Amendment to "provide humane conditions of confinement[,] . . . ensure that prisoners receive adequate food, clothing, shelter, and medical care, and . . . 'take reasonable measures to guarantee the safety of inmates.'"[106] What, however, is the scope of this duty? What conduct, with what state of mind, would represent a constitutional failure of care? In *DeShaney v. Winnebago County*, Chief Justice Rehnquist explained that "when the State takes a person into its custody and holds him there against his will, the Constitution imposes upon it a corresponding duty to assume some responsibility for his safety and general well-being."[107] This "affirmative duty to protect" arises "from the limitation which [the State] has imposed on [the detained individual's] freedom to act on his own behalf."[108] The state's obligation, in other words, arises from prisoners' total dependence on prison officials, a function of the government's own decision to incarcerate people under conditions depriving them of the capacity to meet their own needs.[109] Picking up on this theme, *Farmer* emphasized just how dangerous prisons are and how vulnerable prisoners would be without state aid. As Justice Souter put it, "Having incarcerated persons with demonstrated proclivities for antisocial criminal, and often violent, conduct, having stripped them of virtually every means of self-protection and foreclosed their access to outside aid, the government and its officials are not free to let the state of nature take its course."[110]

If prisoners are wholly dependent on state officials for their basic needs, if they are living in locked facilities in close quarters with people who are possibly dangerous, and if this state of affairs is at the root of prison officials' Eighth Amendment obligations toward the people in their custody, then Chief Justice Rehnquist was right to identify this duty as an *affirmative* one—not a passive obligation on the part of prison officials to respond to problems they happen to come across, but an ongoing responsibility to pay attention to what is happening in the prison, to monitor, to investigate, to stay on top of potential threats to prisoners' well-being. The basic question for this context thus ought to be whether the challenged deprivation was traceable to the defendant's violation of her affirmative duty of care toward the plaintiff. Courts answering this question would need to determine whether prison officials had actual or constructive knowledge of the potential for harm yet failed to take preventative steps, and state officials would be liable if they failed to address serious risks of harm to prisoners about which a reasonably attentive prison official would have known. Courts applying this standard would thus be called upon to scrutinize not only the precise hardships prisoners suffered, but also what steps state officials had taken or failed to take to keep prisoners safe from serious harm and meet their basic needs.

Given the general state of conditions in America's prisons and jails, if this were indeed the governing standard, we might expect to find the courts in an almost constant posture of condemning prison conditions as unconstitutional. Yet in practice, the vast majority of claims alleging unconstitutional conditions in prisons and jails are denied. To be sure, most potential claims fail on procedural grounds. But even for prisoners able to navigate the procedural obstacles and win a hearing on the merits, successful prison conditions claims are still relatively rare—thanks in no small part to operative standards that allow courts to dismiss such claims without having to look too closely at the actual lived experiences of the people the state has chosen to incarcerate.

Substitute Question/Presumption: In *Wilson v. Seiter*, the Court framed the issue for doctrinal purposes as whether prison officials had been deliberately indifferent to prisoners' basic human needs.[111] The question left unanswered was what state of mind deliberate indifference represents. Three years later, in *Farmer v. Brennan*, the Court resolved this issue.[112] The petitioner, federal prisoner Dee Farmer, was a trans woman who had yet to undergo successful gender reassignment surgery. Pursuant to Federal Bureau of Prisons (BOP) policy in place at the time, Farmer was housed in men's facilities. In March 1989, she was transferred to the federal penitentiary at Terre Haute and, after a stint in administrative segregation, was placed in general population, where she was "beaten and raped by another inmate in [her] cell." Farmer sued, alleging that placing her in general population in a men's high-security facility constituted deliberate indifference to the substantial risk of physical harm she faced in such a setting.

The District Court, finding deliberate indifference to require "actual knowledge of a potential danger" and finding the defendants to "lack the requisite knowledge," granted summary judgment. In the Supreme Court, Farmer argued for an objective reading of deliberate indifference, a standard that would instantiate the affirmative duty of care Chief Justice Rehnquist affirmed in *DeShaney*. This interpretation, effectively a gross negligence standard,[113] would require only that, under the circumstances, prison officials should have known of the high risk of placing Farmer in a men's general population unit. The BOP argued, with the District Court, for a subjective standard of criminal recklessness, on which a failure of prison officials to actually realize the risk would immunize them from constitutional liability.

The *Farmer* Court sided with the government. It held that successful Eighth Amendment prison conditions claims require a showing that defendants actually realized the risk of harm. As the Court put it, "a prison official cannot be found liable under the Eighth Amendment for denying an inmate humane conditions of confinement unless the official knows of and disregards an excessive risk to inmate health or safety; the official must both be aware of facts from which the inference could be drawn that a substantial risk of serious harm exists, and he must also draw the inference."[114] The *Farmer* majority acknowledged that "a factfinder may conclude that a prison official knew of a substantial risk from the very fact that the risk was obvious"—an exception by no means empty, since it allows courts to assume defendants are aware of dangers that are generally recognized. But in *Farmer*, the Court was also careful to point out that "[w]hether a prison official had the requisite knowledge of a substantial risk is a question of fact," and "'we know that people are not always conscious of what reasonable people would be conscious of.'"[115]

After *Farmer*, the question is not whether prison officials failed to take adequate steps to protect prisoners from excessive risks to their health and safety. It is whether prisoners faced a substantial risk of serious harm, the existence of which defendants actually, subjectively recognized. In this way, the Court established a frequently dispositive substitute question—did prison officials actually realize the risk of harm?—that operates to divert judicial attention away from prisoners' daily lived experience and into the internal workings of correctional officers' minds. To answer this substitute question, courts need only establish what the defendant actually knew. If, because she was just not paying attention, a prison official had no idea that some prisoner or prisoners in her custody faced a substantial risk of serious harm, under *Farmer*, there is no constitutional violation—even if the danger was glaringly obvious or well understood, even if a reasonable person in the defendant's position *would* have realized the risk, and even if she herself would have realized it if she only had been alert to potential dangers.

Certainly, in those cases where prisoners can prove that defendants realized the risk, courts will need to delve into the details of prisoners' experience. But the threshold question will always be that of what was in the defendant's conscious mind, which is a difficult showing for prisoners to make. The so-called "problem of other minds" makes it hard enough for any party to prove that someone in fact knew what they claim they did not know. Then there is the challenge prisoners face in convincing factfinders to credit the claims of a convicted offender against the word of a uniformed officer claiming lack of knowledge, not to mention how hard it can be to build a case around external evidence when, being locked up and indigent, it can be next to impossible to get any discovery. Add up these difficulties, and in practice, *Farmer's* actual knowledge threshold becomes very hard for prisoners to get past.

The *Farmer* standard, however, does not only introduce a frequently dispositive substitute question for Eighth Amendment prison conditions claims.[116] It also establishes a broad *presumption of constitutionality* that operates to shield a large portion of what goes on in prisons and jails from judicial scrutiny. Notwithstanding *Farmer's* assertion that "'the treatment a prisoner receives in prison and the conditions under which he is confined are subject to scrutiny under the Eighth Amendment,'"[117] after *Farmer*, unless some prison official can be proved actually to have known of the risk of harm, prison conditions will raise no constitutional issue. *Farmer's* holding thus converts prison officials' constitutional duty of care from an ongoing affirmative duty to attend to prisoners' basic needs into an episodic obligation, triggered only when they happen to be paying attention. In this way, most of what goes on in the prison—however disturbing—becomes per se constitutional and thereby irrelevant to courts deciding Eighth Amendment prison conditions claims.

Deference: By contrast with *Strickland* and the Eighth Amendment gross disproportionality cases discussed above, *Farmer* did not explicitly assert the need for deference. But it did not have to. The imperative of judicial deference to prison officials has been the dominant theme of the Court's prison law jurisprudence for the past 40 years.[118] Indeed, so strongly has the Court emphasized the judicial obligation of deference to prison officials' judgments, and so responsive have lower courts been to this imperative, that it is possible to identify a broad "culture of deference that constrains federal courts from interfering in prison affairs."[119] This cultural pressure manifests in intangible yet powerful benefits for prison officials defending against constitutional claims, including the tendency of courts to construe facts in prison officials' favor and to demand limited evidentiary showings in support of their positions.[120] Courts applying the *Farmer* standard do so against this backdrop, which means that the imperative to defer will inform the application of this standard whether or not the *Farmer* Court explicitly required it.

Indeed, the imperative of judicial deference to prison officials goes still further in this context, arguably shaping the *Farmer* standard itself. Justice Souter framed *Farmer's* holding as necessitated by the language of the Eighth Amendment; in the prior case of *Wilson v. Seiter*, the Court had found that "[i]f the pain inflicted is not formally meted out as *punishment* by the statute or the sentencing judge, some [subjective] mental element must be attributed to the inflicting officer before it can qualify [as punishment]."[121] But *Wilson's* reasoning does not withstand scrutiny,[122] and once this (pretextual) justification is removed, it is hard not to see *Farmer's* holding as a product of the Court's determination to create a zone for the exercise of official discretion undisturbed by constitutional imperatives. *Farmer* grants prison officials immunity from judicial scrutiny even in cases involving obvious dereliction of duty. The courts' obligation to defer in this context is thus written right into the standard, prohibiting courts from considering the reality of prisoners' lived experience even when the issue before them is whether the prison conditions shaping that reality are unconstitutional.

D. Fourteenth Amendment Claims of Race Discrimination in Jury Selection after Batson *and* Elem

It is no secret that African Americans are overrepresented in the criminal justice system. The reasons for this disparity are myriad and complex, and explaining them is well beyond the scope of this chapter.[123] It does, however, seem clear that the American criminal system is rife with racial discrimination, and that the legitimacy of this system—its consistency with our core constitutional commitments—depends on ongoing efforts to identify and dismantle the levers of such discrimination.

One primary context for race discrimination claims in the criminal process has been the racially motivated use of peremptory strikes to shape juries. In *Batson v. Kentucky*, the Court affirmed that "[s]election procedures that purposefully exclude black persons from juries undermine public confidence in the fairness of our system of justice," and that "the Equal Protection Clause forbids the prosecutor to challenge potential jurors solely on account of their race[.]"[124] *Batson* has come in for considerable criticism for, among other things, emphasizing the rights of prospective jurors to "colorblind jury selection"[125] over the rights of defendants to "free[dom] from racially discriminatory jury verdicts";[126] for the way it presumes that race bias affects the proceedings only when prosecutors intentionally discriminate against jurors;[127] and for a too-narrow focus on jury composition as the means to combat racial discrimination in the criminal process.[128] But for our purposes, *Batson* is notable for having done little even to prevent racially motivated peremptory strikes. Thanks to how the doctrine has been shaped, courts can easily dispose of *Batson* claims even in cases where a modicum of scrutiny would support a finding that a juror was purposely struck based on race.

In *Batson*, the Court created a three-step process for addressing claims of race bias in jury selection. First, the defendant bears the burden of making a *prima facie* case of "purposeful discrimination in selection of the venire."[129] At that point, the burden shifts to the prosecution. This second step is the heart of the inquiry. It requires that the prosecutor provide a "race-neutral explanation" for the decision. And not just any facially neutral explanation will do; under *Batson*, the prosecutor "must articulate a neutral explanation related to the particular case to be tried." Third and finally, "[t]he trial court then will have the duty to determine if the defendant has established purposeful discrimination." According to the *Batson* Court, this determination "largely will turn on [an] evaluation of [the prosecutor's] credibility."

Implicit bias and the subtleties of race discrimination can make it hard to say for sure when a peremptory strike was exercised on racial grounds.[130] Still, there are mechanisms judges could apply both at the moment of the strike and on appellate review to strengthen their ability to identify and expose racially motivated peremptories. In efforts to ferret out pretext, trial courts could press the prosecution[131] on their reasons for exercising the strike and then evaluate the plausibility of those reasons. The doctrine could also require prosecutors to provide race-neutral reasons specifically relevant to the case at hand or grounds "for believing those factors will somehow affect the person's ability to perform his or her duties as a juror."[132] Indeed, *Batson* itself emphasized that proffered race-neutral reasons must be "related to the particular case to be tried,"[133] thus seeming to invite the creation of standards to guide courts in answering the basic question embodied in *Batson*'s third step, i.e., whether the prosecutor purposely exercised her peremptory challenges "on account of race."[134]

From the outset, *Batson* had little constraining effect on the jury selection process. Although in theory, the doctrine creates space for a more searching inquiry, judges proved reluctant to too closely scrutinize proffered reasons, seemingly because they did not want to "impugn the integrity of the prosecutor, an officer of the court."[135] Courtroom dynamics thus created pressure on judges to accept virtually any explanation for a challenged strike, so long as it was "not explicitly about race."[136] These dynamics, and their apparent neutralization of *Batson*'s disciplining effects on the ground, might have prompted the Court to create doctrinal mechanisms to mitigate trial courts' inclination to defer to prosecutors and to presume the validity of their facially neutral explanations. Instead, in the 1995 case of *Purkett v. Elem*,[137] the Court chose to frame the governing doctrine so as to reinforce these tendencies, effectively all but immunizing prosecutors from successful *Batson* challenges.[138]

Deference, Presumption, and Substitute Question All in One: In *Purkett v. Elem*, the prosecutor used his peremptory challenges to strike two black men from the jury panel. The defendant raised a *Batson* objection, and the prosecutor explained that he "'struck [juror] number twenty-two because . . . he had long hair hanging down shoulder length, curly, unkempt hair. Also, he had a mustache and a goatee type beard. And juror number twenty-four also has a mustache and goatee type beard. . . . I don't like the way they looked, with the way the hair is cut. . . . And the mustaches and the beards look suspicious to me.'"[139] The trial court overruled both objections, the jury was impaneled, and Elem was convicted.

Elem appealed unsuccessfully all the way to the Eighth Circuit, where he finally prevailed. To satisfy *Batson*'s second step, the appeals court held, "'the prosecution must at least articulate some plausible race-neutral reason for believing those factors will somehow affect the person's ability to perform his or her duties as a juror.'" Applying this standard, the appeals court found "that the 'prosecutor's explanation for striking juror 22 . . . was pretextual,' and that the state trial court had 'clearly erred' in finding that striking juror 22 had not been intentional discrimination."[140]

The Supreme Court took the case, and, in a *per curiam* opinion, sided with the state. The Court objected not to the specifics of the burden the Eighth Circuit sought to impose on the prosecution, but to the fact that it had tried to impose any burden at all. According to the Court, *Batson's* second step "does not demand an explanation that is persuasive, or even plausible." Instead, all that must be shown is the "facial validity of the prosecutor's explanation."[141] Brushing aside *Batson's* requirement that the reason proffered must be "related to the particular case to be tried," *Elem* made clear that so long as "a discriminatory intent is [not] inherent in the prosecutor's explanation," any reason at all—however "silly or superstitious," however "implausible or fantastic"—will do. According to the Court, it is not until the third step, when the trial court must determine whether the defendant has met his or her burden to prove purposeful discrimination, "that the persuasiveness of the justification becomes relevant[.]" At that stage, the Court allowed, the trial court confronting "implausible or fantastic justifications may (and probably will)" find them pretextual. However, the Court insisted, "to say that a trial judge *may choose to disbelieve* a silly or superstitious reason at step three is quite different from saying that a trial judge *must terminate* the inquiry at step two when the race-neutral reason is silly or superstitious."

On its face, the Court's stance may seem like empty formalism. If the court is to find a proffered explanation implausible on its face, what does it matter if the judge grants the motion at step two or step three? In fact, however, the distinction the Court draws here is highly material. According to the Court, the Eighth Circuit erred because it asked entirely the wrong question. Instead of focusing as it did on "the *reasonableness* of the asserted nonracial motive," it should have been determining the "*genuineness*" of that motive. In other words—and here is the key move for our purposes—the issue the trial court must decide is not the plausibility of the prosecutor's stated motive, but her sincerity in offering it.

Granted, as the Court takes care to remind us, under *Batson*, the finding at the third stage is to turn "primarily on an assessment of [the prosecutor's] credibility[.]"[142] But what, it might be wondered, of *Batson's* equally clear directive that the prosecutor's race-neutral reasons "be related to the particular case to be tried?" *Elem* appears to regard these two directives as incompatible—is the standard reasonableness or genuineness? But the suggestion of incompatibility seems off-base, or at least to lose sight of the purpose of the inquiry. How else is a court to determine the genuineness of the explanation, if not by seeking to assess its plausibility? At a minimum, it might fairly be thought—along with the Eighth Circuit—that judges would want to hear "some plausible race-neutral reason for believing [that the stated] factors would somehow affect the person's ability to perform his or her duties as a juror" before concluding that the prosecutor's proffered justification was sincere.[143] Absent some rationality standard for smoking out pretext, all courts would have to go on in identifying purposeful discrimination at *Batson*'s step three would be demeanor, which seems problematic if the aim is to root out purposeful discrimination based on race. For one thing, a practiced prosecutor could evade *Batson* purely by feigning sincerity.[144] More to the point, we are back to the very problem trial courts initially encountered when, in order to grant *Batson* claims in the face of facially neutral explanations, judges would have to say explicitly that "they did not believe the prosecutor," thus "essentially calling the prosecutor a liar."[145] Except that, after *Elem*, trial courts now lack the ability to disallow explanations—and thus to grant relief under *Batson*—even when those explanations bear no relation "to the particular case to be tried." As *Elem* made crystal clear, even a "silly or superstitious" reason may count, as long as it is race-neutral on its face.[146]

Elem does not explicitly mandate deference or establish a presumption of constitutionality as a formal doctrinal matter. On its face, all *Elem* does is ease the burden on prosecutors at the second step, while reserving the power to the courts at step three to disbelieve the reason given. But *Elem* achieves the same effect as if it *had* affirmatively mandated deference and a presumption of constitutionality. By denying trial courts any standards for assessing rationality[147]—and thus any tools for ferreting out pretext—*Elem* effectively requires that judges defer to prosecutors so long as their explanations are facially neutral. After *Elem*, prosecutors can defeat a *Batson* objection merely by providing a facially neutral explanation, whether or not it bears on the case. In practice, therefore, the doctrine implicitly creates a strong presumption that facially neutral reasons do not conceal purposeful discrimination. And if *Elem* hinders trial courts' efforts to look behind prosecutor's proffered explanations to smoke out improper motives, it all but forecloses reviewing courts from finding for defendants on appeal. If the trial courts' determinations are solely based on credibility, with no weight at all placed on the rationality of the justification, trial courts' *Batson* dismissals will be entitled to "'great deference.'"[148] On appeal, so long as the record reflects a facially race-neutral explanation, the appeals court must presume (following the trial court) that the strike is not racially motivated.

In effect, after *Elem*, the question courts must ask when deciding *Batson* claims is not whether the prosecution in fact engaged in purposeful discrimination on account of race, but whether the proffered reason was race-neutral on its face. Unlike our prior examples, the substitute question dispositive for this context does not require a pivot to a wholly different issue, but merely an easing of the basic question, from "was the prosecutor's strike racially motivated?" to "was the proffered reason for the strike facially neutral?" This difference may simply be a function of how largely ineffectual as a practical matter *Batson* has been at disciplining prosecutors who strike jurors on account of race. Here, all that was needed to keep courts from directly confronting the basic question was to shift the inquiry from one inviting critical scrutiny to one making clear that no such scrutiny is necessary or expected.

III. The Myth of Constitutional Enforcement in the Criminal Context

It is no secret that courts rarely find for prisoners—a group that includes most people challenging their convictions, sentences, or punishments. This is true even when such claimants manage to get a hearing on the merits. What I have sought to show here is how this predictable effect is achieved as a doctrinal matter. Through the systematic deployment of the three evasive maneuvers I have labeled *deference, presumption,* and *substitute question,* the United States Supreme Court has crafted legal doctrines for the criminal context under which, despite a façade of meaningful constitutional review, the state nearly always wins. And there is a second, arguably more pernicious effect of this dynamic, which is that appeals courts faced with constitutional challenges to the outputs of the criminal system are effectively guided toward affirming the constitutionality of those outputs without ever directly considering the facts before them in light of basic constitutional values. This is so even when the governing legal standards nominally embody these values. As a result, every day, courts around the country hear cases with facts that would make a layperson's jaw drop, facts that call into serious question the normative legitimacy of the criminal justice system, and yet find no constitutional problem.

The argument offered here is not meant as a per se objection to any of the three evasive mechanisms I identify. For example, taken alone and employed judiciously, judicial deference may be perfectly appropriate, as, say, when required by *Chevron*[149] or the political question doctrine. And what I have labeled "substitute question" arguably serves valid purposes in some constitutional contexts, as with the equal protection inquiry into the appropriate level of scrutiny for a challenged regulation or statutory enactment.[150] Indeed, even as to the claims I discuss, some use of deference, presumption, and substitute question may not be inappropriate. For example, it would be reasonable for courts to accord some presumption of constitutionality to legislatively authorized penalties—as the Court arguably does when it reads the Eighth Amendment narrowly, as protecting only against "gross disproportionality."[151]

The problem arises with the systematic mass deployment of these moves, which among other concerns generates the impression of a Court determined to direct judicial scrutiny as much as possible away from what is really going in the nation's courtrooms, jails, and prisons.[152] It is especially troubling that this repeated judicial recourse to the full set of evasive techniques occurs in the criminal context, a setting in which the intrusiveness of state power is both at its zenith and disproportionally deployed against society's most politically, economically, and culturally disenfranchised citizens—most notably, poor people of color. It is one thing if, mindful of what Alexander Bickel famously called the "counter-majoritarian difficulty," the Court makes use of available evasive tools to avoid deciding constitutional questions that might yet be effectively addressed by the political branches.[153] But in the criminal context, the counter-majoritarianism of judicial review is precisely what is called for. It is hard to find a minority more despised and politically disempowered than prisoners, and if the fundamental protections in the Bill of Rights for people accused and convicted of crimes are to have any meaningful content, their enforcement cannot be left to the political branches.

There are many explanations that may account for why the Court forbears from, as Lawrence Sager puts it, enforcing these constitutional provisions to their "full conceptual limits."[154] Although this is not the place for a full assessment of possible reasons, two points bear making. First, the standard arguments typically offered to justify judicial under-enforcement of constitutional norms—federalism, separation of powers, relative institutional competence, fear of opening the floodgates to lawsuits, etc.—ring hollow when those who wind up paying the price for judicial abdication are not society's elites but instead its most marginalized citizens.[155] Second, even assuming that valid institutional reasons justify the phenomenon explored here, to embark on such a justificatory project, the *why* of extreme judicial evasion in this context, is to concede the main point of this chapter—that constitutional protections for people caught up in the American criminal system are manifestly, acutely, judicially underenforced.

It might be argued that, even when the Court fails to fully enforce constitutional norms, the "underenforced margins" of those underenforced norms remain fully binding on government officials.[156] But however compelling this claim is in theory, in practice, the relevant state actors in the criminal context—police officers, prosecutors, defense attorneys, legislators, correctional officers, and so on—*do* look to the courts to discern the reach of their constitutional obligations.[157] The judicial monopoly over constitutional interpretation that shapes the American constitutional scheme means that, when courts underenforce applicable norms to the degree seen here, the government's conduct receives the imprimatur of constitutionality, however problematic that conduct may be.

If review courts are not meaningfully holding state actors to constitutional account, neither checking nor even condemning abuse or excess in the exercise of the state's penal power, we have to ask: what role, exactly, is the institution of judicial review performing in the American criminal justice system? What purposes does it serve? If the courts are not disciplining the criminal system—a site that presents strong temptations for state officials to cut constitutional corners—who is? And if the answer is no one, what does this mean for the degree to which citizens should collectively regard the outputs of the criminal system as consistent with the core constitutional commitments essential to the legitimate exercise of the state's penal power? These are not easy questions. But if the picture of profound systematic judicial underenforcement I have painted here is an accurate one, they demand serious consideration.

NOTES

1 I owe a particular debt of thanks to Sasha Natapoff, for her generous engagement and incisive substantive contributions through innumerable drafts of this chapter. I also thank Hadar Aviram, Sam Bray, Richard Fallon, Josh Kleinfeld, Chris Kutz, Jon Michaels, Richard Re, Danny Richman, David Sklansky, Clyde Spillenger, Carol Steiker, and participants at the Southern California Criminal Justice Roundtable, the UCLA Summer Faculty Workshop, the Stanford Criminal Justice Roundtable, and the Roundtable on Theorizing the Criminal State co-sponsored by Loyola, NYU, and UCLA and held at NYU in April 2014. I also thank Scott Dewey, Maxwell Harwitt, Megan Lollar, Scott Satkin, Ariel Werner, and Ben Woolley for excellent research assistance, and the Dean's Office at UCLA and the Center on the Administration of the Criminal Law at NYU for their support of this project.

2 The exception is capital cases. As Justice Breyer noted in his remarkable dissent in *Glossip v. Gross*, "Between 1973 and 1995, courts identified prejudicial errors in 68% of the capital cases before them. State courts on direct and postconviction review overturned 47% of the sentences they reviewed. Federal courts, reviewing capital cases and habeas corpus proceedings, found error in 40% of those cases." 135 S. Ct. 2726, 2759 (2015). These striking statistics raise an obvious question: how to explain the difference between judicial treatment of claims brought by prisoners in the capital and noncapital contexts? This broader question is beyond the scope of the present chapter, although I intend to return to it in future work. For insightful discussion of the exceptionalism of the judicial treatment of capital cases, see Carol S. Steiker & Jordan M. Steiker, *Opening a Window or Building a Wall? The Effect of Eighth Amendment Death Penalty Law and Advocacy on Criminal Justice More Broadly*, 11 U. Penn. J. Const. L. 155 (2008).

3 *See* Meredith J. Duncan, *The (So-Called) Liability of Criminal Defense Attorneys: A System in Need of Reform*, 2002 BYU L. Rev. 1, 3–4, 7–11 (discussing "unconscious, inebriated, and otherwise incompetent lawyering").

4 *See* Caren Myers Morrison, *Negotiating Peremptory Challenges*, 104 J. Crim. L. & Criminology 1, 39 (2014) (discussing cases from Kentucky, Wisconsin, and Mississippi in which African American defendants were convicted by all-white juries yet no *Batson* violation found).

5 *See supra* note 2.

6 This effect is operative even after accounting for the inevitable loss of constitutional meaning arising from the need for judicially manageable standards. See Richard H. Fallon, Jr., *Judicially Manageable Standards and Constitutional Meaning*, 119 Harv. L. Rev. 1274 (2006).

7 I owe this observation to Sasha Natapoff.

8 *See, e.g.*, Graham v. Florida, 560 U.S. 48 (2010).

9 *See, e.g.*, Lafler v. Cooper, 132 S. Ct. 1376 (2012).

10 *See, e.g.*, Brown v. Plata, 563 U.S. 493 (2011).

11 *See, e.g.*, Daryl J. Levinson, *Rights Essentialism and Remedial Equilibration*, 99 COLUM. L. REV. 857 (1999); Roderick M. Hills, Jr., *The Pragmatist's View of Constitutional Implementation and Constitutional Meaning*, 119 HARV. L. REV. F. 173 (March 2006).

12 *See, e.g.*, Fallon, *supra* note 6, at 1317; Lawrence Gene Sager, *Fair Measure: The Legal Status of Underenforced Constitutional Norms*, 91 HARV. L. REV. 1212, 1213 (1978).

13 Although in doing so, I acknowledge an unresolved and likely contentious question as to how great a gap between meaning and doctrine a constitutional democracy ought to tolerate.

14 To adapt Fallon's formulation, in the constitutional criminal context, governing doctrine is not nearly "close enough," and thus not nearly "good enough." Fallon, *supra* note 6, at 1297 ("Close enough is good enough.").

15 No doubt, assuming this claim is valid, a pragmatist may draw different conclusions and perceive different implications than I would. But the basic claim itself should not on its face be at odds with the pragmatist view.

16 *See* ELIZABETH GREENBERG ET AL., NAT'L CTR. FOR EDUC. STATISTICS, LITERACY BEHIND BARS: RESULTS FROM THE 2003 NATIONAL ASSESSMENT OF ADULT LITERACY PRISON SURVEY 4–5, 13 (2007), *available at* https://nces.ed.gov, quoted in Lynn S. Branham, *Cases and Materials on The Law and Policy of Sentencing and Corrections* (St. Paul, MN: West Publishing, 9th ed., 2012), 558–59.

17 28 U.S.C. § 2254 (d)(1).

18 Harrington v. Richter, 562 U.S. 86, 101 (2011).

19 Carol S. Steiker, *Counter-Revolution in Constitutional Criminal Procedure? Two Audiences, Two Answers*, 94 MICH. L. REV. 2466, 2469 (1996).

20 *Id.*

21 This defense applies only in damages actions. Prisoners seeking injunctions have their own remedial obstacles to overcome.

22 Stephen R. Reinhardt, *The Demise of Habeas Corpus and the Rise of Qualified Immunity: The Court's Ever-Increasing Limitations on the Development and Enforcement of Constitutional Rights and Some Particularly Unfortunate Consequences*, 113 MICH. L. REV. 1219, 1245 (2015) (quoting Harlow v. Fitzgerald, 451 U.S. 800, 818 (1982)).

23 Ashcroft v. Al-Kidd, 131 S. Ct. 2074, 2083 (2011) (quoted in Reinhardt, *supra* note 22, at 1247).

24 In the Prison Litigation Reform Act (PLRA), Congress stipulated that no prisoner can file a lawsuit challenging the conditions of their confinement "until such administrative remedies as are available are exhausted." See 42 U.S.C. § 1997e (a) (2006).

25 See Ashcroft v. Iqbal, 556 US 662 (2009). See also Alex Reinert, *The Impact of Ashcroft v. Iqbal on Pleading*, 43 URBAN LAWYER 559, 562–63 (2011).

26 See Arizona v. Fulminante, 499 U.S. 279, 307 (1991) (listing 17 cases, each representing a constitutional right the violation of which at trial the Court has found to
constitute harmless error).

27 Note that as to this category, the two-step process allows courts to avoid addressing the question of whether a constitutional violation occurred by skipping right
to the second question, for example, whether the trial error, even if it occurred,
was nonetheless harmless, or whether the conduct in question, even if found to
be unconstitutional, violated a clearly established right. In this way, even as to this
category of cases, courts are able to avoid reaching the basic question.

28 See Richard H. Fallon, Jr., *Foreword: Implementing the Constitution*, 111 Harv. L.
Rev. 56 (1997); see also *id.* at 57 ("A crucial mission of the Court is to implement
the Constitution successfully. In the service of this mission, the Court often must
craft doctrine that is driven by the Constitution, but does not reflect the Constitution's meaning precisely.").

29 These examples are meant only to be illustrative, not exhaustive. Other examples
include Whren v. United States, 517 U.S. 806 (1996), and McCleskey v. Kemp, 481
U.S. 279 (1987).

30 If there is something to this argument, many questions necessarily arise. How,
for example, are we to explain what amounts to a broad (although by no means
absolute) judicial abdication of the obligation to enforce the Constitution in the
criminal context? What distinguishes those cases and contexts that represent the
relatively rare exceptions? Is the criminal context an exception, or is minimal judicial enforcement a broader phenomenon? If the criminal context is not unique,
are there nonetheless reasons to be particularly concerned about the implications
of judicial abdication in this class of cases? This set of inquiries—exploration of
which is beyond the scope of this chapter—begins to suggest the breadth of the
challenge, both theoretical and practical, posed by my central claim.

31 Gideon v. Wainwright, 372 U.S. 335 (1963) (extended to non-felonies carrying possible jail time in Argersinger v. Hamlin, 407 U.S. 25 (1972)).

32 Strickland v. Washington, 466 U.S. 668, 685 (1984).

33 *See, e.g.*, Reece v. Georgia, 350 U.S. 85, 90 (1955) ("The effective assistance of
counsel in [capital cases] is a constitutional requirement of due process which no
member of the Union may disregard.").

34 *See* Stephen B. Bright, *Counsel for the Poor: The Death Sentence Not for the Worst
Crime but for the Worst Lawyer*, 103 Yale L.J. 1835, 1843 (1994) (providing several
egregious examples of ineffective assistance of counsel that nonetheless resulted
in a death sentence for the defendant and no action by the judge); Sanjay K.
Chhablani, *Chronically Stricken: A Continuing Legacy of Ineffective Assistance of
Counsel*, 28 St. Louis U. Pub. L. Rev. 351, 376–79 (2009) (providing details
of several instances in which criminal defense attorneys slept through parts of
their client's trial, displayed racist attitudes toward their clients, or were under the
influence of alcohol or drugs during the trial).

35 *See* Bright, *supra* note 34, at 1835 (lawyer in death case failed to locate hospital records that could have corroborated client's testimony of domestic abuse at the hands of the victim).

36 Chhablani, *supra* note 34, at 364 (lawyer accepted plea offer without knowing client's prior record).

37 Strickland, 466 U.S. at 709 (Marshall, J., dissenting) (arguing that such objections could be made subject to "uniform standards").

38 Chhablani, *supra* note 34, at 363 (quoting an ABA study which found that in one quarter of the death sentences upheld by the Tennessee Supreme Court, the defendant's lawyer had failed to present any mitigating evidence).

39 466 U.S. 668 (1984).

40 All quotations in this and the ensuing two paragraphs are taken from Strickland v. Washington, 466 U.S. 688, 689–90, 694, 709 (1984).

41 *Id.* at 694 ("A reasonable probability is a probability sufficient to undermine confidence in the outcome.").

42 *Id.* at 690 (further noting that "[b]ecause of the difficulties inherent in making the evaluation, a court must indulge a strong presumption that counsel's conduct falls within the wide range of reasonable professional assistance.").

43 350 U.S. 91 (1955).

44 Michel v. Louisiana, 350 U.S. 91, 93 (1955).

45 *Id.* at 92.

46 *Id.* at 100–1.

47 *Id.* at 101.

48 *Id.* (emphasis added).

49 As the Court notes, Mahoney had already died by the time *Michel* was decided in December 1955. *See id.* at 101 n.7.

50 The Court seemed particularly concerned with preserving Mahoney's reputation. But surely it is no grounds for condemnation that an elderly man with an incapacitating illness proved unequal to the challenging task of adequately representing a client charged with a capital crime.

51 *See* Stephen F. Smith, *Taking Strickland Claims Seriously*, 93 MARQUETTE L. REV. 515, 522, 537 (2009) (describing the way *Strickland*'s performance prong allowed for the insulation of attorneys' judgments "against judicial scrutiny by uttering the magic words of 'strategy' and 'tactics.' . . . Whenever an attorney committed an error, all that seemed necessary was for the attorney to say 'strategy' and, lo and behold, even the most egregious and prejudicial errors could be made to vanish."). Three recent Supreme Court cases appear to indicate an emerging willingness of the Court to closely scrutinize counsel's performance and to find IAC on grounds that would ordinarily have failed to trigger a judicial finding of constitutional violation under *Strickland. See* Rompilla v. Beard, 545 U.S. 374 (2005); Wiggins v. Smith, 539 U.S. 510 (2003); Williams v. Taylor, 529 U.S. 362 (2000). (Hence Smith's speaking of Strickland's failings in the past tense in *Taking Strickland Claims Seriously. See supra.*). But each of these cases was a death

penalty case, and, as Steiker and Steiker show, there are strong reasons to doubt that the increased scrutiny of attorney performance these cases demonstrate will be applied to noncapital claims. *See* Steiker & Steiker, *supra* note 2, at 190–200. Indeed, as they note, "there is a risk that special treatment of capital cases is *premised* on its inapplicability to the much larger and much more potentially destabilizing mass of ordinary criminal defendants." *Id.* at 199.

52 *See* discussion, *supra* note 51.

53 Strickland, 466 U.S. at 694.

54 *Id.* at 695.

55 *Id.* at 696.

56 *See id.* at 697 ("[A] court need not determine whether counsel's performance was deficient before examining the prejudice suffered by the defendant as a result of the alleged deficiencies. . . . If it is easier to dispose of an ineffectiveness claim on the ground of lack of sufficient prejudice, which we expect will often be so, that course should be followed.").

57 See Jeffrey Levinson, *Don't Let Sleeping Lawyers Lie: Raising the Standard for Ineffective Assistance*, 38 AM. CRIM. L. REV. 147, 171 (2001) (describing *Strickland's* prejudice prong as "a perverse application of the harmless error rule").

58 *See* Duncan, *supra* note 3, at 24–27.

59 Strickland, 466 U.S. at 690.

60 *Id.* at 686.

61 *See* Harmelin v. Michigan, 501 U.S. 957, 997–98 (1991) (Kennedy, J., concurring in part and concurring in the judgment) (controlling opinion).

62 *See* Solem v. Helm, 463 U.S. 277, 294 (1983).

63 *Id.* at 290–91.

64 *Id.* at 291.

65 *Id.* at 292–93; *but see id.* at 308–10 (Burger, C.J., dissenting) (rejecting each of these claims).

66 Harmelin, 501 U.S. at 1005 (Kennedy, J., concurring in part and concurring in the judgment).

67 *See* Christopher J. DeClue, *Sugarcoating the Eighth Amendment: The Grossly Disproportionate Test Is Simply the Fourteenth Amendment Rational Basis Test in Disguise*, 41 SOUTHWESTERN L. REV. 41 533, 533 (2012) ("[S]uccessful Eighth Amendment challenges to noncapital sentences are exceedingly few and far between.").

68 *See, e.g.*, Collins v. Harrington, No. EDCV 10–1236 MMM (FFM), 2011 WL 9150940 (C.D. Cal. June 13, 2011) (35 years to life for attempted criminal threats and making annoying phone calls); Lackey v. Texas, 881 S.W.2d 418 (Tex. App. 1994) (35 years for shoplifting clothing worth $145); United States v. Yirovsky, 259 F.2d 704 (8th Cir. 2001) (15 years in prison for being a felon in possession of a single bullet, which he kept in a box); United States v. Gupa-Guillen, 34 F.3d 860 (9th Cir. 1994) (8 years and 4 months for illegal reentry into the country after deportation); Ries v. Garcia, 390 F.3d 1082 (9th Cir. 2004) (a life sentence for petty

theft); Deroulet v. People, 48 P.3d 520 (Colo. 2002) (36 years for burglary). Several of these cases were taken from the list of "Selected Cases Holding That the Sentence Imposed *Is Not* Grossly Disproportionate to the Offense," found in the Appendix in DeClue, *supra* note 67, at 572–79. The cases listed here only scratch the surface; DeClue's Appendix runs for eight full pages. In the same vein, Sara Taylor surveyed "over one hundred federal appellate court cases addressing Eighth Amendment challenges to noncapital sentences, chosen at random and including cases from all circuits[.]" She found just "one case in which a court overturned the sentence in question": *Ramirez v. Castro*, 365 F3d. 755 (9th Cir. 2004), in which the defendant got 25 years to life under California's three strikes law "for attempted theft of a $199 VCR from a department store[.]" Taylor also surveyed over 200 state court cases, and found "similar trends to those in federal courts[.]" *See* Sara Taylor, *Unlocking the Gates of Desolation Row*, 59 UCLA L. REV. 1810, 1837–38 (2012) (collecting cases).

69   *See* Julia L. Torti, *Accounting for Punishment in Proportionality Review*, 88 N.Y.U. L. REV. 1908, 1934–37 (2013).

70   These aspects include the arguably confusing guidance the Supreme Court's own application of the threshold *Harmelin* factor has provided to reviewing courts hearing these claims; see Lockyer v. Andrade, 538 U.S. 63, 72 (2003) (observing that "our precedents in this area have not been a model of clarity"), the Court's failure to provide any guidance as to how a court should weigh the defendant's prior offenses, and the longstanding disagreement among the justices as to the legitimacy of considering the various factors Justice Powell offered in *Solem v. Helm* for distinguishing more serious from less serious offenses.

71   Harmelin, 501 U.S. at 998 (Kennedy, J., concurring in part and concurring in the judgment) (quoting Rummel v. Estelle, 445 U.S. 263, 275–76 (1980)).

72   445 U.S. 263 (1980).

73   Weems v. United States, 217 U.S. 349, 366–67 (1910).

74   Rummel, 445 U.S. at 272, 274.

75   Solem, 463 U.S. at 304, 317 (Burger, C.J., dissenting).

76   Harmelin, 501 U.S. at 998, 999 (Kennedy, J., concurring in part and concurring in the judgment) (quoting Solem, 463 U.S. at 274).

77   Ewing, 538 U.S. at 28.

78   Hutto v. Davis, 454 U.S. 370, 370–371 (1982).

79   Davis v. Zahradnick, 432 F. Supp. 444, 453 (1977).

80   Davis v. Davis, 585 F.2d 1226 (4th Cir. 1978); Davis v. Davis, 601 F.2d 153 (4th Cir. 1979).

81   *See* Hutto v. Davis, 445 U.S. 947 (1980).

82   Davis v. Davis, 646 F.2d 123 (4th Cir. 1981).

83   Rummel, 445 U.S. 263, 272 (1980).

84   Hutto, 454 U.S. at 384. There were arguably ample grounds for a court to reach this conclusion. *See id.* at 384–86 (1982) (Brennan, J., dissenting).

85   Hutto, 454 U.S. at 374.

86 *Id.* at 374–75.

87 Harmelin, 501 U.S. at 1025–26 (White, J., dissenting).

88 *Id.* at 1005 (1991) (Kennedy, J., concurring in part and concurring in the judgment). Interestingly, Justice Kennedy's conclusion in this regard was supported by the extreme example established in the prior case of *Hutto v. Davis. See* Harmelin, 51 U.S. at 1004 (comparing Harmelin's punishment to that received by Davis).

89 Well before *Harmelin*, the Court had found the death penalty to be unconstitutionally disproportionate for the rape of an adult woman. *See* Coker v. Georgia, 433 U.S. 584, 600 (1977).

90 Consider, for example, these cases cited by Sara Taylor, all of which were upheld by state courts post-*Harmelin*: "25 years to life for theft of two cassette players and three bottles of cologne totaling $70 where defendants had prior criminal convictions; 25 years to life for theft of $149 MP3 player from Target; 25 years to life for possession of a firearm by a felon; 25 years to life for housebreaking." Taylor, *supra* note 68, at 1838.

91 *See* Ewing, 538 U.S. at 28.

92 *Id.* at 29 ("His crime was certainly not 'one of the most passive felonies a person could commit.'") (quoting Solem, 463 U.S. at 296).

93 *Id.*

94 *Id.* at 30. Even Justice Scalia conceded that Justice O'Connor's discussion in Ewing, "in all fairness, does not convincingly establish that 25-years-to-life is a proportionate punishment for stealing three golf clubs." *See id.* at 31 (Scalia, J., concurring in the judgment).

95 Youngjae Lee, *The Constitutional Right against Excessive Punishment*, 91 VIRGINIA L. REV. 677, 734 (2002).

96 *Id.* at 29–30.

97 *See id.* at 30–31. *See also* Lee, *supra* note 95, at 734 ("Some may argue that the *Ewing* Court . . . merely applied an extremely deferential version of the proportionality test, but given the emphasis the Court placed on California's deterrence and incapacitation rationales in virtually every paragraph of the opinion, it is impossible to read the opinion in that way.").

98 Ewing, 538 U.S. at 25 (quoting Harmelin, 501 U.S. at 999).

99 Some might argue that, deterrence and incapacitation being legitimate penological goals, it is appropriate for the Court to expand its analysis beyond a retributive weighing of crime versus penalty to consider whether the sentence is grossly disproportionate in light of these other more institutional goals. But even were this the animating idea behind Justice O'Connor's opinion in *Ewing*, any determination of gross disproportionality in light of these goals would still require consideration of the facts to determine whether, under the circumstances, the penalty at issue is a reasonable way to achieve these goals or is instead grossly excessive. To support Ewing's sentence, for example, the government should have had to show that the penalty was not grossly disproportionate to what was necessary to achieve the state's deterrence goal, or that the state's interest in incapacitating Ewing war-

ranted a sentence of this magnitude. Had a court undertaken this analysis, it may well have found that the burden a 25-year mandatory minimum sentence represents was grossly excessive given the likely benefits to society of incapacitating an addict and small-time hustler like Ewing or deterring his relatively minor crimes. Yet far from directing courts to consider a revised version of the basic question, one focusing on deterrence and/or incapacitation, Justice O'Connor instead demanded only a rational basis showing as to the authorizing statute itself—a very different inquiry—and then affirmed Ewing's sentence without even considering the possibility that a statute authorizing what are effectively life sentences for even minor nonviolent offenders is sure to yield penalties grossly out of proportion to the state's interest in incapacitating petty offenders or deterring their petty offenses. For an alternative, nonevasive approach, *see* Smith v. Regina, [1987] 1 S.C.R. 1045 (Can.) (striking down a statute because it authorized a 7-year mandatory minimum sentence for any crime, no matter how minor, coming within the ambit of the statute, even though no case so minor that it "would certainly be considered by most Canadians to be . . . cruel . . . ha[d] actually occurred").

100 Estelle v. Gamble, 429 U.S. 97, 102 (1976); *see also* Wilkerson v. Utah, 99 U.S. 130, 135 (1879) (citing cases "where the prisoner was drawn or dragged to the place of execution, . . . [or] emboweled alive, beheaded and quartered" as examples of tortures forbidden by the Eighth Amendment).

101 *See* Estelle, 429 U.S. at 103.

102 Rhodes v. Chapman, 452 U.S. 337, 347 (1981).

103 Farmer v. Brennan, 511 U.S. 825, 828 (1994).

104 *See* Estelle, 429 U.S. at 103–4 (1976).

105 *See* Farmer, 511 U.S. at 833 (1994).

106 *Id.* at 832 (quoting Hudson v. Palmer, 468 U.S. 517, 526–27 (1984)).

107 DeShaney v. Winnebago County Department of Social Services, 489 U.S. 189, 199–200 (1989).

108 *Id.* at 200.

109 *See id.* (explaining that the state's duty of care toward prisoners arises because "the State by the affirmative exercise of its power so restrains an individual's liberty that it renders him unable to care for himself"). *See also* Sharon Dolovich, *Cruelty, Prison Conditions, and the Eighth Amendment,* 84 N.Y.U. L. REV. 881, 911–23 (2009) (defining this obligation as the state's "carceral burden").

110 Farmer, 511 U.S. at 833 (citing DeShaney, 489 U.S. at 199–200, along with other opinions; internal citations and quotation marks omitted): *see also* Estelle, 429 U.S. at 103 (1976) ("An inmate must rely on prison authorities to treat his medical needs; if the authorities fail to do so, these needs will not be met.").

111 *See* Estelle, 429 U.S. at 104 (holding that "deliberate indifference" to prisoners' "serious medical needs" violates the Eighth Amendment).

112 Farmer v. Brennan, 511 U.S. 825 (1994).

113 For discussion, see Dolovich, *supra* note 109, at 943–64.

114 Farmer, 511 U.S. at 837.

115 *Id.* (quoting 1 W. LaFave & A. Scott, Substantive Criminal Law § 3.7 335 (1986)). On remand, applying *Farmer's* recklessness standard, the jury found for the defendants.

116 *Farmer* does provide reason to think that prisoners who can demonstrate ongoing harms and who seek injunctions should not be defeated by *Farmer's* recklessness standard, since if such evidence is established, "the defendants could not plausibly persist in claiming lack of awareness." Farmer, 511 U.S. at 846 n.9. But this concession does not help those prisoners whose harms are complete at the time of filing and thus seek only damages, or prisoners who, lacking counsel, face insurmountable obstacles to demonstrating the systemic violations that may have yielded an injunction were the case brought by well-resourced attorneys. Nor does *Farmer* address the way the recklessness standard, operating as a substitute question, may allow courts to avoid having to determine the existence of an "objectively intolerable risk" if the plaintiff cannot effectively demonstrate defendants' knowledge.

117 Farmer, 511 U.S. at 832 (quoting Helling v. McKinney, 509 U.S. 25, 31 (1993)).

118 *See* Dolovich, *supra* note 109, at 961 n.306. *See also* Sharon Dolovich, *Forms of Deference in Prison Law*, 24 Fed. Sentencing Rep. 245 (2012) (arguing that judicial deference is the "primary driver of the Court's prisoners' rights jurisprudence" and exploring the various ways such deference shapes the doctrine in this area).

119 Mikel-Meredith Weidman, *The Culture of Judicial Deference and the Problem of Supermax Prisons*, 51 UCLA L. Rev. 1505 (2004).

120 *See* Dolovich, *Forms of Deference, supra* note 118, at 246.

121 Wilson v. Seiter, 501 U.S. 294, 300 (1991) (italics in original).

122 *See* Dolovich, *supra* note 109, at 895–907 (arguing this point in detail).

123 Among the many important works addressing this vital issue are Michelle Alexander, The New Jim Crow: Mass Incarceration in an Age of Colorblindness (2012); Douglas A. Blackmon, Slavery by Another Name: The Re-Enslavement of Black Americans from the Civil War to World War II (2009); David Cole, No Equal Justice: Race and Class in the American Criminal Justice System (1999); and David Oshinsky, "Worse than Slavery": Parchman Farm and the Ordeal of Jim Crow Justice (1997).

124 Batson v. Kentucky, 476 U.S. 79, 87, 89 (1986).

125 *See* Tania Tetlow, *Why* Batson *Misses the Point*, 97 Iowa L. Rev. 1713, 1714 (2012).

126 Susan N. Herman, *Why the Court Loves* Batson: *Representation-Reinforcement, Colorblindness, and the Jury*, 67 Tulane L. Rev. 1807, 1814 (1993) ("[G]iven a choice between enhancing representation and protecting defendants, the Court is more interested in serving the former goal.").

127 *See* Antony Page, Batson's *Blind-Spot: Unconscious Stereotyping and the Peremptory Challenge*, 85 B.U. L. Rev. 155 (2005).

128 *See, e.g.*, Herman, *supra* note 126, at 1813–14 (describing *Batson* as an "attempt to provide the Court with a judicially modest, procedurally based response to racism").

129 All quotations in this paragraph are taken from Batson v. Kentucky, 476 U.S. 79, 94–98 (1986).

130 *See* Page, *supra* note 127 (on implicit bias in jury selection).

131 *Batson* also applies to prospective jurors struck by the defense. But since the issue here is the role played by judicial review in safeguarding the integrity of the state's exercise of its penal power, I focus here only on the possibility that defendants might be convicted by juries the composition of which was influenced by racially motivated prosecutorial strikes.

132 Elem v. Purkett, 25 F.3d 679, 683 (8th Cir. 1994).

133 Batson, 476 U.S. at 98.

134 *Id.* at 97–98.

135 Nancy S. Marder, Batson *Revisited*, 97 IOWA L. REV. 1585, 1592 (2012) ("If the trial judge scrutinizes the reason further, it would be as if the trial judge did not believe the prosecutor and were essentially calling the prosecutor a liar.").

136 *Id.* at 1591.

137 514 U.S. 765 (1995).

138 As of this writing, the Court has heard argument on but not yet decided *Foster v. Humphrey*, a capital case in which prosecutors used peremptory strikes to remove all four black prospective jurors from the venire. The defendant lost in the Georgia Supreme Court, despite having presented evidence that, "during jury selection, [prosecutors] highlighted each black prospective juror's name in green—on four different copies of the jury list—and wrote that the green highlighting 'represents blacks,'" circled on "each black juror's questionnaire . . . the response "black" next to a question about race, . . . and referred to three black jurors as "B#1," "B#2," and "B#3" in their notes." Mark Joseph Stern, *Georgia Justice*, SLATE, May 27, 2015, www.slate.com. If the Court does reverse on *Batson* grounds—and, given the facts, it is hard to see how it cannot—this would be of a piece with the recent reversals by the High Court of three death sentences on IAC grounds, further reinforcing the gap in the degree of judicial scrutiny as between capital and noncapital cases. For more on this point, see *supra*, notes 2 and 51.

139 All quotations in this and the ensuing three paragraphs are from Purkett v. Elem, 514 U.S. 765, 766–69 (1995).

140 The prosecution had provided a second reason for striking juror 24, which appears to have satisfied the Eighth Circuit panel. *Id.* at 766.

141 According to the Court, "unless a discriminatory intent is inherent in the prosecutor's explanation, the reason offered will be deemed race-neutral." *Id.*

142 *Id.*

143 *Id.* at 767 (quoting Elem, 25 F.3d 769, 683 (1994)).

144 *See, e.g.*, Jack McMahon, *Fear of a Black Jury*, HARPER'S MAGAZINE, July 2000, http://harpers.org.

145 Marder, *supra* note 135, at 1592.

146 To this, it might be argued that requiring some showing of plausibility fails to credit the way trial lawyers may cleave to personal superstitions as regards jurors—a standing practice of, say, striking architects or travel writers or people with purple shirts with no good reason except a personal intuition developed over time. But the inherent difficulty in smoking out pretext in the *Batson* context means that any meaningful prohibition on racial discrimination in jury selection may require that, in this one context, prosecutors may not be able to indulge their ungrounded intuitions. That is, *Batson*'s requirement of race-neutral reasons "related to the particular case to be tried" may be necessary simply because no crisp way exists to preserve space for both fancy and nondiscrimination. *Elem* makes a pretense of doing so. But in practice, its standard protects fancy at the expense of nondiscrimination.

147 This move is directly analogous to the refusal by the *Strickland* majority to specify basic minimum duties of defense counsel for purposes of IAC claims. *See supra*, Part II.A.

148 *Id.* at 1592 (quoting U.S. v. Chinchilla, 874 F.2d 695, 698 (9th Cir. 1989)).

149 Chevron v. NRDC, 467 U.S. 837, 842–43 (1989) ("[I]f the statute is silent or ambiguous with respect to the specific issue, the question for the court is whether the agency's answer is based on a permissible construction of the statute.").

150 I owe this example to Clyde Spillenger.

151 See, e.g., *Vinter v. United Kingdom*, App. Nos. 66069/09, 130/10 & 3896/10, 38 (Eur. Ct. H.R. 2013), http://hudoc.echr.coe.int (noting that "issues relating to just and proportionate punishment are the subject of rational debate and civilized disagreement," and thus that legislatures "must be allowed a margin of appreciation in deciding on the appropriate length of prison sentences for particular crimes").

152 The use of these strategies in cases involving law enforcement creates an equally disturbing effect, especially in light of the nation's long history of racially charged policing practices. *See, e.g.,* Whren v. United States, 517 U.S. 806 (1996).

153 *See* ALEXANDER M. BICKEL, THE LEAST DANGEROUS BRANCH 16, 111 (1962): Pamela S. Karlan, *Exit Strategies and Constitutional Law: Lessons for Getting the Least Dangerous Branch out of the Political Thicket*, 82 BOSTON UNIVERSITY LAW REVIEW 667, 669 (2002) (identifying several such tools—Bickel's "passive virtues"—including doctrines like standing and ripeness and practices like deciding statutory issues instead of constitutional ones and denying *certiorari*).

154 *See* Sager, *supra* note 12, at 1221.

155 Some other possible explanations—indifference, a judicial desire not to upset the status quo, judicial timidity in the face of pointed political animus, or even animus on the part of judges themselves toward people caught up in the criminal system—would be even less valid. Perhaps the most sympathetic possible explanation is that the Court is afraid more capacious enforcement would provoke a political backlash, sparking an institutional standoff and costing the Court institu-

tional capital without making an appreciable difference on the ground. Certainly there is no evidence that state legislators are independently willing to adequately fund indigent defense or to seriously scale back criminal sentences or reduce overcrowding in their carceral facilities, and it is conceivable that some lawmakers may well flout judicial orders rather than comply with constitutional directives to take such steps.

156 *See* Sager, *supra* note 12, at 1221.

157 *See* Steiker, *supra* note 19, at 2535–37 (explaining this effect in the case of police officers).

7

Taking the Constitution Seriously?

Three Approaches to Law's Competence in Addressing Authority and Professionalism

HADAR AVIRAM

The post-Warren Courts' routine findings of constitutional compliance by law enforcement, the courtroom apparatus, and correctional agencies, are of no surprise to anyone studying the American criminal process. Legal realists have long come to regard doctrinal niceties as tools that render legitimacy to intrusive, abusive, and punitive state practices.[1]

But upon closer examination, the Supreme Court's usage of constitutional standards as a way to "kosherize" inferior defense quality,[2] prosecutorial misconduct,[3] and correctional abuses[4] (Dolovich's examples), as well as policing practices,[5] prosecutorial discretion,[6] and plea-bargain abuses,[7] merits deeper attention. When the Supreme Court performs the shift in question and focus that Dolovich identifies, does it "believe" in what it says, or is it cynically exploiting constitutional doctrine to garner legitimacy? And if the Constitution is more than mere window dressing to advance the interests of the powerful, in what ways is it "real"?

In this response, I juxtapose two common approaches to criminal courtroom policy: the legal model approach and the sociological-empirical approach. Each approach offers a valuable interpretation of legal policies and goals, emphasizing certain factors that account for legal practices in the field; however, each of them fails to account for certain factors, thus incompletely explicating the criminal process. I then use Niklas Luhmann's systems theory as a third approach that takes both the Constitution and its limitations seriously. As I argue, systems theory complements doctrinal analysis and socio-legal critique by showing how the very nature of constitutional communications limits their usefulness for criminal justice reform.

The Legal Model Approach: The Constitution as a Value Choice

One perspective on the post-Warren Courts' forgiving approach toward the criminal justice apparatus views the Constitution as a vehicle for advancing one set of legal values over another. A convenient starting point is Herbert Packer's "Two Models of the Criminal Process."[8] Analyzing the Warren Court revolution as it was occurring, Packer transcended the government/defendant dichotomy that dominated contemporary discourse,[9] arguing that the due process revolution consisted of a shift along a continuum between two "ideal types."[10] On one end lay the crime-control model, which prioritized efficiency, advocating for reliance on police and prosecution powers under the assumption that any defendant that made it past these checks into the trial system was "presumptively guilty." This model relied on bargaining and finality and shied away from trials and appeals.[11] On the other end lay the due-process model, which prioritized avoidance of wrongful convictions, treating the criminal justice apparatus with suspicion and allowing for constitutional challenges and ample post-conviction review.[12] Charles Whitebread and Christopher Slobogin argue for a subsequent pendulum swing back toward crime control in the post–Warren Court era, identifying four themes:[13] a focus on factual guilt/innocence, echoing Packer's "presumption of guilt,"[14] a shift from bright-line constitutional rules to flexible, "totality of the circumstances" tests,[15] greater belief in the integrity of the police and prosecution,[16] and greater deference to state courts.[17] Packer himself, a due-process enthusiast, expressed on his deathbed in the early 1970s disillusionment with the Warren Court's project.[18]

Many have used Packer's models as a springboard for suggesting their own models, which were regarded as preferable[19] or more realistic representations of the criminal process.[20] But even Packer's analysis, which imbues the Court's constitutional stance with a more nuanced worldview than mere partisanship, is fraught with the naïveté of what Hunt and Wickham call the "intellectual insularity" of legal scholarship.[21] For Packer, whether the justices subscribe to crime control or due process, they are still, in good faith, applying universal principles to specific cases[22] by classifying real-life situations into preexisting legal "ideal types,"[23] which they apply universally and objectively.[24] This approach does not see the Court as a political institution embedded in the broader socioeconomic, racial, and political context.

Packer would perceive Dolovich's examples as a manifestation of the crime-control model. Creating and reinforcing low expectations from defense attorneys is a vote of confidence not only in public defense, but also in the initial screening process by the police and the prosecution; if a case has made it to trial, the defendant is likely guilty anyway, and guaranteeing the quality of his defense is less crucial. This approach explains not only the performance prong of *Strickland*,[25] but also its prejudice prong: the defendant was probably rightfully convicted and, therefore, any post-conviction debate about defense flaws is moot. Similarly, *Batson*[26] and *McCleskey*[27] can be explained as a crime-control expression of faith in the system's fairness; the defendant's probable guilt makes the possibility of racial bias less worrisome. Both of these scenarios, as well as the third—the case of correctional practices—also strongly indicate the Courts' crime-control commitment to finality and impatience for post-conviction inquiries.

But these three cases also expose the weaknesses of a Packerian approach as the ultimate path to understanding the post-Warren Courts. Why does the Court place such trust in public defense? Does the Court's faith in the system's ability to overcome errors override what the justices surely know about racial discrimination and minority overrepresentation?[28] And how does the Court benefit from its wholesale support of correctional practices?

Finally, the Packerian approach lacks historical sensitivity. It tells us little about why the Warren Court shifted from crime control to due process and why the pendulum has swung back. These questions are better addressed by the second approach.

Sociolegal Approaches: The Constitution in Service of Institutional Legitimacy and Political Entrenchment

The second approach is more frequently espoused by social scientists examining the criminal process, often using empirical tools. For simplification purposes, this approach encompasses various perspectives that see the Court as one of many sociopolitical institutions, with pragmatic concerns, interests, and obligations beyond adherence to a set of values promoted by constitutional provisions.

I identify two strains within the sociolegal approach. The first focuses on factors endogenous to the criminal process, and on the Court's role as an institution within the system. Such works advocate rejecting the notion of the system as a rational apparatus with a single goal in mind,[29] opting instead to see it as constructed of many individuals with different and often conflicting roles, and handling a variety of professional, administrative, and personal constraints.[30] While this literature emerges mostly from lower-court ethnographies, it is nonetheless relevant to the conversation about the Supreme Court in that it draws attention to the "real" reasons why the Court accommodates incompetent lawyers and thinly veiled racially motivated jury selection tactics. The Supreme Court affirms the experiences of state judges who routinely encounter the "repeat players" in the system: defense attorneys and prosecutors.[31] Since the continued collaboration of these participants is essential to keep the wheels of the criminal justice machine turning, their interests are accommodated at the expense of those of the defendants, who are "one-shotters."[32] This principle holds for federal litigation of state correctional practices—the court is well aware of the need to procure the state's collaboration, and therefore gears itself more toward conciliatory compromises and consent decrees.[33]

This literature is particularly useful regarding Dolovich's first example—ineffective assistance of counsel—because in that situation, the defense attorneys' interests line up with those of the court and against their clients. Described in early examples of this literature as "con men" who trick their clients into pleading guilty to save everyone's time,[34] the lawyers quickly develop proficiency in identifying prototypes of cases—"normal crimes"—and perfect ways of negotiating for pleas based on these generalizations.[35]

The second strain examines the creation and administration of the criminal project as a product of the larger social structure, focusing on its reinforcement of patterns of power and inequality. Works by Marxist social historians and conflict criminologists address the emergence of laws aimed mainly at controlling and oppressing disenfranchised populations, mostly by criminalizing their behavior, such as vagrancy[36] and

poaching[37]—crimes created and enforced to protect the property interests of powerful social groups. Similarly, such accounts highlight the
stratifying effect of drug policy,[38] death penalty enforcement,[39] and the
deliberate choices involved in the criminal prosecution of slaves in the
American South.[40] The emergence of penal practices, often shrouded
in therapeutic, ostensibly benevolent reforms, is also interpreted as systemic support for oppression.[41]

Scholars disagree on the level of autonomy they ascribe to law within
the power structure. Instrumental Marxists go as far as to claim that law
is entirely subservient to the mode of production.[42] Structural Marxists espouse a more nuanced approach, acknowledging that law retains
a certain level of autonomy; rather than automatically supporting the
interests of power groups, the law sometimes offers hope to weaker
groups, thus maintaining its appearance of universal and equal application and guaranteeing that, in the long run, the power structure will
prevail.[43]

These approaches clearly support Dolovich's observation that the
Court obtains legitimacy by supporting the interests of power groups.
For example, by supporting the fiction of adequate criminal representation via the "effective assistance of counsel" test, the Court justifies
abusive and punitive practices. The defense attorney's presence becomes
a fig leaf behind which injustices can hide. Similarly, the façade of racial blindness diverts attention from the myriad racialized practices in
the criminal process. And finally, the assertion that inmates are being
punished for their crimes—with all practices associated with their incarceration conveniently labeled as "punishment" and "not punishment"—
masks the severe deprivation of fellow humans' basic material, social,
and medical needs. Even the sporadic exceptions to this pattern of
finding counsel's assistance to be adequate—for example, *Lafler*[44] and
Frye[45]—nevertheless conform to this overall paradigm. This handful of
victories creates an illusionary impression of equality and justice, numb-
ing us to the robust body of opposite decisions.

The problem with this approach is its non-falsifiability. When the
Court rules for the state, we ascribe that to its support of the existing
power structure. When it rules in favor of the defendants or inmates, we
ascribe that to the need to maintain false consciousness and legitimacy.
The answer to when, and why, the Court might choose one course of ac-

tion over another might be close to Dolovich's: when the abuse of power is so blatant that a pro-government decision would cause outrage, the Court shies away from it and gives a handout to the disenfranchised. The extent to which the Court succeeds in predicting the reaction to its rulings is an index of its political astuteness.

But even if it is profitable for the Supreme Court to support the system at the expense of the disenfranchised and downtrodden, why is the Constitution such a convenient vehicle? Doreen McBarnet best phrased this weakness in her book *Conviction*, arguing that sociologists have been remiss in examining only the operation of justice, not the law itself:

> [T]he question underlying sociological analysis of the criminal justice process always seems to be concerned with why the people who routinely operate the law also routinely depart from the principles of justice. . . . What is barely touched on is the nature and role of the law itself. . . . The assumption has been in effect that law incorporates rights for the accused, and the problem has been simply to ask why and how the police and courts subvert, negate or abuse them.[46]

If the Constitution is such a powerful legitimizing tool, why is its ability to provide satisfying solutions to real problems so limited?

A Third Approach: The Constitution and Its Interpretation as an Index of How Law Treats Authority and Professionalism

The third approach transcends the doctrinal insularity of the Packerian perspective, as well as the dismissiveness toward law, and the Constitution, of the sociolegal perspective. While the legal or political consequences of the Court's approach matter, of course, this approach examines the issue through a discursive lens: how does law, in itself, think? This "discursive perspective,"[47] inspired by Niklas Luhmann's systems theory,[48] focuses not on the ontological nature of reality, but on the role of the Constitution in propagating a given view of reality. It helpfully illuminates law as a system without cynically sacrificing the importance of law itself to the result.

For our purposes, the relevant aspect of systems theory is its concern with law's boundaries, self-production, and relationship with external structures. Luhmann aims at accounting for what law is and is not, and at explaining its interaction with other systems:

> A systems theory observation of the legal system would not be limited to self-description (which is limited to law's understanding of its environment), but would be able to look at the relationships between the legal system and other social systems. In particular, through the concept of structural coupling, the theory would be able to examine the social conditions of law's autonomy: the ecological dependencies of the system.[49]

The unit of analysis for the theory is a "communication." Luhmann defines "law" as a set of legal communications, which converse with each other and refer to each other.[50] It is through these communications that law attains a "mind" and a perspective independent from, and unrelated to, that of human legal actors.[51] What distinguishes legal and non-legal communications is their function: the maintenance (stabilization) of expectations (e.g., that actors in the criminal justice system will adequately represent defendants, guarantee racial neutrality, and treat inmates decently) in the face of disappointments (e.g., an unprofessional lawyer, a racially biased jury, or an abusive prison warden). The main distinction made by legal communications in respect to these behaviors is the legal/illegal dichotomy.[52] The communications that determine which behaviors will be deemed "legal" and which will be regarded as "illegal" are contingent upon the concept of justice, which often manifests itself through equality (the equal/unequal distinction).

These distinctions made by the system's communications and operations are exclusive to the system. Law, like other systems, is an autopoietic system, in which "everything that is used as a unit by the system is produced by the system itself."[53] Since the system consists of communications, and the communications use distinctions unique to law, it can converse only with itself, using its own terms and distinctions:

> The autopoietic view of society as a system of social communications . . . draws a clear distinction between individuals and society, with the latter consisting of communications and nothing but communications. Attempts to transfer moral precepts, which have served the individual well in his or her interpersonal relationships, to the level of social per-

formance, result invariably in these precepts being reconstituted as legal, political, religious, scientific or economic communications, which refer back, not to morality, but to law, politics, religion, science, economics, etc, for their authority and legitimacy.[54]

Importantly, as a self-sufficient, self-perpetuating system, law supplies its own legitimacy using internal tools and referring back to them for validity.[55]

Law, argues Luhmann, operates in a universe of systems, and addresses questions that come up in other systems. These questions, however, do not translate well across systems, because systems are "cognitively open" but "operationally closed" to each other; they can communicate *about* each other but not directly *to* each other. Whenever a system is "irritated" by an external event, or an external perspective from a different discipline, a "structural coupling" between the two systems may occur: the first system may choose, through its own operations and distinctions, to select the second system; it then communicates about the second system using the first system's own distinctions, vocabulary and inner logic.

Law's form of operative closure is "normative closure"—while maintaining cognitive openness, and being exposed to other systems through the cases presented to the system or the operation of political institutions that surround it, law chooses to assimilate issues and events based on its fundamental legal/illegal distinction.

When the Constitution is "irritated" by evidence of unprofessional defense attorneys, racial biases, or cruel and indifferent jailers, it has to "translate" this evidence to a question it can comprehend and answer. These big problems have to be reduced to binary questions—namely, whether a given practice with which the system is confronted falls above or below a certain threshold—before they can be addressed by legal communications.

Note the systemic "poverty" of the Court's approach in Dolovich's examples, and its inadequacy in capturing and addressing them properly. Effective assistance of counsel—or, more clearly put, whether counsel performance is "legal/illegal" in the sense that it falls beneath some minimum threshold—is a very limited way to address quality, professionalism, agency, budget constraints, and any other issue stemming from the dark side of *Gideon*. Similarly, a deep conversation about the ways in which racism affects the criminal process is translated to the impoverished, limited binary question of whether the outcome was "legal/illegal," decided based on whether it was "unequal enough" to fall beneath the legality threshold. And broad questions about our trust in the humanity and professionalism of correctional staff, which could raise issues of causality and situational dynamics,[56] are translated to the impoverished, limited binary question of whether the treatment of the inmates was legal/illegal in the sense that it fell beneath a minimum threshold of conditions.

In these three situations, and many more, the Constitution has to confront questions to which it is cognitively open: what professionalism means, how professionalism affects justice, and how professionalism may be promoted. But its limitations and internal rules mean that it can only converse *about* these issues (and not *with* other systems that might tackle these questions differently) in a normatively closed way, that is, through its binary threshold framework.

This also explains another discontent Dolovich identifies and analyzes: setting constitutional standards not only "kosherizes" current practices, but also acts as a barrier to future litigation. Law's self-referential qualities ensure that the next time an "irritant" invades the legal conversation, it will refer back to itself, its usual modes of understanding and decision, and its operative rules in providing an answer. This limitation is built into the world of constitutional communications.

What systems theory offers us is a modicum of modesty when expecting great things from the courts. If what we need are better defense attorneys, juries, and correctional officers, investing our hopes in the flawed instrument of constitutional communication will prove hollow indeed.

NOTES

1 This would be a social science "law in action" answer to the "law in the books" doctrinal analysis of such case law. Roscoe Pound, *Law in Books and Law in Action*, 44 AM. L. REV. 12 (1910).

2 Strickland v. Washington, 466 U.S. 668 (1984).

3 Batson v. Kentucky, 476 U.S. 79 (1986).

4 Ruffin v. Commonwealth, 62 Va. 790, 796 (Va. 1872).

5 Terry v. Ohio, 392 U.S. 1 (1968).

6 United States v. Armstrong et al., 517 U.S. 456 (1996).

7 McMann v. Richardson, 397 U.S. 759 (1970).

8 HERBERT PACKER, THE LIMITS OF THE CRIMINAL SANCTION (1968).

9 Peter Arenella, *Rethinking the Functions of Criminal Procedure: The Warren and Burger Courts' Competing Ideologies*, 72 GEO. L.J. 185 (1983).

10 Packer's usage of ideal types has been seriously criticized: Stuart MacDonald, *Constructing a Framework for Criminal Justice Research: Learning from Packer's Mistakes*, 11 NEW CRIM. L. REV. 257 (2008).

11 *Id.*

12 Some dispute that the two models are ideal types, arguing instead that due process is an ideal and crime control represents the reality: Malcolm Feeley, *Two Models of the Criminal Justice System: An Organizational Approach*, 7 L. & SOC'Y REV. 407 (1972). Others argue that due process has two aspects, formalism and fairness: Hadar Aviram, *Packer in Context: Formalism and Fairness in the Due Process Model*, 36 L. & SOC. INQUIRY 237 (2011).

13 CHARLES WHITEBREAD & CHRISTOPHER SLOBOGIN, CRIMINAL PROCEDURE: AN ANALYSIS OF CASES AND CONCEPTS 4–5 (5th ed., 2008).

14 An example of this would be the focus, in habeas proceedings, on "actual innocence" as the only ameliorative door to an otherwise almost inaccessible proceeding. Murray v. Carrier, 477 U.S. 478 (1986); Kuhlmann v. Wilson, 477 U.S. 436 (1986).

15 Such as the standards for evaluating anonymous tips for purposes of probable cause: *see, e.g.*, Illinois v. Gates, 462 U.S. 213 (1983).

16 The reliance on the factual basis for a plea bargain, which allows the court to accept a plea bargain from a defendant who still maintains his innocence: North Carolina v. Alford, 400 U.S. 25 (1970).

17 Harmless error doctrine has greatly expanded.

18 Aviram, *supra* note 12.

19 John Griffiths, *Ideology in Criminal Procedure, or a Third "Model" of the Criminal Process*, 79 YALE L.J. 359 (1970); John Griffiths, *Review: The Limits of Criminal Law Scholarship*, 79 YALE L.J. 1388 (1970); Keith Findley, *Toward a New Paradigm of Criminal Justice: How the Innocence Movement Merges Crime Control and Due Process*, 41 TEX. TECH L. REV. 133 (2009); Kent Roach, *Four Models of the Criminal Process*, 89 J. CRIM. L. & CRIMINOLOGY 671 (1999).

20 MICHAEL KING, THE FRAMEWORK OF CRIMINAL JUSTICE (1981); Aviram, *supra* note 12.

21 ALAN HUNT & GARY WICKHAM, FOUCAULT AND LAW: TOWARD A SOCIOLOGY OF LAW AS GOVERNANCE 40 (1994).

22 KENNETH VANDEVELDE, THINKING LIKE A LAWYER: AN INTRODUCTION TO LEGAL REASONING (1996).

23 David Trubek, *Max Weber's Tragic Modernism and the Study of Law in Society*, 20 L. & SOC'Y REV. 573–598 (1986); MAX WEBER, ON CHARISMA AND INSTI-

TUTION BUILDING (1968); FROM MAX WEBER: ESSAYS IN SOCIOLOGY (C. Wright Mills & Hans Heinrich Gerth, eds. 1991).

24 David Trubek, *Back to the Future: The Short and Happy Life of the Law and Society Movement*, 18 FLA. ST. U. L. REV. 1 (1990).

25 Strickland v. Washington, 466 U.S. 668.

26 Batson v. Kentucky, 476 U.S. 79.

27 McCleskey v. Kemp, 481 U.S. 279 (1987).

28 See the Court's rejection of Baldus's study in McCleskey, *id.*; D. BALDUS, C. PULASKI, & G. WOODWORTH, EQUAL JUSTICE AND THE DEATH PENALTY (1990). For more on the shortcomings of this naïve approach, see Jean-Louis Halperin, *Law in Books and Law in Action: The Problem of Legal Change*, 64 ME. L. REV. 46, 55.

29 Feeley, *Two Models of the Criminal Process, supra* note 12.

30 MALCOLM M. FEELEY, THE PROCESS IS THE PUNISHMENT: HANDLING CASES IN A LOWER CRIMINAL COURT (1979).

31 PETER NARDULLI, THE COURTROOM ELITE: AN ORGANIZATIONAL PERSPECTIVE ON CRIMINAL JUSTICE (1978); JAMES EISENSTEIN & HERBERT JACOB, FELONY JUSTICE (1977); PETER NARDULLI, JAMES EISENSTEIN, & ROY FLEMING, TENOR OF JUSTICE (1988). See more generally Marc Galanter, *Why the "Haves" Come Out Ahead: Speculations on the Limits of Legal Change*, 9 L. & SOC'Y REV. 95 (1974).

32 The bureaucratic hurdles also explain why the process is geared, evidence-wise, toward conviction—DOREEN MCBARNET, CONVICTION: LAW, THE STATE AND THE CONSTRUCTION OF JUSTICE (1981)—and, bureaucratically, toward encouraging defendants to plead guilty and save themselves the process, which is punitive in itself: FEELEY, THE PROCESS IS THE PUNISHMENT, *supra* note 30.

33 MALCOLM M. FEELEY & EDWARD L. RUBIN, JUDICIAL POLICYMAKING AND THE MODERN STATE (1991).

34 Abraham Blumberg, *The Practice of Law as a Confidence Game: Organizational Cooptation of a Profession*, 1 L. & SOC'Y REV. 15 (1967).

35 David Sudnow, *Normal Crimes: Sociological Features of the Penal Code in a Public Defender Office*, 12 SOC. PROBS. 255 (1965).

36 William Chambliss, *A Sociological Analysis of the Law of Vagrancy*, 12 SOC. PROBS. 67 (1964). Chambliss's historical accuracy has been called into question: Jeffrey S. Adler, *A Historical Analysis of the Law of Vagrancy*, 27 CRIMINOLOGY 209 (1989).

37 E. P. THOMPSON, WHIGS AND HUNTERS: THE ORIGIN OF THE BLACK ACT (1975).

38 TROY DUSTER, THE LEGISLATION OF MORALITY (1970).

39 DOUGLAS HAY, ALBION'S FATAL TREE (1975).

40 Eugene Genovese, Roll, Jordan, Roll: The World the Slaves Made (1974); John Noonan, Persons and Masks of the Law: Cardozo, Holmes, Jefferson, and Wythe as Makers of the Masks (1976).

41 Tony Platt, The Triumph of Benevolence: The Origins of the Juvenile Justice System in the United States (1972); Jonathan Simon, Poor Discipline: Parole and the Social Control of the Underclass, 1890–1990 (1993); David Rothman, Conscience and Convenience: The Asylum and Its Alternatives in Progressive America (1980); Stanley Cohen, Visions of Social Control: Crime, Punishment and Classification (1985); Ruth Rosen, The Lost Sisterhood: Prostitution in America, 1900–1918 (1982).

42 Georg Rusche & Otto Kirchheimer, Punishment and Social Structure (2003[1939]) (arguing that modes of punishment over time address the economic needs generated by the mode of production).

43 Alan Stone, The Place of Law in the Marxian Structure-Superstructure Archetype, 19 L. & Soc'y Rev. 39 (1985); Isaac Balbus, Commodity Form and Legal Form: An Essay on the "Relative Autonomy" of the Law, 11 L. & Soc'y Rev. 571 (1977).

44 Lafler v. Cooper, 132 S. Ct. 1376 (2012).

45 Missouri v. Frye, 132 S. Ct. 1399 (2012).

46 McBarnet, Conviction, supra note 32, at 4–5.

47 Niels Åkerstrøm Andersen, Discursive Analytical Strategies: Understanding Foucault, Koselleck, Laclau, Luhmann (2003). By using the term "discourse," I intend to distinguish between this perspective and the ontological descriptions of the two paths described earlier; this must not be confused with usages of the term "discourse" in postmodern literature irrelevant to this project.

48 While Luhmann's theory is applicable to social systems in general, he has applied it to particular systems, including law, in specific projects. Niklas Luhmann, Social Systems (1995); Niklas Luhmann, Law as a Social System (2004). Luhmann's ideas on law as a social system have been further expanded upon by Teubner: Gunther Teubner, How the Law Thinks: Toward a Constructivist Epistemology of Law, 23 L. & Soc'y Rev. 727 (1989).

49 Introduction to Luhmann, Law as a Social System, supra note 48, at 47.

50 Some of the criticism of systems theory is aimed at this definition, which ignores the role of individuals within the system, and is therefore alien to traditional sociology. Roger Cotterell, Law's Community: Legal Theory in Sociological Perspective (1997).

51 Teubner, supra note 48.

52 Jean Clam, The Specific Autopoiesis of Law: Between Derivative Autonomy and Generalised Paradox, in Law's New Boundaries: The Consequences of Legal Autopoiesis (Jiri Priban & David Nelken, eds. 2001); Luhmann, Social Systems, supra note 48.

53 ANDERSEN, *supra* note 47.

54 Michael King, *You Have to Start Somewhere*, in CHILDREN'S RIGHTS AND TRADITIONAL VALUES 3 (G. Douglas & L. Sebba, eds. 1998).

55 Stanley Fish, *The Law Wishes to Have a Formal Existence*, in THE FATE OF LAW (A. Sarat & T. R. Kearns, eds. 1991).

56 STANLEY MILGRAM, OBEDIENCE TO AUTHORITY: AN EXPERIMENTAL VIEW (1974); C. Haney, W. C. Banks, & P. G. Zimbardo, *Study of Prisoners and Guards in a Simulated Prison*, 9 NAVAL RES. REVS. 1 (1973); C. Haney, W. C. Banks, & P. G. Zimbardo, *Interpersonal Dynamics in a Simulated Prison*, 1 INT'L J. CRIMINOLOGY & PENOLOGY 69 (1973).

8

Making Prisoner Rights Real

The Case of Mothers

LISA KERR

The idea that prisoners do not forfeit legal identity and constitutional protection by reason of their confinement is now widely accepted as a matter of formal law. Beginning in the 1970s and in many cases since, the US Supreme Court has mandated that the rule of constitutional law must run behind prison walls. No reasonable lawyer, judge, or prison warden would now suggest otherwise, and the idea of constitutional rights for prisoners should, in theory, be a significant constraint on both the administration and lived experience of imprisonment. The delineation of rights in the prison context is, however, a more complicated story. The details of specific acts of interpretation of constitutional law for the prison context tend to depart from the grand metaphor that there is "no iron curtain" between prisons and the Constitution.[1]

The idea that constitutional law extends to the prison must mean that rights enjoyed in the community continue during incarceration, so long as they are compatible with the objectives of incarceration and the prison as an institutional form.[2] US courts confirm this principle in general, but fail to meaningfully fulfill it in particular cases. Courts easily deny claims even where prisoners are able to demonstrate the practical compatibility of a right with imprisonment as a matter of fact. Judges defer to the preferences of prison administrators and their bare assertions as to what is burdensome, expensive, or risky in the institutional context to justify extinguishing or seriously constraining even the most fundamental rights. In this sense, prison law is a field filled not only with the standard problem of gaps between *law on the books* and *law in action*, but with gaps between a general legal principle (that prisoners retain constitutional rights) and specific instances of legal interpretation (where rights are easily subordinated to institutional preferences).

One particularly vivid example, explored in this chapter, appears in the legal treatment of the claims of incarcerated mothers who seek to remain with newborn infants. In recent years, the number of states that elect to provide prison nurseries has increased, likely due to a substantial increase in rates of female imprisonment. The growth of prison nurseries confirms the potential compatibility of mother-infant unification with incarceration.[3] To date, however, US law has not even gestured toward the idea of constitutional protection for any maternal custody interests of prisoners. There is no recognized right to be considered for mother-infant unification programs, and no fixed duty for prisons and jails to make them available.[4] Relatedly, the topic of custody rights for incarcerated mothers does not appear on the strategic constitutional litigation agendas of US rights organizations. On this topic and more generally, the substantive content of the constitutional doctrine that applies to prisons allows a prisoner's claim to be extinguished based on little evidence and with a standard of review unknown in other areas of state action that implicate fundamental rights. The idea that constitutional law applies to prisons can no longer be contested as a matter of formal law, but a principled account of retained constitutional rights for prisoners has scarcely been grappled with abstractly, let alone delivered with regularity on the ground.

The topic of maternal custody rights, particularly with respect to newborn infants, highlights the stark difference in the content of rights enjoyed in the community versus in the prison. The family unit, in many of its forms, enjoys a near-sacred status in American law and the wider culture. In constitutional terms, the right to rear a child and make decisions in matters of family relationships is considered fundamental. This status assures protection under the Fourteenth Amendment and careful judicial scrutiny of any abridgement.[5] On the right to breastfeed, state interference outside the prison has attracted strict scrutiny, meaning that there must be "sufficiently important state interests" to justify any infringement, paired with measures that are "closely tailored to effectuate only those interests."[6]

In addition, the medical benefits of breastfeeding for both mother and child are now so widely endorsed that it has become what Linda

Blum calls the emblematic practice of "moral motherhood."[7] Women in the community have to cope with the multiple forms of surveillance and coercion arising from the "hegemonic medical endorsement" of breastfeeding.[8] Meanwhile, the legal system allows the prison system to automatically extinguish the breastfeeding dyad, and for the infants of incarcerated mothers to suffer the psychological and physical losses that are presumed to follow. Women prisoners are most often separated from infants within hours of a birth, even where the foster system is the only alternative for placing the infant. Postnatal women are returned to prison with engorgement and mastitis and also face the prospect of permanent loss of parental rights.

Prisoners have been the occasional beneficiaries of judicial protection under the general heading of familial interests, but only in the clearest of cases that raise little administrative burden for the prison. In *Turner v. Safley*, the US Supreme Court struck down a ban on prisoner marriages, reasoning that the categorical ban at issue in the case was not "reasonably related to legitimate penological objectives" and was thus an impermissible burden on the "right to marry."[9] This aspect of the *Turner* case does not, however, signal a deep jurisprudential commitment to the familial interests of prisoners. The Court elected not to apply strict scrutiny, but found that the marriage ban was not even "reasonably related" to a legitimate penological goal. The holding was no doubt colored by the fact that prisoner marriages absorb no state resources and raise no plausible security concerns.

The claims of incarcerated women who seek to retain physical custody of newborn infants raise more difficult issues. Protection of the family unit in this form clearly demands positive action in the prison system, which explains but does not justify greater hesitation from courts; the fulfillment of rights does occasionally require affirmative steps rather than just a prohibition on abuse and irrational deprivations. But like many marginalized families in the community, female prisoners do not enjoy the benefits of devotion to the cultivation of family life that pervades US political, legal, and social discourse.[10] Where the state interferes with the rights of mothers and infants through incarceration, the judiciary tends to yield uncritically to the consequences.

Comparative perspective sheds critical light on the state of US law and helps to specify *how* constitutional litigation and judicial reasoning could attend more carefully to the meaning of retained rights for prisoners on this topic. For much of its history, judicial review in Canada has been similarly deferential on topics of prison administration, and has similarly delegated the issue of prison nurseries to the policy preferences of legislatures and prison officials. Until recently, only the federal prisons and a few provincial jails allowed eligible mothers to remain with infants and young children while incarcerated, and there was no recognized constitutional right to be considered for the programs. The decided cases suggested that any such claims would fail given one 1994 holding and a general trend wherein Canadian courts defer expansively to administrators who assert institutional imperatives.[11]

A more recent Canadian decision, explored in detail here, breaks sharply from that pattern and serves as a model of judicial scrutiny of the prospect of meaningful familial rights in the prison context. In *Inglis v. British Columbia (Minister of Public Safety)*, a trial judge considered a large evidentiary record and found that it demonstrated the compatibility and indeed the benefits—from both a public health and penological perspective—of facilitating an option for mothers and infants to remain together in the jail context.[12] In short, mother-infant programs can align with both the penological objectives and administrative demands of the prison. The *Inglis* case shows how judicial investigation into specific empirical questions is required so as to faithfully pursue an ideal of retained rights for prisoners. The case also confirms that it is possible for judges, in a constitutional posture, to discern the consequences of penal policies, and to insist that the effects of such policies align with the official goals of the system.

The criminal justice system often operates in ways that compromise its official goals of family reunification, successful prisoner reentry, and preserving the safety and well-being of children.[13] As Issa Kohler-Hausmann helpfully suggests in her contribution to this volume, we should cease being surprised at the fact of disconnect between things like a formal purpose and the actual operation of a system.[14] We should, instead, turn our attention to the precise details and mechanisms by which legal rules become disconnected practices. In that spirit, this chapter considers the logic by which the judiciary denies the interests that incarcerated mother and child have in remaining together, and how that denial compromises both the promise of constitutional law for the prison context and, in many cases, the social outcomes that the criminal justice system delivers.

The chapter concludes that a large part of the problem in US law is that the *Turner v. Safley* standard directs courts to condone rights infringements where some lesser means of exercising a right is offered. *Turner v. Safley* holds that rights infringements can be justified in the light of four factors: whether the policy is "reasonably related" to "legitimate penological objectives"; whether an alternative way of exercising the right is open to the prisoner; whether accommodation of the right would impact prison staff, other inmates, and prison resources; and whether there are "ready alternatives" to the infringement that the prison could employ instead.[15] Sharon Dolovich has aptly characterized the *Turner* test as "creating a space in which prison officials can violate constitutional rights if they can show that doing so facilitates the running of the prison."[16] The Court's elaboration of each factor supplied the language for lower courts to frame deference as a legal mandate.[17]

In *Overton v. Bazetta*, for example, the Supreme Court considered a prison restriction on visits by minor children where parental rights had been terminated. The Court accepted the argument from correctional officials that a parent could send a letter to a child as an acceptable alternative to a visit—ignoring the issue of the age of the child and any literacy issues that might prevent both child and parent from making good use of this option.[18] In a ruling that reflects a weak principle of retained rights and a highly deferential posture to the assertions of correctional officials, the Court accepted the state's argument that the restrictions promoted internal security by reducing the total number of visitors and limiting disruption caused by children.

Judicial reasoning in the *Inglis* case models an alternative approach, in the way that the court rejects the suitability of lesser alternatives that would likely be endorsed under the *Turner* standard. Correctional officials in *Inglis* argued that new mothers could make do without a nursery program. The jail suggested that pregnant defendants could ask for sentence reductions, for placement in the federal prison system with its nursery program, or for enhanced visiting with their newborns in the jail and the pumping and storage of breast milk. The court examined each option, but concluded that these alternatives did not amount to meaningful fulfillment of the interests at stake and instead mandated that the jail continue to facilitate the option of access to prison nurseries. The *Inglis* case confirms the crucial step that courts must be willing to take in order to make prisoner rights real: to insist that constitutional law must protect the *full expression of rights* that are compatible with incarceration, rather than endorsing a view of rights as *subordinate to institutional preferences*. The latter simply amounts to a view of prisoner rights as defeasible interests, secondary in importance to administrative expedience.

I turn now to a selection of cases in which incarcerated women have attempted in various ways to use US courts to protect their custody interests as new mothers, and the terse analysis that has been deployed to deny such claims, suggesting the limited viability of constitutional arguments. I then compare the *Inglis* decision, where dozens of expert witnesses and multiple constitutional arguments fill a lengthy judgment, and where we see the crucial judicial moves that underpin a remarkable but logical interpretation of the idea that prisoners retain constitutional protection. The case generates a roadmap for faithful pursuit of the widely endorsed principle of retained rights in a way that accords with the judicial role. The implications of the approach are relevant not only to incarcerated mothers but to the project of principled legal control over the vast range of deprivations that incarceration entails.

Defining Imprisonment to Preclude Rights

The growth of female incarceration in the US renders the subject of the legal rights of incarcerated mothers increasingly urgent. In a story that is now well known, the 1970s saw a convergence of social and political factors that led to the widespread adoption of legislation stripping judges of discretion in favor of guideline and mandatory sentencing. In the federal system and many states, judges lost the ability to order community sanctions for the many female defendants who appeared before them as the sole caretakers of children. These legislative factors, combined with the war on drugs, produced a vast increase in numbers of non-violent incarcerated women.[19] Between 1980 and 2008, the number of women in US prisons increased sixfold, rising from 11 to 69 per 100,000 people.[20] The increased rate of male incarceration was about half of that—rising from 275 to 957 per 100,000 people.[21] In 2012, there were 201,200 women in penal institutions, up from a number closer to 10,000 in the early 1970s.[22]

The legal struggles of incarcerated pregnant women have been focused in recent decades on securing access to prenatal and postpartum healthcare and nutrition, adequate responses to pregnancy-related emergencies, and limits on the use of restraints during delivery.[23] Significant progress has been achieved on the topic of perinatal shackling: several states and the federal government have now passed legislative and policy reforms ordering prison officials to stop using shackles in almost all cases.[24] A majority of US jurisdictions, however, still lack law and policy on the topic, despite legal holdings that such practices violate contemporary standards of decency and are prohibited by the Eighth Amendment.[25] While shackling reforms are headed in the right direction, the prevalence of the practice remains a disturbing example of penal policies that defy a humane or sensible understanding of pregnancy and childbirth. While shackling affects female prisoners of all races today, Priscilla Ocen argues that the persistence of the US practice is connected to the historical devaluation, regulation, and punishment of the reproductive rights of black women.[26] In practice, women are often still shackled even in jurisdictions where it is explicitly banned.

Of course, the question of whether incarcerated mothers should retain custody of their children is far more complex than the question of whether they should have appropriate access to healthcare and a dignified form of childbirth. Lynne Haney's ethnographic work in California generates a number of warnings about programs designed to keep mother and child together during a custodial sentence, tracing the pains of mothering in the penal context and showing how a promising feminist alternative morphed into its own form of power and control.[27] Moreover, litigation is an unlikely context within which to effectively resolve a delicate web of interests such as those that arise in connection with mother-child prison programs. The striking point, however, is that US courts have not even attempted the task. In the standard authorities cited on this subject, courts have simply rejected the notion that maternal custody rights could ever survive incarceration. As a result, states are not forced to seriously grapple with their treatment of the mother-infant pairing.

In the 1976 case of *Pendergrass v. Toombs*, for example, the Oregon Court of Appeals rejected a woman's claim in a two-paragraph decision, relying on presumptions that persist in the legal system today.[28] The petitioner was pregnant at the time she was sentenced and committed to the Oregon Women's Correctional Center. She was taken to a local hospital for the birth of her child. A few days later, she was separated from the child and returned to the Correctional Center. The Superintendent of the Correctional Center refused to grant her temporary leave so that she could be with and breastfeed her child. In its decision, the court accepted that there is a constitutional right to raise one's children, and that, in the "unlikely event that a governmental unit would attempt to interfere with breastfeeding by a free citizen," such action would undoubtedly be held to be unconstitutional. But breastfeeding is a right that is incompatible with incarceration: "during a period of incarceration that right must give way to the right of the state to incarcerate." To hold otherwise "would be to hold that no parent of an unemancipated minor child can be imprisoned for commission of a crime." Incarceration means separation, no matter the effects or alternatives.

Another standard citation on this topic comes from Mississippi, where Diane Southerland sought an injunction to prevent the state from interfering with her breastfeeding of her infant son.[29] The 1986 Fifth Circuit opinion reports that Southerland had received what appears to be a very severe sentence: five years for embezzling $388.21. At the time she was sentenced, Southerland was pregnant. She gave birth while in custody and commenced breastfeeding immediately. Two days later, the state attempted to remove Southerland from the hospital, and two days after that the district court heard her injunction application. At the hearing, she presented evidence on the benefits of breastfeeding and the particular risk of allergies and diabetes faced by her son in the absence of it. The district court denied the application, and denied an application for a stay pending appeal. The opinion reports a unique act of clemency, where the Mississippi governor granted a temporary suspension of sentence pending the appeal such that Southerland could remain with her child while the appeal was heard.

In a brief decision denying the appeal, the Fifth Circuit took care to confirm the central principle of modern penal law: that Southerland did not forfeit constitutional protections by reason of her incarceration. But the court moves rapidly to confirm another equally clear principle: that prisoner rights are subject to restrictions, such as the institutional needs of prison facilities. The crux of the court's approach, which is broadly representative of judicial reasoning in prisoner cases, appears in the following paragraph:

The considerations that underlie our penal system justify the separation of prisoners from their spouses and children and necessitate the curtailment of many parental rights that otherwise would be protected. In this case, allowing Southerland to breast-feed would impair legitimate goals of the penal system. The state's interest in deterrence and retribution would be undermined by allowing temporary suspensions for female prisoners who choose to breast-feed or by attempting to house nursing infants. Such accommodation also would interfere with the maintenance of internal security. Moreover, the Mississippi penitentiary system does not have the proper facilities or resources to take care of nursing infants. The added financial burden of infant care would further undercut important goals of the already heavily burdened prison system. Plaintiffs argue that the state should transfer Southerland to a minimum security center that generally houses property offenders, where she might be able to nurse Matthew. However, it appears that these centers are not equipped to handle infants, and that even this limited approach would create substantial problems for the Mississippi penal system. The accommodation of nursing prisoners who share Southerland's circumstances is not compatible with the objectives of the penal system.[30]

Packed into this paragraph are several of the standard features of judicial resistance to careful scrutiny of prisoner claims. Internal security and resource allocation are cited as legitimate reasons for denial of a right, though we learn no details about what the costs or risks of such programs would actually be. The notion that constitutional modes of confinement may properly require some level of resource allocation or affirmative state burden is implicitly rejected. The prison system is "already heavily burdened" at the time of this 1986 opinion, although we get no concrete data or temporal comparator. While we learn that Mississippi does not currently have facilities for housing mothers with infants, the court does not query, and perhaps counsel failed to address, whether change is possible nor the relevance of evidence that such possibilities exist in other jurisdictions. The purposes of deterrence and retribution are cited, but there is no argument as to why such principles would be undermined by arranging for mother-infant unification. The court proceeds as if separation of mother and child is in fact the definition of the state's punishment. Imprisonment is defined so as to preclude recognition of the right. The court frames the problem in such a way that empties the constitutional duties—duties that it acknowledges and formally accepts—of all meaningful content.

Turning to the rights of the child, the Fifth Circuit in *Southerland* recognized that a child's right to personal association with a parent was not "wholly lacking" constitutional protection from governmental interference.[31] However, here too the court simply accepts the status quo and a definition of imprisonment that denies the right. The court reasons that children suffer many adverse consequences when a parent is imprisoned, such as loss of the parent's earning power, but that there was clearly no state obligation to limit or ameliorate those consequences. Under this logic, the loss of one right justifies the loss of another. The court accepts the medical evidence that this child had an interest in breastfeeding that was "a good bit stronger" than that of the usual child, but the court was satisfied that the plaintiff's expert "admitted" that termination of breastfeeding "would not be life threatening."[32] Satisfied that the child would only suffer harms short of death, the court found that the state had a legitimate interest—namely to avoid a "material burden on the prison system"—that overrode the interests of the child to breastfeed.[33]

Contrary to the presumptions at the heart of these holdings, the real world confirms that prison nurseries can be compatible with imprisonment, and that they can be designed so as to protect prisoner interests while still allowing discretion to affect individual cases. New York State runs the oldest continuously operated prison nursery program in the country, first established in 1901.[34] The legislation says that women prisoners "may" retain physical custody of newborn infants for one year, unless the chief medical officer of the correctional institution certifies that the mother is "physically unfit" to care for the child. The child is able to remain in the correctional institution for such period "as seems desirable for the welfare of the child, but not after it is one year of age." Cases brought by women seeking access to the program are thus matters of statutory interpretation rather than freestanding rights claims. The New York courts have tended to protect access to the program, holding that the statute implies a standard of "best interests of the child" as the governing principle in placement decisions.[35] The history of the New York program confirms that mother-infant unification is not, in fact, incompatible with the prison context. Security issues, the best interests of the child, and the allocation of resources can be balanced and managed, in this case over the course of many decades.

The constitutional and statutory cases are illuminating to consider together. The first involves constitutional claims by female prisoners that they should retain physical custody of a newborn child, primarily to bond and breastfeed. These claims are rejected in light of easily accepted narratives about the inevitable features of imprisonment. The second line of cases concerns statutory interpretation, brought by women in New York seeking access to prison nurseries long provided for through legislation. The constitutional cases accept a definition of imprisonment that necessarily excludes infant mothering, whereas the New York statutory cases protect the functioning of a program that we learn has been compatible with imprisonment for over a century. In the constitutional cases, courts admit that prisoners retain rights, but such rights are so narrowly conceived that little evidence and little analysis is needed to extinguish them.

Retained Rights in Comparative Light

Like the US, Canadian courts have often articulated standards of extreme deference to prison administrators, both before and after the 1982 advent of the *Charter of Rights and Freedoms*,[36] and despite the fact that the *Charter* places a burden on government to justify any infringement of rights. To be sure, there are certain issues where Canadian prisoners have had success in the courts. As one example, in *Sauvé v. Canada (Chief Electoral Officer)* the Supreme Court of Canada struck down a legislative ban on prisoner voting, reasoning that the right to vote explicitly granted to all citizens in section 3 of the *Charter* cannot be infringed for "symbolic and abstract reasons" but rather demands a justification grounded in evidence that the government failed to provide.[37] The case was expressively significant, but the voting right is occasional and entails little burden for prison administrators.[38] Like the US, cases where rights claims are adjacent to daily operational imperatives tend to generate outcomes far more deferential to the administrative context.

Canada has long had a federal program for eligible women to keep custody of children younger than four years old, but in recent years criteria for admission tightened such that the program now exists in name only.[39] The outright cancellation of a similar provincial program sparked the *Inglis* case. Prior to *Inglis*, it seemed that there was little constitutional basis upon which to insist on mother-infant unification. In a 1994 case, Mary Ann Turner had recently given birth to a baby boy.[40] She was on a short sentence, with less than two months remaining before she was eligible for release. Because of her security classification, Turner was unable to access the "open living unit" where women are eligible to apply to have their infant children live with them. Turner did not challenge the decision to keep her at a more secure level of custody, which was based on previous escape attempts and substance abuse violations. But Turner did ask the court to permit her baby to live with her in the more secure setting, pending her imminent release.

The reviewing court denied the application, emphasizing that a mother-infant program *was* available for women considered to be a lower security risk by the prison. That reasoning seems fair enough, but the court went further to make several remarks suggesting that all constitutional claims on this subject would be weak. In an echo of the US reasoning, the court observed that people who go to jail are "separated from their children" and that such inevitable separation could not be considered "cruel and unusual punishment." The court also rejected the idea that the separation of mother from child amounted to gender discrimination, reasoning that men have even less opportunity for custody of their children while incarcerated. Finally, the court found that "it simply would not be safe" for women to have children in the secure custody area, but the court did not specify what, if any, evidence had been presented to support that assertion.

While the holding in this 1994 trial decision may have been justified on its particular facts, the court seemed to shut the door generally. The court defined imprisonment so as to preemptively justify extinguishing the right: going to jail simply means family separation. The court used a formal equality framework to deny the unique severity of incarceration for women and their children, concluding that women were no worse off than men. Finally, the court made clear that little evidence would be required to support institutional concerns about safety and risk. The

Inglis case—skillfully litigated with a robust evidentiary record, in an era when the frame of formal equality had been explicitly rejected in Canadian law—generated a far different judicial response.

The Inglis Case: Contesting a Decision from Out of the Blue

The plaintiffs in *Inglis v. British Columbia (Minister of Public Safety)* were former inmates of Alouette Correctional Centre for Women (Alouette) and their children. The litigation arose from a decision to cancel a program, in place in some form since 1973, permitting mothers to have their infants with them while they served sentences of provincial incarceration of two years or less (the Program). Access to the Program was contingent upon approvals by the Ministry of Children and Family Development, acting pursuant to legislation that emphasized the best interests of the child.[41] Mothers with babies were housed in a separate structure within Alouette, which included equipment for children and a safe play area, with nursing staff present for any first aid needs throughout the day. Correctional officers staffed the unit 24 hours per day, and each was trained in infant CPR. Physicians and public health nurses regularly visited the infants.[42]

In a judgment that was not appealed, the trial court ruled that the provincial government's decision to close the Program was unconstitutional, violating both equality rights under section 15 and "security of the person" protections under section 7 of the *Charter*. In the section 7 analysis, the court held that the separation of mother and child constituted "serious state-imposed psychological stress."[43] The remainder of the section 7 test required the court to analyze whether that deprivation was "in accordance with the principles of fundamental justice."[44] Because of the way that the decision to cancel the Program was made, discussed in greater detail below, the court found those principles were not satisfied.

In the equality analysis under section 15, the court found that the cancellation of the Program "increased the disadvantage" of an already vulnerable population, and that such disadvantage was related to the protected grounds of race, ethnicity, disability, and sex.[45] The trial judge accepted that the Program cancellation affected prisoners who are both female and disproportionately Aboriginal, which entailed present and historical experiences of addiction and abuse, mental health issues, poverty, foster or institutional care, and child apprehension.[46] The court followed the decision of the Supreme Court of Canada in *Quebec v. A*, where Justice Abella confirmed a substantive equality approach and put the test as follows: "if the state conduct widens the gap between the historically disadvantaged group and the rest of society rather than narrowing it, then it is discriminatory."[47]

The key factual findings concerned the decision to cancel the Program. The main decision-maker, prison director Brent Merchant, testified that he cancelled the Program because of his view that infants do not fall within the "mandate" of corrections.[48] Merchant made the standard move: asserting that incarceration itself extinguished the right. But the trial judge turned to the facts. After finding that constitutional rights were engaged, Justice Ross moved to ask whether such rights were or could be compatible with incarceration. Critical to the outcome was the fact that the record revealed the longstanding, successful operation of the Program and similar programs in the Canadian federal system and abroad. Notably, Justice Ross pointed to New York State as evidence of the potential success of such programs.[49]

A range of experts confirmed the benefits of the Program.[50] The medical evidence indicated that babies in the Program were healthy, happy, and developing at a normal rate.[51] The court cited a "consensus of international health experts" that infants should be exclusively breastfed until age six months and on demand until age two, and that breastfeeding is important for the infant's psychosocial development and healthy immune system.[52] The court also found that breastfeeding provides health benefits to mothers, including lower rates of breast and ovarian cancer and Type II diabetes and reduced risk of post-partum depression.[53] The court's attention to these topics suggests a view that compromised health is not a proper part of a sanction of incarceration.

Evidence from developmental psychology was also central. The court considered the harm caused by insecure attachment in infants, which follows from interruption in maternal bonding in the two-to-ten-month period. The evidence made clear that successful attachment is related to the ability to form future intimate relationships, retain emotional balance, find happiness and satisfaction being with others, and rebound from disappointment and misfortune.[54] Particularly in the immediate post-partum period, staying together delivers significant health and psychosocial benefits to both mother and child.[55] The significance of these interests, to both mother and child, made clear that the case engaged important constitutionally protected interests. The goal being pursued by the government in cancellation had to be an important one in order to survive judicial review.

But evidence of an important governmental objective was absent. The jail conducted no research on the costs and benefits of the Program before cancelling it. The decision to cancel came abruptly in the midst of its successful operation, with the evidence indicating that Merchant had become irritated when he was not notified in advance of a decision to admit a particular mother and infant. What began as slight resistance escalated over time—Merchant had "soured" on the program when he decided to cancel it.[56] Under cross-examination at trial, even government witnesses invariably agreed on the benefits of the Program and the total absence of actual safety incidents, maintaining only that the question of whether the benefits outweighed the risks must be assessed on a case-by-case basis.[57] This was, in fact, how the Program had always been conducted, given the involvement of the relevant children's ministry in placement decisions. The court concluded, in sum, that the decision to eject the Program from the jail was not the sort of studied decision that could properly extinguish the interests that prisoners maintain while incarcerated.

The prisoner director in *Inglis* testified about his view that the jail's task is, primarily, to deliver the secure custody of inmates. The court had a different view, reasoning that inmates are to be secured while retaining whatever rights are compatible with the custodial setting.[58] The key findings of fact were thus the longstanding domestic and international success of prison nurseries. Comparative and historical perspective makes clear what is possible.

The Inglis Legal Analysis

There are four additional dimensions to the *Inglis* reasoning that represent key components of the concept of retained rights in prison. First, Justice Ross found that offers to protect a lesser version of a prisoner right is not, without more, an adequate justification for impairment.

Perhaps most notably for a legal field that has seen so much judicial reticence to scrutinize the claims of prison officials, her method was to analyze the logical and evidentiary plausibility of the alternatives that the government offered up, rather than accepting the suggestions at face value. Second, Justice Ross refused to treat the jail as an entity sealed off from ordinary society. She analyzed the risks and benefits of the Program in light of the limited alternatives that the community could offer. Third, Justice Ross refused to allow the jail to operate in a closed legal compartment where only correctional law applies. She brought family law concepts to bear upon the question of the jail's legal duties as a public institution. Finally, Justice Ross rejected the idea that incarceration can simply be defined as the legitimate cause of any rights infringements. She examined the empirical possibilities rather than defining incarceration so as to preclude the recognition and accommodation of the right.

RESISTING LESSER RIGHTS

Recall that under US law, the *Turner v. Safley* standard has seen courts condone rights infringements where the government points to some lesser means of exercising the right. The *Inglis* defendant asked the Canadian court to take a similar approach, pointing to measures that the institution had taken, or could take, to ameliorate mother-infant separation, such as: encouraging prosecutors and the courts to impose community-based sentences, enhanced visitation, facilities for pumping, storing, and delivering breast milk, and the possibility of transfer to a federal institution (where mother-infant programs still formally exist).[59] Justice Ross interrogated the proffered alternatives by delving into the workings of sentencing law, the substance of the expert evidence, and the realities of prison administration.

Regarding the sentencing option, Justice Ross said that while pregnancy or parenthood can be a factor taken into account at sentencing, mandatory minimum sentences and other restricted offenses prevent judges from imposing community-based sanctions in at least some cases.[60] Regarding the promise of visits, she noted that the expert evidence made clear that even enhanced visitation does not afford an adequate opportunity for the infant to attach to the parent.[61] Finally, Justice Ross noted the obvious practical difficulties with pumping and storing breast milk, and noted that transfer to a federal institution was only a theoretical possibility, given the lengthy federal assessment process and the comparatively short length of sentences for women sentenced to provincial institutions.[62] There were alternatives to the right of mothers and infants to remain together, but with minimal scrutiny it was clear that they did not approach satisfactory fulfillment of the interests at stake.

PRISON NOT SEALED OFF

The government in *Inglis* attempted to justify its cancellation of the Program by arguing that it could not guarantee the safety of infants. In response, Justice Ross resisted treating the jail as an entity sealed off from ordinary society, either judicially or sociologically. Rather, she considered it to be just one institutional space on the spectrum of environments that a child, and particularly a child of an incarcerated person, may come to experience. The court went further and examined in detail the evidence on risks for children in government care, citing evidence that these children are more likely to be diagnosed with a health condition, more likely to be prescribed mental health-related drugs, more frequently admitted to hospital, four times more likely to be diagnosed with a mental disorder, and much more likely to die of both natural causes and external causes than children in the general population.[63] The court accepted that the jail context raised some possibility of harm to infants, but Justice Ross found that there was a risk of harm to infants in virtually any environment, particularly foster care as well as with relatives in the community.

The jail did submit evidence indicating "low-grade harms" that infants face in the custodial context.[64] The first claim under this heading was that, in the past, mothers would occasionally break a rule that infants were to sleep in cribs rather than with them. Justice Ross accepted that it was best practice for infants not to sleep in the same bed as mothers, but she also found that "the practice is widespread in the community and throughout the world."[65] To the extent it was a risk to an infant, it was not one arising exclusively from the custodial environment. There was also evidence that persons other than mothers and designated babysitters would occasionally break the Program rules and touch the babies. Once again, Justice Ross noted that it was impossible to imagine that "in the community or in foster care that only mothers or approved caregivers would touch infants."[66] The risk of harm associated with the jail was contextualized in light of ordinary community experience.

Finally, Justice Ross cautioned against approaches that would immunize penal decisions from scrutiny, such as allowing prison administrators to apply a standard of "guaranteed safety" to their decisions.[67] This standard would be "particularly inappropriate" in this case, given that babies affected by the decision would have to be placed somewhere, and "anywhere they are placed is associated with some level of risk."[68] The concept of retained rights for prisoners means that the prison is not an exceptional space within which any level of risk justifies any type of institutional response.

NO LEGAL COMPARTMENTALIZATION

The government in *Inglis* argued that the only relevant law governing their work is Canada's Corrections and Conditional Release Act and the subsidiary jail policies. This plea for legal insulation occurred because the jail insisted that it was not required to consider family law concepts in its penal administrative decisions.[69] In response, Justice Ross developed a broad conceptualization of the state and its sources of responsibility in administering incarceration. She held that the principle of "best interests of the child" was relevant to the "legislative and social context" of the constitutional issues to be decided in *Inglis*.[70]

In an unprecedented but principled judicial move, Justice Ross rejected "compartmentalization" of the punishment context and the law that applies there.[71] Corrections was responsible for considering and applying the full range of sources of domestic and international law, all of which make clear that "the best interests of the child" apply to "all state actions."[72] With the Program abolished, decisions about infant custody could no longer be made in light of the full range of proper factors. Justice Ross described the problem with the new "blanket exclusion" as follows:

Now instead of a decision based on the best interest of the child following a consideration of all relevant factors, including the importance of continuity in the child's care, the quality of the relationship the child has with a parent and the effect of maintaining that relationship, there is a blanket exclusion that takes into consideration neither the needs and circumstances of the mother nor those of the child.[73]

When the full picture of family law is brought back into sight, the jail would have to recognize that cancelling the Program would result in at least some children being put into foster care. The question as to whether that option is preferable had to be an open one. In sum, Justice Ross found that the government could not avoid the full range of legal obligations that bear upon it by segregating the custodial context from the rest of public law. She conceptualized the jail as simply one mechanism of the government, responsible to the full spectrum of law governing state action. She held that the jail could not "circumvent the requirement to consider the best interests of the children affected by relying on the fact that a different arm of the state would be actually seizing the children."[74] Relatedly, corrections is responsible for seeking input from other agencies before making decisions that would affect other aspects of public administration. Justice Ross found that, on the facts of this case, "when the other agencies expressed concern over the decision, they were ignored."[75] She insisted upon the unity of government when she assessed its conduct under constitutional light.

TESTING CAUSATION

Prisoner cases are often defended on the basis that imprisonment is the inevitable cause of any and all subsequent rights infringements. This standard argument appeared in *Inglis* too—the government even cited the US *Southerland* decision to suggest that the Program is "fundamentally inconsistent with imprisonment itself."[76] The government argued that any separation of mother and infant is not caused by the cancellation of the Program, but rather flows from the custodial sentence. In other words, the separation was caused by the actions of the plaintiffs, whom the criminal justice system had already adjudicated and designated responsible. But Justice Ross scrutinized the suggestion that incarceration itself was the cause of mother-infant separation, finding that "there is nothing in the criminal law, policy or objectives that requires the separation of mothers and infants as a consequence of a criminal sentence."[77] The history of the Program proved the government's claim wrong.

To summarize, the *Inglis* court conducts a holistic analysis of the justifications offered by the state for its rights infringement. The inquiry undertaken by the court goes well beyond the standard question of whether accommodation of a right would encumber the prison or generate some level of risk for those working and living in the institution—queries that could be enough to extinguish a claim under current US law. The *Inglis* court conducts a comprehensive analysis of what Sharon Dolovich has called the "state's carceral burden," namely the price society must pay for the decision to incarcerate.[78] Under this framework, the individual may be removed from shared public space, but the state assumes an ongoing positive obligation to meet basic human needs throughout the administration of the custodial sanction; the incarceration of pregnant women and new mothers entails a positive duty to facilitate an option for the mother-infant pair to remain physically together, in conditions appropriate for childrearing. Even where the government may face certain costs in order to protect the right, those costs may be part of the state's burden, incurred by the election to make use of incarceration.[79]

Conclusion

Several contributions in this volume critique the ways that legal rules are transformed and defeated when they are interpreted and operationalized by actors on the ground. In most jails and prisons, however, there are no nursery programs and no legal doctrines with which to demand them. There can be no occasion to critique the *law in action* where legislation is absent and where the judiciary has yet to make a first interpretive move of constitutional standards.

New York State is one of the few places where the key issue is enforcement of a legislative scheme. The New York law contains only two bars to admission to prison nurseries: if the mother is "physically unfit" to care for her child, and if staying in the nursery would not be "desirable for the welfare" of the child, which state courts have repeatedly interpreted as a test about the "best interests of the child." Within this legal frame, advocates struggle on the ground to maintain a principle of individualized decision-making for a wide range of women and fight against practices that would automatically bar women with particular criminal records and child welfare histories. At Bedford Hills, critics point to delays in processing applications and problematic security and programming protocols that prevent mothers and other prisoners from participating as caregivers in the program.[80]

In most US jurisdictions, however, prison nurseries do not exist and states are under no hard legal pressure to develop them. And while successful constitutional litigation rarely ends a conversation, on many occasions it has started one. Indeed, the victory in *Inglis* is far from the end of the story. A lengthy and elaborate process of policy development, with input from all stakeholders, has followed in the wake of the decision that new mothers effectively have a constitutional right to apply to access a prison nursery program.[81] The effect of the judgment in terms of the quality of the nursery and fair access to it remains to be seen, but the articulation of constitutional boundaries has compelled action on the topic. Perhaps most significantly, the *Inglis* court refused to allow a seemingly random change of mind among low-level officials to determine significant dimensions of state punishment. Even those concerned with the quality and effects of prison nursery programs likely agree that the rights engaged by the topic merit reasoned interpretation.

The *Inglis* court thought that prisoners retain constitutional rights unless such rights are incompatible with the unavoidable features of the prison. The key difference from US approaches to date is that *Inglis* demands that the government adduce support for its assertions about the necessary features of incarceration, treating the issue of whether particular rights are compatible with imprisonment as an open empirical question. Ironically, the Canadian judge points to the few US prison nursery programs as evidence of what is possible—as evidence that automatic mother-infant separation is not, in fact, one of the unavoidable features of imprisonment. This is clearly not the *Turner v. Safley* standard of judicial review, which favors the preferences and resource priorities of prison officials as the key determinants of the scope of prisoner rights.

The *Turner* Court stressed that running a prison is an "inordinately difficult undertaking that requires expertise, planning, and the commitment of resources, all of which are peculiarly within the province of the legislative and executive branches of government."[82] There are few areas of constitutional interpretation that would *not* raise such issues, but prisoner cases have attracted a particularly hesitant posture. Judicial deference to prison officials is also often articulated on the grounds of lack of judicial expertise, only to be accompanied by a refusal to come to know more. This is perhaps most striking in those cases where prisoner claims are dismissed on summary application, where courts prefer the presumed good faith expertise of prison administrators over the ordinary testing of facts through trial process.[83] It was only once the evidence in *Inglis* was laid out at trial—particularly the insights from attachment theory and the medical benefits of breastfeeding, paired with the dearth of evidence showing the downsides of the Program—that the public and penal interest in maintaining close bonds between mother and infant became so clear. This may even explain why the government did not appeal, as officials were exposed to an evidentiary showing that was not canvassed internally prior to cancellation of the Program. Thoughtful litigation educated not only the judge, but also the officials at the jail.

The *Southerland* court did not deny the right to breastfeed an infant and remain united by denying the notion that prisoners retain rights. Such a position would now be anachronistic. But the acknowledged right was too quickly defined as incompatible with imprisonment itself. Rather than allowing the criminal justice system to generate negative social effects with no pushback, the *Inglis* court pushed for benefits to outweigh costs and demanded sensible connections between the long-range goals of the system and its present-day actual operation. Rather than treating the prison as an exceptional space, where the difficulties of managing problematic residents can justify any managerial approach, the court constructed penal facilities as ordinary state institutions responsible to the full spectrum of public law commitments and values. In a great many other prisoner cases, courts fail to delineate meaningful boundaries within which prison policies can be forced to progress. The result is that the fundamental rights of prisoners can be the contingent product of local policy trends, rather than matters bounded by higher law.

NOTES

Thanks to Sharon Dolovich for substantial feedback on this chapter. Thanks also to Benjamin Berger, Kyle Kirkup, Darryl Robinson, and Jacob Weinrib for important comments and discussion.

1 *Wolff v. McDonnell*, 418 US 539 (1974), at 555–556.
2 This principle is endorsed, among other places, in the majority decision in *Hudson v. Palmer*, 468 US 517 (1984), at 517: "prisoners enjoy many protections of the Constitution that are not fundamentally inconsistent with imprisonment itself or incompatible with the objectives of incarceration."

3 Women's Prison Association, *Mothers, Infants and Imprisonment: A National Look at Prison Nurseries and Community-Based Alternatives* (2009), at 4–5 (www.wpaonline.org.), noting that nine states have prison nursery programs in operation or under development. With the exception of the program at Bedford Hills Correctional Facility in New York, all other prison nurseries opened within the last 20 years.

4 Of course, some if not many incarcerated mothers would not participate in such programs, either because they do not want to parent in the penal setting or because their specific histories do not satisfy reasonable admission criteria. This chapter is focused on the issue of the right to apply to mother-child programs, and the question of the state's duty to make them available.

5 See, for example, *Santosky v. Kramer*, 455 US 743 (1982). But for an argument that courts do not consistently apply strict scrutiny in the childrearing context, see Jeffrey Shulman, *The Constitutional Parent: Rights, Responsibilities, and the Enfranchisement of the Child* (New Haven, CT: Yale University Press, 2014).

6 See *Dike v. School Board*, 650 F. 2d 783 (1981), where a public school teacher successfully challenged a rule that she could not breastfeed her child during a duty-free break. The Fifth Circuit held in favor of the teacher and remanded for a determination of whether the school's regulations were justified on the basis of sufficiently important governmental interests and closely tailored to effectuate only those interests.

7 Linda Blum, *At the Breast: Ideologies of Breastfeeding and Motherhood in the Contemporary United States* (Boston: Beacon Press, 1999), at 43.

8 *Ibid.*

9 *Turner v. Safley*, 482 US 78 (1987).

10 Of course, this discourse is contradicted by actual policies on the ground in the non-prison context as well, such as by the fact that the United States is one of the few countries in the world that does not mandate a period of paid maternity leave at the national level, and that protects only 12 weeks of unpaid maternity leave. See International Labour Organization, "Maternity and Paternity at Work: Law and Practice Across the World" (Geneva: International Labour Office, 2014), at 16.

11 See Debra Parkes, "A Prisoners' Charter? Reflections on Prisoner Litigation under the Canadian Charter of Rights and Freedoms," *University of British Columbia Law Review* 40:2 (2007): 629–676; Lisa Kerr, "Contesting Expertise in Prison Law," *McGill Law Journal* 60:1 (2014): 43–94.

12 *Inglis v. British Columbia (Minister of Public Safety)*, 2013 BCSC 2309.

13 Parental incarceration is generally associated with negative effects on the future prospects of children, and those with incarcerated mothers encounter more "risk factors" for poor life outcomes, including substance abuse and mental illness. Elizabeth I. Johnson and Jane Waldfogel, "Children of Incarcerated Parents: Multiple Risks and Children's Living Arrangements," in David Weiman, Bruce Western, and Mary Patillo (eds.), *Imprisoning America: The Social Effects of Mass Incarceration*, (New York: Russell Sage Foundation, 2004). For a systematic review

of the literature, including attention to the methodological problems in discerning the effects of parental incarceration, see Joseph Murray and David P. Farrington, "The Effects of Parental Incarceration on Children," *Crime and Justice* 37:1 (2008): 133–206.

14 Issa Kohler-Haussman, "Jumping Bunnies and Legal Rules: The Organizational Sociologist and the Legal Scholar Should Be Friends," this volume.

15 Part of the *Turner* decision upheld a regulation that prohibited prisoners from corresponding with prisoners at other institutions, regardless of their relationship. The Court admitted that the prison could simply monitor prisoner communications so as to prevent any correspondence that would threaten safety and security, but found that this would impose more than a *de minimis* cost on the prison. The Court accepted, further, that the regulation does not deprive prisoners of all means of expression, but simply bars communication with a limited class of people, and upheld the ban on that basis. *Turner* at 89–93.

16 Sharon Dolovich, "Forms of Deference in Prison Law," *Federal Sentencing Reporter* 24:4 (2012): 245–259, at 246.

17 *Ibid.*

18 *Overton v. Bazetta*, 539 US 126 (2003).

19 The drug laws changed the composition of the female prison population: in the 1980s, most women in prison were convicted of either violent crimes or property offenses, and only 12% percent were incarcerated for a drug offense. By the late 1990s, violent offenders made up only 28% of the female population, and drug offenders were 35%. See Candace Kruttschnitt and Rosemary Gartner, "Women's Imprisonment," in Michael Tonry (ed.), *Crime and Justice: A Review of Research*, vol. 30 (Chicago: University of Chicago Press, 2003), Table 3.

20 Candace Kruttschnitt, "Women's Prisons," in Michael Tonry (ed.), *Oxford Handbook of Crime and Criminal Justice* (New York: Oxford University Press, 2010), Table 2.

21 *Ibid.*

22 Roy Walmsley, "World Female Imprisonment List," 2nd ed. (2012), International Centre of Justice, Kings College London (www.prisonstudies.org).

23 See Ellen Barry, "Pregnant Prisoners," *Harvard Women's Law Journal* 12 (1989): 189–203.

24 Brett Dignam and Eli Y. Adashi, "Health Rights in the Balance: The Case against Perinatal Shackling of Women behind Bars," *Health and Human Rights Journal* 16:2 (2014): 8–18.

25 *Women Prisoners of District of Columbia Department of Corrections v. District of Columbia*, 877 F. Supp. 634 (D.D.C. 1994), *vacated in part, modified in part*, 899 F. Supp. 659 (D.D.C. 1995).

26 Priscilla A. Ocen, "Punishing Pregnancy: Race, Incarceration, and the Shackling of Pregnant Prisoners," *California Law Review* 100 (2012): 1239–1311.

27 Lynne Haney, *Offending Women: Power, Punishment, and the Regulation of Desire*, (Berkeley: University of California Press, 2010); Lynne Haney, "Motherhood as

Punishment: The Case of Parenting in Prison," *Signs* 39:1 (Autumn 2013): 105–130, at 107.

28 *Pendergrass v. Toombs*, 546 P.2d 1103 (1976).

29 *Southerland v. Thigpen*, 784 F. 2d 713, 717 (5th Cir. 1986).

30 *Southerland* at 716.

31 *Southerland* at 717.

32 *Southerland* at 718.

33 *Southerland* at 718. The doctrine of "legitimate interest" in restricting the rights of incarcerated people stems from *Pell v. Procunier*, 417 US 817 (1973). The state interest asserted in the cases tends to be something along the lines of "maintaining the orderly and efficient operation of its criminal justice system."

34 N.Y. Correct. Law § 611 (McKinney 2003 & Supp. 2014). For a leading study on the New York prison nurseries, indicating that infants in these settings experience secure attachment at rates comparable to healthy community children, see M. W. Byrne, L.S. Goshin, and S. S. Joestl, "Intergenerational Transmission of Attachment for Infants Raised in a Prison Nursery," *Attachment and Human Development* 12:4 (2010): 375–393.

35 *Apgar v. Beauter*, 347 N.Y.S. 2d 872 (Sup 1973); *Bailey v. Lombard*, 420 N.Y.S. 2d 650 (Supp. 1979). While the *Bailey* court sided with the institutional defendant on the facts of the specific case, the court rejects several of the institution's arguments in a way that ensures ongoing access to the program. The court dismissed the suggestion that keeping infants in jail creates unacceptable security hazards, and found that a decision based on these factors alone would be arbitrary and capricious, emphasizing that the only relevant test was the statutory principle of individual best interests of the child. The court identified four factors that were proper to consider: the availability of facilities adequate to insure the child's health and safety, the mother's psychological health and parenting background, the crime for which the mother was convicted as it might reflect on her parenting capabilities, and the length of the mother's sentence (654). In a description of the holding that is prescient of the *Inglis* holistic mode of analysis, Mary Deck describes how "the *Bailey* court directed the sheriff to weigh the benefits and detriments of parental care in jail against the effects of placing the child in foster care." Mary Deck, "Incarcerated Mothers and Their Infants: Separation or Legislation?," *Boston College Law Review* 29:3 (1988): 689–713, at 702; *Bailey* at 654.

36 *Canadian Charter of Rights and Freedoms*, Part I of the *Constitution Act*, being Schedule B to the Canada Act 1982 (UK), 1982, c 11.

37 2002 SCC 68 at para. 23.

38 For arguments about how the *Sauvé* case is not representative of the tone and substance of judicial review of prisoner rights in Canadian law, see Debra Parkes, "Prisoner Voting Rights in Canada: Rejecting the Notion of Temporary Outcasts," in Christopher Mele and Teresa A Miller (eds.), *Civil Penalties, Social Consequences* (New York: Routledge, 2005), at 238; Efrat Arbel, "Contesting Unmodu-

lated Deprivation: *Sauvé v. Canada* and the Normative Limits of Punishment," *Canadian Journal of Human Rights* 3:2 (2015): 121–141.

39 See the *Office of the Correctional Investigator's Annual Report* (Ottawa: Office of the Correctional Investigator, 2009–2010) noting that eligibility restrictions announced by the government in 2008 resulted in de facto abolition of the federal mother-baby program.

40 *Turner v. MacMillan*, 1994 CanLII 1218 (BCSC).

41 *Child, Family and Community Service Act*, R.S.B.C. 1996, c. 46.

42 The additional elements of the Program are described at para. 73 of *Inglis*. A system was in place regarding eligibility, MCFD involvement, babysitting and other personnel issues, behavioral requirements for mothers, and arrangements with a local hospital for delivery services.

43 *Inglis* at para. 395.

44 The full text of section 7 is: "Everyone has the right to life, liberty and security of the person and the right not to be deprived thereof except in accordance with the principles of fundamental justice."

45 The full text of section 15(1) is: "Every individual is equal before and under the law and has the right to the equal protection and equal benefit of the law without discrimination and, in particular, without discrimination based on race, national or ethnic origin, colour, religion, sex, age or mental or physical disability."

46 *Inglis* at para. 544.

47 *Quebec (Attorney General) v. A*, 2013 SCC 5, at para. 332.

48 *Inglis* at para. 481.

49 *Inglis* at para. 465.

50 Expert witnesses who recommended the Program included a nurse within federal corrections (para. 84); a Ph.D. in sociology and health education with relevant research experience (para. 89); a physician with a background in obstetrics and addiction (paras. 93–94); a psychologist with extensive experience in corrections (para. 255); the prison physician at Alouette during the pendency of the Program (para. 262); and a law professor who advised that similar programs were available in modern prisons across the world, including the US, Europe, Australia, and New Zealand (para. 76).

51 *Inglis* at paras. 78 and 265.

52 *Inglis* at para. 329.

53 *Inglis* at para. 330.

54 *Inglis* at para. 334.

55 *Inglis* at para. 328.

56 *Inglis* at para. 318.

57 *Inglis* at paras. 289–292. On the lack of risk facing the infants, see paras. 171, 184, 186, and 292.

58 *Inglis* at para. 379.

59 *Inglis* at para. 400. For a summary of the evidence cited by the defendants on alternatives, see para. 435.

60 *Inglis* at para. 401.

61 *Inglis* at para. 402.

62 *Inglis* at para. 402. Justice Ross also observed that the argument regarding transfer to federal institutions contradicted the rest of the government's argument: "this suggests to me that, notwithstanding submissions made in the litigation, Corrections recognized that the prison environment is not necessarily incompatible with a safe and nurturing environment for infants" (para. 468).

63 *Inglis* at para. 485, citing Jane Morely, Q.C., and Dr. Perry Kendall, "Joint Special Report—Health and Well-Being of Children in Care in British Columbia: Report 1 on Health Services Utilization and Mortality" (September 2006), a joint publication of the Child and Youth Officer for British Columbia and the Provincial Health Officer.

64 *Inglis* at para. 437.

65 *Inglis* at para. 463.

66 *Inglis* at para. 463.

67 *Inglis* at para. 483.

68 *Inglis* at para. 484.

69 The defendants argued, in particular, that "the concept of the best interests of the child is not applicable and that Mr. Merchant was not obliged to consider or to attempt to maximize the best interests of the children affected by his decision." *Inglis* at para. 434.

70 *Inglis* at para. 358, following settled law that "the analysis of rights under the *Charter* must be contextual," citing *Winnipeg Child and Family Services v. K.L.W.*, 2000 SCC 48, at para. 71.

71 *Inglis* at para. 369.

72 *Inglis* at para. 370.

73 *Inglis* at para. 474.

74 *Inglis* at para. 454.

75 *Inglis* at para. 451.

76 *Inglis* at para. 405.

77 *Inglis* at paras. 407 and 410.

78 Sharon Dolovich, "Cruelty, Prison Conditions, and the Eighth Amendment," *New York University Law Review* 84:4 (2009): 881–979, at 892.

79 The question of the cost of the Program was not a central part of the litigation, but this is another topic where Justice Ross scrutinized the foundations of the state's plea for deference. The defendants alluded to scarce resources and the need for efficiency. Counsel asserted that the resource-intensive nature of the program required the "disproportionate re-allocation of operational resources, such as full-time medical staff, staff trained in infant care and infrastructure itself, away from programs with proven effectiveness that serve larger groups within the correctional system" (*Inglis* at para. 439). But Justice Ross pointed to both the minimal evidence actually filed on cost and held further that it could not trump the analysis. She noted that Merchant admitted in his testimony that cost was not

a factor in his decision, which was consistent with other evidence of the generally low cost of the Program (*Inglis* at para. 471).

80 For a recent comprehensive study, see Tamar Kraft-Stolar, *Reproductive Injustice: The State of Reproductive Health Care for Women in New York State Prisons* (Report of the Women in Prison Project of the Correctional Association of New York, 2015), at 123–134.

81 See "Guidelines for the Implementation of Prison Mother-Child Units in Canada" (June 2014, Penultimate Version) (on file with the author).

82 *Turner* at 84–85. Also see *Jones v. N.C. Prisoners' Labor Union, Inc.*, 433 US 119, 126 (1977), noting that "the realities of running a penal institution are complex and difficult"; and *Procunier v. Martinez*, 416 US 396, 404–405 (1974), citing "Herculean obstacles" to maintaining order and discipline, preventing unauthorized access or escape, and rehabilitating prisoners.

83 Doctrine in this area stipulates that "substantial deference" will be offered to the "professional judgment" of prison administrators, which means that even where there is a serious factual dispute at the heart of a case, claims can be dismissed where the defendant alludes to the fact of "professional judgment" (*Overton v. Bazetta*). Constitutional claims can be dismissed even on summary application, where the mere assertion of the "professional judgment" of prison administrators is enough to entitle the prison system to judgment in advance of trial (*Singer v. Raemisch*, 593 F.3d 529 (7th Cir. 2010), and *Beard v. Banks*, 548 US 521 (2006)).

PART III

Getting Situated

Actors, Institutions, and Ideology

The criminal process is comprised of thousands of institutions and millions of individual actors. Criminal justice policies have powerful politics and histories that influence what they mean and how they work. These essays bring to bear the disciplinary insights of sociology, criminology, organizational theory, and critical race theory to make sense of the highly situated, contextual reality of the criminal process. Just as importantly, they remind us to think in interdisciplinary ways about inherently interdisciplinary phenomena.

Mona Lynch, The Situated Actor and the Production of Punishment: Toward an Empirical Social Psychology of Criminal Procedure

Priscilla Ocen, Beyond Ferguson: Integrating Critical Race Theory and the "Social Psychology of Criminal Procedure"

Issa Kohler-Hausmann, Jumping Bunnies and Legal Rules: The Organizational Sociologist and the Legal Scholar Should Be Friends

9

The Situated Actor and the Production of Punishment

Toward an Empirical Social Psychology of Criminal Procedure

MONA LYNCH

Introduction

As numerous scholars and commentators have noted, the United States underwent a punitive revolution in the late 20th century resulting in the dramatic expansion of correctional populations in the state and federal systems. Beyond the consequence of locking up significantly higher numbers of people, this revolution also greatly expanded the reach of myriad forms of criminal justice surveillance, intrusion, and control into communities, in a pattern with clear demographic and geographic correlates. These transformations, however, could not have occurred without very specific changes to how criminal justice operates in thousands of local jurisdictions around the country. So while sentencing law reforms helped create the capacity for the consequent penal expansion, it took local level action to change the way front-line criminal justice actors treated the problem of crime and justice in their day-to-day practices.

Although local-level criminal justice operations figure prominently in the distribution and growth of the "carceral state" (Beckett and Murakawa, 2012, 221), much of the scholarly focus has been on either the very front end of the punitive transformations (as well as at the structural end of the scale), particularly political and legislative activity; or at the back end, especially as reflected in aggregated incarceration rates.[1] Moreover, the empirical body of work that does address the role of local policing and trial courts in the punitive changes has tended to focus more on criminal justice *outcomes* (both in terms of formal arrests and final sentences), rather than on underlying *processes*. Sociologically oriented criminologists, in particular, have conducted a large body of research on predicates of arrests and sentence outcomes, and have been concerned with developing largely quantitative empirical models that specify the legal and extra-legal variables thought to predict those outcomes. Yet such models do not directly measure criminal justice actors' cognitions, behavior, or interpersonal interactions, and instead must rely upon indirect inferences about causal triggers of the measured effects (Ulmer, 2012). Thus the theorizations of arrest and adjudication processes, whether action is characterized as driven by "uncertainty avoidance" (Albonetti, 1987), "focal concerns" (Ulmer, 2012), or "racial threat" (Novak and Chamlin, 2012) remain somewhat speculative. Additionally, despite their increased statistical sophistication, quantitative outcome-based models are unable to include key variables that are either irreducible to quantitative indicators or that are not contained in outcome data sources.

Consequently, large gaps exist in our empirical knowledge about key decision-making stages in the contemporary day-to-day operations of American criminal justice, especially early-stage prosecutorial decision-making on whether and what to charge (and its relationship to police charging), and the less formal plea negotiation process that is central to adjudication in most cases (Engen, 2009). In short, local criminal justice is a key, but understudied and undertheorized, driver in contemporary mass incarceration and corollary expansions of criminal justice sanctioning (Lynch, 2011a). Furthermore, the increased racial inequality among those subject to criminal justice intervention emerged in large part from transformed local processes (Alexander, 2010), yet the mechanisms by which racial subordination occurs within the dispersed and autonomous network of local systems are not fully understood.[2]

More abundant and more varied *empirical* scholarship is called for to address, for instance, how novel policing strategies and front-line practices, especially around drug law enforcement, have developed in ways that widen racial disparities (Beckett, Nyrop, and Pfingst, 2006; Lynch, 2012; Mitchell and Caudy, 2013); how expanded prosecutorial power to control sentence outcomes, which resulted from formal legal changes to sentencing structures, has transformed both charging and plea bargaining (Berman, 2010; Gershman, 1991; Stith, 2008); and how judges have adapted to the changing legal and political landscape (Weiss, 2006), particularly as caseloads have dramatically increased at the same time that judicial sentencing discretion has diminished (Gertner, 2007).

More fundamentally, theoretical explanations of criminal justice proliferation could be enriched by greater attention to the mechanisms by which mass incarceration happened. Most prevailing sociological explanations begin and end with structural-level analytic frames of reference, looking to large-scale institutional transformations for explanations of the American "punitive turn" (Hallsworth, 2000), with less attention to its multifarious actualizations on the ground. Many structural accounts—such as those pointing to the rise of "neo-liberalism" as a correlate to penal change, or those linking penal changes to the emergence of risk logics and technologies—may at once overstate the relationship between criminal justice institutions and broader paradigm shifts and underspecify the mechanisms of mutual influence (see Karstedt, 2010). As a consequence, many theoretical understandings of such change lack a clear and convincing account of both the actors and the actions, writ small, who collectively have driven the punitive expansion of criminal justice that we have witnessed, particularly in the US. If local criminal justice systems (and the criminal justice actors and workgroups that people them) are the hubs that translate and put into motion formal legal change to produce punishment outcomes, there is room for much more precise specification of those system features, contexts, actors, and actions.

In this chapter, I aim to delineate a distinctly social psychological empirical research agenda that centers upon on-the-ground criminal justice operations in the US. I deliberately conceptualize this proposed endeavor as a *social psychology of criminal procedure* in order, first, to directly connect with legal scholarship that addresses how American criminal law is made and put into action (including its constitutional boundaries), and second, to emphasize the process and flow of criminal justice, as propelled by system actors, rather than just the outputs (which are plenty studied). In the next section, I step back from the criminal justice setting to conceptualize the situated actor. I begin with insights from social psychology to develop a more theoretically and empirically grounded model of individuals as nested in organizational contexts. That conceptualization forms the basis for understanding organizational action, which I delineate in the following section by modeling the interdependent and variously influenced flow of decision-making within organizational settings. I conclude by returning to the criminal justice context to suggest an empirical research agenda, in part by delineating what a social psychology of criminal procedure would look like.

The Situated Actor

In many social scientific accounts of the criminal justice system, those who occupy the central operational roles remain undertheorized as social psychological beings. This is partly the product of sociological dominance in the criminological field. In particular, as noted above, macro-sociological research tends toward analyses of structures and institutions, with less concern for individual-level action. On the other hand, a purely individual-level psychological approach to understanding the organizational life that characterizes criminal justice systems discounts the impact of group-level influences (Fine, 2012), as well as the immediate contextual and broader institutional impacts on behavior. The predominant empirical paradigm for (non-clinical) psychologists is the laboratory experiment, typically designed to measure individual-level responses to precisely administered independent variables in a tightly controlled environment. As such, the complex constraining/impelling conditions that characterize bureaucratic organizations, where decisions are rarely autonomously made by individual actors, are not easily replicable in the lab.[3]

The concept of the "situated actor" offers a fruitful starting point by building on micro-level social scientific insights into social behavior. The notion of a situated actor has in some sense evolved as a reaction to the (often implicit) assumption of the rational actor that derives from economics but pervades other disciplines as well. It recognizes that choices for human action are always constrained by immediate context, local culture, and broader structural conditions, so "rationality" is always contingent. "Situated rationality," then, implies that making sense of human decision-making requires an analysis that is context-specific, recognizing the bounds of group norms and values that help create the universe of possibility in a given time and place (Douglas, 1992; Swidler, 1986). Along similar lines, neo-institutional sociologists recognize that embedding analyses within the structural bounds of social institutions, which themselves operate on logics that are not always purely rational or technologically efficient, is a necessary predicate to empirical studies of organizational life (Edelman and Suchman, 1996).

Where anthropology and micro-sociology provide a rich understanding of the cultural norms and values that help construct meaning for actors (see especially Fine, 2012), social psychology has been particularly insightful about the role of immediate contextual factors on the "situated actor." The sub-discipline of social psychology emerged in the early 20th century, partly in response to mainstream psychological theories premised on the idea that personality traits and other dispositional factors accounted for the variety of ways individuals differentially think and act. Those understandings assume within-subject consistency across time and place, as well as between-subject variability as a function of individual differences in those psychological features.

Beginning with Lewin (1936),[4] who first formulated the person-situation dynamic, a long line of research has demonstrated that situational forces often have more explanatory power than dispositional factors on social behavior (Fiske, 2009; Ross & Nisbett, 1991). Classic social psychological studies have demonstrated the power of situational influences in inducing conformity, even when the conformer knows he is agreeing with an incorrect conclusion (Asch, 1956); obedience, even when it appears to involve subjecting others to torture and harm (Milgram, 1965); and bystander assistance (or non-assistance) to strangers needing help (Latane and Darley, 1969). The situationist model is not merely a Skinnerian behaviorism; situational stimuli are assigned an affective valence by the actor, aiding the cognitive interpretation of situational meaning. Central to this construal process are the interrelationships, including positional dynamics, between those involved in a given setting, which will differentially exert influence as a function of those relationships, as will broader cultural norms that dictate appropriate responses to situational stimuli (Reis, 2008).

Building on the basic premise that situations shape individual social behavior through an interpretive process, a long line of social psychology has also examined how group identities generally, and the assignment of roles more particularly, influence thoughts, feelings, judgments, and actions. Early studies demonstrated how intergroup conflict can be overcome by reconfiguring groups and establishing "superordinate" goals that transcend divisions (Aronson, 1978; Sherif, 1958). Conversely, a long line of research demonstrates the ease with which social groups can be manufactured, and outgroup discrimination can be manifested (Abrams & Hogg, 1998; Tajfel, Billig, Bundy & Flament, 1971).

Moreover, the assignment of individuals to institutional roles can have dramatic effects, even in experimental settings. For instance, the assignment of young college men to the roles of either "prisoner" or "guard" in the simulated "Stanford Prison" quickly led to role-based group divisions and extremely dysfunctional and harmful interpersonal and intergroup behavior (Haney, Banks, & Zimbardo, 1973). Psychologically healthy subjects assigned to the guard role became authoritarian, aggressive, unempathetic, and in some instances abusive toward prisoners, while those assigned to the prisoner role became dependent, passive, anxious, and in some cases, dangerously rebellious. The findings "demonstrated the power of situations to overwhelm psychologically normal, healthy people and to elicit from them unexpectedly cruel, yet situationally appropriate behavior" (Haney & Zimbardo, 1998, 719). Findings such as these do not deny that individuals bring different psychological and experiential constitutions to a given situation; rather, they foreground how situational triggers work to impel or impede action. As such, social psychology offers a theoretical and empirical bridge between a more individualistic psychology and a structural sociology that could be better exploited in examinations of criminal justice organizational operations.

Organizational Action: Triggers and Restraints

Social psychology has amply demonstrated that social contexts, and the assignment of people to different roles or groups within them, can both push and pull behavior in a manner not predicted by either "rational actor" or personality-driven theories. Nonetheless, with few exceptions (e.g., Haney, Banks, & Zimbardo, 1973; Pager, 2003, in an employment context), the empirical testing of situational effects using an experimental paradigm have focused more on interpersonal situational contexts, without fully grappling with how more formalized institutional structures, roles, and/or parameters directly impinge on or catalyze behavior. The social contexts of complex, bureaucratic organizations, like those that comprise criminal justice systems, contain multiple push and pull factors that shape organizational action. So while both social psychology and micro-sociology can help deconstruct the relationship between the environmental factors (structures, rules, norms, delineated roles) of social organizations and organizational actors' cognitive, affective, and behavioral expressions, there is room to more fully flesh out the multiple levels of influence on decision-making.

The trick with empirical scholarship on organizational life (as is required for studies of criminal justice operations) is to design research with some precision without completely losing sight of that complex interrelationship between levels of influence. To that end, neither a purely psychological approach (which would isolate analyses to the actors, individually or in relation to each other) nor a purely macro-sociological one (which would focus on larger structural forces and paradigmatic understandings about how the world works) can adequately account for the flow of organizational action.

Gary Alan Fine's explication of the small group, or "tiny public," provides an excellent starting point for unpacking organizational life. As Fine has forcefully demonstrated, social interactions within small group settings function as the critical link between the individual and social structure, producing localized "sedimented understandings" (Fine, 2012, 160) that are based on shared histories, and that serve as lenses of a sort for interpretation and action in any given situation. This model takes history seriously, thereby accounting for continuity in social organization over time, as well as allowing for isomorphic adaptation and change: "By building shared pasts and prospective futures, group culture creates an ongoing social order" (Fine, 2012, 163).

Applying Fine's micro-sociological small group analysis to the more complex arena of organizations, like those that comprise the criminal system, requires attention to several additional elements, as delineated in Figure 9.1, below. This illustrates a full, although not necessarily complete, account of how organizations behave and action is produced. While this illustration models levels of influence as causal forces on action, in the long haul, these really are mutually constitutive, interactive processes, in that organizational action itself shapes and reinforces individual, group, and structural processes. This process not only inculcates the "idioculture" of the organization—the "system of knowledge, beliefs, behaviors, and customs" (Fine, 2012, 36) shared by organizational actors—but also radiates upward and outward as a critical source of social structure.

Moreover, while my account is reminiscent of a Mertonian model of social systems, and owes much to the models put forth by neo-institutional sociologists, it can be distinguished from those approaches in that it better integrates social psychological understandings of the individual in social contexts, and treats organizational actors and intra-organizational actor units as (variable) engines of actions rather than as predictable cogs in the organizational machine. To do so moves beyond the classic conception of the actor as a sum of his psychic makeup who reacts to environmental pressures accordingly (Gerth and Mills, 1954; Merton, 1968). It also moves beyond the traditional sociological dichotomy of organizational actors as either rational beings whose actions are taken to maximize benefits and minimize costs *or* as normative, moral beings who are guided by notions of right and wrong (Edelman and Suchman, 1996)—without reducing the actors to automatons operating without conscious motives or affective responses, who are merely actors "as constituted by institutions" (DiMaggio & Powell, 1991, 12).

The "social structures and paradigms" in this model are comprised of those large institutional features of society that generally persist over significant periods of time, and that may cross sovereign boundaries. This is in part the substance of macro-sociology: the political, economic, communal, and cultural ideological paradigms, institutional arrangements, and structures that form the large social systems in which given societies operate, and the "habitus" that organizes our understanding of the world (Mouzelis, 2000; Bourdieu, 1969). For the purposes of this empirical model, these form a backdrop for framing the other elements, rather than the objects to be directly studied.[5]

The "organizational motives, rules, norms, formal roles, and relationships" in this model comprise the organizational context by defining, both inwardly and outwardly, what the entity is and what it is supposed to do. It further defines the rules and responsibilities that guide the organization's functioning, by translating laws into policies, delineating decision-making protocols, assigning roles and responsibilities to actors, and defining the relationships between roles (including hierarchical arrangements), as well as with the public and/or clientele

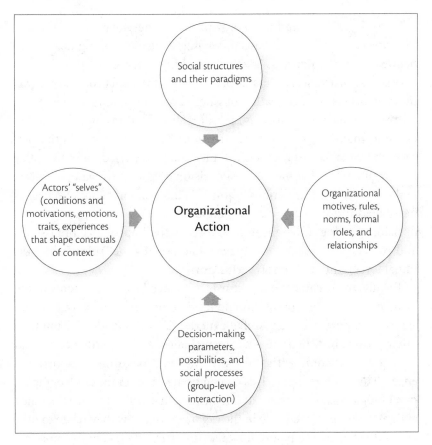

Figure 9.1. Extra- and intra-organizational influences on action

and other organizations. Less formally, the organization imbues norms of operation that are not necessarily inscribed anywhere but that nonetheless get transmitted and acted upon as actors enter and assimilate into the organization (in the criminal court context, see Heumann, 1977). This component might be likened to the "field," at least as conceptualized by Martin (2011), in that it embodies those forces that create the potentiality for action by comprising the *raison d'être* for the organizational existence and the tools and rules for achieving it. This level of influence must be fully fleshed out and empirically investigated in order to construct a comprehensive account of the universe of possibility in the setting.

The triggers of action in an organization generally reside in the formal rules and informal norms governing decision-making discretion, delineated in the figure as "decision-making parameters, possibilities, and social processes." Thus, a prerequisite for explaining organizational action is the delineation of where decision-making power exists (both formally and informally) for all relevant actions; who holds that decision-making power, and whether it is dispersed across multiple actors (and whether group-based or individually exercised) both by policy and by practice; what the range of decision options are (again, both formally and informally defined); how this intra-organizational power is negotiated and shared by distinct actors; and the consequences for rogue decision-making. Inherent in this, then, is the importance of position and role, as well as relations between actors, distinct roles, organizational levels, and divisions (Martin, 2011).

Finally, the organizational actor is influenced by the elements of the "self," comprised of "cognitions and motivations, emotions, traits, experiences." Importantly, part of that experiential self includes the multiple other groups in which the actor participates, and the knowledges and identities that come with those previous and ongoing group experiences. Thus, actors themselves can be fleshed out on those ideographic psychological and experiential dimensions that will influence how they assign meaning to their role in the organization, how they relate to others in the organization, and how they interpret their range of possible actions in that setting. The degree to which these individual level factors influence outcomes will be tempered by the organizational constraints, role constraints, interrelationships, and immediate situational pressures, determined partly by specific factors such as organizational complexity, relative autonomy and individuation of decision-making roles, and consequences for outcomes, both favorable and unfavorable. Individual-level selves will also be shaped by the ongoing experience of being embedded in the organization, so the distinction between role demands and internalized identities will tend to blur over time and as actors deepen their engagement in the setting.

A number of empirical possibilities can be generated by thinking through how contextualized action happens as a function of these organizational elements. For instance, there is a dynamic relationship between the decision-making conditions afforded a given actor and the degree of variation in decision outcomes. To the extent that actors' autonomy is constrained by diffused or hierarchical decision-making mechanisms, and to the extent that decision-makers must act publicly and/or are held directly accountable for their decisions, individual variation (across time and decision-makers) should be expected to be minimized. Conversely, where decision-makers are afforded individual decision-making autonomy, under private and less accountable conditions, individual actors' influence of "self" should be more apparent and the "rules" of decision-making less predictive of outcomes. Finally, to the extent that the organizational rules, norms, and role assignments create group divisions (particularly in people-processing organizations like criminal courts) and depersonalize the consequences of action, we should expect the development of out-group derogation. This can be both intra-organizational among different strata of roles, as well as between organizational actors and those served by (or subjected to) the organization.

What Would a Social Psychology of Criminal Procedure Look Like?

A social psychology of criminal procedure has two mandates, one conceptual and the other methodological. Conceptually, the questions we ask about criminal justice and especially about its effects require that the actors themselves, particularly as embodied in their roles, play a central role in empirical inquiries as variable and complex drivers of institutional behavior. There are at least three categories of inquiry that are ripe for development in a social psychology of criminal procedure that begin with the actors as agents. The first interrogates the process by which formal legal changes get translated into organizational imperatives within local criminal justice settings. How do differently situated actors come to understand policy (and policy changes) and role parameters, and then act on them? Flowing from that, how do the informal processes (discretionary arrests, charging, plea negotiations, etc.) that drive the bulk of case outcomes actually come to be transformed by larger level changes? How do conflicts between "the-way-things-are-done" in any given setting and new mandates that seek to change those practices get resolved? What role do unequal power dynamics among various courtroom participants play in patterns of outcomes?

Second, it is important to examine how the form and substance of criminal matters are conceptualized and acted upon. How do criminal justice actors understand and strategize around the material corpus of criminal cases, such as evidence, "facts," "specific offense characteristics," and defendant features? What narratives are formed by different actors based on this corpus? For instance, while the notion of typical cases and corresponding going rates seem to drive how many criminal matters are resolved even under the same state penal code (Nardulli, Eisenstein, and Flemming, 1988), the corresponding value for a given typical case can vary widely from county to county. Those going rate values have also become much more punitive for some categories of offenses over time, suggesting a need for more direct inquiries asking how group-level understandings of case seriousness are constructed and negotiated over time and across place.

Relatedly, given the expansive growth in criminal cases and the corresponding formal and informal pressures against individualization of defendants, there is a need to examine how, when, and where exceptions to outcome norms happen. How is empathy expressed or constrained by rules, policies, and actors' role demands, particularly under sentencing models that discourage individualization? Who is deemed worthy of empathy and under what conditions, and how does that get transformed into leniency in outcomes? Conversely, when and how do particular cases become exceptionally demonized, and what are the features of those cases in different places, for differently situated actors, and/or at different points in time?

Third, a social psychology of criminal procedure must engage in empirically sophisticated examinations of the reproduction of racial, gender, and class-based inequality and injustice within criminal justice institutions. How are "unwarranted sentence disparities" (Mauer, 2007), especially race- and ethnicity-based inequalities, produced in criminal case contexts? To what extent do societal-level racial ideologies and paradigms shape the organizational context, especially as they enter via criminal justice actors? Alternatively or additionally, are racially biased outcomes in criminal justice produced by ostensibly non-racial organizational policies and practices? In what ways do group identities come to matter in criminal justice systems, particularly in the potential dual derogation presented by the intersection of racial, ethnic, or class bias and criminal othering? Here, we can endeavor to capture the subtle ways that status characteristics of defendants and victims get constructed into case narratives and, ultimately, action. We might also think through how changing role definitions and group memberships/parameters might mitigate racial harms that are the consequence of criminal justice intervention.

Flowing from this set of conceptual imperatives is the question of methodology and what methods are best suited to answer questions about process and action in the criminal system. Studies that specify given outcomes (arrests, convictions, sentences) as dependent variables, then model a series of predictor variables in order to explain them, are unquestionably valuable for certain research questions, but as noted above, they cannot directly provide causal explanations of how social and institutional action happens (see Martin, 2011, for a complex and engaging treatment of this issue). Rather, researchers are left making inferences about the relationships between variables through the elimination of alternative possibilities, often based on theoretical propositions of how such relations are expected to work. Moreover, because such models typically do not directly measure organizational actors' cognitions or behavior, the underlying (often unstated) theory of human behavior is frequently woefully underspecified and overly dependent upon problematic assumptions about why people act as they do.

The methodological gold standard for testing causal relationships, at least in psychology—the experiment—has the potential to be more fully exploited, but the prototypical social psychological experiment of today is situationally and contextually impoverished in its specification of independent variables (i.e., causes) and dependent measures (effects). The most common design usually relies on text or computer-administered stimulus materials, and then measures cognitions rather than behavior to assess the effects of those stimuli. While the current orthodoxy resists alternatives to the lab experiment (Fine & Elsbach, 2000; see also Gergen, 1978; Gergen, 2013), a methodologically robust social psychology of criminal procedure requires a rethinking of how research questions are best answered. This might start by revisiting the discipline's classic and enduring studies, some referenced above, which employed both naturalistic and experimental field methodologies to generate insights (see also Pager, 2007). It also might borrow from other disciplines that aim to explain social behavior through ethnographic field methodologies that more fully articulate the meso-level influences on action. There has been, in the past, a strong tradition in political science and sociology of ethnographies of policing (Herbert, 1996; Lyons, 2002; Manning; 1977; Skolnick, 1966) and criminal courts (Eisenstein, Flemming and Nardulli, 1988; Emmelmann, 1996; Feeley, 1979; Frohmann, 1997; Heumann, 1977; Jacob, 1965; McCoy, 1993), but much less work of this kind has been generated since mass incarceration became full-blown.

Fine and Elsbach (2000, 52) delineate a very useful set of strategies to improve empirical theory-building specific to social psychology, particularly in "interaction domains," which are "collective realities whose meanings develop from the contexts in which they are embedded. They cannot exist without shared understandings and collective meanings, and they cannot be evaluated without data that reflect their dynamic and interactive nature." First, Fine and Elsbach recommend that no single method should ever be seen as capable of doing all the work necessary to generate overarching explanations of any given phenomenon, instead advocating for a multi-methodological approach that relies upon naturalistic, ethnographic data for induction, then experimental data for deduction. They flesh out their protocol by highlighting how researchers can use qualitative interviews to generate hypotheses, employ comparative case studies in naturalistic settings to test hypotheses, and then design more situationally rich, interactional lab studies that repeat conditions but allow for spontaneous and layered responses among participants. We can liken criminal justice organizations to relatively complex "interaction domains" and apply Fine and Elsbach's suggestions to generate multi-methodological, contextually embedded programs of research.

A Concrete Example of the Social Psychology of Criminal Procedure

In order to illustrate, specifically, how the various levels of explanation can help us understand the mechanisms by which local systems contributed to the widening reach of criminal justice in the late 20th century, I offer one small example derived from some previous policy-oriented work I did on a problem of racially selective drug law enforcement and prosecution in Cleveland, Ohio (Lynch, 2011b). I will very briefly describe the research problem, as it were, and then propose a series of empirical research questions that flow from it, followed by a brief analysis of the organizational action revealed here to illustrate the social psychological processes at work.

Beginning in the mid-1980s, in the midst of a national crack cocaine panic, the Cleveland city police department initiated a policy of arresting those in possession of drug paraphernalia for felony drug possession if trace amounts of the drug were detectable on the drug instruments. These cases, initially charged as felonies by law enforcement, were almost always then processed through the local city prosecutor's office (which handles misdemeanors) straight to the Cuyahoga County district attorney's office for felony indictment. The county district attorney's office then routinely sought indictments from the Grand Jury and prosecuted the cases as felonies. The vast majority of these cases settled quickly with negotiated guilty pleas, resulting in felony records for those so convicted. This enhanced police and prosecutorial charging policy placed the city of Cleveland out of step with the rest of the local jurisdictions in Cuyahoga County, as well as with localities across the state of Ohio, since all the other jurisdictions treated these kinds of drug paraphernalia cases as misdemeanors.

During the two and a half decades in which this policy was practiced, those subject to felony charges in drug paraphernalia cases were primarily those in possession of crack cocaine pipes rather than other kinds of paraphernalia, and the majority of those arrested for felony drug possession when they were found only with drug instruments were Black. City officials estimated that during its course of enforcement, each year this policy generated about 1,200–1,500 felony defendants who would not have been had the policy not existed. The practice thus dramatically increased the overall number of felony drug cases in Cuyahoga County's Court of Common Pleas and increased the racial skew of defendants in that court, since suspected drug users who were Black were dramatically overrepresented in the felony drug possession arrests (Lynch, 2011b).

The racial and geographic bias that undergirded this policy was clearly identified as a justice problem for local criminal justice and political actors by early 2002, but there was considerable resistance by police and prosecutors to any calls for reform until finally, almost seven years later, the Cleveland mayor intervened and ordered the police to discontinue the practice. The first major challenge to this policy came in the form of a Grand Jury report submitted to the presiding judge of the Cuyahoga County Court of Common Pleas, in which the foreperson raised concerns about the degree to which those charged in such low-level offenses were minorities while the system actors all tended to be White, suggesting there was "an Apartheid feel" to the indictment process in the low-level drug felony cases. The foreperson also released the report to the local newspaper, the *Plain Dealer*, which ran a news story about the issue, followed by a set of editorials critical of the racially disproportionate impact of the "war on drugs" both nationally and in Cuyahoga County specifically.

Over the next four years, there were several other well-publicized confrontations about the policy within the Court of Common Pleas, leading in one case to an explosive conflict between a sitting judge, who was critical of the policy and made that clear in his instructions to the Grand Jury, and the county district attorney. That incident not only generated considerable media coverage but ultimately involved the state Supreme Court, which litigated a challenge by the district attorney against the judge's "biased . . . judicial activism" in instructing the Grand Jury about the geographic disparities underlying the charging policy. Despite the explicit set of concerns expressed—even by powerfully situated members of the criminal justice system—about the geographically and racially disparate impact of the policy, the police and the county prosecutor continued the arrest and charging practices unabated. In late 2008, under pressure from a broad coalition of individuals and groups in the city, the Cleveland mayor announced that he would direct the chief of police to change the policy. In March 2009, the city officially dropped the felony drug paraphernalia arrest policy, and the Cleveland police chief ordered officers to charge such cases as misdemeanors under the Cleveland municipal code (see Crocker, 2004, and Lynch, 2011b, for more details about this episode). This change was formally mandated by way of a divisional notice issued by the police chief and adopted into the policies and procedures governing Cleveland officers.

This sustained incident has many features that have surfaced in criminal justice systems around the nation during the rise of mass incarceration. Among these common features are the targeting of crack cocaine–related offenses for disproportionally harsh treatment, the kind of geographic law enforcement focus in particular "problem" areas (in this case, it was not only within the city limits, but in the poorer Black-majority neighborhoods within the city), the important role that drug cases played in the increase in felony caseloads, and the systemic denial of the racial effect of such practices. As such, it is exemplary of one prominent mode by which criminal justice expansion occurred.

How might a social psychology of criminal procedure be deployed to unpack the underlying practices described above? Among the research questions that might be posed are: How did the drug paraphernalia felony arrest policy get conceived of, enacted, and routinized in this single jurisdiction, and why in practice were crack pipes the primary felony-generating paraphernalia? Why did prosecutors in both the city and county take action to ratify these arrests as felony charges? Why was the practice so resistant to change even after its racially disparate impacts were made clear to system actors? What changed to allow for remedial reform in the late 2000s?

The first question, as to how the policy came to be and was put into action, requires a close, partly retrospective empirical examination of the police, both management and line officers, to uncover the motivations and triggers for the expansive interpretation of the Ohio penal code needed to generate the paraphernalia felony arrests. Primary documents might be mined for insights about why the Cleveland police innovated as they did. And indeed, one motivational trigger becomes clear from turning to such documents, namely, that the police union collective bargaining agreement with the city provides for substantial overtime pay for officers who are called to court when not on duty. This incentive is part of the "collars for dollars" motivation (Levine and Small, 2008) that is particularly prevalent in drug arrests, since they are much more likely to be proactively produced than are other felonies. In this jurisdiction, the felony charge in particular ensures "court time" overtime pay, since felonies are subject to Grand Jury indictment, prosecutors typically call arresting officers to court to be ready to testify, and most such officers are not on regular duty when these proceedings are in session. As a result, these officers are guaranteed three to four hours of time-and-a-half overtime pay (depending on their shift time), even if their testimony lasts only minutes.

Moreover, the "crack pipe" felony arrests apparently were particularly easy to make. As one critical Grand Jury foreperson (who was a retired municipal court judge from Cleveland's municipal court) put it in her 2006 report, "I got the impression that in many cases police go out and essentially 'shot fish in a barrel.' They know the so called 'high drug areas' so they go to the locations, pick up a couple of crack users, arrest them, get an indictment and conviction, get some overtime, keep the crime statistics up and repeat the same cycle" (Connally, 2006, 11). In short, the foreperson asserts a two-part causal hypothesis that is social psychological at its core: (a) Jurisdiction-specific monetary incentives prompt patrol officers to make low-level drug arrests; and (b) crack users in geographically targeted neighborhoods are sought out for arrests due to the ease with which those arrests can be made. Thus, an explanation of the front end of the process calls for an empirical focus on the relationship between the organizational parameters, especially the rules and norms that govern both police compensation and arrest discretion, and the context-specific decision-making parameters and possibilities in which officers operate in their daily jobs.

Further empirical examination might deploy comparative field observations and interviews of front-line police to develop an account of how they conceive of their daily work and its imperatives, specifically in relation to making drug arrests, within otherwise-comparable agencies either with or without direct financial incentives to make such low-level felony arrests. Experimental research could specifically isolate this hypothesized relationship through the use of analogical contexts and could examine whether and how the process of imposing harm for personal gain is psychologically reckoned with by those who do so. A long line of social psychology, from cognitive dissonance theory to attribution theory, might be deployed to uncover how such action is justified and rendered appropriate.

The foreperson's observations also implicate the second and third research questions I posed, which concern why a racially discriminatory practice like this could take hold, be spread throughout the system by distinct organizational actors, and prove so resistant to change. This problem is directly tied to intergroup dynamics and the relationship dynamics between different roles within the system. First, those putting the policy into practice likely relied upon the derogation of those targeted for arrest and prosecution in order to justify and/or deny the significance of its consequences. In this case, the police proactively targeted a cumulatively derogated population—poor, Black, crack users—and implemented this practice in the 1980s, a time when crack cocaine use was especially demonized. The inflow of such defendants into the courts then functionally reinforced racial stereotypes about both criminality and the prototypical crack abuser, which was signaled in this particu-lar case by the presiding judge's dismissal of concerns about underly-ing racial bias. Thus, when the issue of racial disparate impact was first raised by the Grand Jury foreperson in 2002, the presiding judge told the reporter covering the story that "because of the social and economic aspects of life . . . minorities are committing more crimes," as he brushed off charges that the system might be biased (Naymik, 2002, B2).

Moreover, there is evidence that both the presiding judge and the prosecutor responded, at least publicly, to the various challenges to this practice through a narrowly drawn lens of their particular occupational roles, which served to delegitimize the charges of bias. The prosecu-tor dismissed the arguments that such cases should not be brought as felonies by referencing only his role as a prosecutor, suggesting he need not make an excuse for "presenting crimes that meet standards of prob-able cause" (Naymik, 2002, B2). Similarly, the presiding judge viewed the problem with these low-level felony cases only as one that affected his organization's efficiency. Thus, he voiced to the reporter the court's sentiment that "[w]e wish [the prosecutor's office] would reduce some of them to misdemeanors to lighten our load" (Naymik, 2002, B2), signal-ing how his position in the system dictated this analytic frame. Using the lens of each of their organizational roles, these actors implicitly denied a place for empathic consideration of the harms caused by the policy. Rather than focusing on internal, individual-level explanatory causes such as implicit bias (which has become a dominant perspective in psychology), fruitful empirical examinations might build on the group process ethnographic approach (Fine, 2012) to unpack how meaning-making occurs for differently situated actors in the varied contexts of local criminal courts.

We can also see the momentum that occurred as arrested persons were institutionalized as "cases"—once they enter the system, even if primarily as the result of shooting-fish-in-a-barrel law enforcement, the actors at court subsequently propelled them forward through the court process by viewing them through a narrow organizational lens as mere cases to be processed. Indeed, the kinds of questions asked to initiate prosecutions—Can I get a Grand Jury to indict? How can we process and dispose of these cases efficiently?—not only lose sight of the fairness and justice ideals, but can and often do contravene them (see Natapoff, this volume). Again, with the backdrop of a paradigmatic "war on drugs" ideology that was especially pervasive regarding crack at the time this policy was instigated, once such cases were made a reality—as normative fodder for the criminal justice machinery—organizational forces across the different arms of the system kept the cases moving in a flow that was difficult to impede. In order to effectively document and assess how these patterns develop, empirical examinations might focus on uncovering how the specific features and parameters of different organizational roles shape the construal process of who criminal defendants are and what constitutes a prosecution-worthy case. This would constitute a first step to explaining the persistence of the crack pipe felony prosecutions even in the face of highly publicized and vigorous challenges to them.

The process of reform in this case is also explainable through the multilevel social psychological framework I have proposed. In this case, the coalition that spurred remedial action by the mayor used several strategies that were able to overcome the out-group derogation upon which the practice relied, and thereby combatted the racial blindness that characterized the systemic resistance. First, in written and spoken communications, the group (and its representatives) redefined the out-group members—the criminal defendants charged with drug possession felonies—as part of an "us" of the community, including whole families who were economically harmed by the policy since felony convictions are so detrimental to obtaining employment. The coalition's name, Citizens for a Safe and Fair Cleveland, also did some of the work to reconstitute group boundaries by defining itself as representative of the city as a whole. It made compatible two noble values—public safety and fairness under law—that are implicitly treated as incompatible by law enforcement policies that rely upon racial profiling or stereotyping. Thus the group projected an aspirational mission that was inclusive and reflective of positive justice values (Lynch, 2011b).

The group also communicated a cooperative agenda that took as a given the realities of the racially disparate impact of the policy, suggesting that it "look[ed] forward to continu[ing] to work with city and county officials towards finding a resolution that will be equal to all and keep our streets safe" (Citizens for a Safe and Fair Cleveland, 2008). As such, it endeavored to partner with those responsible for the policy to achieve the super-ordinate goal of fairness and safety for the community. Finally, the group composition itself implicitly spoke for Cleveland as a diverse but united community that was also inclusive of those directly harmed by the policy, in that it was a racially and socio-economically diverse group reflecting the demographics of the city. It included several prominent, well-respected community leaders, who added to the power and diversity of the group, and whose participation in a well-attended and well-publicized town hall meeting that the coalition organized helped catalyze a rising chorus in several press outlets that the policy had to change. As noted above, that change came from the mayor's office, which had the power to stop the flow into the system by ordering the police chief to establish and implement the new policy. While the county district attorney never reformed, the mayor's action had a pro-phylactic effect on his charging behavior by shutting down the pipeline of "crack pipe" cases to his office.

This intervention suggests underlying mechanisms that may be pin-pointed through experimental research, building on existing group paradigm work on inclusiveness (i.e., Levine, Prosser, Evans & Reicher, 2005) by manipulating group definitions to test for their influence on policy preferences and commitments. It also suggests an opening for examining the role of group-level emotion in inclusion and exclusion (see Lynch, 2011b, for a fuller discussion of this).

Conclusion: Why This Agenda?

From an intellectual standpoint, the overemphasis in empirical research on formal sentencing outcomes, decontextualized from the more mundane norms of case processing, leaves us with an inaccurate under-standing of the criminal justice transformations we have experienced over the last several decades. Moreover, due to sociology's dominance in the field of criminology, the empirical account of criminal justice actors is thin and imprecise. As I suggest here, a full understanding of crimi-nal justice practices requires fleshing out those fundamental human processes as they are shaped by the specific conditions that comprise the constituent organizations as complex social spaces.

More pragmatically, in order to mitigate the high costs exacted by our contemporary criminal justice system, it is critical that we identify the contributory processes as they occur on the ground. We can begin to develop empirically grounded and smaller-scale policy interventions that can help as jurisdictions struggle to address the unsustainable fiscal and human costs wrought by mass incarceration and corollary criminal justice expansion (see Lynch, 2011a, for a discussion of what these might look like). Given that we know that formal legal change is always transformed and sometimes subverted when put into practice, focusing only on statutory change at the state and/or federal level will likely not provide adequate remediation. Rather, any rollback efforts will have to include a diffuse network of localized strategies to intervene on triggers of action within individual organizations in order to be sustainable. To do so, academic scholars need to forge productive partnerships with both social change activists and criminal justice practitioners to make their work externally valid, policy-relevant, and—ideally—deployable in reform mobilization efforts.

I have advocated for a research agenda that, while rigorous, emphasizes smaller, highly contextualized examinations as the appropriate approach to address many unanswered questions about how the criminal system operates, proliferates, and produces injustice. While it is clear that the most important triggers of punitive criminal justice can only be sufficiently studied using this kind of methodological approach, it also poses two significant challenges. The first is the problem of access. The empirical answers that we generate about the causes and consequences of mass incarceration and punitive criminal justice are to a substantial degree shaped by data availability. Thus, to the extent that outcome data are becoming more accessible in a period when direct institutional access (at least to outside researchers) has become much more limited, it is more difficult than ever to launch a full version of the program of research recommended here. In particular, it is widely understood that changes to the prosecutorial role (and the accretion of power in that role) are substantially responsible for the expanding numbers of people criminal justice controls (Pfaff, 2011), but the empirical understanding of how that changing role is realized in practice is nearly nonexistent.

The second challenge that confronts us has to do with how empirical scholarship is understood and utilized in the legal and policy worlds. Even if we are able to gain the kind of access needed to study decision-making processes in the manner I have suggested, such findings may be marginalized outside of academic settings. The form, rather than the substance, of social science research often plays an important role in its ability to impact policy-makers, such that quantitative research, particularly of the kind that relies upon official forms of aggregated outcome data, is privileged. Changing conceptions in the policy and legal realms of what rigorous research looks like, to include studies comprised of naturalistic qualitative field data and experimental simulations of real-world conditions, may become more difficult than ever as quantitative modeling techniques grow more sophisticated and dazzling.

NOTES

1 As such, it is also overly concerned with the very harshest manifestations of contemporary penal practices, ignoring the more pervasive and perhaps equally harmful ways that criminal justice has been transformed for those accused and convicted of very-low-level offenses (Natapoff, 2012; Beckett and Herbert, 2009; Harris, Evans, and Beckett, 2011).

2 There does exist a large, somewhat cohesive body of quantitative work, especially within criminology, that examines "unwarranted disparity" in criminal justice outcomes (Engen, 2009), but this kind of research necessarily although sometimes problematically homogenizes key variables across time and place (Lynch, 2011a). It also does not lend itself to directly explaining the processes by which race and ethnicity, gender, and class come to matter in arrests, charging, and adjudication (Ulmer, 2012).

3 This partly explains why psychology and law scholarship relevant to criminal justice is so fractured, with a proliferation of work on laypersons' more limited roles in criminal justice in the form of simulated juror studies, experimental work on eyewitness identification issues, and studies examining interrogation effects, but a relative dearth of research on the more common, day-to-day practices of organizational actors such as discretionary arrest decision-making, prosecutorial charging, and plea negotiations.

4 As Martin (2003) points out, Lewin is one of social science's first field theorists. As such, his articulation of the actor-environment has conceptual overlaps with, and was influential on, the more widely known and cited sociological versions of field theory.

5 Just as I carve out a space for this level of analysis, so should macro-sociologists attend to the on-the-ground realizations of paradigm shifts in order to make convincing claims (see Mouzelis, 2000).

REFERENCES

Abrams, D., & Hogg, M. A. (1998). Prospects for research in group processes and intergroup relations. *Group Processes and Intergroup Relations, 1*, 7–20.

Albonetti, C. (1987). Prosecutorial discretion: The effects of uncertainty. *Law and Society Review, 21*, 291–313.

Alexander, M. (2010). *The new Jim Crow: Mass incarceration in the age of colorblindness.* New York: New Press.

Aronson, E. (1978). *The jigsaw classroom.* Thousand Oaks, CA: SAGE Publications.

Asch, S. E. (1956). Studies of independence and conformity: I. A minority of one against a unanimous majority. *Psychological Monographs: General and Applied, 70*(9), 1–70.

Beckett, K., & Herbert, S. (2009). *Banished: The new social control in urban America.* New York: Oxford University Press.

Beckett, K., & Murakawa, N. (2012). Mapping the shadow carceral state: Toward an institutionally capacious approach to punishment. *Theoretical Criminology, 16*, 221–244.

Beckett, K., Nyrop, K., & Pfingst, L. (2006). Race, drugs and policing: Understanding disparities in drug delivery arrests. *Criminology, 44*, 105–138.

Berman, D. (2010). Afternoon keynote address: Encouraging (and even requiring) prosecutors to be second-look sentencers. *Temple Political and Civil Rights Law Review, 19*, 249–441.

Bourdieu, P. (1969). Intellectual field and creative project. *Social Science Information, 8*, 189–219.

Citizens for a Safe and Fair Cleveland (2008). *Study Shows African Americans More Likely to be Charged with Drug Felonies.* Retrieved from www.safefaircleveland.org.

Connally, C. E. (2006). *Grand Jury Report, April 26, 2006.* Retrieved from www. safefaircleveland.org.

Crocker, P. (2004). Appointed but (nearly) prevented from serving: My experiences as a Grand Jury foreperson. *Ohio State Journal of Criminal Law, 2*, 289–302.

DiMaggio, P. J., & Powell, W. W. (1991). Introduction. In W. W. Powell & P. J. DiMaggio, eds., *The new institutionalism in organizational analysis.* Chicago: University of Chicago Press.

Douglas, M. (1992). *Risk and blame: Essays in cultural theory.* London: Routledge.

Edelman, L., & Suchman, M. (1996). Legal rational myths: The new institutionalism and the law and society tradition. *Law and Social Inquiry, 21*, 903–941.

Eisenstein, J., Flemming, R., & Nardulli, P. (1988). *The contours of justice: Communities and their courts.* Boston: Little, Brown.

Emmelman, D. (1996). Trial by plea bargain: Case settlement as a process of recursive decisionmaking. *Law and Society Review, 30*, 335–360.

Engen, R. (2009). Assessing determinate and presumptive sentencing—making research relevant. *Criminology and Public Policy, 8*, 323–336.

Feeley, M. (1979). *The process is the punishment: Handling cases in a lower criminal court.* New York: Russell Sage.

Fine, G. A. (2012). *Tiny publics*. New York: Russell Sage.

Fine, G. A., & Elsbach, K. D. (2000). Ethnography and experiment in social psychological theory building: Tactics for integrating qualitative field data with quantitative lab data. *Journal of Experimental Social Psychology, 36,* 51–76.

Fiske, S.T. (2009). *Social beings: Core motives in social psychology*. New York: Wiley.

Frohmann, L. (1997). Convictability and discordant locales: Reproducing race, class, and gender ideologies in prosecutorial decisionmaking. *Law and Society Review, 31,* 531–556.

Gergen, K. J. (1978). Toward generative theory. *Journal of Personality and Social Psychology, 36,* 1344–1360.

Gergen, K. J. (2013). Qualitative inquiry and the challenge of scientific status. In N. K. Denzin & M. D. Giardina, eds., *Global dimensions of qualitative inquiry,* 29–45. Walnut Creek, CA: Left Coast Press.

Gershman, B. (1991). The new prosecutors. *University of Pittsburgh Law Review, 53,* 393–458.

Gerth, H. H., & Mills, C. W. (1954). *Character and social structure: The psychology of social institutions*. New York: Taylor & Francis.

Gertner, N. (2007). From omnipotence to impotence: American judges and sentencing. *Ohio State Journal of Criminal Law, 4,* 523–539.

Hallsworth, S. (2000). Rethinking the punitive turn: Economies of excess and the criminology of the other. *Punishment and Society, 2,* 145–160.

Haney, C., Banks, C., & Zimbardo, P. (1973). Interpersonal dynamics in a simulated prison. *International Journal of Criminology and Penology, 1,* 69–97.

Haney, C., & Zimbardo, P. (1998). The past and future of U.S. prison policy: Twenty-five years after the Stanford Prison Experiment. *American Psychologist, 53,* 709–727.

Harris, A., Evans, H., & Beckett, K. 2010. Drawing blood from stones: Legal debt and social inequality in the contemporary United States. *American Journal of Sociology, 115,* 1753–1799.

Herbert, S. (1996). *Policing space: Territoriality and the Los Angeles Police Department*. Minneapolis: University of Minnesota Press.

Heumann, M. (1977). *Plea bargaining: The experiences of prosecutors, judges, and defense attorneys*. Chicago: University of Chicago Press.

Jacob, H. (1965). *Justice in America: Courts, lawyers and the judicial process*. Boston: Little, Brown.

Karstedt, S. (2010). New institutionalism in criminology: Approaches, theories and themes. In E. McLaughlin & T. Newburn, eds., *The SAGE Handbook of Criminological Theory,* 337–359. Thousand Oaks, CA: SAGE Publications.

Latane, B., & Darley, J. M. (1969). Bystander apathy. *American Scientist, 57,* 244–268.

Lewin, K. (1936). *Principles of Topological Psychology*. New York: McGraw-Hill.

Levine, M., Prosser, A., Evans, D., & Reicher, S. (2005). Identity and emergency intervention: How social group membership and inclusiveness of group boundaries shape helping behavior. *Personality and Social Psychology Bulletin, 31*(4), 443–453.

Levine, H. G., & Small, D. P. (2008). *Marijuana arrest crusade: Racial bias and police policy in New York City, 1997–2007.* New York: New York Civil Liberties Union.

Lynch, M. (2011a). Mass incarceration, legal change and locale: Understanding and remediating American penal overindulgence. *Criminology and Public Policy, 10,* 671–698.

Lynch, M. (2011b). Crack pipes and policing: A case study of institutional racism and remedial action in Cleveland. *Law & Policy, 33,* 179–214.

Lynch, M. (2012). Theorizing the role of the "war on drugs" in US punishment. *Theoretical Criminology, 16,* 175–199.

Lyons, W. (2002). *The politics of community policing: Rearranging the power to punish.* Ann Arbor: University of Michigan Press.

Manning, P. K. (1977). *Police work: The social organization of policing.* Cambridge, MA: MIT Press.

Martin, J. L. (2003). What is field theory? *American Journal of Sociology, 109,* 1–49.

Martin, J. L. (2011). *The explanation of social action.* New York: Oxford University Press.

Mauer, M. (2007). Racial impact statements as a means of reducing unwarranted sentencing disparities. *Ohio State Journal of Criminal Law, 5,* 19–46.

McCoy, C. (1993). *Politics and plea bargaining: Victims' rights in California.* Philadelphia: University of Pennsylvania Press.

Merton, R. (1968). *Social Theory and Social Structure,* 2nd ed. New York: Free Press.

Milgram, S. (1965). Some conditions of obedience and disobedience to authority. *Human Relations, 18,* 57–76.

Mitchell, O., & Caudy, M. S. (2013). Examining racial disparities in drug arrests. *Justice Quarterly,* 1–25. DOI:10.1080/07418825.2012.761721.

Mouzelis, N. (2000). The subjectivist-objectivist divide: Against transcendence. *Sociology, 34,* 741–762.

Nardulli, P., Eisenstein, J., & Flemming, B. (1988). *The tenor of justice: Criminal courts and the guilty plea process.* Urbana: University of Illinois Press.

Natapoff, A. (2012). Misdemeanors. *Southern California Law Review, 85,* 101–162.

Natapoff, A. (this volume). The penal pyramid. In S. Dolovich & A. Natapoff, eds., *The new criminal justice thinking.* New York: NYU Press.

Naymik, M. 2002. McMickle blasts justice system; grand jury process "had an apartheid feel," NAACP ex-leader says. *Cleveland Plain Dealer,* February 26, B2.

Novak, K. J., & Chamlin, M. B. 2012. Racial threat, suspicion, and police behavior: The impact of race and place in traffic enforcement. *Crime and Delinquency, 58,* 275–300.

Pager, D. (2003). The mark of a criminal record. *American Journal of Sociology, 108,* 937–975.

Pager, D. (2007). The use of field experiments for studies of employment discrimination: Contributions, critiques, and directions for the future. *Annals of the American Academy of Political and Social Science, 609,* 104–133.

Pfaff, J. F. (2011). The myths and realities of correctional severity: Evidence from the National Corrections Reporting Program on sentencing practices. *American Law and Economics Review*, *13*(2), 491–531.

Reis, H. T. (2008). Reinvigorating the concept of situation in social psychology. *Personality and Social Psychology Review*, *12*, 311–329.

Ross, L., & Nisbett, R. (1991). *The person and the situation: Perspectives of social psychology*. New York: McGraw-Hill.

Sherif, M. (1958). Superordinate goals in the reduction of intergroup conflict. *American Journal of Sociology*, *63*, 349–356.

Skolnick, J. H. (1966). *Justice without trial: Law enforcement in democratic society*. New York: Wiley.

Stith, K. (2008). The arc of the pendulum: Judges, prosecutors, and the exercise of discretion. *Yale Law Journal*, *117*, 1420–1497.

Swidler, A. (1986). Culture in action: Symbols and strategies. *American Sociological Review*, *51*, 273–286.

Tajfel, H., Billig, M. G., Bundy, R. P., & Flament, C. (1971). Social categorization and intergroup behavior. *European Journal of Social Psychology*, *1*, 149–178.

Ulmer, J. (2012). Recent developments and new directions in sentencing research. *Justice Quarterly*, *29*, 1–40.

Weiss, J. C. (2006). Tough on crime: How campaigns for state judiciary violate criminal defendants' due process rights. *New York University Law Review*, *81*, 1101–1136.

10

Beyond Ferguson

Integrating Critical Race Theory and the "Social Psychology of Criminal Procedure"

PRISCILLA OCEN

In August 2014, the streets of Ferguson, Missouri erupted in protest over the death of Michael Brown, an unarmed 18-year-old African American, who was fatally shot by a Ferguson police officer.[1] Brown's killing was preceded by the death of Eric Garner, a 43-year-old, unarmed African American man who died after a New York police officer employed a banned chokehold maneuver during an arrest. Brown and Garner were two of many unarmed African Americans killed by police annually.[2] Although available data are incomplete, the FBI reports that approximately 400 people are killed by police annually,[3] and of those 400, approximately one-quarter are African Americans.[4] The same study reveals that African Americans between the ages of 18 and 24 are 21 times more likely to be killed by police than their white counterparts.[5]

The deaths of Brown and Garner at the hands of police are the most extreme examples of what many contend is a pattern of excessive force against people of color, particularly African Americans. In the months following the deaths of Brown and Garner, there were numerous taped incidents of police use of deadly force against African Americans,[6] most notably Walter Scott in South Carolina.[7] Despite this persistent pattern and the profound dissatisfaction with policing in communities of color, very few officers are disciplined or prosecuted by the state.[8] This dynamic was brought into high relief as St. Louis County and Staten Island Grand Juries failed to indict the officers that killed Brown and Garner, setting off new waves of protests in Ferguson, New York, and elsewhere.

What accounts for the persistence of police abuse against people of color and the failure of prosecutors to hold officers responsible? To answer this question, Critical Race theorists forcefully describe the racialized nature of legal doctrine, the ways in which law constructs institutions, enables particular forms of discretion, and authorizes racially discriminatory outcomes.[9] Indeed, Critical Race theorists assert that policing and incarceration operate as particular forms of racial domination, facilitated through state violence, surveillance, and control; they contend that the racial disparities within police use of force are not aberrational, but instead constitute a fundamental component of the criminal justice system. The violence, regulation, and control over racialized communities by the criminal justice system are manifestations of racial subordination that also serve to reinforce and perpetuate such subordination. To bolster these and other normative claims regarding the relationship between race and law, many Critical Race theorists argue for greater integration of empirical projects that can demonstrate the insights of Critical Race Theory (CRT) with respect to the racialized operation of the criminal justice system.[10]

In her essay for this volume, Mona Lynch presents an empirical model that may serve as a point of interaction between CRT and empirical projects that specifically examine the role of race in criminal justice outcomes. In particular, the model proposed by Lynch enables examination of the ways in which institutional settings shape the actions of individuals, bridging the discursive gap between structural and individual theoretical engagements with the criminal justice system. Without such a comprehensive analysis, Lynch contends, those interested in exploring how the criminal justice system functions will lack a robust understanding of troubling outcomes like the disproportionate police use of deadly force against African Americans. In calling for a "social psychology of criminal procedure," Lynch argues that scholarship on the criminal justice system must address the "complex interrelationship between levels of influence," particularly with respect to local actors and the decision-making processes that lead to institutional outcomes. Conceptualizing and examining individual action within various systems enables a focus on the local-level criminal justice operations that are often overlooked by scholars despite their profound impact on policing and aggregate rates of incarceration.

Understanding how state institutions function is tremendously important for Critical Race theorists and advocates who work on behalf of the racially marginalized, given that "the state plays a major role in structuring race and racism."[11] In this essay, I describe Lynch's model and suggest two potential points of interaction between the model and CRT. On the one hand, I note the ways in which Lynch's model can provide an empirical basis for theoretical claims advanced by CRT. In particular, I highlight the ways in which the social psychology of criminal procedure can empirically ground CRT's claim that race and racism are foundational aspects of the modern criminal justice system. On the other hand, I describe the ways in which Lynch's model can incorporate some of the normative and methodological insights of CRT. Specifically, I suggest that the model can engage CRT's normative claim that race and law are mutually constitutive, that law constructs and reinforces racial inequality. Methodologically, the model can more explicitly examine the ways in which "outsider voices" shape institutional outcomes. By "outsider voices," I refer to CRT's commitment to centering voices from the margins so as to fundamentally shift perceptions of social institutions. I argue for the explicit inclusion of external actors, such as community activists, who are often unaccounted for in empirical projects despite their important role in driving institutional action.

Macro- and Micro-Analysis of Criminal Justice Outcomes and the "Social Psychology of Criminal Procedure"

In her articulation of the "social psychology of criminal procedure," Lynch provides a conceptual and methodological framework for exploring discretionary actions that produce outcomes within the criminal legal system. In so doing, Lynch joins a growing literature calling for a more integrated empirical analysis of processes, actors and institutions. Indeed, recognizing the various actors within institutional settings such as legislatures and executive agencies, many scholars have critiqued sociological and legal approaches that are either too narrowly structuralist or individualist in their orientation.[12] Similarly, Critical Race theorists have called for a more integrated model of analysis of race and racial discrimination under the banner of Critical Race Realism and Critical Race Empiricism, both of which employ empirical analysis to understand discrimination by legal actors and institutions.[13] Although not without concerns regarding empiricism's compatibility with the broader canons of CRT,[14] Critical Race theorists have taken this "turn to social science,"[15] often integrating social psychological scholarship on implicit bias, which is understood to result from the cognitive categorization process that produces unconscious negative associations between racial groups and harmful stereotypes. As Laura Gómez and others have noted, empirical methodologies can be marshaled to advance the theoretical understanding of race and racial dynamics as complex and rooted in historical and social processes.[16]

In her essay here, Lynch extends the insight of this socio-legal literature by connecting the institutional to the individual actor in the criminal justice system. Because the criminal justice system has historically and contemporarily served as significant site of racial subordination, her model provides a point of interaction for sociologists, social psychologists, and Critical Race theorists who have called for empirical projects that can measure how race shapes criminal justice outcomes. Importantly, while much of the literature highlights the need for microanalysis, here Lynch presents a specific and sequential framework for evaluating individual behavior within institutions by articulating a multi-methodological analysis of institutional context, individual action, and the individual's relationship to organizational outcomes.

Central to the four components of inquiry within the model is the treatment of "situated actors" as "complex drivers of institutional behavior" in the criminal legal system rather than automatons effecting institutional directives. The situated actor is an individual within an institution whose behavior and expressions of rationality are contingent upon institutional context, culture and social dynamics. As such, situated actors are "shaped by the specific conditions that comprise the[ir] constituent organizations." Alongside the situated actor, the institutional environment is conceived of as a co-agent in determining outcomes, either by constraining or enabling individual action. As Lynch has noted elsewhere, "Institutional factors may play more of a role on behavior than the personality characteristics or dispositions of actors within institutions."[17] Indeed, the institutional context grounds the actor's behavior and may cause the actor to operate in ways that are not "always purely rational or technologically efficient." She asks empiricists and others studying the criminal legal system to take account of these interactions when assessing why the criminal justice system functions in the way that it functions.

The introduction of the "situated actor" into the model proposed by Lynch is a significant contribution to the study of criminal justice outcomes. Indeed, for decades social psychologists have studied the ways in which situations, not dispositions, account for much of human behavior.[18] Taking situations seriously results in what Jon Hanson and David Yosifon call "a realistic vision of humanity."[19] As Lynch notes, the situational actor challenges the legal fiction that either the individual or the institution is dispositive in producing organizational outcomes. Thus, scholarly focus on individual action and institutional outcomes rather than institutional processes obscures the dynamic interactions that lead to outcomes.

Moreover, focus on the situational actor rather than the dispositional actor also raises questions about how law interrogates outcomes. For example, in the context of anti-discrimination law, which is the basis for many of the challenges to discriminatory criminal justice outcomes, the inquiry tends to center on individual intention. Did a police officer intend to discriminate? If we take theories of situational action seriously, this is the wrong question. Instead, courts and scholars should direct their attention away from the individual animus and toward the ways in which institutional settings or cultures shape individual action to produce discriminatory effects. Critical Race scholars have raised similar concerns regarding the intent standard. Indeed, Critical Race scholars have noted the ways in which the intent standard establishes an impossibly high burden of proof that functions to insulate racial discrimination from challenge.[20] Scholars have also asserted that individual intent is not the primary driver of discrimination; rather, such discrimination occurs as a result of institutional practices and cultures that shape individual actions and organizational outcomes.[21] As such, the situated actor and Lynch's model provide an opportunity for engagement with CRT's claims that the intent standard is insufficient to address the complex drivers of discrimination in the criminal justice system.

With the institution and the situated actor as the primary sites of analysis, the model begins by identifying "organizational action." Under the model, organizational action is derived from the collective action of small groups with shared histories that produce social outcomes. According to Lynch, such groups serve as a "critical link between the individual and social structure." For example, the number of convictions and the racial disparities within rates of convictions would constitute organizational outcomes produced by the collective action of prosecutors in a particular jurisdiction. Often, legal analysis by CRT scholars focuses on such racially disparate organizational action, utilizing the fact of disproportionality to make broader arguments about the discriminatory operation of the criminal justice system and to critique the failure of legal doctrine to disrupt such inequality. Lynch's model, however, presses scholars to go further in their analysis and examine the precise ways that organizational context contributes to specific outcomes.

Indeed, the model proposes an assessment of organizational norms and the responsibilities of actors within institutions that produce organizational action. As Lynch has noted elsewhere, "These are the formal laws, internal policies, procedural rules, and the unwritten norms that dictate how business gets done in a given institution, comprising, in part, the institutional parameters."[22] In examining this component of the model, a researcher might examine the formal mandates of the organization, the formal policies or regulations employed by the organization, roles assigned to actors within the organization, external regulations imposed on the organization, and the specific institutional culture in which actors make decisions. For example, in the context of criminal prosecutions, this component of the model would require an examination of the mission of the prosecutor's office, and the institutional expectations of prosecutors that shape their behavior. Here, a researcher might inquire into the ways in which "bias [is] implicitly inscribed in policies, procedural rules, and practices."[23]

In what is described as the "institutional parameters" that constrain individual decision-making and autonomy, the model delineates the immediate context in which discretion and decision-making occurs within institutions. In particular, it explores the discrete factors that shape or predict behavior within the institution as actors negotiate policies, practices, and other constraints in their efforts to perform what they understand to be their organizational role. Here, researchers investigating racially disparate conviction rates might ask, for example, whether there are areas where prosecutors have more discretion and whether those areas are associated with increased racial disparity. These areas that enable discretion are ripe for analysis given, as Victor Quintanilla has noted, individuals may express "bias subtly and in ways that can be rationalized under conditions of situational ambiguity: when norms are unclear, when situations are ambiguous, when the correct choice is unclear, where bias against minority-group members can be rationalized on some factor other than race."[24] Lastly, through what Lynch calls the "actor's self," the model calls for an examination of the cognitions and motivations of actors within institutions. At the micro-level, the characteristics of actors, including implicit and explicit biases, may have a bearing on individual action within the institution. Notwithstanding the importance of these kinds of dispositional factors, Lynch notes that actors are not governed solely by their individual characteristics nor do they have unfettered discretion to shape institutional outcomes. Rather, their individual actions are guided by institutional cultures that shape and give context to their use of discretion. Here, researchers may examine the implicit and explicit biases of actors and other characteristics that may have a bearing on individual action within the institution.

Taking each of the specific areas of inquiry together, the social psychology of criminal procedure draws our attention away from the formal operation of law and institutions and directs it toward an empirical examination of how law and institutions function as a practical matter. As such, the model can elucidate the important questions raised by CRT regarding the precise relationship between institutions, individuals, and racialized outcomes. The model outlined by Lynch is an interdisciplinary project that is consistent with the development and evolution of CRT's emphasis on structural discrimination, as it examines the ways in which structures and the actors within them produce criminal justice outcomes. The model proposed by Lynch raises nuanced questions and offers conceptual and methodological frameworks for the analysis of criminal justice outcomes by focusing on four discrete components that are ripe for empirical analysis. Moreover, as I note below, the model can also interrogate and perhaps support CRT's normative claims that formal criminal legal rules effectuate, rather than eliminate, racial domination.

Accounting for Race: Empirically Engaging CRT's Claims Regarding Race Subordination and the Criminal Law

Institutional actions and outcomes do not occur in a vacuum. Rather, institutions are shaped by historical contexts that are rooted in and reproduce race, gender, and class inequalities. Lynch acknowledges the ways in which social structures that cross jurisdictional boundaries persist over time, including economic or political systems that are steeped in racial ideologies, and are thus constitutive elements of organizational action and institutional functioning. In what she calls a "substantive imperative," Lynch asserts that the social psychology of criminal procedure "must engage in empirically sophisticated examinations of the reproduction of racial, gender, and class-based inequality and injustice within criminal justice institutions." With respect to race, racial inequality, and mass incarceration, Lynch's model integrates questions of racial ideology and invites empiricists to consider "[t]o what extent . . . societal-level racial ideologies and paradigms shape the organizational context, especially as they enter via criminal justice actors." Through this inquiry, the model can serve as an important vehicle to examine how racial ideologies seep into all aspects of organizational actions and outcomes. Importantly, the model's inquiry into societal-level racial ideologies can draw upon CRT's normative insights regarding the relationship between racial domination and social structures.

Indeed, Critical Race scholars have suggested that race is an enduring and fundamental organizing principle in the United States generally and in the criminal justice system specifically. They have long asserted that race and racial bias are essential, rather than aberrational, components of the criminal justice system. According to Critical Race scholar Ian Haney López, "Even absent malice, race remains a powerful astringent that thoroughly suffuses American society—one that especially continues to distort those major institutions in American life steeped in racial oppression, such as the crime control system."[25] Historically, Blackness and criminality have been linked in the United States and used as a justification for various forms of racial subordination.[26] For example, African Americans were subject to special forms of policing in the post-Reconstruction era through the enactment of the "Black Codes," which criminalized conduct such as "vagrancy," alcohol consumption, unemployment, and gun ownership. African Americans arrested for such crimes could be subject to punishment in chain gangs or convict leasing camps. As such, criminal punishment became another mechanism for the exploitation and subordination of African Americans. In the Jim Crow era, law enforcement was often absent in African American communities or complicit in violently policing the boundaries imposed by segregation. Policing was, in a very real sense, "separate and unequal."

This relationship between race and crime did not, however, cease with the formal abolition of de jure segregation. Instead, it was leveraged to justify a punitive shift in criminal policy, leading to increased rates of incarceration, particularly among African Americans.[27] Opponents of civil rights utilized the language of crime to capitalize on growing anxieties about racial unrest and broader demands for social inclusion. As political scientist Vesla Weaver notes, "The same actors who had fought vociferously against civil rights legislation, defeated, shifted the 'locus of attack' by injecting crime onto the agenda. Fusing crime to anxiety about ghetto revolts, racial disorder—initially defined as a problem of minority disenfranchisement—was redefined as a crime problem, which helped shift debate from social reform to punishment." During this political shift, anti-Black rhetoric and imagery was used to justify an ever-expanding criminal justice system and ever-expanding police presence in Black communities.

While this is a reductive account of the relationship between race and the institutions that comprise the criminal justice system, it certainly suggests that contemporary institutions and individual actions are embedded within histories of racial subordination. By drawing upon theoretical traditions which assert that individuals and institutions operate in particular political and historical contexts that are deeply racialized, Lynch's model can help scholars and advocates determine whether and to what extent race affects the criminal justice system at every stage of the model. Moreover, examination of racial ideologies and histories of subordination presents a significant opportunity to empirically engage CRT's observations regarding the centrality of racial ideology within criminal justice systems.

Looking to the Bottom: Expanding Conceptions of the "Situated Actor"

Just as CRT can benefit from the empirical inquiry propounded by the social psychology of criminal procedure, so too can the model benefit from important methodologies articulated by CRT. In particular, the model could benefit from an expansion of the subjects of inquiry to include those affected by police violence and those advocating for change within the criminal justice system as what I refer to as "externally situated actors." CRT, led by scholars such as Mari Matsuda, advocates for a theoretical methodology that privileges the experiences and perspectives of those who are subordinated by law. In her seminal article "Looking to the Bottom: Critical Legal Studies and Reparations," Matsuda suggests that "[l]ooking to the bottom—adopting the perspective of those who have seen and felt the falsity of the liberal promise—can assist critical scholars in the task of fathoming the phenomenology of law and defining the elements of justice."[28]

Although Lynch very briefly discusses community activists in the application of her model, how such activists figure into an institutional context as situated actors is not entirely clear within the model itself. Explicitly incorporating external actors, such as community activists, into the current model, however, could uncover the dynamic interaction between internal and external actors, who are most often impacted by organizational action within the criminal justice system. Indeed, community activists shape how the institution's mission is articulated and perceived in society, as well as how the institution effectuates its regulations, policies and practices. Advocacy and activism performed by external actors may shape how internally situated actors understand their roles and duties and further influence how discretion is deployed. Thus, the interaction between internal and external actors is critical to understanding outcomes.

Moreover, examining the role of externally situated actors in organizational action brings into view differing perspectives about the relationship between race and the criminal justice system. The inclusion of external actors allows researchers to move beyond formal descriptions of institutional missions to the lived reality of those who interact with criminal justice institutions. Since the deaths of Michael Brown and Eric Garner, for example, African American advocates have lamented that anti-Black racial bias within the criminal justice system is not an aberration, but the norm.[29] They contend that the disproportionate use of deadly force against African Americans is part of a historical pattern of state regulation and denigration of Black bodies. The perspective of such external actors is often unaccounted for in empirical studies of institutional operation and individual use of discretion. Lynch's model, however, has room for an analysis of how affected communities experience criminal justice policies, as well as an interrogation of how community actors press for reform. Inclusion of these voices "from the bottom" can provide a fuller account of individual action and institutional change.

Analyzing Race and Discretion and Prosecuting Police Use of Deadly Force

How might the empirical model proposed by Lynch, as informed by the perspective of external actors, assist in understanding the prosecutorial charging decisions reached in Ferguson or in New York? According to the model, it must first be acknowledged that while the two decisions were undoubtedly local, they were reached in the context of macro-institutional dynamics, or what Lynch calls "structures and paradigms," which have been shaped by race and racial exclusion at the national level. Thus, the analysis could begin with an engagement of the claim, frequently theorized by Critical Race scholars, that many of the institutions that comprise the criminal justice system have historically been deployed to contain the "threat" presented by non-whites, the poor, and other marginalized groups. Therefore, beginning with an inquiry into the relationship between race and criminal justice institutions would signal the centrality of broader social paradigms and ideologies within the model.

In Ferguson, for example, the shooting death of Michael Brown took place less than a mile from the burial place of Dred Scott, whose case famously prompted the assertion that African Americans had "no rights which the white man was bound to respect"[30]—a statement that continues to have particular resonance in light of the impunity with which police are perceived to act in African American communities. The racial landscapes of both New York and Ferguson have been shaped by redlining and exclusionary housing policies that resulted in segregated housing patterns.[31] Such patterns enable police to be deployed to regulate racially isolated and impoverished communities. The politically powerful are thus able to direct resources toward "tough on crime initiatives" against minority communities without directly affecting affluent communities.[32]

Grounded in this racial context, the social psychology of criminal procedure calls upon researchers to examine "organizational actions."

The organizational action or outcome to be examined here is the failure of prosecutors to pursue charges against police officers who use deadly force against unarmed African Americans. At this stage in the model, we might ask the location of shootings, the characteristics of the victims, including their racial and gender identities, and whether officers were prosecuted. Many internal and external actors have attempted to document these outcomes. According to one study, police have killed at least 7,000 people in the last 15 years;[33] over the same period of time, only 54 officers have been criminally prosecuted for deadly use of force.[34] These outcomes take place within a broader environment of racialized law enforcement practices such as broken windows policing and racial profiling. These forms of policing lead to high degrees of adversarial contact between police and citizens in racially marginalized communities, some of which result in deadly uses of force by police. Further, as Critical Race theorists have noted, the practices of police and prosecutors occur within the context of ostensibly "colorblind" policies and institutional spaces, yet the outcomes of such policies disproportionately affect African Americans and increase their vulnerability to state violence.

The organizational outcomes or actions described above (i.e., racial profiling and police use of deadly force) occur as a result of what Lynch calls "organizational motives, rules, norms, formal roles, and relationships." Here, the model asks researchers to examine the organizational context, including rules that constrain or enable institutional actors such as prosecutors pursuing criminal charges against police who use deadly force. As a formal matter, prosecutors and district attorney's offices have a unique role, one that is vested with a high degree of autonomy and discretion; prosecutors are vested with sole responsibility for making charging decisions in criminal cases[35] and are admonished by the American Bar Association to "refrain from prosecuting a charge that the prosecutor knows is not supported by probable cause."[36] Prosecutors must weigh the available evidence and determine whether a criminal charge is appropriate. Once a prosecutor decides to proceed with a criminal charge, prosecutors may take a case to trial or settle with a criminal defendant via plea bargain.

Next, the model investigates the "immediate institutional context" in which decisions are made and the ways in which institutional norms shape the behavior of actors. This inquiry could include the behavior of internally as well as externally situated actors, specifically, prosecutors and advocates on behalf of communities affected by police violence. A researcher might ask: what are the rules and procedures for bringing charges? Are charges less likely when the victim is a person of color who is injured by whites or members of law enforcement? Who do internally and externally situated actors understand to be the primary constituents of the prosecutor's office? The model's ability to generate empirical data regarding these questions can, depending on what is found, provide empirical grounding for CRT's claim that racial bias affects all aspects of the criminal justice system, including the initiation of criminal prosecutions when the victim is a person of color. Such data can also be useful in determining whether particular points of discretion are associated with racial disparities in prosecutorial charging decisions and, if so, whether the institutional culture contributes to such disparities.

As noted above, prosecutors rarely exercise their discretion in favor of prosecuting police officers for homicide offenses.[37] This stands in contrast to non-officer-involved criminal cases, when probable cause is almost never questioned. For example, the Bureau of Justice Statistics reports that federal prosecutors presented 162,000 cases to Grand Juries in 2010 and indictments were returned in all but 11 cases.[38] In a few high-profile cases, due to pressure from external actors, prosecutors have submitted evidence to a Grand Jury to determine whether the available evidence supports a criminal charge. It is at this charging stage that prosecutors have vast discretion that produces organizational outcomes. They can choose to submit a case to a Grand Jury rather than a judge. The use of discretion in this way facilitates a lack of transparency and accountability for outcomes.

In both Ferguson and Staten Island, the local prosecutors convened Grand Juries to hear the evidence and determine whether there was probable cause for an indictment. This process is very uncommon in state criminal cases.[39] In most criminal cases, the decision to file charges rests primarily with the prosecutor's office and must be justified during an appearance before a judge. In another highly unusual move, the prosecutors allowed the jurors to hear testimony from the officers that were the subject of the Grand Jury's investigation. Typically, during Grand Jury proceedings, prosecutors present only evidence that suggests the defendant's guilt, not their innocence. According to news reports, the

St. Louis Grand Jury was presented with "witnesses who both supported and contradicted Officer Darren Wilson's account, three autopsy reports, bloodstains and shell casings."[40] A similar approach was taken in Staten Island and has been subject to significant critique.[41] Critics suggested that prosecutors presented conflicting evidence in an attempt to ensure that an indictment would not be returned against the officers.

The use of the Grand Jury in these cases shifted the site of organizational action out of the prosecutor's office and into the domain of a secretive Grand Jury. When the Grand Jury failed to indict the officers who killed Brown and Garner, the prosecutors pointed to the Grand Jury's use of discretion to explain this outcome, notwithstanding the fact that their charging decisions and approach to the Grand Jury process likely contributed to the failure to indict. Moreover, the secret process and the failure to secure indictments led many external actors to allege that local prosecutors were selectively enforcing the law and manipulating legal processes in order to protect police officers. As a result of this fragmentation of the criminal justice proceedings, external actors could not hold the prosecutors directly accountable for failing to criminally charge officers for the killing of unarmed African American men and women.[42]

Examining processes used by prosecutors in cases involving police use of deadly force could generate important empirical data and normative insights regarding the nature of prosecutorial discretion and the internal constraints that produce racially disparate organizational outcomes. For example, scholars argue that prosecutors decline to pursue charges against police officers accused of excessive use of force in order to preserve their relationship with law enforcement. Indeed, prosecutors rely on police officers to collect evidence, investigate crimes and serve as witnesses in criminal cases. Therefore, alienating law enforcement officers might undermine the ability of prosecutors to identify other crimes and secure convictions.

While this "prosecutorial structural location" explanation may account for some of the failure to prosecute police for use of deadly force, the model can also examine alternative explanations, such as legal standards that place significant evidentiary burdens on prosecutors and therefore make it more difficult to successfully prosecute police officers for deadly use of force. To determine which explanation is most probable, researchers could examine the decisions of internally situated actors in other institutions that intersect with local prosecutors' offices, such as state petit juries and the federal Department of Justice (DOJ). With respect to petit juries, even when police are tried for homicide offenses that stem from deadly use of force, state juries have failed to convict. Moreover, DOJ routinely fails to pursue criminal charges against police officers who use deadly force, often due to insufficient evidence. Neither petit juries nor federal prosecutors are reliant on local police agencies and yet they often fail to impose criminal sanctions upon officers for deadly use of force. The determinations made by jurors and federal prosecutors may support the claim that the legal standards that evaluate the "reasonableness" of an officer's fear of the victim in such cases are significant barriers to prosecution and discourage prosecutors from bringing charges. Consequently, communities of color are left unprotected against police violence. In this example, the application of Lynch's model can assist researchers as they weigh competing explanations for the failure to indict law enforcement officers and marshal empirical evidence in support of reforms.

Another element analyzed by the model is the "actor's self." By this, Lynch refers to the psychological aspects of an institutionally situated actor, which include "cognitions and motivations, emotions, traits, experiences." Researchers examining the actor's self can test the claim that implicit racial biases contribute to institutional outcomes, such as the failure to criminally prosecute police officers. Indeed, racism, as a pervasive social dynamic, not only shapes how resources are allocated at the institutional level, it also shapes how individuals interpret and value others. Numerous studies have demonstrated that unconscious racial bias may play a role in how actors exercise discretion and guide institutional outcomes.[43] In the criminal context, prosecutors are called upon to independently weigh evidence to determine whether they believe probable cause exists to support the initiation of a criminal proceeding. Race and implicit racial bias may play a role in how such actors assess evidence, particularly when the alleged perpetrator is a white police officer and the victim is African American. For example, social psychologists have documented the effect of implicit racial biases on official decision-making across a range of settings, including law enforcement.[44] These studies demonstrate that African Americans are seen as more criminal, more aggressive, and more violent than their white counterparts. Racial biases may therefore cause prosecutors to more readily accept an account of an African American as a deadly aggressor or a police officer's assertion of fear of serious bodily injury at the hands of the victim. It also may cause prosecutors to devalue eyewitness accounts of people of color or to empathize less with victims. Researchers utilizing this model can design studies to test out these and other hypotheses.

The failure of prosecutors to prosecute police officers who kill unarmed civilians, however, is not uncontested. Prosecutors and jurors are not the only actors that shape organizational actions. Rather, externally situated actors, such as activists and the families of victims, place demands on institutions, shape institutional decision-making, and create the possibility for change. For example, following the announcement of the non-indictments, communities around the country protested the lack of accountability for police who use deadly force against African Americans. Activists staged disruptive public "die-ins" and generated hashtags such as "Black Lives Matter" and "I Can't Breathe," which quickly spread via social media. Activists demanded independent federal prosecutions of officers that use deadly force, the implementation of citizen review boards with the power to discipline and terminate officers, the prohibition of racial profiling in law enforcement, and the demilitarization of police departments.[45] New York Times columnist Charles Blow called this collective expression of outrage "a new age of activism."[46]

In response to the protests, President Barack Obama convened a meeting at the White House with activists and policy makers to discuss policing reform. Following the meeting, the president announced plans to fund body cameras for police officers, and Attorney General Eric Holder announced a federal investigation into the death of Eric Garner. The attorney general also endorsed the idea of independent investigators of police use of deadly force, and the U.S. Department of Justice released new guidelines on the use of race in policing in an effort to curb racial profiling. Further, shortly after the highly publicized death of Freddie Gray, an African American man who sustained a fatal injury while in police custody in Baltimore, city officials announced that criminal charges were being filed against officers allegedly involved in his death. Announcing those charges, Baltimore district attorney Marilyn Mosby noted that the indictments were, in part, a response to the community's demands for transparency and accountability. With protests ongoing as of the writing of this essay, it is clear that actors outside of the formal criminal justice system are having a significant effect on reform efforts that any model designed to capture the role of race in the criminal justice system should acknowledge and analyze.

Conclusion

Mona Lynch's essay on the social psychology of criminal procedure is an important contribution to the legal, sociological, and empirical literature on the criminal justice system. It demonstrates how advocates and scholars can use empirical methods that engage how situated actors behave, how they deploy their discretion, and how such actions produce racially disparate outcomes in criminal justice institutions. It also offers a methodology by which CRT scholars can empirically support claims regarding structural racial inequality within various systems at both micro- and macro-levels at a time when the racially disparate outcomes of the criminal justice system are undergoing significant critique from within and without the system. Such an approach enables CRT scholars and advocates to better understand the discrete processes that produce racially disparate outcomes and may thereby enable more effective reforms. At the same time, the model also presents an opportunity to engage CRT methodologies such as "looking to the bottom" to better understand how the activists and communities that are most impacted by the criminal justice system respond to and shape criminal justice outcomes. For the communities calling for justice in Ferguson, New York, and elsewhere, such an approach can assist them in developing the tools the system so desperately needs to deconstruct its stubborn inequality.

NOTES
1 Julie Boseman & Emma G. Fitzsimmons, *Grief and Anger Follow Shooting Death of a Teenager*, NY TIMES, Aug. 10, 2014, www.nytimes.com.
2 James Queally, *Man's Death after Apparent Chokehold to Be Probed*, LA TIMES, Jul. 18, 2014, www.latimes.com.
3 Jaeah Lee, *Exactly How Often Do Police Shoot Unarmed Black Men?*, MOTHER JONES, Aug. 15, 2014, http://m.motherjones.com; Rob Barry & Coulter Jones, *Hundreds of Police Killings Are Uncounted in Federal Statistics*, WALL ST. J., Dec.

3, 2014, www.wsj.com (noting that the reported numbers are woefully understating the number of police uses of deadly force).

4 Kevin Johnson, Meghan Hoyer, & Brad Heath, *Local Police Involved in 400 Shootings per Year*, USA TODAY, Aug. 15, 2014, www.usatoday.com.

5 *Id.*

6 A. J. Vicens and Jaeah Lee, *Here Are 13 Police Killings Captured on Video*, MOTHER JONES, May 20, 2015, www.motherjones.com.

7 *Id.*

8 Reuben Fischer-Baum, *Allegations of Police Misconduct Rarely Result in Charges*, FIVETHIRTYEIGHT, Nov. 24, 2014, http://fivethirtyeight.com.

9 Devon W. Carbado, *(E)racing the Fourth Amendment*, 100 MICH. L. REV. 946, 968 (2002); Ian F. Haney López, *The Social Construction of Race: Some Observations on Illusion, Fabrication, and Choice*, 29 HARV. C.R.-C.L. L. REV. 1, 3 (1994); Cheryl I. Harris, *Equal Treatment and the Reproduction of Inequality*, 69 FORDHAM L. REV. 1753, 1762 (2001); Cheryl I. Harris, *Whiteness as Property*, 106 HARV. L. REV. 1709, 1716–21 (1993).

10 *See, e.g.*, Devon Carbado & Daria Roithmayr, *Critical Race Theory Meets Social Science*, 10 ANN. REV. L. & SOC. SCI. 149 (2014); Victor D. Quintanilla, *Critical Race Empiricism: A New Means to Measure Civil Procedure*, 3 UC IRVINE L. REV. 187 (2013); Laura E. Gómez, *Understanding Law and Race as Mutually Constitutive: An Invitation to Explore an Emerging Field*, 6 ANN. REV. L. & SOC. SCI. 487 (2010); Osagie K. Obasogie, *Race in Law and Society: A Critique*, reprinted in RACE, LAW AND SOCIETY 468–69 (Ian F. Haney López ed., 2007).

11 Gómez, *supra* note 10.

12 Lawrence D. Bobo & Cybelle Fox, *Race, Racism, and Discrimination: Bridging Problems, Methods, and Theory in Social Psychology Research*, 66 SOC. PSYCH. Q. 319–332 (2003) (calling for a social psychology of race, racism, and racial discrimination).

13 *See, e.g.*, Gregory Scott Parks, *Toward a Critical Race Realism*, 17 CORNELL J. L. & PUB. POL'Y 683 (2009).

14 Dorothy A. Brown, *Fighting Racism in the Twenty-First Century*, 61 WASH. & LEE L. REV. 1485, 1487–89 (2004).

15 Jerome M. Culp, Jr., Angela P. Harris, & Francisco Valdes, *Subject Unrest*, 55 STAN. L. REV. 2435 (2003).

16 LAURA GÓMEZ, MISCONCEIVING MOTHERS: LEGISLATORS, PROSECUTORS AND THE POLITICS OF PRENATAL DRUG EXPOSURE (1997); *see also* Shaun Ossei-Owusu, *Gimme Some More: Centering Race and Gender Inequality in Discretion Discourse*, 18 AM. U. J. GENDER SOC. POL'Y & L. 607 (2010).

17 Mona Lynch, *Institutionalizing Bias: The Death Penalty, Federal Drug Prosecutions, and Mechanisms of Disparate Punishment*, 41 AM. J. CRIM. L. 91, 110 (2013).

18 Jon D. Hanson & David Yosifon, *The Situation: An Introduction to the Situational Character, Critical Realism, Power Economics and Deep Capture*, 152 U. PA. L. REV. 129, 155 (2003).

19 *Id.*

20 Girardeau A. Spann, PURE POLITICS IN CRITICAL RACE THEORY: THE CUTTING EDGE 25 (Richard Delgado & Jeanine Stefancic eds.).

21 Daria Roithmayr, *Locked in Inequality: The Persistence of Discrimination*, 9 MICH. J. RACE & L. 31 (2003).

22 Lynch, *supra* note 17, at 115.

23 *Id.*

24 Quintanilla, *supra* note 10, at 199.

25 Ian F. Haney López, *Post-Racial Racism: Racial Stratification and Mass Incarceration in the Age of Obama*, 98 CAL. L. REV. 1023, 1060 (2010).

26 *See, e.g.*, KHALIL G. MUHAMMAD, CONDEMNATION OF BLACKNESS: RACE, CRIME AND THE MAKING OF MODERN AMERICA (2011).

27 *See, e.g.*, MICHELLE ALEXANDER, THE NEW JIM CROW: MASS INCARCERATION IN THE AGE OF COLORBLINDNESS (2010); BRUCE WESTERN, PUNISHMENT AND INEQUALITY IN AMERICAN DEMOCRACY (2006); Loïc Wacquant, *The New "Peculiar Institution": On the Prison as Surrogate Ghetto*, 4 THEORETICAL CRIMINOLOGY 377 (2000); Velsa Weaver, *Frontlash: Race and the Development of Punitive Crime Policy*, 21 STUDIES AMER. POL. DEV. 230 (2007).

28 Mari J. Matsuda, *Looking to the Bottom: Critical Legal Studies and Reparations*, 22 HARV. C.R.-C.L. L. REV. 323, 324 (1987).

29 Albert Burneko, *The American Justice System Is Not Broken*, CONCOURSE, Dec. 3, 2014, http://theconcourse.deadspin.com.

30 Dred Scott v. Sanford, 60 U.S. 393, 407 (1857).

31 DOUGLAS MASSEY & NANCY DENTON, AMERICAN APARTHEID (1993).

32 *See, e.g.*, David Dante Trout, *Screws, Koon, and Routine Aberrations: The Use of Fictional Narratives in Federal Police Brutality Prosecutions*, 74 N.Y.U. L. REV. 18 (1999).

33 Erin McClain, *One Year After Ferguson: Why Nobody Knows How Many People Are Killed by Police*, NBC NEWS, Aug. 10, 2015, www.nbcnews.com.

34 Kimberly Kindy and Kimbriell Kelly, *Thousands Dead, Few Prosecuted*, WASH. POST, April 11, 2015, available at www.washingtonpost.com.

35 *See* JONATHAN SIMON, GOVERNING THROUGH CRIME: HOW THE WAR ON CRIME TRANSFORMED AMERICAN DEMOCRACY AND CREATED A CULTURE OF FEAR 39 (2007).

36 ABA Rule 3.8(a).

37 Taylor Kate Brown, *The Cases Where US Police Have Faced Killing Charges*, BBC NEWS, Dec. 5, 2014, www.bbc.com.

38 Phillip Blump, *The Rarity of Federal Grand Jury Not Indicting, Visualized*, WASH. POST, Nov. 24, 2014, www.washingtonpost.com.

39 Laurie L. Levenson, *The Future of State and Federal Civil Rights Prosecutions: The Lessons of the Rodney King Trial*, 41 UCLA L. REV. 509, 547–48 (1994).

40 David Zucchino, *Prosecutor's Grand Jury Strategy in Ferguson Case Adds to Controversy*, LA TIMES, Nov. 26, 2014, www.latimes.com.

41 Jeffrey Toobin, *How Not to Use a Grand Jury*, NEW YORKER, Nov. 25, 2014, www.newyorker.com.

42 *Cf.* SAMUEL WALKER, TAMING THE SYSTEM: THE CONTROL OF DISCRETION IN CRIMINAL JUSTICE 1950–1990 13 (1993).

43 Justin D. Levinson & Robert J. Smith, *The Impact of Implicit Racial Bias on the Exercise of Prosecutorial Discretion*, 35 SEATTLE U. L. REV. 795, 797 (2011–2012) (collecting studies); Christine Jolls & Cass R. Sunstein, *The Law of Implicit Bias*, Faculty Scholarship Series, Paper 1824 (2006); Jerry Kang et al., *Implicit Bias in the Courtroom*, 59 UCLA L. REV. 1124, 1142 (2012); Cynthia Lee, *Making Race Salient: Trayvon Martin and Implicit Bias in a Not Yet Post-Racial Society*, 91 N.C. L. REV. 1555 (2013).

44 *See* sources cited *supra* note 43.

45 Ferguson Action, *Ferguson Activists Meet with President Obama to Demand End to Police Brutality Nationwide*, Dec. 1, 2014, available at http://fergusonaction.com.

46 Charles M. Blow, *A New Age of Activism*, NY TIMES, Dec. 8, 2014, http://mobile.nytimes.com.

11

Jumping Bunnies and Legal Rules

The Organizational Sociologist and the Legal Scholar Should Be Friends

ISSA KOHLER-HAUSMANN

Introduction

In the brilliant and bizarre film *Bartleby*, there is a scene in which an office worker sits at his desk, watching a pink bunny windup toy.[1] It is the type of toy that, after being wound up, jumps in the air. And yet each time the toy jumps in the air the office worker is startled: he jolts out of his chair and then settles back to a calm, observant posture, only to be jolted again when the bunny again jumps into the air repeatedly. The scene is hilarious. It is hilarious because it is funny to be consistently surprised by someone or something doing what is in its nature to do.

There is a way in which we scholars studying the relationship between "law on the books" and "law in action" might look like the funny office worker with the wind up bunny toy in *Bartleby*: we are consistently surprised by things that, given the nature of what we are looking at, should not surprise us at all.[2] A familiar conceptual move is to posit *law on the books* as a set of clear commands dictating an obvious real-world incarnation that should naturally occur as a law in action. If it fails to do so, we tend to view the factors identified as coming between law on the books and law in action as distorting influences.

But we know from years of quality scholarship on the topic that the fact that law in action does not match law on the books is as predictable as the fact that a windup jumping bunny toy will jump after being wound up. In fact, we might even go so far as to say that the law on the books versus law in action distinction is susceptible to the type of critique that Judith Butler levies at sex versus gender. Just as Butler claims

246

sex was "always already gender" because our sexed bodies have no obvious unmediated meanings prior to the interpretive and constructive sociocultural practices that constitute them as gendered bodies, perhaps law on the books was always already law in action because there are no obvious, unmediated meanings of legal rules prior to the interpretive and constructive sociocultural practices that constitute them as legal rules in practice.[3]

Perhaps, it might be argued, it is somewhere between a conceptual mistake and an unintelligible proposition to hold that law in action is a set of cultural and social practices instantiating, interpreting, and practicing law on the books, because the social activity of law is precisely *what we mean* when we use the term *law*. This is what John Dewey holds in maintaining that the creation and application of law are of a piece: "A given legal arrangement *is* what it *does*, and what it does lies in the field of modifying and/or maintaining human activities as going concerns. Without application these are scraps of paper or voices in the air but nothing that can be called law."[4]

We need not settle these questions of semantics and analytic jurisprudence in order to agree that we ought to no longer startle at the jumping bunny. Legal rules are selectively used and enforced, legal processes are subverted and transformed, and legal actors diverge from their officially sanctioned roles. This we know.

Of course, something unsurprising can still be of interest. Furthermore, something unsurprising as a matter of empirical expectations can still be disappointing or even deeply problematic as a matter of social legitimacy or legal fairness. But I want to suggest that an excessive focus on the theme of a surprising disconnect risks obscuring the mechanisms that systematically structure legal outcomes and mischaracterizing the means by which they do so. And a careful understanding of precisely how legal rules become actual practices and outcomes is essential for reform initiatives seeking to get legal actors to act in a certain way.

This chapter proposes that old debates about formal goals and actual practice on the ground in one field—organizational sociology—offer valuable lessons for how legal scholarship might approach the space between ideals and action in another field—the study of law. So the legal scholar interested in how law works on the ground should be friends with the organizational sociologist who has studied the relationship between organizational plans and organizational action. That friendship can yield important insights into this line of inquiry, especially in the criminal justice field.

As Mona Lynch's contribution to this volume states, the expansion of the United States' penal operations over the last few decades is not just a story of changes in legislation but a story about operations: "[L]ocal criminal justice systems (and the criminal justice actors and workgroups that people them) are the hubs that translate and put into motion formal legal change to produce punishment outcomes."[5] Therefore, as she urges, if we want to understand the role of law in America's penal expansion, we must understand precisely how legal rules are given life and operationalized inside organizations. Because Lynch's contribution to this volume eloquently spells out the importance of taking an organizational perspective on the study of local criminal justice operations and offers up a social psychological approach for doing so, I want to focus on another intellectual offering that organizational sociology has for such a study of criminal law.

The insight I wish to borrow from organizational sociology essentially consisted in a conceptual shift: moving from conceptualizing formal organizational rules and structure as providing immediate and clear directives for action to conceptualizing them as tools or plans that must always be made sense of and implemented in concrete action settings. The first part of this chapter explores and develops that insight. If we apply the insight to the study of legal action, it means starting from the premise that legal actors always need to make a practical determination about what the law means in the first instance in constrained action settings. This move opens up new lines of inquiry, such as looking at how local solutions to immediate problems inside legal organizations become institutionalized as established ways of doing the law in a field of activity or how and why variation in the law's use or disuse is produced over time and place. The remainder of the chapter takes up two topics discussed elsewhere in this volume to explore a bit more precisely the value added to the study of criminal law from this conceptual shift. The two topics I address are subjects the authors in this volume have carefully explored to document the substantial costs to fairness and legitimacy produced by the gap between the law's ideal in formal specification and operation in its real-world incarnation. I explore a different side of those topics, which is to think through how to approach explaining the divergence and the precise shape it takes over time.

Taking It Way Back

Ever since Weber offered up his ideal type of bureaucracy, scholars have been picking at components of the concept and asking to what extent any actually existing organization fits the definition or to what extent legal rational authority is actually achieved in the proffered fashion. One strand of the enterprise began by positing a distinction between the formal and informal organizational structure. The formal organization was the official design that usually set out something like a Weberian ideal type of bureaucracy with defined hierarchal offices delimited by spheres of competence, bound together to achieve a specific end with an abstract set of rules for doing so. The value of positing the concept of the formal organization was to highlight how, according to someone's plan, things ought to be working: "The relevance of the known qualities of things becomes very apparent when one considers that it must be at least possible for them to be related in ways that the idealization stipulates."[6]

Sociologists studying actual existing organizations proposed that inside (and sometimes in opposition to) formal organizations grew informal organizations, entities that are "not simply idiosyncratic deviations but *form consistent patterns that are new elements of the organization*."[7] In fact, the claim of Blau and other early organizational sociologists was that "bureaucratic structures continually create conditions that modify these structures" because operations create new needs and new problems.[8] Or, as Selznick explained, formal organizations must move from plan to action by selecting specific technologies of execution inside of concrete social and institutional environments. These environments are not merely passive habitats of their activity. Rather, they contain elements that the organization must work and engage with as the organization undertakes a specific course of action. In so doing, the organization's actions generate "involvements" and "commitments" that necessarily and inexorably transform the plans of organizations as they unfold in the real world over time.[9]

Thus, the space between organizational plan and action is a feature of the different sorts of thing they are:

> Plans and programs reflect the freedom of technical or ideal choice, but organized action cannot escape involvement, a commitment to personnel or institutions or procedures which effectively qualifies the initial plan. *Der Mensch denkt, Gott lenkt* . . . . We are inescapably committed to the mediation of human structures which are at once indispensable to our goals and at the same time stand between them and ourselves.[10]

So, after a generation of studies consistently finding the existence of elements and practices inside organizations that were not established or anticipated by formal organizational plans, the field came to accept that this insight should no longer be offered as a satisfying conclusion to the research program. Rather, it ought to be the premise of the research program.

In one of my favorite formulations of this conclusion, Etzioni argued that approaching the study of organizations by asking to what extent their operations conformed to formal plans generated predictable findings thoroughly dependent upon the model's assumptions. He noted that "goals, as norms, as sets of meanings depicting target states, are cultural entities," whereas "organizations, as systems of coordinated activities of more than one actor, are social systems."[11] Therefore, it should come as no surprise that comparing "the blueprint of an organization . . . a set of symbols on paper" to the actually existing organization, which is "a functioning social unit," will repeatedly yield findings showing that the organization in actual practice operates quite differently from the organization in idealized conception.[12] Or, as Egon Bittner put it, "It has been one of the most abiding points of interest of modern organizational research to study how well the programmatically intended formal structures of organizations describe what is going on within them, and what unintended, unprogrammed, and thus informal structures tend to accompany them."[13]

Perhaps, one line of scholars argued, it makes sense to think of the existing practices inside an organization less as an "informal" organizational structure than as the actual "situated determinations of what the rules, procedures, policies and goals of the organization actionably consist in."[14] That is,

The very features of the bureaucrats' circumstances which are often identified as factors leading to the modification or violation of formal rules
and occasioning the emergence of alternative "informal rules" may in
fact be the features which bureaucrats consult in order to decide what the
formal rules might reasonably mean and what it would take to employ
them *in the first instance*.[15]

In sum, a school of organizational sociologists urged a move away
from an external deductive approach that takes the formal, officially
stated plans of an organization as the point of departure and then analyzes the barriers to effectively realizing the official goals or reasons for
deviation from formal plans of action. They urged a move toward an internal and inductive approach that takes the practical circumstances of
daily activities as a point of departure and asks how rules are interpreted
and made use of in the ongoing course of activity. The reason for such
a move was not some a priori commitment to negating the ontological
status of formal organizations or their constitutive rules, but rather a
desire to enhance explanatory gratification. Ultimately, the claim was
that it was *unsatisfying* to consistently conclude there was a difference
between formal plans and actual practices and *unproductive* to characterize those elements responsible for that difference as distorting influences because that approach seemed to assume the answer to the most
interesting questions.

The rejected approach seems to assume that abstract rules have obvious and specific meanings in the world of action, meanings that are
clear and immediately available to actors in specific choice situations.
But it is precisely the fact that we don't live in such a world and that,
with respect to much of the activity we are keen to understand, abstract statements do not direct obvious and specific courses of action
that leads us to study the object in the first place. Most of the time, the
meanings of rules are susceptible to many interpretations and moments
of application are characterized by resource constraint and uncertainty.
We find ourselves back in the messy lived environments of social life,
asking how actors make sense of what rules mean and demand of
them. How do actors manage to apply rules under conditions of complex and competing demands, resource constraint, and informational
uncertainty?

Applying this insight to the study of law, I claim that if we want to *understand*—and by that I mean render intelligible—the space between plan and execution or between law on the books and law in action, then we want to ask what exactly the frontline legal actors are doing with legal rules and how they interpolate them into an ongoing course of meaningful (although not necessarily beneficial) social action. If we fail to do so, our reform activities may be plagued by unintended consequences because that unaccounted-for residual will turn into a new line of action.

In the next section I apply the lessons from organizational sociology to the sociology of law. In so doing, I hope not to "confuse similarity with identity."[16] Organizational rules are not identical to statutes, and organizational plans are not identical to institutionally prescribed roles in legal systems. My claim is not that the two can be perfectly equated. Nonetheless, I do believe insights achieved in the former domain can be successfully leveraged into the latter because there are certain points of analytic similarity: both organizational and legal rules make out a set of formal directives outlining how things ought to operate, who has which powers, and what activities are authorized under what conditions. Actors must then operationalize these rules in order to do their work. Although there is much dissimilarity, one benefit of analogizing law to organizational rules is to highlight inclusion in the concept of law of those "power-conferring" or role-defining rules beyond the Austinian sanction-backed commands so frequently studied in criminal law.[17] The actors populating living criminal justice systems are working with (or under) all types of legal rules—those detailing proscribed behavior and authorized sanctions, those conferring powers and capacities, those defining roles and statuses, those prescribing and proscribing methods of conducting business, and many others difficult to easily categorize. Furthermore, the claim that actors must operationalize these rules for law to become *law* is not reducible to (although it is compatible with) realist or critical claims that legal rules are "indeterminate," meaning that legal actors fill in the gaps with idiosyncratic preferences, hegemonic ideology, or other extralegal considerations. Even those that take the internal view of law—in the Hartian sense—must decide *what it means* in concrete action settings to "guide and evaluate conduct in accordance with rules."[18]

Two Examples and What Organizational Sociology Has to Do with It

The remainder of this chapter takes two insights about the current operations of the criminal justice system proffered in this volume and explores how the contribution I developed above from organizational sociology might open up a set of research questions. In the course of exploring these lines of research, I propose some substantive ideas about the topics. Nonetheless, it is my aim in this short chapter not to defend any particular hypothesis but to propose what hypotheses inspired by the insight from organizational sociology might look like.

Two of the most notable developments across the multitude of jurisdictions that constitute America's "criminal justice system" over the last 30-plus years are the adoption of determinate sentencing regimes and the establishment of, and then iterative increases in, statutory minimum sentences.[19] Although these are conceptually and legally distinct classes of reforms, they followed a similar logic that swept the criminal justice field starting in the early 1970s and often were passed within close temporal proximity in various jurisdictions. On the books, these statutes significantly increased the punishments available to state actors. But what unfolded over this period was extreme variation in their use and possibly even systematic downward departure from authorized sentences. In fact, it is precisely these statutes that some scholars have pointed to as an explanation for a transformation in the mode of criminal law administration. Rachel Barkow here and elsewhere has argued that the prosecutor's office (namely in the federal system) plays a quasi-administrative role in the criminal justice system as opposed to being one party in an adversarial system. Her insight is not limited to noting that the actual operations of the criminal justice systems diverge from the ideal of formal adversarial justice. The insight is particularly interesting, I submit, because it extends to the precise *way* in which the operations diverge from the adversarial ideal and what might account for this fact.

Consider one of the leading states to adopt draconic mandatory minimums: New York. In 1973 Nelson Rockefeller, the moderate Republican governor of New York since 1958, announced a dramatic shift from what had been a steady course of (at times compulsory and at times voluntary) medicalized treatment of drug offenders. Within the year, a slightly modified version of his initial bill was passed, and the various statutory reforms came to be known as the Rockefeller Drug Laws.[20] These laws provided for some of the longest mandatory minimum sentences for drug crimes, including elevating the sale of one ounce (or possession of two ounces) of narcotics such as cocaine and heroin to a class A-I felony (on par with homicide and first-degree kidnapping), carrying a mandatory *minimum* sentence of 15 to 25 years with a maximum of life.[21]

Despite an emboldening political climate for carceral drug policies and signals from the state legislature conveying the punitive spirit of the statutory amendments, the substantial and extensive changes to the penal law passed in 1973 did not translate into significant correctional outcomes for almost eight years. Figure 11.1 shows that prison sentences imposed from felony drug arrests began their steep upswing in the mid-1980s, almost a decade after the passage of the Rockefeller Drug Laws. The state trends were largely driven by trends in New York City. According to one source, the share of the state's prison population committed for drug offenses increased very slightly from 1972 (11 percent) until 1977 (12 percent) and then fell again (9 percent) by 1980 only to increase sharply after that to over 35 percent by the early 1990s.[22]

Behind these trends was an array of shifts at each level of criminal justice processing, demonstrating that this massive change in formal law on the books had a varying and evolving effect on law in action. Noticeably, the number of drug felony arrests in New York declined in the years immediately after the passage of the law until the early 1980s, after which drug arrests as a percentage of total felony arrests doubled from 1985 until 1994.[23] Figure 11.2 displays the total number of dispositions from felony drug arrests, the percentage of those dispositions taken in Supreme Court (the court with jurisdiction to impose felony conviction and sentence), and the percentage of felony drug arrests resulting in prison sentences, available from New York State's Department of Criminal Justice Services (DCJS) over the years 1979 through 2013. Although the DCJS does not provide continuous data before 1979, other sources report that felony drug arrests, indictments, and conviction rates for felony drug crimes decreased in New York City between the enactment in 1973 and 1976.[24]

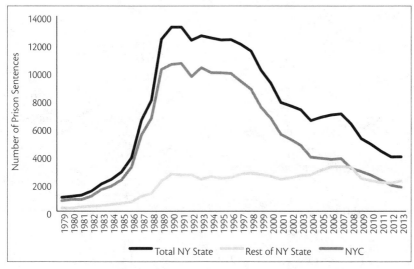

Figure 11.1. Prison Sentences from Felony Drug Arrests, New York City and New York State, 1979–2013

The percentage of dispositions from felony drug arrests taken in Supreme Court—which is the best available measure of indictments from felony arrests—began to rise sharply only in the mid-1980s.[25] According to other sources reporting data before 1979, the indictment rate from felony drug arrests actually decreased significantly between 1973 and 1976, from about 39 percent to 25 percent. However, the prison-sentencing rate from drug felony cases increased during this period, with one reason being that the law strictly limited plea bargaining on class A drug felonies after indictment (the restriction was slightly loosened in 1976).[26] In fact, those restrictions on plea bargaining were a source of frustration to many court actors: prosecutors resented statutory limits on their professional autonomy, and by reducing the incentive to plead early, the restrictions created significant backlogs in felony courts.[27] But as Figure 11.2 shows, the increase in the percentage of felony drug cases resulting in prison sentences did not begin its precipitous climb until the mid-1980s. Again, this is almost a decade after the enactment of the Rockefeller Drug Laws. For comparison, Figure 11.3 shows the trends for violent felony dispositions over the same time period of 1979 through 2013.

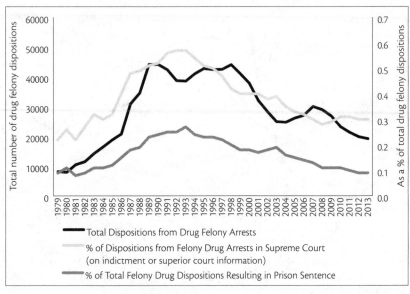

Figure 11.2. Total Drug Felony Dispositions, Supreme Court Disposition Rate and Prison Sentence Rate, New York City, 1979–2013

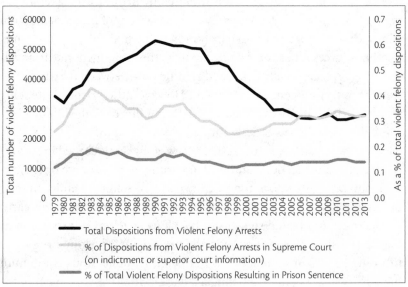

Figure 11.3. Total Violent Felony Dispositions, Supreme Court Disposition Rate and Prison Sentence Rate, New York City, 1979–2013

Again, the mere fact that a statutory change does not immediately and mechanically translate into outcomes should not surprise us. Laws don't apply themselves; someone somewhere must do things and make choices. But why would the adoption of penal statutes in which substantial prison sentences attach automatically upon conviction to specific offenses change not just outcomes but also the character of criminal law administration? One answer is that criminal statutes specifying mandatory minimums change the interactional dynamics of the various actors that compose the criminal justice system. It does so because they are—like other organizational actors—engaged in an ongoing meaningful enterprise. They are *doing something* with the rules and procedures that structure the criminal justice system. And to make sense of what the New York State criminal justice actors did with a new set of rules, we need to study the precise commitments and resources with which they were operating and to get a sense of how they understood the ongoing enterprise of which they were a part. The question is, "how is it that members of an organized setting go about finding the sense, import, and actionable features of rules and other rational constructions within, and with respect to, and by their artful management of, the actual contingent situations of their use."[28]

One compelling hypothesis suggested by the data presented here is that these new laws changed how prosecutors approached plea bargaining and how other actors in the system—namely, judges, defense attorneys, and defendants—strategically reacted. Certainly the dominance of plea bargaining is not a recent development. Most historical accounts estimate it was the primary mode of case disposition in urban and federal jurisdictions in the United States at least by the beginning of the 20th century—by some estimates accounting for somewhere between 50 and 90 percent of dispositions.[29] As Figure 11.4 shows, trials were nearly extinct as a means of securing guilt by the late 1970s. But the claim of Barkow and others, as I understand it, is that the distinctive feature of a quasi-administrative system is not just that prosecutors are avoiding trials as a means of establishing legal guilt.[30] Rather, the claim is that under the current sentencing regime the upshot of avoiding trials as a means for establishing legal guilt means that prosecutors are able to exercise combined adjudicatory and sentencing authority.

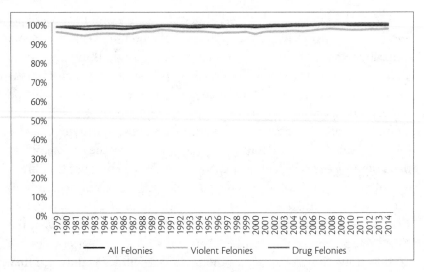

Figure 11.4. Percent of Convictions by Plea: All Felonies, Violent Felonies, and Drug Felonies, New York City, 1979–2014

And if we start with an organizational perspective, it makes sense that plea bargaining under a legal regime with mandatory minimums is driven by different considerations, imperatives, and logic than under a legal regime in which a finding of guilt to a specific offense does not automatically trigger (or dramatically narrow) a sentence. This approach opens up a particular set of empirical questions and hypotheses. For example, to what extent is the emergence of a quasi-administrative method of criminal law administration made possible by the continuity, as opposed to rupture, of the professional roles or self-understandings of prosecutors? Perhaps prosecutors in the United States have long felt that it was their prerogative and duty to assess probable guilt and estimate proportionate blameworthiness of defendants in carrying out their jobs. But what it means to do so responsibly and how they can do so are determined only in particular legal and political environments.

Historical studies have found variation in plea bargaining practices based on different sentencing regimes as far back as the mid-19th century. According to George Fisher, prosecutors engaged different case resolution practices with liquor cases, where the statutes specified mandatory sentences for specific offenses, than they did with other criminal cases, where statutes did not.[31] With the former category they would, as we say today, initially "overcharge" and then bargain to get the defendant to plead to an offense carrying a sentence the prosecutor deemed appropriate.[32] If what prosecutors were doing with criminal law was not only trying to dispose of cases or maximize convictions but also trying to secure, under various constraints, what they consider a substantively satisfactory outcome from the encounter, then they would adjust their strategic case processing decisions when specific sentences automatically attach (or drastically narrow the range) upon conviction.

Another set of interesting questions triggered by this insight is to ask what accounts for the variation in the use of prosecutorial quasi-administrative power. Returning to the story of the Rockefeller Drug Laws, the dramatic rise and fall in the absolute numbers of felony drug arrests terminating in prison sentences over the life span of the Rockefeller Drug Laws is breathtaking. As shown in Figure 11.1, in 1979 there were 751 drug felony convictions imposing a prison sentence. At the height of the upward trend in 1991, there were 10,590 felony drug convictions imposing a prison sentence in New York City—an increase of more than 1,300 percent. The upward trends were partly driven by a substantial increase in felony drug arrests (which raises another interesting question). But they were also driven by a significant increase in indictments, felony convictions upon indictment, and prison sentences imposed upon conviction. And these trends reversed without major statutory change. In 1991 over 90 percent of felony drug cases that had been transferred to superior court resulted in a felony conviction, after which the trend began to decline down to about 80 percent in the early 2000s and down further to about 60 percent in 2013. The prison-sentencing trend started to decrease significantly before the two rounds of major statutory changes that were enacted in 2004, under Governor Pataki, lowering the mandatory minimums, and again in 2009, under Governor Paterson, eliminating many, but not all, mandatory minimums for drug offenses. By 2004 the number of prison sentences imposed from felony drug arrests had already declined to 3,877—down 63 percent from its peak in 1991. Thus, it is evident prosecutors used their quasi-administrative power differently over time.

This brings us back to jumping bunnies. If we start from the proposition that legal actors are social actors, that they encounter legal rules as tools or impediments in an ongoing course of activity, then we would not expect legal rules to mechanically direct outcomes. But we would expect legal rules to influence organizational and institutional dynamics within their respective fields of operation. And in those legal fields things such as political movements and professional understandings are not confounding distorting variables that warp an otherwise natural progression between law on the books and law in action. Rather, they are the very material that makes law what it is as a felt social force. Thus, one final important line of inquiry about statutes such as the Rockefeller Drug Laws is to examine how they do not merely reflect a political reality but also actively construct that reality and thereby make possible a particular set of uses of the law, such as punitive exclusion of large populations.[33]

Another example from this volume demonstrates the opposite trend: continuity in certain practices of criminal justice organizations despite legal change. Sasha Natapoff in this volume and elsewhere has noted that it might be an understatement to say that due process ideals are not realized in the lower reaches of the penal pyramid. As she points out, the lack of process to determine facts means that, with respect to lower criminal courts, "it is hard to maintain that the system is authentically motivated by defendant culpability because the players rarely stop to check whether defendants are innocent or not."[34] Given the fact that commentators and courts have long complained of the "shocking fact-finding deficiencies of lower courts," we might wonder why this fact seems so impervious to changing legal structures.[35]

If the criminal justice actors in lower criminal courts are not using criminal procedures to sort the guilty from the innocent in order to convict those factually guilty of specific offenses and to impose a formal criminal punishment *because* of guilt, then what are they doing? Perhaps the persistent divergence of lower criminal court adjudicative practices from the ideal of due process is explained by a succession of novel proximate causes. Again, the specifics of the legal, political, and organizational environment might be the point of departure to ask what legal actors are doing with the rules they have at their disposal.

Consider Caleb Foote's study of the processing of vagrancy-type offenders in the early 1950s. Foote observed hundreds of trials of defendants accused of vagrancy, drunkenness, or disorderly conduct over three years in a Philadelphia magistrate court and concluded that the routine summary procedures lacked "most elementary requirements of a fair hearing."[36] On a representative day, "[d]efendants were tried, found guilty and sentenced in the elapsed time of seventeen seconds from the time that the first man's name was called by the magistrate through the pronouncing of sentence upon the fourth defendant."[37] He noted that many defendants were quickly adjudicated guilty on the basis of appearance, ascribed status, or minimal statements from arresting officers and then rapidly committed to the House of Corrections for a term of months. But he also noted that many others were quickly *discharged* with orders to leave Philadelphia or go back to the part of town "where they belonged," or were allowed to avoid being processed at all if they could produce evidence of an outbound bus ticket or steady employment.

What's organizational sociology got to do with it? The proposed line of inquiry suggested from the lessons belabored above would be to discern what immediate ends-in-view the actors in this system had and how they accordingly interpreted and made use of the legal tools at their disposal. Foote argued that vagrancy laws were being repurposed to their initial use during pre-Elizabethan and Elizabethan England as antimigratory measures to control newly freed labor after "the break-up of Feudalism and its resulting economic dislocation."[38] In Foote's research site the actors were similarly concerned with maintaining control over certain physical spaces of the city by excluding unattached labor. The link between component criminal justice organizations was essential to his story. The police were using broad criminal statutes proscribing vagrancy and habitual drunkenness as a general grant of authority to expel and exclude certain populations from the physical space of the city, what the police called *civic sanitation*.

In this setting, the frontline court actors (who at the time did not include many defense attorneys) considered the criminal process as a mere roadblock. Process was not so much ignored as inconsequential to what they understood their task to be (and they clearly believed it to be a legitimate task): to expel unemployed or transitory populations from public spaces.[39] So, if process as a means to determine factual guilt needed to be avoided to get directly to the criminal penalty, then it would be ignored. But, correspondingly, if process as a means to determine innocence needed to be avoided to allow the court to *discharge* a defendant who showed he was willing to leave town, who was employed, or who demonstrated stable residence in Philadelphia, then it would also be ignored.[40]

As Foote notes, even if there had been a more robust process, it is not clear it would have altered the fates of many defendants since the substantive criminal provisions—the "law being applied"—was so broad that the terms of the offense was no limiting principle at all on the exercise of judicial authority.[41] Furthermore, there were few levers for defendants to pull to try to force an unwilling court to intercede a careful factual inquiry into guilt between accusation and punishment (or nonpunishment).

Indeed, it was precisely these twin critiques—that the most common low-level offenses charged were so broad there was little fact-finding work for lower courts to do, and that defendants had shockingly little leverage to demand fact-finding work—that led reformers in the next two decades to challenge both vague statutes and sparse procedure. And that movement was largely successful, at least in its immediate goals. Between 1962 and 1972 most "status" offenses were struck down as either unconstitutionally vague or lacking a constitutionally required intentional act.[42] Over that same time period the Warren Court's "due process revolution" unfolded, in which the Supreme Court elaborated a series of procedural protections as constitutionally required in various governmental undertakings, including in the criminal justice domain for our present purposes.

Those reform movements led Malcolm Feeley to revisit the site of lower criminal courts in the 1970s. Indeed, the empirical puzzle of his book was why, in the "full bloom" of the due process revolution, so few defendants took advantage of their newly awarded rights to demand a more rigorous process between arrest and penalty.[43] He found that they often declined to do so because it was rarely in their (at least short-term) interests to do so. The relatively minor sanctions meted out to misdemeanor defendants were often dwarfed in comparison to the procedural costs suffered from arrest, pretrial detention, appearance, attorney fees, lost work, and court delays. As captured by the iconic title *The Process Is the Punishment*, Feeley argued that in lower criminal courts the "locus of court-imposed sanctions shifts dramatically away from adjudication, plea bargaining, and sentencing to the earlier pretrial stages."[44]

What is fascinating is that despite a significant change in the legal rules structuring the site of lower criminal courts, the defining feature of lower courts identified in earlier eras—the criminal process was not being used to sort the guilty from the innocent—persisted. However, the actual meaning and use of this feature were transformed in the site and time of Feeley's study.

The holdings and rules that constituted the due process revolution was large and diverse. But for the most part, they consisted in the non-compulsory right of a defendant to demand a certain process before a certain determination could be made or the inability of the state to use certain evidence obtained in unauthorized ways *in trial*. Many commentators and activists hoped that, taken together, these new rights and duties (especially the right to counsel in any criminal case terminating in a custodial sentence) would have the effect of making courts orient their activities toward finding guilt using authorized procedures.[45] But it is important to note that the form of most of these new rules was not a command to the state that "you must undertake these procedures in each and every case," but rather "if you want to do X, you must do it P way," or "if you want to do X, you must do Y first." Proceeding from the insight that legal rules are tools available to actors engaged in ongoing courses of meaningful activity in a concrete setting, we might see these new rules as an occasion for actors to ask, "Well, do we really need to do X in order to get what we want out of this encounter?"[46]

And what Feeley found was that in this new environment, for the most part, many prosecutors and judges did not feel the need to do X in order to get what they wanted out of the encounter, where X usually stood for a substantial formal punishment or even an official finding of guilt. Feeley found that prosecutors decided to *nolle prosequi* more than one-third of the cases and offered noncustodial sentences in the grand majority of the guilty pleas.[47]

Courthouses are interactional sites where the observed patterns are the outcome of many actors making strategic decisions in reaction to the choices of other actors. Feeley's account was not just that defendants forwent trials and due process rights because they were too burdensome. His account was that defendants forwent them *in exchange* for a disposition proposed by prosecutors and ratified by judges.[48] What did prosecutors and judges get out of this exchange? How did they understand or seem to practice their immediate grounded goals of doing work in this legal site with those legal rules? Feeley found that most prosecutors and judges were concerned with what he termed *substantive justice*, delivering some appropriate response given a quick, yet individualized, assessment of the alleged criminal act and the defendant as a person.

Here, not only were defendants often seeking to avoid process in lieu of a quick disposition, but also the very fact that defendants had experienced costly impositions and burdens was interpreted as a conclusion— indeed a punishment—sufficient to satisfy the immediate goals of the frontline actors administering criminal justice. And part of the explanation Feeley found for this was that in this space at this time, these cases were "universally labeled as 'garbage', 'junk', 'trash', 'crap', penny ante', and the like."[49] So the process being the punishment for such "junk" cases (at least in the majority of cases) was enough.

Over 30 years later my own research revisited misdemeanor courts at a time when the valence around such cases had decidedly changed. No longer mere "junk," these cases were held out as the key to maintaining order and safety in public spaces in the policing models pioneered in New York City under the ambiguous banner Broken Windows, quality-of-life, or order-maintenance policing. Yet I found the same fact reported by Foote, Feeley, Natapoff, and others: these were not courts where, by and large, process was used to sort the guilty from the innocent. However, certain changes in the legal, political, and organizational environment made the broad fact of a disconnect acquire a much different meaning in this site and time. I found that although the criminal process was rarely used to sort out factual guilt, it *was* actively used to test and monitor the defendants flowing through the courts. In fact, this active new use of the criminal process to assess, discipline, and surveil substantial populations of largely young minority men hauled into lower courts from these policing tactics could be said to have given rise to a new model of criminal law administration, what I have termed the *managerial model*.

In Foote's study the police activities that brought in misdemeanor arrests were largely about expelling and excluding specific migratory populations from key public spaces, and in Feeley's study the policing activities were largely about interrupting unseemly but not intolerable behaviors in a reactive manner. In my study, the expansion of misdemeanor arrests over the past 20 years in New York City was the result of a particular policing model that posited intensive enforcement against low-level crimes as the linchpin of urban crime control. The policing of low-level offenses was proactive and targeted at residential and commercial spaces alike and at established (i.e., nonmigratory) populations. The goal was not to banish populations from the city or interrupt a particular bad act, but to transform spaces and to track and sort people in the city. The model held out that by doing so the police could not only abate certain quality-of-life issues but also reduce serious violent crime by establishing "order" in urban neighborhoods and by identifying risky individuals. Law enforcement explicitly sought to increase the formal records kept from each encounter and to make sure records about the individuals they encountered persisted within an official state repository. These policing tactics in New York City ended up sweeping in very large numbers of people who had no prior criminal convictions at the time of their arrests.[50] And the lower courts of New York City had to process those individuals, who for the most part stood accused of relatively minor transgressions (marijuana or narcotics possession, turnstile jumping, petty theft, minor assault), under extreme resource constraint.

I found that in New York City, the lack of criminal process was less about actors trying to avoid it to expeditiously get to the exercise of coercion (whether that was a jail sentence, expulsion, or release with a demand to get to work), a set of inconvenient burdens that dissuaded defendants from pursuing formal adjudication of their case, or even a collection of informal means by which judges and prosecutors punished defendants (although that certainly happened). The story about the lack of process in this site was primarily a story about frontline actors using the various tools of the criminal process as a means to sort, engage, and regulate defendants over time. For example, prosecutors were often willing to offer and judges were willing to accept dispositions that involved temporary "marking" of defendants—creating a record of the criminal justice encounter that could be accessed by the public and others in the criminal justice system only for a limited amount of time. These nonconviction dispositions became one of the most common tools for dealing with new entrants to the misdemeanor justice system. In fact, as the lower courts were flooded with ever-higher volumes of misdemeanor cases, the disposition category that grew the fastest was not criminal convictions, but dismissals.[51]

The procedural hassles of case processing represented a series of opportunities to engage defendants in official encounters with state authority, to discipline and reform their behavior. Defendants must not only confront these procedural hassles, but their efforts to discharge and overcome the procedural hassles are also evaluated as a performance by judges and prosecutors. Defendants' later experiences in lower court often depended on how well and responsibly they bore up under the earlier demands of procedural hassle. Defendants who performed satisfactorily were often able to exit the system, whereas those who failed—by failing to show up to court or to a community service or program assignment, or by getting rearrested with a pending case—were pushed deeper into the system. I found that when low-level offenses were imbued with import in a particular urban control project that intensively policed certain spaces and populations, the lower courts were engaged in a long-term relationship with misdemeanor defendants. Not only was process the punishment for a particular encounter, but it was also a useful opportunity to learn about and gauge the defendant, to decide whether it was worth the judicial resources to further engage the individual.

In sum, this brief discussion of lower courts is an example where a persistent disconnect between law on the books and law in action—namely, the failure to regularly engage the criminal process to sort on guilt or innocence—is produced differentially over time. The prior discussion of the Rockefeller Drug Laws shows a different trend—radically changing legal outcomes over the life span of a (fairly) stable statute. Both examples are offered toward the same end. Starting from the premise borrowed from organizational sociology—actors populating living legal institutions must always make sense of the rules that structure their field of operation in order to move from theory to action and they do so in situated spaces of resource and informational constraint—generates a set of research questions about how legal rules are fundamentally always interpolated into the course of ongoing activity. The ongoing projects of organizational actors are not distortions to an otherwise obvious incarnation of an abstract principle; they are the very sources that shape how legal actors think of what the rule means in the first instance.

I conclude by emphasizing, at the risk of stating the obvious, the important role for carefully noting the space between theory and action. Institutions that perform weighty roles such as declaring a person guilty of a crime and deploying the state's power to punish are designed with certain protections and safeguards. It is precisely those protections and safeguards that are supposed to offer legitimacy to such weighty acts. That legitimacy is challenged when those designed protections and safeguards do not operate in practice. The legitimacy concerns raised by the two examples discussed in this chapter—the operation of a quasi-administrative prosecutor's office inside of a nominally adversarial system and the routine disposition of cases with little factual or legal deliberation in lower criminal courts—are detailed elsewhere in this volume, so I will not cursorily cover what has been carefully documented elsewhere. I wish to simply note in closing that reform activities benefit from sociological investigation of the sort proposed here: not only careful documentation of the space between law on the books and law in action but also attentive analysis of the precise factors that shape how frontline legal actors come to understand law on the books in the first instance. If we fail to account for what they are doing with the legal rules and tools at their disposal, then reform activities will be plagued by unintended consequences because, well, the jumping bunny jumps. Laws, like formal organizational plans, do not manifest as social practices by formal enactment. Situated social actors must make sense of rules and decide what they mean in particular action settings. Therefore, we must understand the particular commitments, constraints, and conceptualizations of current legal actors working with the rules we hope to change if we wish to change the outcomes produced by those rules.

NOTES

1 *Bartleby*, directed by Jonathan Parker (2001) (adapted from Herman Melville's short story *Bartleby, the Scrivener* [1853]).

2 There is a long history of law and society scholars studying what has been termed the *gap* question. See, for example, David Nelken, "Gap Problem in the Sociology of Law: A Theoretical Review," *Windsor Yearbook of Access to Justice* 1 (1981): 44 (discussing an academic schism between sociology of law and sociolegal studies as characterized by the former criticizing the latter for making "implausible assumptions concerning the way in which norms might be expected to affect conduct"), and Carroll Seron and Susan Silbey, "Profession, Science and Culture: An Emergent Canon of Law and Society Research," in *The Blackwell Companion to Law and Society*, ed. Austin Sarat (New York: John Wiley & Sons, 2008), 30–59 (documenting law and society scholarship on various subject matters—from courts to policing to administrative agencies—and noting most of the seminal

scholarship is focused on documenting the gap between law on the books and law in action).

3 Judith Butler, *Gender Trouble: Feminism and the Subversion of Identity* (London and New York: Routledge, 2011), 10. Butler's claim is that those "immutable" physical characteristics that we call sex are as contested as what features constitute gender; and we cannot think of them as providing some material structure upon which the superstructure of gender is constructed because the very act of selecting and rendering relevant certain traits is at the same time the production of sex and gender. Of course, one does not need to accept Butler's view on sex and gender to entertain the possibility of such a critique regarding the distinction between law on books and law in action.

4 John Dewey, *The Later Works of John Dewey, 1925–1953: Essays, Reviews, and Miscellany, 1939–1941* (Carbondale: Southern Illinois University Press, 1988), 118. For an extended discussion of the "identity question" of law from a rigorous philosophically analytic approach, see Scott J. Shapiro, *Legality* (Cambridge, MA: Harvard University Press, 2011).

5 Mona Lynch, "The Situated Actor and the Production of Punishment: Toward an Empirical Social Psychology of Criminal Procedure," this volume.

6 Egon Bittner, "The Concept of Organization," *Social Research* 32, no. 3 (October 1, 1965): 244.

7 Peter Michael Blau, *The Dynamics of Bureaucracy; A Study of Interpersonal Relations in Two Government Agencies* (Chicago: University of Chicago Press, 1955), 3.

8 Ibid., 9.

9 Philip Selznick, "Foundations of the Theory of Organization," *American Sociological Review* 13, no. 1 (February 1, 1948): 32, doi:10.2307/2086752; Philip Selznick, *TVA and the Grass Roots: A Study of Politics and Organization* (New Orleans: Quid Pro Books, 2011), 64.

10 Selznick, "Foundations of the Theory of Organization," 32. The German phrase means "the human being thinks, God directs."

11 Amitai Etzioni, "Two Approaches to Organizational Analysis: A Critique and a Suggestion," *Administrative Science Quarterly* 5, no. 2 (September 1, 1960): 258.

12 Ibid., 259.

13 Bittner, "The Concept of Organization," 239.

14 Don Zimmerman, "Tasks and Troubles: The Practical Bases of Work Activities in a Public Assistance Agency," in *Explorations in Sociology and Counseling*, ed. Donald A. Hansen and Jessie Bernard (Boston: Houghton Mifflin, 1969), 338.

15 Ibid., 341 (emphasis added).

16 Malcolm M. Feeley, "The Concept of Laws in Social Science: A Critique and Notes on an Expanded View," *Law & Society Review* 10, no. 4 (July 1, 1976): 502.

17 Herbert Lionel Adolphus Hart, *The Concept of Law* (Oxford: Oxford University Press, 2012); Feeley, "The Concept of Laws in Social Science," 498, 504.

18 Scott J. Shapiro, "What Is the Internal Point of View?," *Fordham Law Review* 75 (2006): 1157.

19 Prior to 1970, very few states prescribed mandatory minimums for the great majority of penal law offenses—with the exception of life sentences for murder in some jurisdictions. Michael Tonry, *Sentencing Matters* (Oxford: Oxford University Press, n.d.), 6; Ram Subramanian and Ruth Delaney, *Playbook for Change? States Reconsider Mandatory Sentences* (Vera Institute for Justice), www.vera.org. As of the late 1980s it seems almost every state had replaced indeterminate with determinate sentences over a large portion of the specific offenses in the penal code or had set substantial mandatory minimums for indeterminate sentences, thereby narrowing the band of possible sentences for each designated offense.

20 Act of May 22, 1973, ch. 276, sec. 9, Crim. Proc. § 70.00, N. Y. Laws 1044–45 (McKinney); Julilly Kohler-Hausmann, "'The Attila the Hun Law': New York's Rockefeller Drug Laws and the Making of a Punitive State," *Journal of Social History* 44, no. 1 (2010): 75.

21 N.Y. Penal § 70.00 (McKinney 1987) (establishing sentence minimum and maximum for class A-I felonies); N.Y. Penal § 220.43 (McKinney 1980) (classifying possession of two ounces as A-I felony); N.Y. Penal § 220.21 (McKinney 1980) (classifying sale of one ounce as A-I felony); N.Y. Penal §§ 125.25 and 125.27 (McKinney 1987) (classifying homicide as class A-I felony); N.Y. Penal § 135.25 (McKinney 1987) (classifying kidnapping as class A-I felony); N.Y. Penal § 70.00 (McKinney 1987) (terms of imprisonment for felony crimes).

22 David F. Weiman and Christopher Weiss, "The Origins of Mass Incarceration in New York State: The Rockefeller Drug Laws and the Local War on Drugs," in *Do Prisons Make Us Safer?: The Benefits and Costs of the Prison Boom*, ed. Steven Raphael and Michael A. Stoll (New York: Russell Sage Foundation, 2009), 88.

23 Ibid., 95.

24 Joint Committee on New York Drug Law Evaluation, *The Nation's Toughest Drug Law, Evaluating the New York Experience: Final Report of the Joint Committee on New York Drug Law Evaluation [of] the Association of the Bar of the City of New York [and] Drug Abuse Council* (Association of the Bar of the City of New York, 1977); Weiman and Weiss, "The Origins of Mass Incarceration in New York State."

25 New York Department of Criminal Justice Services (DCJS) data, on file with the author; was provided for only the years 1979–2013. In New York the superior court can impose felony sentences on either an indicted felony arrest or a case proceeding on "superior court information" when the defendant waives the right to a grand jury. So the superior court disposition rate is the best approximation of the indictment rate, i.e., prosecutors going forward with felony charges.

26 Shortly after it was enacted, N.Y. Crim. Proc. § 220.10 was amended by Act of August 3, 1973, ch. 1051, sec. 16, Crim. Proc. § 220.10(6)(a), N.Y. Laws 1993, 1998 (McKinney) to prohibit a plea of guilty to any offense below a class A felony after the defendant had been indicted of a class A felony (A-I and A-II could plead to A-III but no lower; A-III could not plead below A-III). By 1976 the statute was amended to require a plea of guilty to at least an A-III felony if the indictment charged an A-I or A-II felony and to require a plea of guilty to at least a class C

felony if the indictment charged an A-III felony. These restrictions were only applicable to indictments of crimes under Penal Law 220 (Controlled Substances); the 1976 version allowed for a guilty plea to any felony for indictments to class A and B felonies under other provisions of the Penal Law. Guilty Pleas and Sentencing, ch. 480, secs. 1–2, Crim. Proc. §§ 220.10 (5)(a–c), 220.20 (i), 1976 N.Y. Laws 1104, 1104–1105 (McKinney).

27 According to the Bar Association evaluation, the average disposition time for a drug felony doubled between 1973 and 1976, and court actors expressed frustration at their inability to use plea bargaining as a way of managing administrative overload. Joint Committee on New York Drug Law Evaluation, *The Nation's Toughest Drug Law, Evaluating the New York Experience*, 17–19, 28.

28 Zimmerman, "Tasks and Troubles," 241.

29 Albert W. Alschuler, "Plea Bargaining and Its History," *Columbia Law Review* 79 (1979), 6, 26–30. Some put the rise of plea bargaining even earlier, e.g., George Fisher, *Plea Bargaining's Triumph: A History of Plea Bargaining in America* (Stanford, CA: Stanford University Press, 2003), 36.

30 I use the term *quasi-administrative* because it has features of an administrative system by adaptation and practice, not by design. This is, as Barkow points out, precisely the problem, as an inadvertent quasi-administrative system does not have the procedural protections of an intentional administrative system.

31 Fisher, *Plea Bargaining's Triumph*.

32 Ibid., 49–51.

33 Julilly Kohler-Hausmann, "Guns and Butter: The Welfare State, the Carceral State, and the Politics of Exclusion in the Postwar United States," *Journal of American History* 102 (2015): 87–99.

34 Alexandra Natapoff, "The Penal Pyramid," this volume.

35 Debra Livingston, "Police Discretion and the Quality of Life in Public Places: Courts, Communities, and the New Policing," *Columbia Law Review* 97 (1997): 596.

36 Caleb Foote, "Vagrancy-Type Law and Its Administration," *University of Pennsylvania Law Review* 104 (1956): 644.

37 Ibid., 605.

38 Ibid., 615–19, quotation at 615.

39 Ibid., 613.

40 Ibid., 619–20.

41 The offenses processed in court were largely "status" type offenses such as vagrancy, habitual drunkenness, and some borderline "act" type of offenses such as disorderly conduct, which at the time were drafted with maximum vagueness. As Foote points out, the laws were "of use" to police as a weapon precisely because of such vagueness. Ibid., 609, 630.

42 Many of the "status" crimes were struck down between 1962 and 1972, in *Robinson v. California*, 370 U.S. 660, 666–67 (1962), *Powell v. Texas*, 392 U.S. 514, 532–34 (1968) and *Papachristou v. City of Jacksonville*, 405 U.S. 156 (1972). As Deborah

Livingston has documented, criticism such as Foote's prior to the due process revolution, that "assembly-line justice meted out in lower criminal courts for offenses like drunkenness, disorderly conduct, vagrancy, gambling, and prostitution . . . was itself one of the surest signs that the criminal sanction was being misapplied," was part of the argument for expanding constitutional and procedural controls over police discretion during the Warren Court era. Livingston, "Police Discretion and the Quality of Life in Public Places," 586.

43 Malcolm Feeley, *The Process Is the Punishment: Handling Cases in a Lower Criminal Court* (New York: Russell Sage Foundation, 1979), xxiv, 31.

44 Ibid., 30.

45 *Argersinger v. Hamlin*, 407 U.S. 25, 33 (1972). The case did not extend the Sixth Amendment right to counsel to all criminal cases, but rather held that no person could be incarcerated, even for a very short period of time, if he or she were not represented by counsel (and had not waived that right).

46 To be clear, I am not proposing that actors necessarily explicitly ask that question, but rather that the question presents itself in their daily activity as a series of punctuated moments in which choices have to be made under conditions of uncertainty and resource constraint.

47 Feeley, *The Process Is the Punishment*, 127, 138, 249, 255. Feeley reported that about 5 percent of the convicted cases resulted in a jail sentence.

48 Ibid., 69, 150–67.

49 Ibid., 4.

50 Issa Kohler-Hausmann, "Mass Misdemeanors and Managerial Justice," *Stanford Law Review* 66 (2013): 641 (noting that in 1990 there were 53,152 people arrested for misdemeanor crimes who had no prior criminal convictions, and by 2010 that number reached over 130,000).

51 Ibid., 642. As the total number of misdemeanor case dispositions more than doubled from 1993 (the year before the widespread policing changes) to 2011 (the recent peak of misdemeanor arrests), the number of misdemeanor convictions went up by only about 21 percent and the absolute number of dismissal dispositions increased by over 235 percent between 1993 and 2011.

PART IV

Humanizing the Question

The criminal process is the primary mechanism through which our democracy touches, marks, burdens, and governs millions of people. What sort of system *should* it be? What principles of humanity and democracy *should* guide it so as to give us confidence in its legitimacy? These essays explore that age-old question, driven by new insights from the spectacular failures of mass incarceration and race-based policing.

Jonathan Simon, The Second Coming of Dignity

Jeffrey Fagan, Dignity Is the New Legitimacy

12

The Second Coming of Dignity

JONATHAN SIMON

Introduction: Criminal Justice, Law, and Dignity

At the beginning of the 19th century, as the modern European nation state was emerging out of the Napoleonic wars, a German law student (twenty-three years old) named Paul Johann Anselm von Feuerbach formulated what we all might recognize as the central premise of modernity in criminal law and criminal justice. In its English translation it reads: "There's no crime and hence there shall not be punishment if at the time no penal law existed" (Hall, 1937). For simplicity's sake, and consistent with many criminal law casebooks, I will call this the legality principle. For some two centuries, Feuerbach's legality, and its vernacularizations (he did, consistent with many 19th-century scholars, put it in Latin) into various national constitutional doctrines (e.g., the prohibitions on ex post facto and vague laws), have served as a banner and something more than that for the progress of limiting the arbitrariness and severity of punishment in modern society.

In this essay I would like to suggest that we have reached the end of the time when that remarkable slogan can lead us forward either sociologically or jurisprudentially, and that we should replace it (or more precisely supplement it) with another one, born closer to our own time, which can be called the dignity principle.[1] There are many possible models for it, especially the language of Article 5 of the *Universal Declaration of Human Rights* which provides: "No one shall be subjected to torture or to cruel, inhuman or degrading treatment or punishment." Because dignity is only implied there in the negative of torture, cruelty, and degradation, it might be desirable to reformulate it as a positive right to the recognition of dignity: "There shall be no crime and no punishment without respect for human dignity." I want to suggest that as a broad guide, this dignity principle, alongside the traditional legality principle, can provide the right path forward to reforming the criminal justice system after years of distortion and abuse, in ways that will protect the dignity of both those who are caught up in the criminal process, and those front-line state workers that we ask to carry out criminal justice.

The current dignity wave that is moving through both law and society is actually the second one to follow the great shock of World War II and the mass atrocities associated with that conflict (above all, the Holocaust, the reaction to which most historians agree formed the essential core of contemporary legal dignity). The first wave produced the great 20th-century human rights treaties, as well as varying national constitutional developments. In the US, the Warren Court's criminal procedure revolution in the 1950s and 1960s owed a great deal to this first post-war dignity wave, as did the somewhat later wave of sentencing reform and limited substantive criminal law decriminalizations that took place during the 1970s.

By the 1980s, a contrary trend of punitiveness and racially marked prosecution of crime had overtaken the first wave of dignity reforms, coopting some of their elements (e.g., determinate sentencing) and working around others (e.g., constitutional criminal procedure) to produce mass incarceration (Alexander, 2010; Garland, 2001; Simon, 2007; Simon, 2012; Wacquant, 2009; Zimring & Hawkins, 1991) and varieties of wars on crime/gangs/drugs. The result is a policing, justice, and punishment system as degrading as any that has been produced inside a liberal democracy and comparable to that of illiberal states like Apartheid South Africa and the post-Stalin Soviet Union (Simon, 2014).

After reviewing the appeals of the legality principle and summarizing arguments for dignity, I will address some reasons for skepticism about dignity. My conclusion is that the great banner reading *"nulla poena sine lege"* must now be, not lowered, but joined by another banner of "no crime and no punishment without respect for human dignity." While this is a work of normative sociological jurisprudence it is not intended as idealism. Legality and dignity are both values that can motivate and mobilize citizens, but they are not talismans that can magically overcome inertia and interests on their own.

Legality

Feuerbach's statement of the legality principle made his career. He was eventually appointed to professorships at the universities of Jena and Keil and authored the progressive Bavarian penal code of 1813. Feuerbach's passion was to limit judges in penal matters to the penal code, a cause that faired less well in common law countries generally, and in the United States in particular, than on the Continent. But even where common law powers remain on the edges, the principle of legislative supremacy is a near universal in modern legal systems, including the United States. While legislatures have rarely acted with the kind of systematic penal policy that Feuerbach and his contemporaries (like Bentham and Thomas Jefferson) imagined, courts in the 20th century have labored hard to treat the often-archaic common law language of state crimes as a set of well-defined public policies. Indeed, the futility of this pursuit is one of the grounds on which I believe legality today seems to be failing us.

Even though courts play a key role in defining the elements of crimes, they do so generally attempting to implement the legislature's will, often trumping other traditional interpretive concerns like leniency and clarity. During a period of harsh crime politics such as the US experienced over the past forty years, when legislators reliably sought to enhance penal severity in almost every imaginable way, the judicial pursuit of legislative intent alone can become a tool to increase severity and cease altogether to be a restraint.

It is no accident that Feuerbach's thesis caught the tide of modern parliamentary sovereignty as it swept Europe, bringing with it the modern political system and the body of administrative law that we think of as the modern state. For much of this period, tying criminal justice reform to this legality principle reliably yoked it to progressive tendencies. This effect was primarily due to two major secular trends that swept the state in the 19th and late 20th centuries, each of which has long been recognized by scholars of criminal justice history.

First, many (but by no means all) states became progressively more democratic, extending voting and participation rights to non-property-holding men and eventually to women. With democratization of the vote came incentives for parliamentary parties to shelter the persons and reputations of their working class constituents. They sought to do so in part by supporting greater efforts to individualize punishments, both in terms of proper due process and consideration of the prospects for reform of the guilty (Garland, 1985).

The legality principle has also tied criminal law and administration to a set of administrative organs that were almost universally becoming more bureaucratic and legally rational (to use Max Weber's famous and helpful term) (Jacobs, 1977; Feeley & Rubin, 1999). From the early modern period to the end of the 20th century, criminal justice institutions in the advanced tier of developed countries became progressively more a function carried out by public bureaucracies subject to rules of administration and thus promised the possibility but not the guarantee of law.[2] Indeed, it is noteworthy that throughout the period of mass incarceration this bureaucratizing process has continued and arguably triumphed. War on crime has helped create a criminal justice system more integrated vertically and horizontally, more law-like and accountable (tamed, in the apt image of Sam Walker's 1993 history of this process), and has at the same time become more destructive and punitive at every stage of the process.

This direction was not constant or without exceptions. But between the end of the 18th century and the end of the 20th, both these progressive tendencies (democracy and bureaucracy) mitigated the harshness and arbitrariness of criminal law, criminal trials, and punishments. To take only the best known example, capital punishment for felonies like armed robbery, burglary, and even theft, which was common in England and colonial North America at the start of the 18th century, became, by the middle of the 19th century, common only for murder—and by the early decades of the 21st century has been abolished by most fully developed countries (the US being a glaring exception) (Garland, 2011). Investigatory and trial procedures, all but summary processes with few professionals or lawyers for all but the rare case until at least the middle of the 19th century, became more and more a contest of lawyers subject to judicial oversight by the end of the 20th (Langbein, 1994). Only after the Supreme Court's *Gideon v. Wainwright* decision in 1963 were lawyers provided routinely to indigent defendants facing state prison (although many urban counties in the North and West had begun far earlier). The fact that mass incarceration was accomplished despite mass legal aid to criminal defendants is another key indicator that legality by itself is not enough. One can argue forcefully that rights like those announced in *Gideon* have never been sufficiently implemented and that a more robust legality principle would take us closer. The position taken here is that without dignity as a parallel value, the bureaucratic and political pressures on legality will assure its thinness and formality.

The mark of both general processes is evident in the formation of modern criminal justice from the end of the 18th century through the middle third of the 20th--albeit everywhere limited and deformed by the principles of "least eligibility" and class hegemony (Rothman, 1972, 1980; Rusche & Kirchheimer, 2003) and by the attractiveness of the penal field to moral entrepreneurs in the neighboring domains of journalism, politics, and law (Platt, 2009; Rothman, 1980). Going back to Cesare Beccaria's *On Crimes and Punishments* (1764) and John Howard's *The State of the Prisons* (1779), the whole process of jailing, prosecuting, and punishing crime (what we have called the criminal justice system since the 20th century) has been an unparalleled public forum for the larger project of creating a rule of law more and more subordinated to the supremacy of legislative will and judicial oversight. The list of successful reforms under this banner include the rise of the penitentiary, the abolition of solitary confinement and chain gangs in the 19th century (although they came back in the late 20th), and the juvenile court. It remains tempting to believe that this process of reform might be restarted in the aftermath of mass incarceration.

However, certain social and political developments arose in the United States in the last decades of the 20th century to severely undercut the capacity of the legality principle to make progress, or even preserve the "gains" of leniency and due process. The most significant of these developments was mass incarceration, which, beginning in the 1970s, transformed criminal justice practices into an increasingly coordinated exercise in harsh punishment directed primarily at minority youth, but also at anyone perceived as a violent or serious criminal.

The promise of expanding democracy for criminal justice reform relied on the incorporation of formerly marginalized groups into the political process and the ability of that process to mediate the severity of criminalization and punishment (Stuntz, 2011). In the United States, the growing power of the white working classes from the turn of the

20th century on, including millions of new immigrants from Southern and Eastern Europe, made itself felt in the reform of criminal justice institutions. Criminologists and reformers advocated for a rehabilitative penal regime based on classification and appropriate treatment and argued that many young people from lower-class and immigrant backgrounds who were convicted of crime were amenable to reform and capable of achieving their full status as citizens (Garland, 1985; Muhammed, 2011; Rothman, 1980). The whole plethora of progressive criminal justice institutions—juvenile courts, probation, and indeterminate sentencing—reflected the success of these efforts as America's great moral panic about European immigration reached its climax in the 1920s. The same process, however, worked far less well for social groups barred from incorporation into the political process by entrenched norms of white supremacy, sexism, religious distrust, and heteronormativity. These groups, and especially those at the intersection of racialization, sexualization of women, or queerness were frequently denied access to these more ameliorative measures, and the criminological discourses that framed the immigrant and lower-class white person suspected of crime as reformable often expressly framed these criminal others as beyond reform.

And with the rise of mass incarceration, and the huge increase in the concentration of criminal justice power on minority communities, these limitations have become overwhelming. The descendants of the European immigrants whose crimes and delinquencies were mitigated by progressive criminal justice policies of the 1920s were no longer targets of the criminal justice system in the 1980s and 1990s. Politicians who appeal to white voters with harsh anti-crime policies that lead to the arrest and prosecution of black and brown citizens (or undocumented immigrants better yet) face little risk of retaliation from isolated and low-voting citizens (or nonvoting in the case of undocumented immigrants) and have little to fear from majority voters. The effort of progressive professionals to ameliorate public desires for harshness on behalf of large white ethnic immigrant communities was never extended to racial minorities.[3]

The transformation of criminal justice agencies into bureaucracies, with all that promises in terms of rationality, legality, and accountability, historically led to some improvements in criminal justice practices (compare pretrial practice today to that described in Philadelphia by Caleb Foote [1956] in the 1950s). In the era of mass incarceration, a high level of bureaucratic formation has also ceased to operate as a significant break on cruel and degrading treatment. While front-line justice workers including police and correctional officers are far more diverse than they were a generation ago (Sklansky, 2006), the scope and severity of criminal justice treatment, concentrated as it is on racialized populations, has created a gulf between the communities harmed and humiliated by criminal justice encounters and those that feel protected and respected by those encounters. At the same time, the massive expansion and political empowerment of criminal justice agencies has led to an increasing political autonomy of front-line criminal justice professionals from the normative influence of other sectors of civil society (Page, 2011). The attendant cultural valorization of crime control has led professional law enforcers to develop their own powerful interest groups and their own Durkheimian sense of moral entitlement as well as an extraordinary potential for political influence (Page, 2011; Simon, 2007). With the proliferation of harsh criminal laws, even the demand for formal legality has become a weapon of the strong to streamline conviction and harden punishment against the politically weak. In the meantime, more traditional methods of seeking leniency through politics or appeals to mercy have largely disappeared from criminal justice (Bowers, 2014; Stuntz, 2011).

Nowhere is this effect more evident than in American state prisons. The due process revolution that began in the 1960s and 1970s sought to bring greater legality to internal prison procedures and practices, but the result was not the development of correctional systems with greater respect for human dignity. Instead, as it often does, adversarial legalism (Kagan, 2009) ended up producing a reactive culture within prison bureaucracies, which came to view the resulting prisoner rights as ceasefire lines in a war between prisoners and prison administrations over control of the prisons (Simon, 2013a). The lengthy effort to improve conditions in American prisons (most of them legacies of the 19th century) through federal court litigation has generally and persuasively been presented as a successful combination of court pressure and reform leadership by American correctional executives (with the legislatures being driven by both into opening up new funding for prisons). But even accepting that account as largely true, it was predictable that once litigation became an integral part of governing the penal field, America's adversarial logic would make it easy for both prison managers and front-line prison workers to take a zero-sum approach to prisoner rights and to treat legal rights intended to be minimum standards within an uplifting system of professional correctional norms as maximums in an increasingly punitive system. This was exacerbated by historic shifts in the official state goals of prison from rehabilitation to punishment and incapacitation (Travis, Western, & Redburn, 2014).

Both tendencies (populist punitiveness and bureaucratic expansionism) have been evident in the wars on crime, drugs, and terrorism that have reshaped law enforcement agencies and courts over the last several decades in the United States. While formally meeting the legality principle, much of the conduct criminalized by these wars has consisted of preparatory conduct like possession or material assistance, which is easily proven and gives juries little to consider in the way of evaluating the criminality of the defendant. Much like vagrancy at common law, these modern offenses punish the status of being dangerous rather than the creation of prohibited harms or specific risks (Dubber, 2006; Stuntz, 2011). Whatever merits such crime definitions may have one by one, their proliferation in recent decades is a threat to human dignity beyond that posed by the common law of England. During the recent war on terror, the criminalization of assistance to terror organizations or plots at a very inchoate stage has led some observers to claim that the legality principle is being displaced altogether by a form of preemptive justice (Zedner, 2009). Although the current wars on drugs and terror may be winding down, the broader link between governmental power and fear of crime remains largely intact. Legislative supremacy, combined with a sense of national emergency, can and will continue to produce dramatic reductions in legal protections for individuals, all within the scope of respect for legality.

The principle of legality holds that crimes, criminal procedures, and punishments must be bound before and after by law. When assessed through the lens of mass incarceration, it is clear that this principle no longer assures progress toward a more humane and civilized system of criminal punishment, one that strives to achieve social goals while protecting human dignity.[4] The quantitative growth in the scale of imprisonment, and the qualitative turn toward harsh and degrading prison sentences with little in the way of hope for improvement and restoration while in prison—and indeed some reasonable fear of deterioration, pain, and suffering—is undeniable.

There is good reason not to abandon the legality principle. We do, however, need something more if we are to confront and redress the damage that mass incarceration has done to the civil and human rights of Americans—especially minorities with a long legacy of racial discrimination (African Americans, Native Americans, Latino Americans)— and to prevent its spread to other societies prone to many of the same late-modern tendencies.[5] That something more needs to show promise in operating independently of, and sometimes contrary to, patterns of populist crime politics. It needs a history of overcoming racialized lines of empathy that allow penal excess to remain invisible to the majority. It must also be capable of sustained contestation with the slippery slope toward cruel, inhuman, and degrading treatment inherent in the situation of prolonged incarceration. I am not alone in suggesting that that something might be, could be, dignity.

Dignity

As seen through the lens of long-term constitutional history, and even, in the nearer term, that of post–World War II jurisprudence, the US Supreme Court today is engaged in a dignity "revolution." The United States is not alone in this regard, or even in the lead. Indeed dignity has been an increasingly prominent value in modern legal systems internationally since the middle of the 20th century. This term, for example, has been given pride of place in such foundational documents of the contemporary age as the *Universal Declaration of Human Rights*, in the reconstructed legal systems of post-war Europe (particularly Germany), and in regional human rights treaties like the *European Convention on Human Rights* and the more recent *European Union Charter of Rights*. For present purposes, what is particularly noteworthy is the rising salience of dignity arguments in the US Supreme Court, which is the only legal institution capable of using dignity values to directly confront the political power of populism and penal bureaucracies in the United States (Garland, 2011; Henry, 2010).

In Europe, dignity has spawned a body of public law that has directly engaged national prison bureaucracies with specific, practical normative guidance and public evaluation (van Zyl Smit & Snacken, 2009). For example, the European Prison Rules, promulgated by the legislative arm of the Council of Europe (the body of nations signatory to the *European Convention on Human Rights*, a group overlapping with but somewhat larger than the European Union), create a detailed body of standards for prisons addressing a wide variety of prisoner needs essential to conserving human dignity, including contact with family and access to health and educational resources as close as possible to those available to free citizens. While this largely soft-law corpus is not invariably or immediately respected by those governed by it, there are strong reasons to believe it has operated to resist penal populism and the bureaucratically driven culture of dehumanization. Forging a similarly strong version of dignity seems to be a promising avenue for confronting America's distended and degrading penal state (Simon, 2014; Travis, Western, & Redburn, 2014).

But some observers have raised trenchant questions about just how effective dignity as a legal value can be in forging policy change in a socio-legal context as different from northwestern Europe as much of the United States is; as the title of a recent article on capital punishment in the US put it, "Texas ain't Tuscany" (Sween, 2014). Indeed, many critics doubt that importing dignity will make us any more European than importing workers' compensation laws in the 1900s or a taste for eating yogurt in the 1970s turned out to. On the extreme end of this view, dignity is just too flabby and squishy to really drive change at all (Pinker, 2008). Even those most sympathetic to dignity, like legal historian James Whitman (2003), have suggested that American history, particularly the absence of a prolonged political struggle with the aristocracy and the extended experience with slavery, have rendered dignity a less powerful norm in the United States. This may explain the relatively weak influence of dignity up until now.

Other commentators, responding to these objections, have presented strong and normatively appealing interpretations of contemporary law that express well the ambitions I would have for a dignity-based struggle to transform criminal justice in America (Waldron, 2012).[6] For present purposes, however, I want to dodge much of this critique by suggesting that everything depends on what questions we ask of dignity and when we ask them. Dignity is not inherently more flabby or squishy than any of the other broad values expressed in the Constitution, values like "equality," "liberty," or "due process." Context and history are crucial.

For example, it is difficult to believe that dignity would have carried much legal significance for gay and lesbian rights advocates seeking to knock down heteronormative limitations on private intimacy, let alone marriage, thirty years ago when the Supreme Court upheld the criminalization of sexual intimacy between adults of the same gender in the privacy of a home (*Bowers v. Hardwick*, 1986). Today, of course, dignity has become a powerful one-word response to the waning appeals made to populist hostility against same-sex marriage. Has dignity changed its meaning? Yes, in part—a far larger portion of the living and meaning-generating share of the American population imagined gay sex as something involving criminality or mental illness, positions then well supported by organized religion, social science, and medicine. Dignity is also being used to highlight somewhat different aspects of the human condition, not sex or privacy per se, but relationships, and the possibility of love. As a result, in part, of the political struggles of sexual minorities to claim their own human dignity, the culture had also changed, bringing expanded respect for the role of intimacy and relationships in a decent human life (*Lawrence v. Texas*, 2003; Rubin, 2015).

In the domain of criminal justice, we have a different problem. Dignity arguments were very effective thirty and more years ago in promoting reforms that turned out to be deeply problematic and which have led to the opposite, even more degrading outcomes. Indeed criminal justice reform has almost always claimed to be about dignity, but to what end? (McLennan, 2008; Platt, 2009).

Dignities

If dignity means everything, it means nothing, and it certainly will not convince many American judges that they can use it to meaningfully apply the broad language of the Fourth, Fifth, Sixth, and Eighth Amendments. A recent analysis by Professor Leslie Henry of what she calls the "jurisprudence of dignity," on the Supreme Court's usage of dignity, suggests that variation is not necessarily randomness (Henry, 2010).

Henry borrows language philosopher Ludwig Wittgenstein's concept of a "family resemblance," a set of features shared by individual examples that overlap but for which no core elements can be isolated. On Henry's account, dignity has overlapping meanings that have emerged at distinctive moments in United States political and legal history and which continue to have relevance in contemporary law and to share overlapping features while remaining distinct. Professor Henry's five clusters are "institutional status as dignity," "equality as dignity," "liberty as dignity," "personal integrity as dignity," and "collective virtue as dignity."

Henry's analysis usefully reveals dignity as a legal concept with layers of meaning. For most of our constitutional history, dignity meant mostly "institutional status as dignity." Dignity by status dates from the earliest Greek and Roman conceptions, when dignity was uniquely associated with those of high status and conceptualized as anchored in that hierarchical structure. The United States at its founding renounced the power to ennoble an aristocracy, but the Supreme Court's use of dignity to describe states and courts suggests that some aspects of aristocratic privilege shifted that hierarchical sense of dignity to the state itself and to its officials. For much of the next century and a half, dignity is discussed mostly as a property of government, especially states and courts. Thus dignity, to the extent it had any relevance to criminal justice institutions in the first century of our republic, operated mainly to insulate these institutions from review, thus establishing an aristocratic zone of discretion around state courts, police stations, and prisons.

This understanding began to change in the 20th century and accelerated significantly after World War II with the *Universal Declaration of Human Rights*, which, when ratified by the Americans, made the United States a party to a treaty of rights grounded in dignity.[7] It is after the 1948 signing of the *Universal Declaration* that Professor Henry finds a new sense of dignity emerging, now associated not with the hierarchical status of the state and its agencies, but quite the opposite. It is individuals whose equal dignity as citizens is reflected in the state's respect for their liberty. A series of Supreme Court decisions in this period invokes dignity to protect the individual from aggressive efforts by the police to collect evidence in ways that strip suspects of their dignity and from punishments so severe that they endanger their ability to recover their status as equal citizens (*Trop v. Dulles*, 1958). Much of this dignity wave in US constitutional law took place during the Warren Court and the first (and more liberal) part of the Burger Court.

Afterward, starting in the mid-1970s, Professor Henry argues, dignity went into a "period of hibernation during the Burger and Rehnquist Courts" (Henry, 2010, p. 171). The term "hibernation" aptly captures the Supreme Court's dramatic freeze in enforcement of criminal procedure rights and across-the-board retrenchment. The opposite of hibernation might be said to characterize criminal justice at large during this period: in the late 1970s, 1980s, and 1990s, the legal structure of mass incarceration was put in place and the criminal process became increasingly assimilated to the goal of moving young men of color into prison as quickly and for as long as possible (Simon, 2014).

A new wave of dignity jurisprudence is emerging today from the very conservative Court presided over by Chief Justice John Roberts. While this jurisprudence often reflects an alliance of liberal and conservative justices, it is noteworthy that dignity has been cited by some of the most conservative justices and that the Court overall is far more conservative than at the last time of significant activism in the criminal justice field. The most recent Supreme Court cases reflect what Professor Henry describes as her fourth and fifth clusters in the family of meanings she traces in the jurisprudence of dignity: dignity as "personal integrity" and dignity as "collective virtue."

Personal integrity expresses human dignity in its concern for "people who become vulnerable to their circumstances, express unharnessed appetites, and expose their bodily nakedness or mental fragility" (Henry, 2010, p. 212). Note that this conception differs dramatically from the focus on autonomy and rationality that figured so heavily in the Kantian-influenced first wave. Death and suffering are something we share with animals and other life forms, but awareness of our frailty and vulnerability to these dangers are unique to the human condition, and form an enduring basis for protecting the dignity of those who are not perceived as rational and autonomous. Because of this awareness, every person is capable of expressing human excellence or virtue in the most exalted forms in bearing the quotidian burdens of life and death.

Henry discerns a fifth meaning in cases where state actors behave in ways that portray society itself as cruel, uncaring, and inhumane, even if it does not directly disrespect the human dignity of a particular individual. Collective virtue might be best seen as the collective side of dignity as personal integrity, expressed in notions like a "decent society" or "civilized society." As a constitutional matter, dignity as collective virtue may mean state power to override otherwise protected individual choices that would risk the disintegration of a person (and thus the loss of their dignity as personal integrity) and would conversely expose the collective or community imposing or permitting that loss to judgment as indecent, inhuman, or uncivilized (see *Indiana v. Edwards*, 2008, upholding a court's decision to deny a seriously mentally ill defendant the right to represent himself in a criminal trial).

Critics of the ambiguity of dignity have a point. It has meant different things at different moments and all these meanings might well be at work in the term as a legal concept. It is fair to ask which one(s) we intend to invoke as a new principle for criminal law, and whether that meaning is stable and normative enough to join legality as the lead principles for advancing what might be called "the civilization of criminal justice."[8] If we take these different uses of dignity as layers of contextually situated meaning, in which justices draw on historical shifts in cultural understanding to elaborate the often-broad phrases of the Constitution, we have a genealogy, not a cacophony. When courts draw on historically changing meanings in language to interpret the broad phrases of the Constitution, they operate within a well-established common law tradition that can provide both flexibility and a means to restrain judicial subjectivity (Levi, 2013).

Second, raising dignity arguments in areas like the Fourth, Fifth, Sixth, and Eighth Amendments may seem to imply a risky departure from the productive doctrinal frameworks developed by the Warren Court a generation ago to protect individuals caught up in the criminal process (Bowers, 2014). Through a historical lens we can see those doctrines as products of the Court's first major effort to develop dignity as an individual right centered on liberty and equality. A brief review of this period suggests that dignity as understood by reformers in that era led to incomplete and immature criminal justice reforms in ways that may have paradoxically accelerated mass incarceration and helped encourage the Supreme Court's dignity "hibernation." The dignity jurisprudence that is emerging today reflects, in many regards, a continuation or second wave of that first individual rights wave of dignity, but newly refined in ways that look to be much more promising for creating sustainable reform of a now much expanded criminal process.

The First Coming of Dignity

During the first wave of dignity jurisprudence following World War II, dignity was referenced primarily in terms of liberty and equality. Both aspects seem to have been philosophically influenced by the rediscovery of Immanuel Kant's work on dignity and the growing disquiet of legal intellectuals with the totalitarian implications of the penal-therapeutic state (Kant, 1999; Waldron, 2013). Intellectually this meant that first-wave dignity put a lot of emphasis on autonomy and rationality (virtues Kant thought were essential).

Sociologically, this cluster of legal meanings was deeply infused with moral concerns in the aftermath of World War II, including the role of law in promoting racial exclusion and the domination of individuals in total institutions. In the United States, these concerns helped swell broader elite support for the civil rights movement and related movements for reform of college regulations, mental hospitals, and prisons. Struggles for equality were infusing struggles for liberty, and dignity highlighted concerns as various as the lack of respect given to black adult citizens by Jim Crow segregation in the South and outdated university governance principles on campuses (Cohen, 2009).

This period between the 1950s and the 1970s, as dignity values were first influencing the Court, was particularly crucial for criminal justice, as change anchored in dignity proceeded in all phases of the criminal process.

Proceduralizing the Police

Between the late 1950s and the early 1970s, the Supreme Court produced what has been aptly described as a "national code of criminal procedure" (Friendly, 1965) for the police in the United States. Using the Fourth, Fifth, and Sixth Amendments, the Court created a set of knowledge thresholds and warnings between police agents and criminal suspects. This was a remarkable result in many respects given the fact that police forces in the United States are organized at the local level into over fifteen thousand separate agencies. Contemporaneous critics of this revolution thought it would hamper law enforcement. Current critics have argued—none more ably than the late William Stuntz—that this top-down effort at regulation deformed the development of law enforcement, creating a reactive organizational shift toward using drug law as a substantive crime work-around of the procedural limits on investigating conventional crime (Stuntz, 2011).

While this jurisprudence was often framed in terms of privacy and liberty, we can see in retrospect that what unifies doctrines as diverse as *Mapp v. Ohio* (affirming that the exclusionary rule applies in state court where the police have failed to obtain a warrant before entering a house), *Miranda v. Arizona* (requiring warnings before a suspect in custody can be subject to interrogation), and *Terry v. Ohio* (requiring reasonable suspicion before police may stop a person) is a common concern for dignity. The practice of imposing quasi-judicial procedures (or judicially required proceduralism) on the police may not have prevented the police from securing evidence necessary for successful prosecutions as law and order critics of the Court believed. However, it does assure, at least in a minimal sense if honored, that police respect their equal status as citizens. This is one reason, at least, that some conservative justices have been unwilling to completely overrule them.

Due Process Prisons

The Supreme Court's decisions on the Eighth Amendment during this early dignity wave did not do much to illuminate the specific problems of dignity in prisons,[9] but these decisions did seem to signal federal trial courts that they could consider prison conditions (particularly in the deep South, where many legal elites had already come to favor improvement of backwater prisons; Feeley & Rubin, 1999). Between the late 1960s and the early 1980s, the federal courts dropped their historic "hands off" doctrine and began to evaluate prison conditions under the Eighth Amendment's command that "cruel and unusual punishments" not be "imposed." Moved by the often dramatic gap between the social norms of post-war American society and the reality of life inside prisons (many of which continued to operate on 19th-century principles through the 1960s despite the promise that official state penology made of rehabilitation), courts began demanding significant improvements in both conditions and procedures inside the prisons. In drawing out prison standards from the simple language of the Eighth Amendment, federal courts were aided by the relative national consensus behind rehabilitation, and the professionalization of correctional officers nationwide through professional organizations and the Federal Bureau of Prisons (Feeley & Rubin, 1999).[10]

The result was a major wave of state investment in prison building and prison bureaucratization. Prisoners' rights advocates hoped that raising the cost of prisons dramatically, at a moment when prisons were also under attack as penologically counterproductive, might lead to a significant step away from incarceration. Instead, as documented by scholars of mass incarceration, in states like Florida, Arizona, and California, court orders coincided with growing political demands from below (much of it fed by local prosecutors and law enforcement agencies) for more punitive sentencing laws to overcome historic patterns of fiscal conservatism that had acted as a restraint on imprisonment in many Southern and Western states (Lynch, 2009; Schoenfeld, 2010; Simon, 2013a).

Retribution

This first wave of the dignity-driven reform of criminal justice also began to challenge the virtually unreviewable discretion around parole decision-making that was central to mid-20th-century institutions like the juvenile court and the indeterminate sentence (American Friends Service Committee, 1971; Von Hirsch, 1975). By the 1970s, many leading legal academics and judges believed that desert-based retributivism would produce a fairer and even more lenient criminal justice system than one based on discretion and the promise of rehabilitation (Frankel, 1973). Some states entirely adopted determinate sentencing laws, rejecting discretionary release from prison sentences and often espousing an explicit embrace of deserved suffering for crime as the proper purpose of punishment (Simon, 1993). The "just deserts" movement (as it was called in the 1970s) was a kind of early marriage of legality and dignity. Reformers hoped that fixed sentences would work to provide a clearer relationship between legislative will and punishment, assuring that punishment would not be extended by the self-interest (or ill will) of potentially biased state officials, while also limiting punishment to a core of morally deserved deprivations, purified of predictions of future dangerousness or utopian presumptions about reform. Ultimately, however, as a rationale for punishment, retribution proved difficult to distinguish in the political marketplace from incapacitation, a justification that promised both retribution and utilitarian crime reduction through extended prison sentences for felons of all sorts (Simon, 2013b; Zimring & Hawkins, 1995).

Even though many states did not adopt determinate sentencing, retribution and incapacitation rose to become the dominant public rationales for punishment. Yet even when the resulting legislation was actually consistent with these values (many failures of which are now well established), neither offered a reliable basis for restraining punishment or protecting prisoners' rights. For a time, in the 1970s, support for sentencing reform, along with support for prisoners' rights, rose among the mostly legal or academic specialists moved by the first dignity wave. Once fixed, and/or extended, sentences became a way to assure the maximum incapacitation of those convicted of crimes (and presumed likely to commit more crimes if released), and the dignity or well-being of prisoners became invisible. Although retribution was once thought to assure recognition of the prisoner's dignity, it had become very quickly a rationale for ignoring it.

The Death of the Asylum

These movements toward due process in policing and retribution in sentencing had a parallel in the transformation in mental health law in the 1960s and 1970s. During this period, courts ended decades of deference to medical judgment concerning the involuntary hospitalization and treatment of adults with mental illnesses, and legislatures adopted new statutes requiring the state to show an imminent threat of suicide or assault against another before prolonged hospitalization could be ordered (Appelbaum, 1994). Combined with the new retributivism in criminal law, this shift led to a radical separation of the penal and the psychiatric field (or rather, the elimination of a great deal of the public-sector psychiatric field and the purging of psychologically oriented doctrines permitting leniency from much of the criminal justice system). The perverse result by the start of the 21st century was the accumulation of persons with serious mental illnesses inside jails and prisons, and—often due to their difficulty coping with control-oriented regimes—their concentration in the most punitive and high-security portions of the prisons (Haney, 2006; Simon, 2014).

Mass Incarceration and the Hibernation of Dignity

This set of reforms, summarized all too briefly here, demonstrated a common core influence of dignity values on the shape of the criminal justice system during the period of roughly 1950 through 1980. The results were often perverse from our present perspective, undermining the capacity of—and public confidence in—modern corrections and law enforcement as an independent wave of crime and social unrest rolled through America. In many respects, these reforms rolled back the system of social control that existed in America in the period after World War II, shrinking both prison and mental hospital populations, and reducing the legal authority of the police to engage citizens at their discretion. But seen in retrospect, these changes also seemed to have predisposed the system toward mass incarceration, reducing the flexibility of prison sentences, incentivizing police to develop pretextual grounds on which to intervene in suspicious circumstances, and legitimating the imposition of lengthy incapacitative sentences on people convicted of crimes.

So did the first wave of dignity reforms fail? In most respects the answer is yes and no. Police and prisons are in some respects better than they were two generations ago, even as the massive increase in the scale of the latter has meant an overall increase in penal suffering. Asylums have all but disappeared, and while it is common to blame their absence for problems like homelessness and even mass incarceration itself, the relationships are a good deal more complex. Sentencing reform, except for the few places that coupled it with strong restraints on extending sentences, is perhaps the closest to an abject failure.

But a slightly different way to see this mixed record, which will be asserted here, is that these reforms were an incomplete dignity revolution in American criminal justice which must now be completed. The promise of dignity as equality for reform of criminal justice seemed clear enough in the Jim Crow era, when a color line ran visibly through the entire criminal justice system. Dignity means equality of treatment before the law. Likewise, for citizens held in the public mental hospitals of the same era without treatment or a reasonable basis for confining them, or held in a county jail because they could not afford the amount set for bail, dignity as liberty was a compelling remedy.[11] But for those who came after these initial reforms were put in place, which is all of the victims of mass incarceration, once found guilty after a trial that met the modest court-enforced standards created (or a plea bargain in the shadow of a remote trial possibility), dignity as liberty and equality promised very little. For those sentenced to prison, liberty and privacy have ceased to be matters of right altogether under current law, available at the discretion of prison authorities, if at all, and easily withdrawn wherever even the shade of a security rationale urges even more precaution. Equality may be roughly respected at the punishment end of the system, but only the equality of deprivation that has become more complete as the nation grows more confident in the virtue of punishment through imprisonment (and even that may be racially skewed). Of course the courts, and the Supreme Court in particular, might have attempted to broaden out the meaning of dignity in criminal justice, or at least rejected the very narrowing interpretations that they steadily embraced. What followed in the 1980s and 1990s is aptly described as a hibernation of dignity (Henry, 2010). As the wars on crime and drugs transformed local law enforcement agencies and state courts from creaky and inefficient local institutions into formidable engines of harsh criminalization and punishment, the wave of dignity-based jurisprudence that had moved through American courts between 1950 and 1980 subsided.

The Second Coming of Dignity: Bodies, Suffering, and Hope in the Roberts Court

Coming after a period in which dignity has been in hibernation, and before that, a period in which dignity-oriented reforms may have put the US justice system on the track toward mass incarceration, placing much hope on a return of dignity jurisprudence might seem the height of imprudence. But if, as I have argued, much turns on the specific factual contexts and historical meanings in which dignity as a legal concept is refined and interpreted, recent decisions elaborating on dignity as "personal integrity" and a "decent" or "civilized" society (Henry, 2010) provide a promising framework for reforming criminal justice.

Dignity as personal integrity, which recognizes the distinctively human condition of frailty and vulnerability to injury, diseases, and death, requires that people be protected against state actions that fatefully compromise this capacity, or "disintegrate" it, to take up Professor Henry's artful term. Front-line criminal justice actors are particularly likely to be exposed to situations in which dignity as personal integrity is at stake. For example, in *Michigan v. Hudson* (2006), Justice Scalia cited dignity in explaining the common law "knock and announce rule" by which, absent exigent circumstances, the police must announce themselves before forcefully entering a person's private place, even though they are carrying a warrant giving them an entitlement to enter. Requiring the police to knock first and stall their entrance momentarily affords "the opportunity to collect oneself before answering the door" (*Michigan v. Hudson*, 2006). This may seem like a minor concession (and indeed Justice Scalia rejected the application of the exclusionary rule for a violation of it), but it recognizes the centrality of dignity as personal integrity even in a seemingly minor gesture of respect, and even in a context where state security interests are inherently high. If dignity as personal integrity is critical to the Constitution in these circumstances, it may have much more to say about the right of the same person to avoid unnecessary humiliation during the arrest process, pretrial release under the least-intrusive circumstances, respect for privacy in jails and prisons, and the right to keep their prison record private.

Other recent decisions of the Supreme Court exemplify the idea of dignity as "collective virtue," which I argue is consistent with terms like "decency" (as in "evolving standards of decency") and "civilized society." Perhaps the most significant recent invocation of this notion of dignity as decency is the *Brown v. Plata* (2011) decision finding that California's chronically overcrowded and medically underresourced prisons had created a risk of suffering equivalent to torture—one which was "incompatible with the concept of human dignity and has no place in a civilized society." In this case, citing years of efforts by courts to remedy unconstitutional medical and mental health conditions in California prisons, as well as chronic overcrowding, the majority ordered an unprecedented prison population reduction that has played an outsized role in the nation's very tentative trend away from mass incarceration (Carson & Golinelli, 2013).

In comparison with the liberty and equality values of the first dignity wave, the personal integrity and collective decency values expressed in recent Supreme Court cases speak very precisely to the prisoners and former prisoners of mass incarceration, most of whose convictions comply with the legality principle, and many of whom suffer from chronic mental and physical illness. For example, a life without parole (LWOP) sentence for individuals who choose to carry very large quantities of illicit drugs (*Harmelin v. Michigan*, 1991) in defiance of laws threatening that very severe punishment against a feared social menace, seems perfectly compatible with the dignity values of liberty and equality. In upholding Harmelin's LWOP sentence, Justice Kennedy emphasized the prisoner's choice (liberty) to engage in a crime associated with violence (possessing crack cocaine). Likewise, there was no claim that Harmelin was being treated unequally. Presumably, others charged with the same crime and convicted in Michigan received the same sentence.

But if dignity also reflects a respect for personal integrity, a punishment that requires a person to experience aging and death in the isolation of prison regardless of the years they have served or their prison record may be considered unconstitutional even for more serious crimes like aggravated murder. The European Court of Human Rights, Grand Chamber, recently held whole-life sentences for aggravated murder incompatible with human dignity (*Vinter et al. v. United Kingdom*, 2013). That does not mean that every prisoner has an absolute right to release simply because they are experiencing aging or a limited remaining portion of life, only that rigid rules that make remission impossible for such prisoners is incompatible with respect for human dignity.

Looked at as a long arc, beginning in the 1950s with dignity as liberty and equality and continuing in this century with personal integrity and public virtue, dignity has emerged as a mature expression not just of individual human rights, but also of the relationship between individuals and government. I do not mean to suggest that drawing specific meanings from this term for reforming criminal justice will always be easy or uncontroversial. But I am arguing that analysis of contemporary criminal justice practices from this perspective is likely to be productive in giving courts purchase on the ways those practices endanger human dignity in our time.

To provide some more specificity, and examples of the kind of changes that might emerge in a second wave of dignity-driven reforms, I offer several brief examples from across the criminal process.

Substantive Criminal Law: Decriminalizing Possession

The criminal procedure revolution that unfolded during the first wave of dignity's influence on American law aimed at protecting liberty and equality through limiting police discretion. However, the criminalization of possession, especially of drugs, during the subsequent three decades has created a large window of opportunity for police and prosecutors to work around this obstacle of heightened procedural protection. Possession crimes give police wide opportunity to make arrests based on the discovery of evidence in the midst of investigations justified on other grounds (like frisking someone based on reasonable suspicion that they are involved in crime and are carrying a weapon, or that there is a basis to arrest them for some other offense). By attaching lengthy prison sentences to many possession crimes, prosecutors avoid charges that can be frustrated by criminal procedure rights and exert enormous coercion on defendants to abandon any remaining trial defenses and plead guilty. Since police stops and frisks often involve racial profiling, minority communities have experienced a disproportionate share of the extra imprisonment generated by prosecution of possession crimes.

Under the dignity principle, possession crimes themselves should be challenged, especially under the current emphasis on protecting personal integrity and public decency. Dignity in its mature form is incompatible with marking someone as a criminal and subjecting them to sanctions simply because they are in possession of material that has been proscribed by the laws of the state. The criminalization of simple possession presumes that a person intends to use that material in a way that is harmful to others or to society as a whole. With the exception of particularly dangerous material, such as a bomb or assault weapon, or some other item so unreasonably dangerous to public safety as to express a form of criminal recklessness, possession crimes rob citizens of the right to voluntarily conform their behavior to the law. In effect, they are a form of pre-crime that punishes the status of being untrusted by the police.

Policing: Protecting Personal Integrity and Public Safety

Perhaps no area of our current constitutional law of criminal procedure better reflects the limits of legality as a way to protect essential elements of personal integrity and public decency than the "search and seizure" doctrines of the Fourth Amendment (Bowers, 2014). So long as police have "reasonable suspicion" to believe a crime is occurring or has occurred, and cause to believe that an individual may be armed, they can subject that person to the experience of being stopped in public, forced to assume degrading positions, and subjected to an intrusive physical inspection of their clothing and the surface of their body, or a sniff by a dog. If they find evidence that gives them "probable cause" to believe a crime has occurred—no matter how trivial—they can place the suspect under arrest, subject the suspect and their immediate personal property to an even more comprehensive search, and convey them to jail where they may be held for several days before seeing a lawyer or a judge. This remains true even if the police are acting on a pretext, choosing to target the person on the basis of their race, age, and gender rather than their criminal behavior. Between 2004 and 2013, at the height of our long war on crime, New York police used their power to "stop and frisk" more than 4.4 million people.

A dignity principle embedded in the Fourth Amendment would supplement the weak protections of legality with a requirement that these police powers be balanced against the significant loss of both personal dignity and public decency involved through their unbridled (if lawful) use. Police might still stop and frisk people, or arrest them, but only when a contextual analysis of the interaction in terms of its time, place, and manner suggests that the police acted with full respect for the personal integrity of the suspect and for public decency. Against this principle much of the contemporary logic of urban policing would have to be rethought. No doubt many instances of police intervention would need to be highly factual and subjected to the usual limits on judicial second-guessing of police discretion. But other shifts from current doctrine are clearer. The use of minor criminal violations as pretexts for police actions actually based on race (among other factors) would represent a per se violation of the dignity principle, as would arrests for offenses in which no prison or jail time was a possible penal sanction. These actions violate the human dignity of the individuals stopped or arrested, but they also offend the public decency of a community that must witness its citizens systematically harassed or humiliated in front of their loved ones.[12]

Sentencing: Toward a Dignified Social Defense

In the era of mass incarceration, states adopted an extreme version of incapacitation as a penal rationale and courts deferred to it (Dolovich, 2012). I call this version "total incapacitation" to distinguish it from the broad school of incapacitation, or "social defense" as it was primarily called in Europe during the 20th century. Like a highly mutated strain of this broad logic, total incapacitation pursues crime prevention with the following extreme presumptions.

1. All felons present an undeterminable risk of committing the most serious violent felonies like murder, kidnapping, and rape.
2. The risk does not change significantly during the life course.
3. Only secure physical isolation can reliably eliminate the danger of these most violent felonies from these identified felons, and then only by transferring the danger for a limited time to the prison and its staff.

This strain of incapacitation has proven incredibly politically resilient because it creates an inherent trap for politicians who would support leniency. Having established that the public is always better off when a convicted person is incarcerated (because at least some crimes will be prevented), any legal or policy change that would lessen the scope or length of incarceration can easily be viewed as a decision against public safety. For decades this effect has stalled any effort to reform much-criticized law. But the deep recession of 2008–2009, combined with the crisis of mass imprisonment, has begun to break down this consensus (Aviram, 2015). Most recently, in 2014's Proposition 47, California voters overruled timid politicians and enacted a sentencing reform that is expected to result in more than two thousand prisoners being released early.

Here, I want to suggest that one of the most productive uses of the new dignity would be to reshape a legitimate penal rationale for a post–mass incarceration justice system. A good starting point is the failure of dignity ideas in the first wave to provide a politically sustainable alternative to penal incapacitation. The "justice model," as some called it, offered a pure strain of dignity as liberty and equality. Punishment was to be based on retribution or "just deserts" for past wrongs, not on future dangerousness. The ability of retribution to set limits through the appeal of proportionality between crime and punishment fails in the absence of strong conventional norms with which to assign cardinal (rather than ordinal) levels of punishment for crimes.[13] Since just deserts–based determinate sentences could be increased at the will of a legislature (legality going off the rails) and retribution can easily be shot through with broad bands of incapacitative zeal, dignity as retribution could not stop, and may have accelerated, the cascade toward mass incarceration.

The new dignity points us back to the old European idea of social defense (Ancel, 1965). Often cast as illiberal, social defense recognizes the huge social stake in crime (both in causing it and suffering the long-term damage). In an age of dignity, social defense recognizes that both the individual and community have a strong interest in that individual not committing assaults on the dignity of others (because those kinds of assault equally damage the dignity of the actor). Thus, a person who commits such an assault has an interest not simply in being punished for it (the retributive dignity idea of the first wave), but also in reasonable methods of assuring it does not happen again. Mass incarceration rejected any consideration of the latter (in this regard mimicking just deserts), telling its prisoners, in effect, "go to hell, we don't care what you do here, just do your time."

Restorative justice models offer an attractive framework for bringing questions of both past accountability and future prevention into a common and democratically legitimate forum. Long-term sentences, for example, for murder or rape, might be handed down by such a restorative justice circle, which would retain jurisdiction and revisit the sentence and the prisoner over time and repeatedly.

Conclusion: Asking the Right Questions at the Right Time?

"No crime and no punishment without law," the principle of legality, proved a worthy pole star to lead the long arc of criminal justice reform in a direction of leniency and humanity between the early 19th century and the 1980s. Since then, at least in the United States, the principle of legality has proven unable to protect human dignity and public decency against significant pressures for extreme and degrading policing and punishments from populist punitive politics and self-interested penal bureaucracies.

Does "no crime and no punishment without respect for dignity" offer a corrective that can resist these strong features of late modern criminal justice? There are strong claims being made today that it may, and I mean to join those (cited throughout). There are also doubts that a concept so squishy or flabby can provide anything more than a fig leaf of jurisprudential heft to a set of ideals that, as much as they might appeal to some human rights–oriented academics and jurists, are unlikely to win democratic assent.[14]

I close with two defenses of the new dignity talk. First, its squishiness all depends on what questions we ask of it. Consider an example outside the penal field: Does dignity require that we respect a terminally ill patient's request for assistance in dying ahead of his or her illness's schedule? There seems to be spirited arguments on both sides and no clear answer has yet to emerge from the specialist community. But if you ask a different question: whether dignity requires terminally ill patients to have the option of palliative treatment that offers a priority on comfort and quality of life over medical convenience and therapeutic effectiveness, there is a virtual consensus in favor of access to hospice care, which was not true twenty years ago (Gawande, 2014). Many questions of criminal justice will yield similarly clear answers.

Second, dignity has been evolving since the great emergence of human rights norms as general principles in the years after World War II. What I've called the first wave of dignity, with its emphasis on liberty and equality, had and continues to have great salience for the fate of social and cultural minorities (consider the current role in the expansion of gay and lesbian rights), but its influence on criminal justice reforms was limited at best, and destructive at worst. The new dignity wave today presents different aspects that have a more direct and productive relationship to criminal justice. Whether particular policing and penal practices are compatible with respect for personal integrity and public decency will not always be clear or uncontroversial. But the hope is that emphasizing these values will focus courts and other decision makers on the real impact state coercion has on the ability of individuals and communities to retain the humanity of their social relations.

Of course, the application of dignity as a legal concept will bring decision makers against the limits of their own understanding of humanity. Dignity as a force for change tends to work through sympathy, empathy, and a capacity for feeling shame and regret when our actions have violated the dignity of another. All of these important human faculties are profoundly distorted by the impact of racism on the modern state generally, and on the US state in particular.[15] Social systems that degrade racialized populations have been far more tolerated than those that make their mark on those deemed non-racial (or white). Likewise, advances in dignity-inspired human rights, what I call "dignity cascades" (Simon, 2014, p. 133), often lose momentum when their reforms reach racialized populations. Clearly, the long tolerance of the systematically degrading nature of mass imprisonment and militarized policing has made possible the extreme racial disproportion of both enterprises. What is needed is a two-step movement that simultaneously insists on the substantive concessions due the humanity of prisoners and suspects, and demands a widening of that understanding of humanity.

NOTES

1 There is a great wave of scholarship on dignity today (Waldron, 2012; Dan-Cohen, 2002; Whitman, 2003; Van zyl Smit & Snacken, 2009; Henry, 2010; Cohn & Grimm, 2013).

2 No writer invoked this haunting proximity of law and arbitrariness within bureaucracies more than Franz Kafka. For example, "The Judgment" or "In the Penal Colony" in *Franz Kafka: The Complete Stories* (Kafka, 1995).

3 Indeed, Muhammed (2011) argues persuasively that progressive era social scientists helped make their case for white immigrants by demonizing "black crime."

4 Consider the late-20th-century resumption of practices like capital punishment, the chain gang, the provision of substandard medical care, etc.

5 While the US is unique in the portion of its citizens incarcerated by a great degree, many other Western nations experienced a sustained growth in their prison

population since the 1980s, including Ireland, Spain, the United Kingdom, and the Netherlands.

6 Waldron (2012) argues, persuasively in my view, that whatever its moral meanings, dignity in Western law has come to be associated with institutionally specific rights to better treatment for high-status individuals and that the meaning of human dignity as expressed in contemporary human rights law is the normative objective of treating all members of the human community with the special kind of solicitude that was once extended to high-status individuals even when they were being policed or punished.

7 Admittedly, the original intent was clearly to describe aspirations rather than enforceable rights, a move that permitted Joseph Stalin's Soviet Union to be one of the signatories along with the US with its Jim Crow South (Anderson, 2003).

8 As a sociological concept, civilization and civilizing process has been associated with the rise of the centralized nation-state and its monopoly on violence (Elias, 1978). As Zygmunt Bauman has noted, that kind of civilization is all too compatible with rights abuses and even mass murder (Bauman, 1989). In seeking to civilize criminal law through dignity, the civility we seek is a deeper one than this bureaucratic and disciplinary character (although those are also necessary ingredients). That deeper meaning is the one invoked by Chief Justice Warren in *Trop v. Dulles*: "The basic concept underlying the Eighth Amendment is nothing less than the dignity of man. While the State has the power to punish, the Amendment stands to assure that this power be exercised within the limits of civilized standards" (*Trop v. Dulles*, 1958, p. 100).

9 Ironically the strongest use of dignity language in an Eighth Amendment decision came in the 1958 case *Trop v. Dulles*, which dealt with denaturalization as a punishment for desertion in wartime. Two decades later, when the Supreme Court affirmed that poor prison conditions and inadequate medical care could constitute cruel and unusual punishment, there was little invocation of dignity, decency, or civilization (*Estelle v. Gamble*, 1976).

10 As recent research on Southern and Western states shows, that consensus was always extremely patchy, with little support for the rehabilitative concept in states like Texas (Perkinson, 2010) and Arizona (Lynch, 2009). However, the fact that there was at least lip service to this idea across the country and that it was strongly supported by national institutions like the Federal Bureau of Prisons and the American Correctional Association allowed courts to treat this as a consensus.

11 On the lower courts in the era before mass incarceration, see Foote's "Vagrancy Law and Its Administration" (1956, pp. 603–650) and Feeley's *The Process Is the Punishment: Handling Cases in a Lower Criminal Court* (1979).

12 The events in Ferguson, Missouri, in the summer and fall of 2014 reflected growing public revulsion at that kind of indignity inflicted by law enforcement.

13 Which is not to say there are not empirical regularities to be discerned through surveys, experiments, or both. Paul Robinson (2014) proposes "empirical desert,"

where criminal law and sentencing would track popular opinion regarding the relative blameworthiness of crime.

14 Indeed, in the two years since I gave a first draft of this paper, I have repeatedly been told that it is way too optimistic, even by readers who fully agree with its conceptualization of dignity.

15 For the most insightful recent study of how race influences the politics of the contemporary American state, see Haney López (2014).

REFERENCES

Alexander, M. (2010). *The new Jim Crow: Mass incarceration in an age of colorblindness.* New York: New Press.

American Friends Service Committee. (1971). *Struggle for justice.* New York: Farrar Straus & Giroux.

Ancel, M. (1965). *Social defence: A modern approach to criminal problems.* London: Routledge & Kegan Paul.

Anderson, C. (2003). *Eyes off the prize: The United Nations and the African American struggle for human rights 1944–1955.* Cambridge, UK: Cambridge University Press.

Appelbaum, P. (1994). *Almost a revolution: Mental health law and the limits of change.* New York: Oxford University Press.

Aviram, H. (2015). *Cheap on crime: Recession-era politics and the transformation of American punishment.* Berkeley: University of California Press.

Bauman, Z. (1989). *Modernity and the Holocaust.* Ithaca, NY: Cornell University Press.

Beccaria, C. (1995 [1764]). On crimes and punishments. In R. Bellamy (Ed.), *'On crimes and punishments' and other writings.* Cambridge, UK: Cambridge University Press.

Bowers, J. (2014). Probable cause, constitutional reasonableness, and the unrecognized point of a "pointless indignity." *Stanford Law Review, 66,* 987–1050.

Carson, E., & Golinelli, D. (2013). *Prisoners in 2012: Trends in admissions and releases, 1991–2012.* Washington, DC: Department of Justice, Office of Justice Programs.

Cohen, R. (2009). *Freedom's orator: Mario Savio and the radical legacy of the 1960s.* New York: Oxford University Press.

Cohn, M., & Grimm, D. (2013). Human dignity as constitutional doctrine. In M. Tushnet, T. Fleiner, & C. Saunders (Eds.), *The Routledge Handbook of Constitutional Law.* Abingdon and New York: Routledge.

Dan-Cohen, M. (2012). Defending dignity. In *Harmful thoughts: Essays on law, self and morality.* Princeton, NJ: Princeton University Press.

Dolovich, S. (2009). Cruelty, prison conditions and the eighth amendment. *New York University Law Review, 84,* 881–979.

Dolovich, S. (2012). Exclusion and control in the carceral state. *Berkeley Journal of Criminal Law, 16,* 259–339.

Dubber, M. (2006). *Victims in the war on crime: The uses and abuses of victims' rights.* New York: New York University Press.

Elias, N. (1978). *The civilizing process.* Oxford: Blackwell Publishing.

Feeley, M. (1979). *The process is the punishment: Handling cases in a lower criminal court*. New York: Russell Sage.

Feeley, M., & Rubin, E. (1999). *Judicial policy making and the modern state: How courts reformed America's prisons*. Cambridge, UK: Cambridge University Press.

Foote, C. (1956). Vagrancy law and its administration. *University of Pennsylvania Law Review, 104*, 603–650.

Frankel, M. (1973). *Criminal sentences: Law without order*. New York: Hill & Wang.

Friendly, H. (1965). The bill of rights as code of criminal procedure. *California Law Review, 53*, 929–956.

Garland, D. (1985). *Punishment and welfare: A history of penal strategies*. Brookfield, VT: Gower.

Garland, D. (2001). *The culture of control: Crime and social order in contemporary society*. Chicago: University of Chicago Press.

Garland, D. (2011). *Peculiar institution: America's death penalty in an age of abolition*. Cambridge, MA: Harvard University Press.

Gawande, A. (2014). *Being mortal: Medicine and what matters at the end*. New York: Metropolitan Books.

Hall, J. (1937). Nulla poena sine lege. *Yale Law Journal, 47*, 165–170.

Haney, C. (2006). *Reforming punishment: Psychological limits to the pains of imprisonment*. Washington, DC: American Psychological Association.

Haney López, I. (2004). *Racism on trial: The Chicano fight for justice*. Cambridge, MA: Belknap Press.

Haney López, I. (2014). *Dog whistle politics: How coded racial appeals have reinvented racism and wrecked the middle class*. New York: Oxford University Press.

Henry, L. (2010). The jurisprudence of dignity. *University of Pennsylvania Law Review, 160*, 169–232.

Howard, J. (1779). *The state of the prisons*. Warrington: William Eyres.

Jacobs, J. (1977). *Stateville: The penitentiary in mass society*. Chicago: University of Chicago Press.

Kafka, F. (1995). In N. Glatzer (ed.), *Franz Kafka: The complete stories*. New York: Schocken Books.

Kagan, R. (2009). *Adversarial legalism: The American way of law*. Cambridge, MA: Harvard University Press

Kant, I. (1999 [1785]). The metaphysics of morals. In *Kant, practical philosophy*. Cambridge, UK: Cambridge University Press.

Langbein, J. (1994). The historical origins of the privilege against self-incrimination at common law. *Michigan Law Review, 92*, 1047–1085.

Levi, E. (2013). *An introduction to legal reasoning* (2nd ed.). Chicago: University of Chicago Press.

Lynch, M. (2009). *Sunbelt justice: Arizona and the transformation of American punishment*. Stanford, CA: Stanford Law Books.

McLennan, R. (2008) *The crisis of imprisonment: Protest, politics, and the making of the American penal state, 1776–1941*. Cambridge, MA: Harvard University Press.

Muhammed, K. (2011). *The condemnation of blackness: Race, crime, and the making of modern urban America*. Cambridge, MA: Harvard University Press.

National Academy of Sciences. (2014). *The growth of incarceration in the United States: Exploring causes and consequences*. Washington, DC: National Academies Press.

Page, J. (2011). *The toughest beat: Politics, punishment, and the prison officers union in California*. New York: Oxford University Press.

Perkinson, R. (2010). *Texas tough: The rise of America's prison empire*. New York: Picador.

Pinker, S. (2008, May 27). The stupidity of dignity. *New Republic*, www.newrepublic.com.

Platt, A. (2009). *The child savers: The invention of delinquency* (40th anniv. ed.). New Brunswick, NJ: Rutgers University Press.

Robinson, P. (2014). Empirical desert, individual prevention, and limiting retributivism: A reply. *New Criminal Law Review, 17*, 312–375.

Rothman, D. (1972). *The discovery of the asylum*. Boston: Little, Brown.

Rothman, D. (1980). *Conscience and convenience: The asylum and its alternatives in progressive America*. Boston: Little, Brown.

Rubin, A. T. (2015). Resistance or friction: Understanding the significance of prisoners' secondary adjustments. *Theoretical Criminology, 19*, 23–42.

Rusche, G., & Kirchheimer, O. (2003 [1939]). *Punishment and social structure*. New Brunswick, NJ: Transaction Publishers.

Schoenfeld, H. (2010). Mass incarceration and the paradox of prison conditions litigation, *Law & Society Review, 44*, 731–768.

Simon, J. (1993). *Poor discipline: Parole and the social control of the underclass, 1890 to 1990*. Chicago: University of Chicago Press.

Simon, J. (2007). *Governing through crime: How the war on crime transformed American democracy and created a culture of fear*. New York: Oxford University Press.

Simon, J. (2012). Mass incarceration: From social policy to social problem. In K. Reitz & J. Petersilia (Eds.), *The Oxford handbook of sentencing and corrections*. New York: Oxford University Press.

Simon, J. (2013a). Courts and the penal state: Lessons from California's decades of prison litigation and expansion. *California Journal of Politics and Policy, 5*, 252–265.

Simon, J. (2013b). Total incapacitation: The penal imaginary and the rise of an extreme penal rationale in California in the 1970s. In M. Malsch & M. Duker (Eds.), *Incapacitation: Trends and new perspectives*. Surrey: Ashgate.

Simon, J. (2014). *Mass incarceration on trial: A remarkable court decision and the future of prisons in America*. New York: New Press.

Sklansky, D. (2006). Not your father's police department: Making sense of the new demographics of law enforcement. *Journal of Criminal Law and Criminology, 96*, 1209–1243.

Stuntz, W. (2011). *The collapse of American criminal justice*. Cambridge, MA: Harvard University Press.

Sween, G. (2014). Texas ain't Tuscany: How a truism might further invigorate contemporary cost arguments for the abolition of the death penalty. *American Journal of Criminal Law, 41*, 151–188.

Travis, J., Western, B., & Redburn, S. (2014). *The growth of incarceration in the United States* Washington, DC: National Academies Press. Retrieved from https://download.nap.edu.

van Zyl Smit, D., & Snacken, S. (2009). *Principles of European prison law and policy.* New York: Oxford University Press.

Von Hirsch, A. (1975). *Doing justice.* New York: Hill & Wang.

Wacquant, L. (2009). *Punishing the poor: The neoliberal government of social marginality.* Durham, NC: Duke University Press.

Waldron, J. (2012). *Dignity, rank, & rights: 2010 Tanner Lectures.* New York: Oxford University Press.

Waldron, J. (2013). Citizenship and dignity. *New York University Public Law and Legal Theory Working Papers.*

Walker, S. (1993). *Taming the system: The control of discretion in criminal justice 1950–1990.* New York: Oxford University Press.

Whitman, J. (2003). *Harsh justice: Criminal punishment and the widening divide between America and Europe.* New York: Oxford University Press.

Zedner, L. (2009). Fixing the future? The pre-emptive turn in criminal justice. In B. McSherry, A. Norrie, & S. Bronitt (Eds.), *Regulating deviance: The redirection of criminalisation and the futures of criminal Law.* Portland, OR: Hart Publishing.

Zimring, F., & Hawkins, G. (1991). *The scale of imprisonment.* Chicago: University of Chicago Press.

Zimring, F., & Hawkins, G. (1995). *Incapacitation.* New York: Oxford University Press.

CASES

Bowers v. Hardwick, 478 U.S. 186 (1986).

Brown v. Plata, 563 U.S. 493 (2011).

Estelle v. Gamble, 429 U.S. 97 (1976).

Ewing v. California, 538 U.S. 11 (2003).

Harmelin v. Michigan, 501 U.S. 957 (1991).

Indiana v. Edwards, 554 U.S. 164, 176 (2008).

Lawrence v. Texas, 539 U.S. 558 (2003).

Mapp v. Ohio, 367 U.S. 643 (1961).

Michigan v. Hudson, 547 U.S. 586 (2006).

Miller v. Alabama, 132 S.Ct. 2455 (2012).

Miranda v. Arizona, 384 U.S. 436 (1966).

Terry v. Ohio, 392 U.S. 1 (1968).

Trop v. Dulles, 356 U.S. 86 (1958).

Vinter et al. v. United Kingdom, Application nos. 66069/09, 130/10, and 3896/10 (2013).

13

Dignity Is the New Legitimacy

JEFFREY FAGAN

In a recent symposium, a retired federal district court judge made the following observation: If you walk into a judicial conference on criminal law in Europe and use the term "dignity," heads universally nod affirmatively. There is little need for explanation or definition, much less citing precedent or intellectual grounding. Use the term "dignity" in a similar setting with their American counterparts, and eyeballs will roll like numbers and symbols on a lunatic slot machine.

There are perfectly reasonable bases for the divided reaction. To the Europeans, and more recently to the South Africans and other transitional regimes, dignity has concrete meaning in constitutional law, and occupies familiar ground in the moral vocabulary of philosophy and jurisprudence.[1] The Universal Declaration of Human Rights and the International Covenant on Civil and Political Rights, starting points for many new or revised constitutional designs, both mention dignity and link it closely with basic human rights.[2] Dignity is either essential to human rights in these charters, or is perfectly fungible with human rights.

American jurisprudence often wrestles with the term "dignity."[3] At least some of this skepticism is explained by the separation of (continental) European legal regimes from American common law foundations, and the tendency of American legal theorists to see both procedural and substantive rights doing the work of dignity. And dignity appears nowhere in the constitution. But despite its absence there, dignity appears in caselaw on the Fourth, Fifth, Sixth, Eighth, and Fourteenth Amendments, and recent "dignitarian" moves suggest that it may have constitutional weight.[4]

Yet the meaning of dignity in these cases remains not just elusive, but an analytic challenge. Is it a religious term? An expression of a moral norm about the sanctity of the individual and her right to human flourishing? Does it reflect the autonomy and privacy of the individual against an intrusive or coercive state? Is it a placeholder or vessel for a more concrete analysis of rights? And what work does affixing the term "human" do for a serious analysis of rights?

At least some of the distrust of the term "dignity" stems from just this lack of definition. Its definition is both indeterminate and prone to subjective attributions of legal and normative meaning, meaning that is more likely to reflect the definer's priors than a specific set of terms with shared meaning and a firm theoretical foundation.[5] Some refer to a "cult of dignity" that borders on the religious[6] or that substitutes for the more complicated moral questions that are raised by modern bioethics.[7] Given both the vagueness and diversity of the meanings attached to dignity, it may well be a concept that is better defined in the breach than in the affirmative.[8]

Still, we can assume that dignity has its place in law, both in the U.S. and in other legal regimes. One challenge—both for law and for constitutional regulators—is to determine exactly what kinds of remedial measures should follow a breach of dignity. Should these measures address punishment practices, such as execution methods or extended periods of psychologically disfiguring solitary confinement?[9] Or should the remedies address jurisprudential foundations of criminal law and procedure, requiring a reconceptualization of the premises of social and moral prohibitions on specific behavior? Should the remedies preserve those norms but recalibrate proportionality principles to replace draconian punishments with morally informed sanctions that preserve the essential respect that all humans deserve?[10] Should we subjectivize punishments so that we avoid disfiguring harms that inflict cruelty and pain in the name of the state, and thereby allow offenders to suffer deprivations that matter to them while maintaining our respect for their humanity?[11] Would dignity principles mean that our starting points for punishment recognize the status of prisoners as deserving of the respect of the state despite their transgressions?[12] In other words, should we dissolve the barriers of "condition status" (as a prisoner or defendant) to confer a normative personhood status that demands dignity?[13]

And how should we respond to procedural incursions on dignity, such as unwarranted arrests or searches or abrogations of trial rights?

Should respect for the rights of the accused be part of their dignity, or does dignity occupy a different space—and perhaps in a rights-based regime, a smaller space—where we honor those rights for moral reasons that are somewhat apart from conferred rights? How much work can *privacy* do as a vessel for dignity when it appears nowhere in the U.S. Constitution? Should there be a remedy beyond the exclusion of a case when a suspect is denied access to a lawyer, or is unable to confront an accuser, or cannot present mitigating evidence that lessens her blameworthiness? These rights are enshrined in American caselaw and in the Constitution, and at least some are embellished by references to dignity. Should there be a premium on the sanctions imposed for dignity incursions on top of the rights violation? Certainly, conceiving dignity as a jurisprudence independent from the jurisprudence of legality would suggest that, yes, remedies for such violations should indeed go beyond those imposed for rights violations alone.

This is the jurisprudential and intellectual territory that Jonathan Simon's *The Second Coming of Dignity* seeks to occupy and expand. He implicates the legality principle in American jurisprudence as failing to provide workable principles to ensure a "humane and civilized system of criminal punishment" that can assure human dignity.[14] He does not argue to abandon legality as the jurisprudential principle to guide punishment, but to locate dignity alongside legality to provide a moral force against "cruel, inhuman and degrading treatment inherent in prolonged incarceration." He briefly surveys 20th-century theory and discourse on dignity in criminal law and procedure, noting that attempts to constitutionally instantiate dignity into criminal law and procedure were mostly aimed at procedural reforms rather than substantive rules. Simon concludes that the retributive turn in both punishment and procedure starting in the 1970s abandons two core elements of Leslie Henry's nosology of dignity: "personal integrity" and "collective virtue,"[15] elements that speak to the frailty of the individual before the state and the dignity that the state imparts by caring for and about the individual.

This degradation of dignity is the challenge that Professor Simon seeks to expose and reverse. His proposals for injecting dignity into the jurisprudence of criminal law and procedure would undo these harms at each of several critical junctures where dignity has been sacrificed to public security and to retribution. This is Dignity 2.0: a rich blueprint for elevating the status of dignity in the everyday logic and actions of criminal justice institutions. The path is through law, procedure, and perhaps enhanced regulation.

My purpose is not to dispute Simon's exhortation toward instantiating dignity into jurisprudence and policy. My prior is that these measures will in fact enhance the dignity of the criminal law, if only by eliminating many of its features that produce indignities. The implicit moral realignment of punishment principles will also enhance dignity. But such a realignment leaves open the question of how these principles will be subjectively experienced when the state attempts to punish. Encounters with the law, whether with police on the street or behind bars with jailers, are inherently subjectively experienced events where not only may dignity be violated, but where emotional damage is a collateral injury. This essay suggests a complementary design that shifts the analysis to the processual, experiential, and consequentialist features of criminal law and procedure.

Similar to the conferring of legitimacy on criminal law and procedure,[16] dignity in this view is constructed through interactions between the state and the person who falls under the state's gaze, if not its control. Emotions—anger, fear, recognition, or respect, even pleasure at belonging and equality—are the bases of both dignity and legitimacy. Whereas legitimacy is a subjective evaluation of a legal institution, dignity is the byproduct of these interactions, and is a reflected appraisal of the individual as to her belongingness and equality before the law. Meaning, including dignity, is constructed from these interactions through processes that are brought to the situation by both the state actor and the individual. It is that process of interaction and social construction that is an important bridge from legal principles to the realization of dignity.

Feeling Dignified

Assume dignity. That is a starting point for thinking about how we negotiate our dignity over time through interactions with state actors and institutions. Since our concern here is the behavior of criminal legal institutions, we can assume that one brings dignity to a transaction with the police or other legal actors. We assume dignity because these institutions are obligated to honor the equal respect of each citizen.[17] Philosophers such as Alex Honneth and Charles Taylor cite respect and recognition as fundamental human needs. For Honneth, one's worth is intersubjectively understood.[18] In other words, we imagine ourselves as how other people see us, and we understand who we are in and through our relationships with others, through a process of reflected appraisals.[19]

Our dignity derives from this sense of positive dignity: we have "the right to be beyond reproach" and to exercise our rational free will. This allows us to self-govern or self-regulate and therefore achieve autonomy.[20] A person enjoying or expressing her dignity experiences a sense of belonging within the social and political realms that bound everyday life.

Professor Ekow Yankah describes this as the dignity of citizenship: it confers the idea of the worth of the person and her status of belonging and entitlement to rights and respect in society.[21] Whereas Kant starts with free will and autonomy, the citizenship view assumes a social process of interactions between individuals and between the individual and social or legal institutions. We assume our dignity because we belong, not simply because we exist.[22] In other words, we flourish as humans through our participation in social and political communities.[23] Being recognized as being endowed with full social and political equality is part of our belonging, a foundation of our dignity.

Thus, we are endowed with positive dignity by virtue of our membership in the society, as well as by the more widely recognized Kantian vision of dignity's autonomy and privacy, which are highly individualized states. From exercising our citizenship in ways both small (freedom of movement) and large (voting, perhaps even holding office), we derive a sense of recurring validation. It may even be pleasurable, with each interaction or recognition churning the emotions that are aroused by experiencing political and social inclusion. Some of this exercise of dignitarian liberties is social, but much is political. Security and respect are markers of our citizenship, and interactions with state actors who hold the power to confer respect are particularly freighted with emotion. Dignity, then, at least before the state, and especially in the context of the criminal law where liberty is at stake, hangs in the balance of these interactions.

Indignities

Again, assume dignity. It is nurtured, cultivated, shaped, and reinforced through social and political interactions across a wide landscape of interactions, including interactions with legal authorities. Procedurally pleasant encounters can confirm and reinforce citizenship, and in turn, one's social and political dignity. But what are the consequences for dignity of adverse encounters? Of encounters where one's sense of belonging is not simply denied, but undermined and corroded? It is not only punishments that can be disfiguring, as Professors Simon and Steiker point out. Procedural encounters and interactions can also be disfiguring. The consequences are a loss of dignity.

This is a consequentialist view of dignity that goes beyond simply the denial of constitutional rights. It is inherently processual, and indignities are not easily managed by either a reinvigorated legality principle or by a procedure-based regulatory apparatus that responds formally to dignity incursions. The consequentialist view assumes that there are observable, if not measurable, harms that can be physical, social, and even political in the sense that dignity violations violate citizenship and belonging. These harms can be the beginning of a jurisprudence of dignity, a point on which Professor Simon and I are in strong agreement.

The harms that accrue from everyday encounters with police in contemporary criminal justice are the substance of the consequentialist view of dignity in this essay. These front-end encounters with the police under the "new policing"[24] are fertile grounds for petty or pointless indignities or gratuitous humiliations that arise in everyday encounters with the police and those who process arrests.[25] With its emphasis on stopping crimes before they happen, and on police aggressiveness in these proactive encounters, the "new policing" creates a capacious space for police to act on thin bases of suspicion—at times, actuarial or even Bayesian estimates of suspicion—to infringe on freedoms and bodily integrity;[26] in other words, to treat citizens as "objects to be manipulated," as persons whose criminality is assumed (thereby reversing the burden of proof during the encounter), and undeserving of the rights that come with their citizenship.[27] What the Warren Court in *Terry* worried about as a "petty indignity" has grown over nearly 50 years to innumerable pointless indignities or "horribles"[28] with a far wider range of potential harms. The outrages to dignity stand alone and are distinctive in their harms.

Professor Simon cites examples of dignity-violating abuses by police, mainly in the modern era of field interrogations that are the staple of the "new policing": physical degradation, punitive cavity searches of the body, damage to personal property, dog sniffs, and a host of other humiliations. The link to dignity is in the injuries that these acts produce, the incursions on dignity. William Stuntz defined at least four.[29] The first is the unwarranted invasion of the person's privacy—the coercive incursion on one's person or property or even identity robs the citizen of the dignity of control and privacy: for example, an unwarranted police stop and field interrogation that is part of a dragnet or a program of street detentions.[30]

Second is "targeting harm"—being singled out in public by the police and treated like a criminal suspect.[31] The fact that so few stops yield evidence of criminal wrongdoing ensures the spread of the denial of the dignity of innocence, especially among citizens in the more powerless communities. A person might well ask *why me? Why did the police stop me if they had no evidence, if they did it on a hunch that I might be a criminal?* The privacy harm is compounded by the targeting harm, doubling down on the denial of autonomy and, in turn, the incursions on dignity. When done in a public space, as is often the case, the act is a public discounting of worth by state actor. The confusion of *why me* can transform into feelings of humiliation and rage from the experience of being singled out as a criminal, of being stopped and suspected of criminality by a state actor.

The third harm flows from the racial bias in the distribution of these incursions:[32] the signaling of suspicion of criminality—if not criminality itself—on Black citizens simply by virtue of being Black or moving about in a Black neighborhood. When done to Black or Latino people, it becomes a form of public shaming by a state actor that signals to bystanders that Black or Brown or Asian people are not equal to Whites.[33] The indignity also derives in part from the knowledge that their uniqueness as individuals is accorded less respect than that of others. The singling out of Black or Brown people signals that state actors value the autonomy of White people more, accord them greater respect, and regard Whites as more unique than are Black or Brown people.[34]

The verbal and physical violence that often accompanies these encounters is the fourth indignity. These are not discrete either: the damage to dignity from both verbal and physical assaults adds up to more than the sum of their individual pain. The indignity from inaccurate, if not unjustified, police incursions on liberty is compounded by the mix of these harms within any single interaction.[35] Harsh treatment compounds the second and third harm—the assault on the dignity of innocence[36]—by signaling the legitimacy of the predicate of race-based suspicion that seems to have motivated an unjustified police interdiction. First-hand accounts of police encounters make plain the racial degradation, verbal threats, physical violence, and sexual aggression in these encounters.[37]

When someone feels that she had no ability to prevent any of these humiliations, either because she was targeted in the specific incident, or because of features that would make her targeted over and over again, then the feeling of loss of autonomy (loss of control over what happens with one's own life), and the feeling of being treated as less worthy of respect than others (less human), are likely to deepen the subjective feeling of humiliation.[38] A person targeted by police for any of the humiliations and affronts described by Brunson and Weitzer has little to no space to negotiate her dignity.[39] Even encounters involving only minor intrusion on privacy or liberty (such as being stopped on the street by a police officer and being asked to identify oneself), are likely to be experienced as subjectively and cumulatively humiliating if one feels that the stop was mistaken or unjustified, that there is nothing she could have done to stop it from happening this time, and that there is nothing she can do to stop it from happening again and again. This experience of loss of autonomy, in the sense that one's own choices could not have prevented unpleasant encounters with law enforcers, plus the feeling of being treated as someone whose individual circumstances and liberty are less worthy of respect than those of others, are at the heart of the antagonism (or erosion of legitimacy)[40] caused by adverse encounters with law enforcement.

The persistence of indignities inflicted by agents of the law, both to an individual and vicariously to the persons around her, can metastasize into fundamental problems of social exclusion, where a profound sense of loss of recognition, respect, and self-worth follows. In Charles Taylor's work on the self and the importance of recognition, he argues that our identities are deeply moral, that we understand ourselves as moral entities.[41] Denial of basic and essential recognition—or respect or the belonging that accompanies it—means denial of the recognition of others that one is a unique and worthy human being, worthy of social inclusion and worthy of citizenship. In Taylor's view, indignities confer a harsh status: those who suffer indignities are regarded as having weaker moral claims to recognition and respect.

So, indignities cause harms that go beyond the legal violations and the personal harms that individuals suffer. Indignities have social meaning in the sense that their consequences and harms carry weight that affects the ties of groups to legal authority, and to the moral norms that legal actors both express and enforce. More than a legitimacy argument, this suggests that indignities affect the social relationships necessary to have a full and dignified life. Indignities, then, have both individual costs to autonomy and social costs to the capacity of communities to provide the social resources necessary for dignity.

Dignity 3.0

Professor Simon proposes a shift from the formalism of the principle of legality (Dignity 1.0) toward a jurisprudential principle of "no punishment without dignity" (Dignity 2.0). I want to push further, to propose a jurisprudence that moves beyond formality of law and policy and the inherently institutional basis of legitimacy, toward one that recognizes the emotional highway between dignity and legitimacy. This would be Dignity 3.0.

Modern case law treats the source of indignities from policing as technical violations that should merit a constraining response in the form of "cut it out."[42] But technical parsing of constitutional violations strips them of their moral harms and consequences. It minimizes the protections of citizens from the types of indignities from everyday aggressive policing that are evident under order-maintenance tactics. The trend neutralizes and dismisses the emotional residue of indignity. When transformed to a regulatory regime, not only does the risk of indignity harms increase, but the harm is compounded by the dismissal or impossibility of redress.

The cumulative harm to the individual and the aggregate harm to the community from indignities provide reason to consider a jurisprudence of respect or dignity as a means to provide a set of principles for thinking about the harms of order maintenance. This requires more than simply creating mechanisms for redress of dignity harms; in fact, we have recourse such as §1983 remedies and (though subject to a variety of barriers) tort relief. And it requires more than administrative accountability measures where citizens can activate public service amenities such as civilian review boards to correct wrongs, especially when those wrongs may not be viewed as such by the court.[43]

One might see this as merely a move from procedural due process (Dignity 1.0) to asking nothing more than that we take substantive due process more seriously (Dignity 2.0). Perhaps, but there are considerations that might set Dignity 3.0 apart from either of those perspectives. First is the recognition of emotion as the basis of both dignity and legitimacy. We feel good when our dignity is confirmed: when we are treated respectfully, when our privacy and autonomy are honored, when we are accommodated by legal actors because of our status as citizens and persons. We view those institutions as legitimate because they have treated us with respect. We view ourselves with renewed dignity from these encounters. The emotional highway connects the two to a common source.

The second distinction is the method of remedy that indignities would ignite. We can't rely on enhanced training, or even other forms of police oversight that incentivize constitutional compliance, to produce contacts that reinforce dignity, not when constitutional interpretation of what is legal or permissible—even if it produces indignities—is left to police administrators under a narrowly conceived administrative regime of police control. Formal recourse—through litigation, regulation, or the political process leading to statutes—to ensure that everyday interactions avoid indignities and degradation seems to be impotent in the face of hegemonic and enduring police cultures that have been virtually immunized under current remedies.[44] Even when police departments are doing all they possibly can to ensure that their officers are well-trained, rules such as those in *Herring, Whren,* and *Moore*[45] can create the not-so-odd situation that the well-trained officer may be perfectly compliant with constitutional requirements while compiling indignities in the course of her everyday patrol. These everyday indignities could be explicitly rejected under a jurisprudence that recognizes and internalizes the central role of dignity and respect to regulate the relations between citizens and criminal legal actors.

What indicia would a court look to for positive guidance to legal actors when allegations of indignity are made? Stuntz's four harms provide a starting point.[46] But these tell courts when and perhaps how indignities have occurred, and the depth and nature of the harm as well. Translating the actions that led to the harms into jurisprudential principles for preserving dignity also requires us to look inside the social science of legitimacy, and to identify its components.

The aspirations for dignified treatment of individuals who are subject to the power of the state—regardless of whether they run afoul of the state's authority and norms, or if they are innocent but suspected—run deep in both American law[47] and in common law.[48] Those values can serve as guiding principles for state actors and citizens alike in their exercise of authority and power. It is now up to judges to develop the language of dignity and to instantiate its components into jurisprudence and ultimately in the institutional cultures of policing. Dignity may indeed be the new legitimacy.

NOTES

1 Grundgesetz für die Bundesrepublik Deutschland [Constitution] (Ger.); Constitution of the Republic of South Africa, 1996; Manuel Wackenhaim v. France, Communication No. 854/1999, U.N. Doc. CCPR/C/75/D/854/1999 (2002) [French dwarf-tossing case].

2 Universal Declaration of Human Rights, G.A. Res. 217A (III), U.N. Doc A/810 (1948); International Covenant on Civil and Political Rights, G.A. Res. 2200A (XXI), U.N. Doc. A/6316 (1966).

3 See, for example, Leslie Henry, "The Jurisprudence of Dignity," *University of Pennsylvania Law Review* 160 (2010).

4 Vicki C. Jackson, "Constitutional Dialogue and Human Dignity: State and Transnational Constitutional Discourse," *Montana Law Review* 65 (2004); Bruce Ackerman, "Dignity Is a Constitutional Principle," *New York Times*, March 30, 2014, at SR5.

5 See, for example, David A. Hyman, "Does Technology Spell Trouble with a Capital 'T'? Human Dignity and Public Policy," *Harvard Journal of Law and Public Policy* 27 (2003).

6 Stephen Pinker, "The Stupidity of Dignity," *New Republic*, May 28, 2008.

7 Ruth Macklin, "Dignity Is a Useless Concept," *British Medical Journal* 327 (2003).

8 *The Simpsons* offers a brilliant illustration of the definitional vagueness of dignity. In "A Milhouse Divided," an episode of *The Simpsons* from the 1990s, several Simpson friends are playing a game of Pictionary following a dinner party at the Simpsons' home. (Pictionary is a sort of visual version of charades). Kirk Van

Houten (father of Bart's friend Milhouse) draws a shapeless blob on the easel and exclaims to his wife, Luann, who sits looking confused, "It could not be more simple." The timer runs out and he cries, "It's dignity, gah! Don't you even know dignity when you see it?" Luann decides that she can "do better." With the easel turned away from the television audience, she produces a drawing that the viewers never see. But the people in the Simpsons' parlor are ecstatic with recognition: "Oh that's dignity alright" and "Worthy of Webster's."

9 See, for example, *Richard E. Glossip et al. v. Kevin J. Gross, et al.*, Supreme Court of the United States, 14–7955, Oral Argument, April 29, 2015.

10 Joseph Raz, *Value, Attachment and Respect* (2000); Harry Frankfurt, "Equality and Respect," in *Necessity, Volition, and Love* (1999).

11 Adam Kolber, "The Subjective Experience of Punishment," *Columbia Law Review* 109 (2009); David Luban, *Legal Ethics and Human Dignity* (2007), 70–71.

12 Carol Steiker, "To See a World in a Grain of Sand: Dignity and Indignity in American Criminal Justice," in *The Punitive Imagination*, ed. A. Sarat (2014). Steiker includes shaming of prisoners as a dignity violation, as well as the infliction of psychological or physical pain.

13 Jeremy Waldron, "What Do Philosophers Have against Dignity?" (NYU School of Law, Public Law & Legal Theory Working Paper no. 14–59).

14 Carol Steiker agrees, arguing that "the collective aspect of dignity may be . . . more normatively attractive" in an era of mass and harsh incarceration. Steiker, supra note 12 at 21–22.

15 Henry, "Jurisprudence of Dignity," supra note 3 at 169.

16 Tom R. Tyler, "Legitimacy and Legitimation," *Annals of the American Academy of Political and Social Sciences* 593 (2006); Jonathan Jackson, "On the Dual Motivational Force of Legitimate Authority," in *Cooperation and Compliance with Authority: The Role of Institutional Trust*, ed. B. H. Bornstein and A. J. Tomkins (2015); Anthony Bottoms and Justice Tankebe, "Beyond Procedural Justice: A Dialogic Approach to Legitimacy in Criminal Justice," *Journal of Criminal Law and Criminology* 102 (2012).

17 See, for example, South African Bill of Rights § 36: "The rights in the Bill of Rights may be limited only in terms of law of general application to the extent that the limitation is reasonable and justifiable in an open and democratic society based on human dignity, equality and freedom." See also Sharon Dolovich, "Legitimate Punishment in Liberal Democracy," *Buffalo Criminal Law Review* 7 (2004): 314 ("If the idea of a liberal democracy means anything, it means a commitment to what we can think of as the 'baseline' liberal democratic values: individual liberty, dignity, and bodily integrity; limited government; the primacy and sovereignty of the individual; and the entitlement of all citizens to equal consideration and respect").

18 Alex Honneth, *The Struggle for Recognition: The Moral Grammar of Conflicts* (1996); Charles Taylor, *Sources of the Self: The Making of Modern Identity* (1989).

19 Richard Felson, "Reflected Appraisal and the Development of Self," *Social Psychology Quarterly* 48 (1985).

20 Immanuel Kant, *Groundwork of the Metaphysics of Morals*, ed. Mary Gregor (1998), 7–14; Immanuel Kant, *The Metaphysics of Morals*, ed. Mary Gregor (1996), 13–14.

21 Ekow Yankah, "Policing Ourselves: A Republican Theory of Citizenship, Dignity and Policing" (2013), at http://ssrn.com.

22 Professor Ekow Yankah of Cardozo Law School pointed out this distinction; my thanks to him.

23 Ekow Yankah, "Legal Vices and Civic Virtue: Vice Crimes, Republicanism and the Corruption of Lawfulness," *Criminal Law and Philosophy* 7 (2012); Douglas B. Rasmussen, "Human Flourishing and the Appeal to Human Nature," *Social Philosophy and Policy* 16 (1999). Some might simply call this version of dignity "franchise."

24 Phillip B. Heymann, "The New Policing," *Fordham Urban Law Journal* 28 (2000).

25 See Josh Bowers, "Probable Cause, Constitutional Reasonableness and the Unrecognized Point of a 'Pointless Indignity,'" *Stanford Law Review* 66 (2014). Professor Bowers uses the example of the custody arrest of Gayle Atwater in Lago Vista, Texas, for a seat belt violation. Her children were in the car, and the arresting officer did not allow her to drop the children at her house, just a few doors from the arrest location, before taking her into custody. See, generally, Jeremy Waldron, *Cruel, Inhuman and Degrading Treatment: The Words Themselves* (2008). See also Avishai Margalit, *The Decent Society* (1996), 10–11.

26 For an example, see Bernard E. Harcourt, "Unconstitutional Police Searches and Collective Responsibility," *Criminology & Public Policy* 3 (2004), describing a futile cavity search for drugs alongside a public thoroughfare.

27 Waldron, *Cruel, Inhuman and Degrading Treatment*, supra note 25.

28 *Atwater v. City of Lago Vista*, 532 U.S. 318, 321 (2001) (noting the "dearth of horribles demanding redress").

29 William J. Stuntz, "*Terry's* Impossibility," *St John's Law Review* 72 (1998).

30 For an example, see Tracey L. Meares, "Programming Errors: Understanding the Constitutionality of Stop-and-Frisk as a Program, Not an Incident," *University of Chicago Law Review* 82 (2015).

31 See Sherry F. Colb, "Innocence, Privacy, and Targeting in Fourth Amendment Jurisprudence," *Columbia Law Review* 96 (1996).

32 The New York City "stop and frisk" litigation illustrates the breathtaking racial skew in these everyday police encounters. See Report of Jeffrey Fagan, Ph.D. (2010), for *David Floyd et al. v. City of New York et al.*, U.S. District Court for the Southern District of New York, 08 Civ. 01034 (SAS), October 28 (showing that African Americans and Latinos were the targets of over 85% of the 4.4 million "street stops" made by NYPD officers from 2004 to 2009, or approximately 1,700 stops per day of non-Whites).

33 I. Bennett Capers, "Policing, Race and Place," *Harvard Civil Rights–Civil Liberties Law Review* 44 (2009).

34 Capers, id.

35 See Stuntz, "*Terry's* Impossibility," supra note 29.
36 Rinat Kitai, "The Presumption of Innocence," *Oklahoma Law Review* 55 (2002): 267, 270.
37 For examples, see Rod K. Brunson and Ronald Weitzer, "Police Relations with Black and White Youths in Different Urban Neighborhoods," *Urban Affairs Review* 44 (2009): 866–68; Victor M. Rios, *Punished: Policing the Lives of Black and Latino Boys* (2011); Ross Tuttle (dir.), "The Nation, The Hunted and the Hated: An Inside Look at the NYPD's Stop-and-Frisk Policy" (October 9, 2012), at www. youtube.com; Jacinta Gau and Rod Brunson, "Procedural Justice And Order Maintenance Policing: A Study Of Inner⊠City Young Men's Perceptions Of Police Legitimacy," *Justice Quarterly* 27 (2010); Michael Powell, "Police Polish Image, but Concerns Persist," *New York Times*, January 4, 2009, at B1. See also U.S Department of Justice, Civil Rights Division, Special Litigation Section, Investigation of the Ferguson Police Department (March 4, 2015), at www.justice.gov.
38 Judith Resnik and Julie Chi-Hye Suk, "Adding Insult to Injury: Questioning the Role of Dignity in Conceptions of Sovereignty," *Stanford Law Review* 55 (2003).
39 Avishai Margalit describes humiliation as the sense of being deprived of control: "Curtailing the freedom of the other, and making gestures designed to show that the other is severely limited in her control, may constitute a rejection of the other as human." Margalit says this is a way of marking them as subhuman, as a mere object. Margalit, *Decent Society*, supra note 25 at 118.
40 David Beetham, *The Legitimation of Power* (1991). See also Tom R. Tyler and Jeffrey Fagan, "Legitimacy and Cooperation: Why Do People Help the Police Fight Crime in Their Communities," *Ohio State Journal of Criminal Law* 6 (2008); Charles Ogletree, *The Presumption of Guilt: The Arrest of Henry Louis Gates, Jr. and Race, Class and Crime in America* (2012).
41 Charles Taylor, *Sources of the Self: The Making of Modern Identity* (1989).
42 Andrew Taslitz, "Respect and the Fourth Amendment," *Journal of Criminal Law & Criminology* 94 (2003); Wayne Logan, "Police Mistakes of Law," *Emory Law Journal* 61 (2012).
43 See Colb, "Innocence, Privacy, and Targeting," supra note 31 (noting that offenders have to function as their own private attorney general to prevent government misconduct).
44 See Joanna Schwartz, "Myths and Mechanics of Deterrence," *UCLA Law Review* 57 (2009).
45 *Whren v. U.S.*, 517 U.S. 806 (1996) (stating that any traffic offense was a legitimate legal basis for a stop even if conducted for some other law enforcement objective); *Virginia v. Moore*, 553 U.S. 164 (2008) (allowing evidence obtained unlawfully to be used in a criminal prosecution since the arrest was based on probable cause); *Herring v. U.S.*, 555 U.S. 135 (2009) (allowing evidence obtained by negligent error in recording mistaken information in a warrant to be used in a criminal prosecution).
46 Stuntz, "*Terry's* Impossibility," supra note 29.

47 Taslitz, "Respect and the Fourth Amendment," supra note 42; Colb, "Innocence, Privacy and Targeting," supra note 31; Judith Resnik, "Detention, the War on Terror, and the Federal Courts," *Columbia Law Review* 110 (2010); Martha Minow, "Equality and the Bill of Rights," in *The Constitution of Rights: Human Dignity and American Values*, ed. Michael J. Meyer and William A. Parents (1992), 118–28 (discussing how human dignity and equality are embraced in the Bill of Rights, especially in the protections of the First Amendment); George P. Fletcher, "Human Dignity as a Constitutional Value," *Univ. of Western Ontario Law Review* 22 (1984); Neomi Rao, "On the Use and Abuse of Dignity in Constitutional Law," *Columbia Journal of European Law* 14 (2008).

48 Kitai, "Presumption of Innocence," supra note 36.

PART V

The New (Old) Criminal Justice Thinking

None of these questions are new. Neither are many of the answers. For hundreds of years, human beings have been arguing about how to think about the criminal justice process, what it signifies, and what it actually does. The disciplines and intellectual frameworks devoted to the question have changed greatly over time, but certain ways of thinking come and go with regularity. This concluding essay surveys the history of criminology itself, an intellectual history that reveals a remarkable amount about how we ended up with the criminal system we have today.

Mariana Valverde, "Miserology": A New Look at the History of Criminology

14

"Miserology"

A New Look at the History of Criminology

MARIANA VALVERDE

One would think that the fact that criminological teaching and research has been growing exponentially, in the global South as well as the North, with this boom showing no signs of slowing down, would have created an atmosphere of optimism and collective self-congratulation. But, paradoxically, many of the field's theorists feel that the subject is in a deep state of fragmentation and suffers from a loss of purpose. Some of the pessimists—who often cite the field's very success in attracting government and university resources as a worrying symptom—are currently leading campaigns to "save" independent and/or "critical" criminology, exhorting younger scholars to resist the siren song of "administrative" criminology (e.g., Williams and Lippert 2006). Others, on their part, are quietly abandoning criminology, or at least crime and criminal justice. They are redefining the scope of their own work by taking up fields that appear as broader and/or more theoretically lively, such as the study of social regulation and order, the study of risks and risk management, or the study of security (e.g., Wood and Shearing 2007, Ericson and Haggerty 1997, O'Malley 2004, Zedner 2009). Oxford's Lucia Zedner is not alone when she worries whether criminology will stagnate and perhaps even lose relevance if it maintains a focus on crime. In her view, the only way to renovate criminology and make it more relevant is to begin by acknowledging that today risk and security are the key objects of policy concern. Her argument, which appears to be widely shared by theoretically oriented criminologists, is that risk and security (not crime) should be the central objects of research for those whose official profession is criminology. Such a change, in her view, would necessitate learning from and allying with enterprises such as economics, political science, moral philosophy, risk society studies, and international human rights research.

I am very much in sympathy with Zedner's diagnosis—which is hardly surprising, given that my background and training featured no criminology at all, and that, today, I tend to locate my work more within law and society scholarship than criminology proper. But my purpose in this paper is different from the concerns animating scholars such as Zedner. My purpose is neither diagnostic nor curative, in large part because I am unusual among theorists in believing that excellent empirical work on criminal justice institutions and criminal justice policy can get along quite well and make useful contributions to both knowledge and policy, even if criminological theory is either dead or in crisis. Here, then, I do not offer any programmatic vision to save criminology by saving or reinventing criminological theory. Instead, I wish to contribute to the existing discussion about what criminology is or should be in a somewhat tangential and non-programmatic manner. My main objective is to revise the genealogy of the varied pursuits that today go on under the banner of criminology, displacing or decentering crime and the study of crime. This revision, I argue, is not an anachronistic effort to find "the risk society" or "security studies" in embryo form. On the contrary, I will argue that decentering crime in the history of criminology provides a more historically accurate picture of intellectual developments in the nineteenth century that are not properly understood if "crime" is selected out for attention. Looking back at our intellectual ancestors on their own terms, rather than merely picking out isolated comments they made about crime and punishment, results in a very different picture of our history—one that puts the present theoretical crisis in a new light. I will show that if we revise our history to do more justice to the nineteenth-century pioneers who first talked about "the social" as a problem, with crime forming but one element of a larger intellectual and social-legal reform project rooted in the crisis of early industrial capitalism, we may no longer feel quite so anxious about "crime" ceasing to be the central focus of both academic and government interest today.

In particular, I will show that the late-nineteenth-century positivism that is generally regarded as "the beginning" cannot be properly understood unless we go back a few decades, specifically to the 1830s and 1840s. That was the time in which "the social question" first came to the fore in industrializing cities, especially in Britain and France. The conventional periodization seriously undervalues the rich diversity of knowledges of "deviance" and "social control" produced by early- and mid-nineteenth-century European (and Euro-American) thinkers and reformers. Even Lombroso himself (whose role and influence is regularly exaggerated by textbooks that use him as a comic foil to "proper," sociological criminology) is best understood not as a "biological determinist" but rather as one example (admittedly an unusually eclectic and unscientific example) of ways of thinking about normality, social order, and individual deviance that were widely shared across political as well as disciplinary divisions, at a time when there was little interest in drawing any sharp lines between the biological and the cultural, the physiological and the moral. Now that social theory is being transformed through the influence of "actor network theory," specifically Latour's claim that "nature" and "culture" are questionable abstractions produced in binary form by "the modern constitution" of knowledge (Latour 1993), it is a very good time to look back and revise our account of our intellectual ancestors. After Latour, it seems to me, we can no longer continue to repeat the now discredited assumption that there is indeed a dividing line between nature and culture, and that many of our ancestors simply got that line wrong.

Where Does the History of Criminology Begin?

Stanley Cohen, one of the most influential criminologists of the twentieth century, stated as an uncontroversial fact that criminology has two beginnings. One is the moment of Beccaria and the Enlightenment, when utilitarianism and humanitarianism were invented, in no small part through a negative reaction against arbitrary and harsh criminal punishments. The second beginning, Cohen claims, took place in the late nineteenth century, at the time of the invention of criminal anthropology and other knowledges of human abnormality (Cohen 1988). For Cohen there is nothing of relevance to note in between one beginning and the next, between classic legal-political contract theory and the positivism of the late nineteenth century. This picture is seriously problematic (though even more problematic is the fact that many criminology textbooks dispense with Beccaria and the Enlightenment altogether, as if that important moment were relevant to the criminal law but not criminology).

It is true that there is a major historical discontinuity between Cohen's first beginning and his second beginning. Beccaria was focused on governing criminality as a discrete series of acts, willed acts to be precise, and insisted on treating everyone including criminals as equally rational, in sharp contrast to the late-nineteenth-century obsession with documenting deviance. And perhaps more importantly, he was not particularly interested in criminality at all: his real aim was to argue that governing crime is an important matter of state policy, because if criminal punishment is rendered rational, transparent, and humane, then that will transform the state itself and through the state, the society. Thus, in keeping with earlier classical social contract theory, Beccaria's hugely influential model featured only two entities: the (rational) individual, on the one hand, and the "state," on the other. Neither the body of the individual criminal nor the biopolitical entity of "the criminal class"—the two great objects of study in the late nineteenth century—were visible in his work. For Beccaria, criminals as well as legislators are disembodied individual actors who should be encouraged, by the design of the legal system, to make rational choices. As with Enlightenment thinking generally, the emphasis is on what legislators and offenders have in common (rationality), not on differences among different groups of humans.

The disembodied rational actor of Enlightenment thought, the actor that might make an irrational or even an evil choice but who is not (yet) a "deviant" (because normalization has not yet been invented), disappeared from the human sciences as the nineteenth century wore on; law, and especially criminal law, was one of the few spheres in which such an entity continued to play a key role. Therefore, Cohen is, in a sense, correct in restarting the story of criminology in the late nineteenth century—when bodies, families, races, and subpopulations had come to the fore as objects of study—given the stark discontinuity between the strongly biopolitical character of the social and psy-sciences of that time and the earlier Enlightenment framing of the individual. The inventors of psychology, sociology, and criminology had little or no use for either Kantian individuals or for humanity in general; for them, scientific inquiry consisted in differentiating humans from one another, both by elaborating techniques to identify deviant individuals and by defining and studying deviant groups that had not existed in Beccaria's time—the feeble-minded, the born criminal, the homosexual (Garland 1985; Pick 1985; Rose 1990; Foucault 1978).

The psychology, sociology, and psychiatry invented in the last quarter of the nineteenth century and documented, among many other works, in David Garland's *Punishment and Welfare* (1985) were epistemologically poles apart from Enlightenment ideas about universal human rationality; but they were not as new as they claimed to be. The sociology invented by Durkheim, Herbert Spencer, Charles Booth, and the early Chicago School put itself forward as a brand-new enterprise (with Durkheim being particularly successful at selling, arguably through some false advertising, the novelty not only of his work but of the discipline he promoted). And scientific psychology too tried hard to differentiate itself from the philosophical speculation about the human mind that lay in its past (Danziger 1990; Rose 1990). However, these new knowledges, while largely ignoring Enlightenment thought, had very deep roots in the European intellectual ferment of the decades that lie in between Cohen's first beginning and his second.

The forerunners of the sciences born in Cohen's "second beginning" are a diverse array of writers and reformers, virtually none of whom had university positions, who from the 1820s onward sought to draw attention to the dangerous changes brought about by early industrial capitalism and urbanization. Some were conservative philanthropists, like the aristocrat and philanthropist Villeneuve-Bargemont, in France, unknown today but influential in his own day (Procacci 1991). Some were proto-socialists, like Henri de Saint-Simon and his followers in France and Robert Owen and sundry early socialist-feminists in Britain. Some were the medical doctors whose "sanitary walks" in the brand-new slums of cities like Manchester eventually gave rise to public health as a new form of knowledge. Some began to study prostitution as a social and not merely a moral phenomenon, notably Parent-Duchâtelet in Paris and William Acton in England (Parent-Duchâtelet 1836). Given the very diverse political preferences and professional pursuits of the early social reformers and social scientists, it is not surprising that they did not build anything like a coherent group. In most cases they did not succeed in forming any kind of school or influencing state policy (the early public health doctors were unusual in this regard). But, in retrospect, one can argue that while not working together or even, in many cases, knowing about one another, they did collectively create a new type of knowledge, one that by analogy with criminology one can call "miserology."

"*Misère*"—a term sometimes translated into English as "pauperism" or "indigence" (Dean 1985), but whose unique meaning is highlighted by the fact that the musical based on Victor Hugo's famous work is still going, today, under its French name—was the term used for a condition that was thought to be sharply differentiated from old-fashioned poverty. Poverty, the miserologists said, has always existed, and exists still in the countryside; but misery—a hybrid of moral degradation, physical ill health, spatial marginality, and collective despair—was found only among the new urban proletariat (Procacci 1991).

Along these lines, Bentham too made a sharp distinction between "poverty," which was for him a common and not necessarily worrisome condition, and, on the other hand "pauperism"—with the latter term implying a condition of moral decay and inability to improve oneself, not just a low income. Pauperism is arguably the ancestor of today's "welfare dependency," which is like pauperism a term used to indicate a cross-generational decay of the moral fiber, not merely a shortage of material goods; but for our purposes what matters most is that from the 1820s to, say, the publication of Victor Hugo's masterpiece in the 1860s, it was the specter of pauperism that haunted bourgeois Europe. Crime—which at this time came to be regarded as an urban phenomenon—was seen as merely one dimension of this larger phenomenon.

It should be emphasized that the miserologists who laid the groundwork for the later pursuits of urban sociology, criminology, and certain forms of psychology were not necessarily law-and-order conservatives. Some of them, including, of course, Victor Hugo himself, had progressive political affiliations, and expressed considerable sympathy with those denizens of the new slums whose lives made it almost impossible for them to rise even to a state of normal poverty. A notable left-wing miserologist, one of the few whose works are still read, was Frederick Engels, whose miserological treatise *The Condition of the Working Class in England* was what brought him to the attention of Karl Marx, arguably with world-historical consequences. In this important work of early social science, Engels focuses on the "nameless misery" that is particular to factory workers, and, typically for the miserology genre, he claims that the dehumanization of factory work (quite apart from the low wages) produces "demoralization"—and elsewhere in the book, "demoralization and crime," "crime, misery and disease," "want and disease," and, again, "demoralization" (Engels 1887, 119, 121, 26, 211).

An interesting formal feature of the miserology genre is that while miserological accounts feature individuals and houses and streets, often with real names attached, the individuals are treated as mere examples of a group, and specifically examples of what would later come to be called a subculture. Similarly, the social novels that played a major role in the dissemination of miserology obviously feature particular characters, but the characters are always case studies, examples of a type—the fallen woman, the male factory worker who ends up falling into alcoholism, etc. From Elizabeth Gaskell through Eugene Sue to Émile Zola, nineteenth-century "social" novelists communicated to their audiences messages about the systemic problems of industrial capitalism, messages which for many people, including Victorian social reformers, constituted proof that individual moral persuasion was not going to work, and that legislation imposing more humane conditions for industrial labor had become necessary, Adam Smith to the contrary notwithstanding. That miserology was almost completely an extra-university phenomenon cannot be emphasized enough. In the days before social science had made inroads in the universities, novels, plays, and more or less sensationalist journalism were the primary sources of information about the kinds of problems that came to be called "social," supplemented by the "sanitary walks" accounts of public health doctors and the occasional work of proto–social science, such as Engels's.

Today, many people will guiltily admit that they gained much of the knowledge they possess about "the underclass" from realistic television shows such as *The Wire*, but even people who have never gone to university know that there are experts on social problems who are sure to have scientific studies of drug use, crime, and other "social problems" that have more scientific credentials than even the best HBO series. Miserology, by contrast, thrived in the decades just before the great divide separating and ranking the knowledges produced by universities, those produced by journalism, and those produced by realist fiction came into being. Engels's famous Manchester working-class study was, typically, nothing but journalism, indeed amateur journalism. Karl Marx of course worked hard to create a science—not of pauperism, which he would have dismissed as an imprecise hybrid of economic and moral factors, but of the relations of production, which in his view were the underlying cause of the phenomenon known as pauperism. Marx's contemptuous (and often quite inaccurate) dismissal of his predecessors, the so-called "utopian socialists," worked to draw a sharp and enduring line separating work such as his (and later university-based studies) from his miserological predecessors and contemporaries. To that extent, Marx's inaccurate comments about "utopian socialists" had similar effects to the claims made by Chicago School sociology to a superior form of knowledge, one higher than the practically acquired knowledge of philanthropists and social reformers such as Jane Addams. And the conventional history of criminology reenacts this questionable binary opposition separating science (university-based science) from social reform whenever "the origins" of criminology are traced only to the 1890s and not to the earlier, non-institutionalized writings on pauperism, misery, political economy, and social reform that flourished in the 1830s and 1840s. To dismiss miserological accounts of crime of the Victor Hugo type as not belonging even to the prehistory of criminology is simply to repeat, unthinkingly, the self-interested prejudiced views of those who fought hard to discredit their variegated, often ethically committed predecessors in order to establish criminology and sociology as respectable university-based endeavors.

Urban sociology—whose history is intimately entwined with that of criminology—also owes a great deal to the miserological tradition, though it too regularly fails to acknowledge the importance of the more-or-less populist genres that were used by the early students of urban poverty and urban problems (Valverde 1996). One of the books regularly cited as among the first sociological research projects, Charles Booth's massive *Life and Labour of the People (later Life and Labour of the People in London)*, was very significant in giving miserology a quantitative (and also a micro-cartographical) turn (Booth 1889–1891). But while Booth's quest to map every block and to measure deprivation quantitatively renders the work "modern" and scientific—and indeed it is Booth's in-person surveys and mapping techniques that are generally celebrated in the history of sociology—it is problematic to dismiss the overtly moralistic content of his volumes as somehow incidental. His ethical commitments, just like those of the socialist movement, were integral to his research.

An example here will show how problematic it is to reject the ethics while preserving the scientific improvements. Working-class income was a key quantitative variable for Booth and his numerous research assistants. However, the black color that—not coincidentally—he used to indicate the "lowest" grade of street blocks was not a representation of an economic indicator, but rather a composite. When he decided to update his massive study more than a decade after the first volume had appeared in 1889, he made a telling offhand remark: "Drinking habit and the disorderliness resulting from them could not but be continually mentioned in the course of the long walks taken in all parts of London day after day with the picked police officers who were permitted to assist us during the revision of our maps" (Booth 1902, vol. 8, 61). Throughout the work's multiple volumes, demoralization, drinking, and economic deprivation are presented as different facets of the same phenomenon—with the category of "vice" now being central to his discourse, however, having largely replaced the older and less prejudiced terms "pauperism," "indigence," and "*misère*." And just as the black color did not denote a quantitative measure of poverty but rather a hybrid condition, so too the white and yellow colors chosen to indicate "good" streets were not mere markers of wealth but indicators of an equally hybrid condition in which sobriety, intact nuclear families, traditional gender roles, Christian habits, and economic well-being were inseparably intertwined.

Miserology, therefore, took as its object a condition specifically caused by early industrialization—a condition (misery, pauperism) clearly distinguished from older and less historically specific kinds of deprivation. This move would prove foundational for criminology: "crime" in general, crime without any adjectives or qualifiers, is still today identified with the criminality of urban working-class neighborhoods, with other types of criminality requiring a special qualifier (violence against women, corporate crime, white-collar crime, etc.). Secondly, miserology held a resolutely hybrid or (in Latour's terms) non-modern ontology, as seen in Charles Booth's work. Finally, a third knowledge move commonly performed in today's criminological research turns out to also have been invented by the miserologists: the quiet shift from persons to spaces.

Some important miserological works of the last two decades of the nineteenth century emphasized the physical spaces of misery and vice, using the kind of architectural determinist argument that was later used (in the 1940s and the postwar period) to justify urban renewal, and has been revived today with different content, to tear down the very structures that postwar social thinking saw as virtue-inducing as well as healthy. In England, there was a moral panic about the dreadful effects, on sexual morality as well as hygiene, of working-class overcrowding—a panic leading to a Royal Commission on working-class housing and to a whole range of new building regulations. In the US, the Hull House reformers, for example, spent much time and energy developing techniques for evaluating buildings, in the belief that "bad" spaces produced bad social relations.

In general, in both Europe and the US, the 1890s was a decade in which many technical refinements in the measuring of vice and misery were made. A narrow focus on those late-nineteenth-century researchers who studied crime hides from view many who are arguably ancestors of today's criminology, especially those activists who argued that certain "criminogenic" (as we would say now) spaces were featured as the causes of the misery and degeneration of the people living in them. While those focusing on identifying criminals and measuring deviance in *persons* (e.g., Lombroso's criminal anthropology) are included in every account of the history of criminology, the reformers and scientists who focused on the spaces of working-class vice (whether tenements or saloons or bars) have generally been neglected. This neglect is unfortunate, especially given today's interest in spatialization. Of interest to today's urban criminologists is the fact that his beloved, labor-intensive maps seemed to become to Booth more real than the households and people they supposedly represented (as critical cartographers have pointed out in relation to colonial maps and "discovery" maps). At one point Booth tellingly states: "The eye readily notices those black spots which betoken a *miserable* combination of poverty, vice and crime" (Booth 1889, vol. 1, 335; emphasis added).

Urban maps that differentiate streets, and even blocks, from one another in terms of vice and crime, first produced in the US by Hull

House and in England by Booth, are still an important tool of "misero-logical" social science today. But another innovation of the 1890s that has also been excluded from the purview of the history of criminology (and even urban sociology) was the effort made to measure the health of the buildings themselves, primarily by focusing on the flow or lack of fresh air (as mentioned above in relation to London). In New York City, the concern about poor physical and moral health in tenements led to a new ordinance that decreed that all rooms should have windows, a rule that sometimes resulted in windows being created linking two equally drab and dark inside rooms (as the Tenement Museum in lower Manhattan shows). Similarly, the 1880s "overcrowding" crusade in England led to many efforts to measure the health not of people but of buildings. Such efforts are today remembered only by specialized historians of housing and by historians of public health; but they too, in my view, deserve a spot in the history of criminology, given that "housing" was then not a separate subject for either government policy or expert studies, but was rather one facet of the larger question of urban misery. The moral character of buildings, determined by scientific methods such as measuring the amount of air in a tenement room or the number of windows in a house (and usually aggregated to form the character of a neighborhood or street or block), became not just an indicator of the situation of the inhabitants but an object of study in itself, often with deterministic assumptions about the effects of such housing on the inhabitants.

Was Lombroso a Biological Determinist? Toward a Revisionist Reading

Cesare Lombroso's work is generally regarded as inaugurating biological determinism in criminology. Such a reading, however, demands that the explanations and theories of crime and deviance that he provides throughout his work that cannot be made to fit within the scope of "biological determinism" be ignored or treated as inconsistencies that are the result of moral and cultural prejudices seeping into and corrupting his scientific approach. A recent article, for example, by the title of "New Natural Born Killers? The Legacy of Lombroso in Neuroscience and Law," argues that today's neuroscientists, including those concerned with criminological issues such as addiction, aggression, and impulsivity, are the direct heirs of Lombroso; today's neuroscientists, Emilia Musumeci states, "adopt the same paradigm as Lombroso" (Musumeci 2013, 143). As I have argued at more length elsewhere, I believe it is time to revise our view of Lombroso (Valverde 2013). His arguments about the "born criminal" are certainly important predecessors of biomedical explanations of crime, including today's neuroscience; but to select those comments out from a much larger and far more complicated body of work so as to slot them into the chronologically first place in a text on "biological theories of crime" is anachronistic. The standard, presentist account classifies Lombroso as a positivistic biomedical researcher who was just not very good at his job, since his work is shot through with knowledge claims that are not in the least biomedical or even scientific. But might it not be useful to consider putting Lombroso back in his own intellectual context—which was the age of "degeneration." Degeneration theory, if mentioned at all in histories of criminology, is generally dismissed as a scientific, positivist theory that was contaminated from the outside by moralistic, sexist, and racist prejudices. Such an account of Lombroso teleologically assumes that the inherent purpose and logic of investigations of the human body and mind is to be strictly scientific, to be pure and uncontaminated by racism, sexism, and moralism. If we dispense with teleological frameworks for intellectual history and attempt to understand our ancestors on their own terms, we see something quite different. What we see is not proto-science or even pseudo-science but rather a fantastically eclectic epistemology that completely undermines the modern effort to separate natural from cultural explanations. Lombroso's sources of "data" include popular folklore and folk sayings, legal texts, anthropological body measurement charts, psychological case histories (all secondhand), observations made by prison doctors and by French specialists on brothels, and bits of 1840s phrenology, juxtaposed without pause with the latest psychiatric concepts, photographs of Russian prison inmates of uncertain provenance, and the letters of Madame de Stael—just to name a few. If we focus more on his sources of "data" and his formats—rather than on the content of his theories—it is apparent that Lombroso can be seen as the last of the miserologists, rather than as the first criminologist.

Conclusion

In the first couple of decades of the twentieth century, the study of vice, poverty, and crime began to be slowly integrated into universities. University-based social research benefited a great deal from the encouragement and participation of social reformers, frequently motivated by religious or by left-wing political beliefs, who despite their personal motivations believed in using social scientific methods (unlike the resolutely anti-intellectual Salvation Army, one of the key generators of knowledge of "deviance" and urban crime in the late nineteenth century). The settlement movement was in many instances a crucial link between Christian philanthropy, left-wing social activism, and university research. In Toronto, for example, most early settlement houses, dating from the 1920s, were either Protestant or Catholic, but there was also a "university settlement," closely linked to the brand-new Faculty of Social Work.

By the 1950s, however, the social sciences had become much more powerful and institutionalized in universities; and the Cold War environment did not encourage university professors and students to take an active part in community activism and neighborhood social reform. This was the context in which the first criminological research institutes were planned: the Mannheim Centre at the London School of Economics, the Cambridge Institute of Criminology, the Toronto Centre for Criminology. On their part, many sociologists, from the 1950s and 1960s onward, also took up criminology as a productive subfield of scholarship. But while a certain political and ethical commitment did return to criminology (in the critical criminology of the 1970s), the new generation had little or no knowledge of their predecessors, at least nothing earlier than Lombroso. As criminology established itself as a powerful scholarly domain, few people looked back to reflect on the history of the field, and fewer still thought of looking a few decades earlier than the 1880s and 1890s. While the sketch provided here is of necessity very brief and somewhat superficial, further research in the intellectual history of criminology may well restore the social reformers, philanthropists, socialists, journalists, and assorted organic intellectuals of the 1830s and 1840s to their proper place as the pioneers of "criminology."

REFERENCES

Booth, Charles. 1889–1891. *Labour and Life of the People*, 1st ed. (2 vols.). London: Williams and Norgate.

Booth, Charles. 1902–1903. *Labour and Life of the People in London*, 3rd ed. (17 vols.). London: Macmillan.

Cohen, Stanley. 1988. *Against Criminology*. New Brunswick, NJ: Transaction Books.

Danziger, Kurt. 1990. *Constructing the Subject: Historical Origins of Psychological Research*. Cambridge, UK: Cambridge University Press.

Dean, Mitchell. 1985. *The Constitution of Poverty*. London: Sage.

Engels, Frederick. 1887 [1845]. *The Condition of the Working Class in England in 1844*. Translated by Florence Kelley. New York: J. W. Lowell & Co.

Ericson, Richard, and Kevin Haggerty. 1997. *Policing the Risk Society*. Toronto: University of Toronto Press.

Foucault, Michel. 1978. *Discipline and Punish: The Birth of the Prison*. Translated by Alan Sheridan. New York: Pantheon.

Garland, David. 1985. *Punishment and Welfare: A History of Penal Strategies*. London: Gower.

Latour, Bruno. 1993 [1991]. *We Have Never Been Modern*. Translated by Catherine Porter. New York: Harvester Wheatsheaf.

Musumeci, Emilia. 2013. "New Natural Born Killers? The Legacy of Lombroso in Neuroscience and Law," in Paul Knepper and P. J. Ystehede, eds., *The Cesare Lombroso Handbook*. London: Routledge.

O'Malley, Pat. 2004. *Crime and Risk*. London: Sage.

Parent-Duchâtelet, A.J.B. 1836. *De la prostitution dans la ville de Paris*. Paris: J.B. Ballière.

Pick, Daniel. 1985. *Faces of Degeneration: A European Disorder, c. 1848–c. 1918*. Cambridge, UK: Cambridge University Press.

Procacci, Giovanna. 1991. "The Government of Misery," in G. Burchell, C. Gordon, and P. Miller, eds., *The Foucault Effect: Essays on Governmentality*. Chicago: University of Chicago Press.

Rose, Nikolas. 1990. *Governing the Soul*. London: Routledge.

Valverde, Mariana. 1996. "The Dialectic of the Familiar and Unfamiliar: 'The Jungle' in Early Slum Travel Writing." *Sociology* 30, no. 3: 493–509.

Valverde, Mariana. 2013. "Lombroso's *Criminal Woman* and the Uneven Development of the Modern Lesbian Identity," in Paul Knepper and P. J. Ystehede, eds., *The Cesare Lombroso Handbook*. London: Routledge.

Williams, James, and Randy Lippert. 2006. "Governing on the Margins: Exploring the Contribution of Governmentality Studies to Critical Criminology in Canada." *Canadian Journal of Criminology and Criminal Justice* 48, no. 5: 703–719.

Wood, Jennifer, and Clifford Shearing. 2007. *Imagining Security*. Cullompton: Willan.

Zedner, Lucia. 2009. *Security*. London: Routledge.

ABOUT THE CONTRIBUTORS

HADAR AVIRAM holds the Harry and Lillian Hastings Research Chair at U.C. Hastings College of Law and is Vice President of the Western Society of Criminology.

RACHEL BARKOW is Segal Family Professor of Regulatory Law and Policy at NYU School of Law and Director of the NYU Center on the Administration of Criminal Law.

STEPHANOS BIBAS is Professor of Law and Criminology at the University of Pennsylvania Law School and Director of the Supreme Court Clinic.

MEDA CHESNEY-LIND is Chair and Professor of Women's Studies at the University of Hawaii at Manoa.

SHARON DOLOVICH is Professor of Law at the UCLA School of Law and Director of the UCLA Prison Law and Policy Program.

JEFFREY FAGAN is Isidor and Seville Sulzbacher Professor of Law at Columbia Law School and Professor of Epidemiology at the Mailman School of Public Health at Columbia.

LISA KERR is Assistant Professor of Law at Queen's University.

ISSA KOHLER-HAUSMANN is Associate Professor of Law at Yale Law School and Associate Professor of Sociology at Yale University.

MONA LYNCH is Professor of Criminology, Law & Society, and Law at U.C. Irvine, Vice-Chair of the Department of Criminology, Law and Society, and Co-Director of the Center in Law, Society and Culture.

ALEXANDRA NATAPOFF is Associate Dean for Research, Rains Senior Research Fellow, and Professor of Law at Loyola Law School, Los Angeles.

PRISCILLA OCEN is Associate Professor of Law at Loyola Law School, Los Angeles.

DANIEL RICHMAN is Paul J. Kellner Professor of Law at Columbia Law School.

JONATHAN SIMON is Adrian A. Kragen Professor of Law at U.C. Berkeley School of Law and Director of the Center for the Study of Law and Society.

MARIANA VALVERDE is Professor of Criminology at the Centre for Criminology and Sociolegal Studies, University of Toronto.

INDEX